FAME AND THE FO

DOUGLASS ADAIR

ESSAYS BY DOUGLASS ADAIR

FAME

AND THE

FOUNDING

FATHERS

EDITED BY TREVOR COLBOURN,
WITH A PERSONAL MEMOIR BY
CAROLINE ROBBINS
AND A BIBLIOGRAPHICAL ESSAY BY
ROBERT E. SHALHOPE

LIBERTY FUND

This book is published by Liberty Fund, Inc., a foundation
established to encourage study of the ideal of a society of
free and responsible individuals.

𒂼𒄄

The cuneiform inscription that serves as our logo and as
a design element for Liberty Fund books is the earliest-known
written appearance of the word "freedom" (*amagi*), or "liberty."
It is taken from a clay document written about 2300 B.C.
in the Sumerian city-state of Lagash.

2nd printing (2023), printed on demand by Lightning Source, Inc.

Library of Congress Cataloging-in-Publication Data
Adair, Douglass.
Fame and the founding fathers : essays / by Douglass Adair : edited
by Trevor Colbourn, with a personal memoir by Caroline Robbins
and a bibliographical essay by Robert E. Shalhope.
p.   cm.
Originally published: New York : Norton for the Institute of
Early American History and Culture at Williamsburg, 1974.
Includes bibliographical references and index.
ISBN 0-86597-192-7 (hc)   —ISBN 0-86597-193-5
(pb : alk. paper)   1. The Federalist.   2. Constitutional history—
United States.   I. Title.
JK155.A32   1998
973.4'092'2—dc21   98-2875

Liberty Fund, Inc.
11301 North Meridian Street
Carmel, IN 46032
libertyfund.org

CONTENTS

I. ARTICLES AND ESSAYS

II. REVIEW ESSAYS, NOTES, AND DOCUMENTS

PREFACE

MANY DISTINGUISHED SCHOLARS wanted this book and have a
part in it. Its concept is only minimally that of the editor; it is clearly
Douglass Adair's book, albeit regrettably delayed by the editor's
administrative distractions. Its publication owes much to many people: to Virginia Hamilton Adair, literary executor to her late husband;
to Arthur Pierce Middleton and Marvin Harvey for permission to
include articles in which they were collaborators with Douglass Adair;
to Thad Tate, formerly editor of the *William and Mary Quarterly*
(and now director of the Institute of Early American History and
Culture), for his helpful cooperation on questions of copyright; to
Moravian College for permission to include "Fame and the Founding
Fathers"; to the Henry E. Huntington Library and Art Gallery for
permission to reprint Adair's essay in *The Reinterpretation of Early
American History* and his article in the *Huntington Library Quarterly*, and for allowing access to the Adair Papers now on deposit in
San Marino; to the many historians who volunteered their recollec-
tions and professional regard for their late colleague; to Robert E.
Shalhope for his historiographical essay; and to Donald Lamm, vice-
president of W. W. Norton, whose combination of patience and
enthusiasm is reminiscent of the real author of this volume.

But perhaps the most notable contribution comes from Caroline
Robbins, whose "Personal Memoir" appropriately introduces Douglass Adair's essays and articles and confirms what many already
know: it is impossible to consider Adair the historian without recalling Adair the person.

THE EDITOR has been fortunate in the preparation of this volume in having the assistance of the staff of the Institute of Early American History and Culture. With their advice and aid the following editorial method was adopted. Previously published pieces by Adair have been reprinted as they were in their original appearance, except that obvious typographical errors have been corrected and details of spelling, capitalization, italicization, and hyphenation have also been made consistent with the present Institute *Style Sheet.* In the footnotes, the mechanics of citation have also been standardized according to current rules of style, and in some cases, without indication, more bibliographic information has been supplied than was given in the original printing of an article. The two essays herein that are printed from unpublished Adair manuscripts, "The Jefferson Scandals" and "Clio Bemused," have been edited as though they were being prepared for publication in the *William and Mary Quarterly* today.

T.C.

INTRODUCTION

Trevor Colbourn

THIS VOLUME is intended as a sort of valedictory, my farewell to the finest of friends. It is also a posthumous offering to the historical profession, the intellectual testament of an inspired teacher, scholar, editor, and writer that takes the form of a selection of some of the liveliest and the most influential writing by the late and very lamented Douglass Greybill Adair.

It is also, appropriately, a book that Douglass Adair had often been asked to furnish and one that he was increasingly tempted to prepare in the years before his untimely death. "I have a strong professional interest in *book publication,*" he wrote to a colleague in 1960, "since the world of scholarship, as you know, rates one mediocre monograph as more of a scholarly achievement than a dozen brilliant articles." In the same year he confided to a good friend his proposal to compile a collection "under the title Jefferson Scandals and Other Essays— the Horn Papers, my pair on the 10th Federalist, Hamilton's Pseudo- nyms and Religion etc." His purpose, he continued, was "to resurrect them from the old files of the [*William and Mary*] *Quarterly,* where no one ever saw them except a very small circle of constant readers, and make a book." This memorial volume includes all of the essays and articles that Adair had in mind at that time.

Clearly, he underestimated the influence and impact of the *William and Mary Quarterly.* He never realized the full measure of his reputation as the gifted practitioner of a rare style of historical journalism or recognized the high regard in which his articles were held by numerous readers. If Caroline Robbins is correct in her view that Douglass Adair was troubled by "a feeling of rejection by colleagues during life," then he made himself the most tragic victim of skewed self-judgment (ironically, itself a favorite Adair phrase). Those whose professional respect he sought and valued knew him and recognized him for what he was: a man of uniquely brilliant insights whose work they admired and frequently cited. As John Pomfret has observed, "How many times, in speaking to a colleague about Madison, Jay, or Hamilton, has one heard the rejoinder, 'You know, Adair (or Douglass) thinks . . .' " When reviewing Gerald Stourzh's recent book, *Alexander Hamilton and the Idea of Republican Government* (1970), Gordon Wood remarked that "Douglass Adair would have liked this book, for he understood better than most historians the peculiarities of the intellectual world of the late eighteenth century. It is thus especially fitting that this book . . . is dedicated to his memory." It was fitting indeed, for Douglass Adair was the thoughtful and unselfish negotiator of the publication of Stourzh's book, a role he played for other historians many times.

DOUGLASS GREYBILL ADAIR died by his own hand on May 2, 1968. His death was a personal tragedy as well as a public loss. He was a man of rare gallantry, grace, courtliness, wit, and style. To some he seemed an eighteenth-century philosophe who had strayed into the twentieth century by some happy accident.

Adair's curriculum vitae tells too little of the man. Born in New York City, he grew up in Birmingham and Mobile, Alabama, majored in English at the University of the South in Sewanee and then went on to Harvard, where he received an M.A. in 1935. He spent a brief period in Washington, D.C., as research assistant to Walton H. Hamilton, with whom he wrote *The Power to Govern* (1937),[1] and

---

1. He later declared it to be "chiefly the writing of Walton Hamilton; he was extremely generous to add my name on the title page."

then returned to graduate school at Yale. There he was awarded the doctorate in 1943. His study of "The Intellectual Origins of Jeffersonian Democracy" is a minor classic among dissertations. He taught briefly at Princeton before moving to the College of William and Mary, where his association with the *Quarterly* from 1946 to 1955 brought fame to both. For the remaining thirteen years of his life, he contributed by his teaching and scholarship to the distinction of the Claremont Graduate School.

His published writing over these years was substantial and significant. Skill in historical detective work was first revealed in his extraordinary study of "The Authorship of the Disputed Federalist Papers" (1944). This was followed in 1947 by "The Mystery of the Horn Papers," written in collaboration with Pierce Middleton. In 1948 there appeared an edition of Robert Munford's *The Candidates*, co-edited with Jay B. Hubbell. "The Tenth Federalist Revisited" (1951) and " 'That Politics May Be Reduced to a Science': David Hume, James Madison, and the Tenth Federalist" (1957) give evidence of their continuing significance by the number of times they have been reprinted. Adair's sustained concern with the intellectual origins of the Constitution had its most recent exposure in " 'Experience Must Be Our Only Guide': History, Democratic Theory, and the United States Constitution," contributed to *The Reinterpretation of Early American History: Essays in Honor of John Edwin Pomfret* (1966), edited by Ray Allen Billington.

Adair's editorial talents were not confined to the *Quarterly* only. He entered into a happy and productive partnership with John A. Schutz, which resulted in *Peter Oliver's Origin and Progress of the American Rebellion* in 1961 and *The Spur of Fame: Dialogues of John Adams and Benjamin Rush, 1805–1813*, in 1966. Subsequently he embarked upon (but did not live to complete) an edition of David Ramsay's *History of the American Revolution;* at the same time he began work with Martin Diamond on a new edition (with commentary, concordance, and glossary) of *The Federalist* papers; and one of his last interests was an examination of the authorship of the *Annual Register,* to be studied with the aid of computer technology.

What does Adair's work signify for the historiography of early America? In a profession that places value upon being first with a new interpretation, a new insight, Adair's niche is secure. When he wrote his extraordinary doctoral dissertation at Yale, historians were still very much inclined to treat ideas as determined by nonrational economic factors. Adair was among the first to challenge the prevailing views of Charles Beard and his disciples and to consider carefully the classical legacy to the Founding Fathers and their inheritance from the seventeenth-century English republicans. At the time of Adair's death Martin Diamond concluded that "his outstanding merit as a historian and scholar was an acute awareness of the importance of ideas in determining the conduct of men and in shaping affairs. ... This is not to imply that ideas are disembodied forces which explain the whole of human behavior, but only to suggest that ideas achieve a force and life of their own and determine conduct as much as they are themselves determined by external forces."

Some three years earlier Adair himself had attempted a measure of self-identification in a long letter to Robert E. Brown at Michigan State:

I am, of course, as you charge, a historical determinist in the de Tocqueville sense, holding that the experience of each of us draws a circle of wider or narrower dimensions around each of us, and that our freedom of choice and options of necessity take place within this circle. And, of course, as you know, the "area" [sic] of experience that I have been most fascinated in for our eighteenth century friends is the realm of symbolic experience—their reading, their formal college training, etc.—which I feel structured and determined to a significant degree the physical world they saw with their eyes, or didn't see. The *Common* response of a Henry, a Rush, an Otis to the Stamp Act was *not* random, it was a response conditioned by a particular taught view of English Classical history that produced a very specific—

one might say predictable—reaction, although the personal history and temperaments and the particular environments of these men was [*sic*] quite different. . . . It is my own feeling that we really can't break into the eighteenth century semi-closed circle that determined their meaning and expectations when they talked about the limits and possibilities of politics and social organization.

His concern was always with motivation and the frame of reference that can help us to understand that motivation. His discovery of the remarkable relevance of "English Classical history" was one he generously shared with others.

With the marvelously accurate vision afforded by hindsight, we can see his scholarly liaison with Caroline Robbins as quite logical and inevitable, a liaison that furnished the foundation for the definitive contributions of such friends and admirers as Bernard Bailyn, Jack Pole, and Gordon Wood. Adair influenced a generation of scholars whose writing persistently reflects his insight, his curiosity, and his enthusiasm for people, past and present.

Despite his excellent publication list and his obvious influence, Adair often expressed dissatisfaction with his accomplishments, but he did not choose to live to publish the major monograph of which so many colleagues believed him easily capable. When well-intentioned friends chided him on his failure to bring forth his long-expected study of the intellectual origins of Jeffersonian democracy, he would shrug and remark that historians who mattered had already read his Yale dissertation; and he was right to the extent that the list of borrowers resembles a who's who in early American history. He worked in his own way, often content to explore a subject and then contribute his ideas and insights to others who would bring the study to full realization. Frequently Adair's own publications came with the helpful midwifery of friends and admirers like Margaret Kinard at the *Quarterly* or Edmund P. Willis at the 1966 Moravian College Conference.

Adair saw no point in attempting to patent ideas. He enjoyed stimulating others and took satisfaction in their success. Page Smith has remarked that "in my scholarly career I have never known anyone who was so much a source of ideas and inspiration for others as Douglass Adair. For me visits with Douglass were always an opportunity for a kind of intellectual gourmandizing. . . . He made conversations feasts of wit and reason and kindness. I valued his critical judgments more than those of anyone I know."

Such comments occur with remarkable frequency in any discussion of Adair's professional achievement. John Pomfret recalls Adair's "creative enthusiasm," how he was always seeking the idea behind the fact. Jack Greene remembers Adair the critic demonstrating that "criticism need not be negative" and, as Greene observes, that "to be devastatingly generous obviously requires far more imaginative power." As another one of his former students put it, Adair never exercised "a critic's virtuoso at the expense of other men's works, although he could be very exacting in his demands upon his fellow historians." Indeed, he was never less than intellectually honest and never less than kind, a man who found it easier to help others than himself. Lawrence Towner vividly recalls his first encounter—by correspondence—with Douglass Adair: "His response, for me, epitomizes the man he was. It was brilliant; it was kindly; it had half a dozen other subjects in it that he thought, quite rightly, needed investigation (all far better than the subject I proposed); and it represented a commitment then, and forever after, to me as a new friend and, despite the fact I was only a graduate student, a new colleague. That was Douglass Adair."

Perhaps Adair's happiest quality was his infectious enthusiasm, which in turn enhanced his extraordinary talent as a teacher of both peers and students. Indeed, recalls Joyce Appleby, "There was a quality about his relation with the past which went beyond enthusiasm. The past was alive to him—it was life, perhaps, and in his open exploration of history and man through history, he removed the barriers which usually loom up to make the past seem quaint or different."

But Wilbur Jacobs probably savored in a unique if melancholy fashion Adair's influence as teacher. Taking over Adair's seminar at Claremont the semester after his death, Jacobs reported:

The legacy of Douglass Adair seemed everywhere around. Somehow Douglass had unconsciously projected his dynamic personality into the very student body of the graduate school of history. There was scarcely a student I met . . . who was untouched by the Adair magic. Time and again these students seemed to reflect flashes of Adair himself; his creative powers, his eager idealism, his humane spirit, and his chivalrous admiration for the underdog. Sometimes the impact of Adair on students was almost overwhelming, especially when they attempted seminar papers and dissertations on profound topics that seemed to me to be the meat of unfinished books that Douglass had envisioned for himself. . . . He was always so generous . . . that his own work undoubtedly suffered.

Jacobs has another memory, one others have known: "I remember particularly his comradeship at a history convention when he comforted me after a critic on a paper I had read made what I thought was an ungentlemanly commentary. After the session Douglass came up to me, put his arm on my shoulder and said 'Come, let me buy you a drink, and I'll tell you what that fellow was trying to say.' And he did, but coming from Douglass the criticism was a delight to hear."

Such warm remembrances of Adair's counsel in part account for the extraordinarily favorable response from the profession to the recently established Douglass G. Adair Memorial Award. Announced in early 1972 by the Claremont Graduate School and the Institute of Early American History and Culture, the quadrennial award is given for the most significant article published in the *William and*

Mary Quarterly.[2] (The first covered the years 1964 to 1972; the next selection will occur in 1976.)

It is perhaps too evident that it is still difficult to write of Douglass Adair without being far more personal than is professional custom. But perhaps some of the reasons emerge. As Keith Berwick has remarked, Adair's "example and encouragement were constant sources of nourishment" for many of us. We believe the pages that follow will help explain why.

2. It is a remarkable testimony to Adair's impact on his time that sufficient funds were raised in his memory to enable the award committee to set the prize at $500 plus a gold medal. In Mar. 1973 in Claremont, Calif., the first Douglass Adair Award was presented to Edmund S. Morgan for "The Puritan Ethic and the American Revolution," *William and Mary Quarterly,* 3d Ser., XXIV (1967), 1–43.

DOUGLASS ADAIR

A Personal Memoir

Caroline Robbins

AT THE American Historical Association meeting in December 1946, Felix Gilbert brought over to me and introduced a large man who seemed somewhat formal in manner, saying, "You are both interested in Algernon Sidney, I believe." We settled down to talk. Adair was, I realized, southern. I also immediately became conscious of an engaging grin that as friendship progressed and meetings were more frequent, suggested an overwhelming pleasure in encounter and an all-enveloping welcome. On this first occasion I was questioned rapidly but listened to with rare attention, and before our talk ended, I had undertaken to write about Sidney for the *William and Mary Quarterly*. "What is it?" I ignorantly asked—and received a mild rebuke for not knowing this important journal of which, as I was to discover later, Douglass had recently become the editor.

Since 1943 Douglass had taught at the College of William and Mary in Williamsburg, after instructorships at Princeton (1941–1943) and Yale (1939–1941). A master's in history from Harvard in 1935 was followed by three years in Washington before he went to Yale, where he was to receive his Ph.D. degree in 1943. As a research assistant at the Social Security Board (1936–1938), it was in Washington that he collaborated with Walton H. Hamilton on *The Power To Govern: The Constitution—Then and Now* (New York, 1937). A timely book, it also combined for Douglass two lifelong interests: modern politics and the constitutional creation of the Founding Fathers. During his year at Harvard Law School (1933–1934) he had met and courted Virginia Hamilton. They were to have three children— Robert, Douglass, and Katherine Sidney—who no doubt brought their parents the normal quota of anxiety, but also indisputably an enormous amount of pleasure. Such biographical information was achieved slowly, however. In over twenty years of warm acquaintance, we were to converse for hours, after a quick exchange of personal news, about Madison, Jefferson, Hamilton, their antecedents and successors. Reminiscences about childhood and education were in short supply—I was not Boswell, and Adair always had academic problems and questions to discuss.

At this first meeting I told Douglass of my early plans, frustrated by the appearance of Vernon L. Parrington's *Colonial Mind,*[1] to analyze and trace the sea change undergone by emigrant Pilgrims and others this side of the wide Atlantic. He told me of his interest in David Hume and Madison (which was later to be brilliantly illustrated in " 'That Politics May Be Reduced to a Science' " in the August 1957 *Huntington Library Quarterly*), as well as in some seventeenth-century republicans. So a kind of partnership was formed. My article was duly dispatched and, to the accompaniment of the kindest of compliments, torn apart. Even in the printed version (July 1947), incorporating my meek agreement to nearly all suggestions, I discovered an extra sentence I had not fathered and a footnote *a* following my note 27 referring to the third president's use of Sidney. Douglass had been unable to resist inserting a few lines about his own "The New Thomas Jefferson" (*Quarterly*, January 1946), in which the phrase "the mass of mankind has not been born with saddles on their backs . . . ," used by the Virginian, was traced to the dying speech of Richard Rumbold, executed in 1685, two years

1. Vol. I of Parrington's three-volume *Main Currents in American Thought* (New York, 1927–1930).

after Sidney's death. An exchange followed in which Rumbold's own unacknowledged debt to Father Paul (Sarpi) was noticed, and eventually "Rumbold's Dying Speech, 1685, and Jefferson's Last Words on Democracy, 1826," appeared in the *Quarterly* for October 1952. I learned a lot about editorial plans and policies and the methods Douglass used to achieve them. But Keith Berwick has admirably described the third series under Morton, Adair, Bell, Towner, Abbot, and Greene and the "vintage years" in which for nine years Douglass had so large a part.[2]

In the summer of 1947 my husband, Joe Herben, and I visited Monticello and on impulse called up the Adairs asking if we might call on them if we made a long detour through Williamsburg. All suggestions of a motel were brushed aside. Douglass and Virginia made us welcome, introduced us to the children, fed us magnificently. The "Celebrated Mrs. Macauley" was mentioned, and when I remarked that I knew of a lively essay lying dormant in the desk of Lucy Martin Donnelly of Bryn Mawr, I was commissioned to see what could be done to get hold of it for publication. Miss Donnelly was delighted and started at once to revise as I began collecting enough references to Macauley's American friends to fit the subject to the *Quarterly*. Even Miss Donnelly's sudden death in the fall did not stop the project. Edith Finch and I continued work; Douglass declared that footnotes were not necessary and himself began collecting illustrative material. For these pictures he was to write "Catherine Macauley and Her Famous *History*, a Pictorial Commentary," inserted with the prints between pages 186 and 187 of the April 1949 issue in which the article appeared.

But this was a long job. During the summer of 1947 Douglass was fascinated by another problem. In "The Mystery of the Horn Papers" (*Quarterly*, October 1947), Arthur Pierce Middleton and Adair reported the work of a committee sponsored by the Institute

2. "A Peculiar Monument: The Third Series of the *William and Mary Quarterly*," WMQ, 3d Ser., XXI (1964), 3–17.

of Early American History and Culture to investigate a three-volume publication in 1945 of reputed documents. The investigators declared the whole thing a fabrication and probably the work in or around 1930 of one man. As Douglass described the detection involved, the doubts early expressed by Julian Boyd and others, and the steps necessary to uncover the fraud, even my husband, whose American interests focused chiefly on the military history of the Civil War, found the story utterly engrossing. Douglass could talk with an infectious enthusiasm, sparking his listeners to interested rejoinder. He was probably, I think, better in conversation and discussion groups than on the podium. His was an outgoing personality; he liked response, contradiction, commentary, and this would set him off again. He was a great talker, but also a good debater and conversationalist with the sure sense of exchange that such must have.

Nineteen forty-eight was an active year. I arranged a symposium on "The Venetian Commonwealth" in honor of Howard L. Gray, my late chairman and long a teacher of Renaissance history at Bryn Mawr. Douglass agreed to talk on "The Corruption of an Aristocracy: Venice as Viewed by Eighteenth-Century Americans." He and Virginia came to stay at our house the night before the meeting. Talk was lively. Zera S. Fink, whose *Classical Republicans* (1945) we all admired and who was on hand for the same occasion, was at last discovered by Douglass to be male, and the ice broken, many exchanges followed.[3] Douglass was in high spirits but was, alas, compelled to endure the ordeal of ad lib cutting, for his essay came at the conclusion of a morning of good, but overly long, contributions. He had done a fine job and won high praise from many present, including Conyers Read, who had presided over the festival in honor of his old colleague.

In this same month, April, Jay B. Hubbell and Adair printed in

---

3. [This meeting with the author of *Classical Republicans* must have been a surprise for Adair, for in his 1946 *Quarterly* review of that book, he repeatedly referred to the author as "Miss Fink."—Ed.]

the *Quarterly* Robert Munford's play, *The Candidates*, with literary and historical remarks about this drama of the Revolutionary period. In the following January, Douglass was to perform ebulliently in the production of the piece at the College of William and Mary. We were also at this time already discussing Thomas Hollis of Lincoln's Inn and his attempts to maintain and extend English libertarian ideas and practices in colonial America when they were suffering, he keenly felt, an eclipse in England. Since student days I had been casually aware of Hollis as a collector of seventeenth-century materials, but work in the forties in the magnificent Harvard library, where so many early books bore Hollis's inscriptions, comments, and admonitions, had enormously whetted my curiosity. Though William Jackson and Keyes Metcalfe, always generously and professionally helpful, had expressed polite indifference to speculations about the significance of their Hollis holdings, Douglass at once decided the *Quarterly*'s readers should learn about the eccentric republican. I produced an article I thought quite well of, only to receive orders from the Editor—to the tune, to be sure, of cheers and praise—to find the Hollis diary I had referred to as "lost." The Institute, prodded by Adair and benevolently disposed under Carl Bridenbaugh, promised some financial aid for films. In due course the diary was rediscovered, photographed, transcribed, and used in a fresh version of "The Strenuous Whig," which appeared in the July 1950 *Quarterly*. Douglass was a goad, a promoter, a builder-upper, and a superb critic. A long chapter would be needed to relate all the results of suggestions made by him and produced by his slave driving. Hollis books became a passion with both of us, and indeed much of my own scholarly activity was at this time concerned with the Harvard benefactor.

As Berwick has pointed out, special issues devoted to a single theme were among the strongest productions from the Adair editorial portfolio. The January 1951 *Quarterly* was devoted to Douglass's great passion, James Madison, and in it appeared one of his best essays, "The Tenth Federalist Revisited." Later a Hamilton collection of pieces was projected, but dilatory writers left most to Douglass, who published only a small sheaf of notes of his own on the eve of his retirement in 1955. Meanwhile plans were being developed for a "Scotland and America" number. I had a piece on Francis Hutcheson's theory of colonial independence that I wanted Douglass to print. With his customary flair, he was recruiting such then unknown writers as John Clive, Bernard Bailyn, Jack Price, and others. Though by no means all opinions expressed in the April 1954 *Quarterly* were entirely agreeable to the Scots, the total response everywhere was gratifying. At least two famous scholars, a philosopher and a historian, expressed appreciation and surprise. The undertaking was a tremendous success. Whitfield J. Bell, Jr., in addition to his own contribution, had by then taken over the acting editorship, while Douglass was away teaching at the University of Washington at Seattle, and saw the number through the press. As noted, Douglass returned, but in 1955 resigned both from the College of William and Mary and the *Quarterly*. He left plans for several issues ahead, so his influence continued long after his departure.

The Adairs moved to California when Douglass was appointed professor at Claremont Graduate School. Virginia soon joined the English department at California State Polytechnic College. The children grew up and scattered. The house bought at 489 West Sixth Street had, to their delight, a walled garden with a large lawn, camellias, and citrus fruit trees. Both Virginia and Douglass liked the West. Their hospitality was unchanged. During a relatively quiet period in the progress of the fatal disease that had overtaken my husband, we flew out, and were met at the airport, wined, dined, and kept overnight to inspect the new family domain. Then we moved to the Cal Tech Faculty Club in Pasadena. I read at the Huntington and, sitting in the lunch hour among its flower beds and trees, talked as often as possible with Jack Greene and Douglass about our mutual interests.

Douglass had had computers on his mind since the mid-fifties. In 1959 he was already in correspondence with the MIT scientists

Frederick Mosteller and David L. Wallace, whose *Inference and Disputed Authorship: The Federalist* (Reading, Mass., 1964) records work in this field of stylistic detection and acknowledges more than once the help received from Adair. In the *Quarterly* for April and July 1944 Douglass had published his conclusions about the relative share of Madison and Hamilton in the production of papers in *The Federalist*. When he talked to Greene and myself and was about to speak to the scientists at a conference held September 9, 1962, in Minnesota, he was enthusiastic and already fairly certain that his earlier deductions had been confirmed by the machines.

The Adairs took California to their hearts and seized the chance of acquiring one of the remaining "homestead lots" in the Mojave desert. Its address pleased them and us—"Shiloh," Star Route 2, Twenty-nine Palms. During that Huntington summer, with a station wagon loaded with food, ice, and drinks, the four of us drove out past the Joshua trees to spend a night there under the clear, starry desert sky. Douglass wanted me to hear a part of Virginia's play on the Wordsworths; Joe, who was too deaf to listen long, was happy observing the surrounding mountains and odd sparse vegetation. In the difficult days to come, these few hours became Joe's most agreeable recollection of his western stay, and this in spite of warnings from all but the Adairs that no invalid should endure such a trip in summer. A close second in expeditions was afforded by a drive up the coast to a Spanish mission specially selected for us by Douglass and then exploration of the Hearst Castle at San Simeon, its odd assortment of treasures and mementos, and its delicious gardens. As we returned to the public parking lot in the estate bus, the driver reflected on the late Mr. Hearst's love of animals—giraffes and others—of flowers, and of the magnificent scenery all around. The three of us speculated about the possibility that in a hundred years, when controversy was forgotten, California might acquire a patron saint William known chiefly for benevolence and for other characteristics more typical of St. Francis of Assisi than of most tycoons.

The sixties were productive. Unfortunately Douglass's plan for a volume of Washington's correspondence miscarried. But fruitful collaboration with John A. Schutz resulted in an edition of *Peter Oliver's Origin and Progress of the American Rebellion* in 1961 and, five years later, *The Spur of Fame: Dialogues of John Adams and Benjamin Rush, 1805–1813,* with a running commentary on the selected letters. In that year, 1966, Douglass came east to a conference at Moravian College in Bethlehem, Pennsylvania, where he read "Fame and the Founding Fathers," following a paper by Forrest McDonald and a comment by Staughton Lynd that provided material for some of his remarks. The papers and comments delivered at this conference were edited under the title of Douglass's essay by Edmund P. Willis and appeared in 1967. He projected a conference on editorial problems and worked during the summer of 1967 with Virginia on the identification of the pieces contributed by Edmund Burke to the *Annual Register.*

During the sixties, too, the Adairs at long last went abroad in search of books, British origins, the Lake poets, and other matters. Unfortunately we were leaving as they arrived, and I heard less than usual of their doings. Douglass, whom I saw but briefly during our last days in London, seemed depressed at the cold rains of England. But later both reported a very good year and thorough enjoyment of the leave.

Douglass and I, both members of the Institute Council in 1964 and 1965, had two encounters in Williamsburg, where we had not been together since the early days of "Scotland and America." The return gave much pleasure with renewed feelings of homecoming and cheerful meetings with old friends. About this time, too, Douglass III got into what his father called "the hereditary disease of the family"—editing a lively publication, *El Malcriado,* for César Chávez and the United Farm Workers of California. Katherine Sidney spent her junior year at the University of Amsterdam, graduated from Scripps, and while working in Cambridge became engaged to (and later married) Robert Harlow Waugh. The eldest, Robert, was also married and living not too far away. Though Douglass's exuberance was bound to have its reverse moments of depression, I had thought that affairs, which had been gloomy in the mid-fifties, had taken a turn for the better. The last time I saw Douglass Adair was in November 1967 when he came east for an oral history conference and seized the opportunity to spend Thanksgiving with his daughter, Katherine, and the Trevor Colbourns in New Hampshire and then visited myself and Joe, who was in the last weeks of his illness, in Pennsylvania. He could not stay with us, and we drove round the lovely wintry countryside to talk and avoid tiring the invalid. I found Douglass delighting in deciduous trees and stone buildings, and full of plans, apparently contented and happy. After his return in the spring, he sent me a postcard of the beautiful Watts Towers, to see which, he wrote, he and Virginia had "played hookey," and he also suggested an outline plan for my own future activity. The news of his tragic death was as unexpected as it was shocking.

What indications were there for friends? For me there were none at the time, though earlier I had observed moments of gloom, even despair. Hindsight suggests that Douglass was increasingly concerned with fame. He would inquire at large what it might be like to be quoted, appreciated, and admired by contemporaries. The paper at Moravian was eloquent on fame and the Founding Fathers' interest in it. The Adams-Rush letters presented yet another facet of the same theme occupying his attention. He cited Timothy Ford, *Eulogy on John Adams* (*Spur of Fame*, 283): "The desire for posthumous fame is an affection purely intellectual—standing in close connection with the immortality of the soul." But I doubt that reputation or possible lack of it after death troubled Douglass as much as a feeling of rejection by colleagues during life.

A brilliant young man, the early years at the *Quarterly* confirmed all expectations. Yet southern colleges, William and Mary included, offered low salaries, and the rewards of others were more than his for comparable jobs. Douglass gave very generously of his time, scholarship, and creative thinking to Williamsburg. He left there as embittered as a singularly sweet disposition allowed.[4] In the kinder West he did not find all the fulfillment he desired. "Not of course," he once wrote, "if I push with all my strength can I make nice things happen." Action often eluded him for weeks and even months. Review books, letters, papers would stack up; plans collapsed; opportunities passed as relentlessly as the years of scholarly career. Douglass prodded friends to action, criticized results, and urged them to renewed effort with an uncanny insight into what they could best achieve. He threw himself at times into Virginia's many creative activities and into meeting the needs of colleagues. He sent me many a note on matters of mutual interest, and as Joe's illness became more restricting, he also sent him paperbacks on military history, joke books, notes on desert flowers, not to mention airmail packages of fragrant blooms from the Adair garden.

Perhaps he should have been an idea man hired to throw out suggestions in some large university. Of ideas he had plenty to stimulate young and old; the very abundance and speed with which they occurred made it hard for him to finish projects. His out-going qualities perpetually distracted him from private and sustained labors. Yet Douglass never shirked drudgery, as all who felt his editorial gavel will remember. He simply did not find enough time to sit out the many frustrations of finishing his own work, the books that he felt the conventions of his profession as well as his own knowledge and insights demanded. His genius lay in generous and shrewd perception; his fate was possibly determined by a capacity to help others so much more than he could help himself.

4. [In 1965 he reported that "it was fun and slightly strange to be in Williamsburg as a 'distinguished visitor' after having spent so many years there as a low man on the totem pole—'the shining city of my manhood's grief'—and it was the first time I'd really visited since I left in 1955."—Ed.]

DOUGLASS ADAIR AND THE HISTORIOGRAPHY OF REPUBLICANISM

Robert E. Shalhope

WITHIN THE LAST DECADE a sophisticated understanding of eighteenth-century republicanism has emerged in American historiography. Whereas earlier scholars either ignored this concept or viewed it simply as a form of government based on the sovereignty of the people, historians have recently begun to perceive it as a dynamic set of ideas that assumed a vital, shaping role within early American society. Their research has illuminated the distinctive frame of mind that predominated in colonial American society. Americans, drawing heavily upon English libertarian thought, created a unique attitude toward government and society that literally permeated their culture. A consensus, with the concept of republicanism standing for the new world that eighteenth-century Americans believed they had created, quickly formed.

The Americans were convinced that what made republics great (or what ultimately destroyed them) was not force of arms but the character and spirit of the people. Public virtue became the preeminent social good. A people noted for frugality, industry, temperance, and simplicity was good republican stock. But those who wallowed in luxury could only corrupt others. Easily acquired wealth was always gained at the expense of the community. It was the entire society that was crucial, for the public welfare was the exclusive end of good government and demanded a constant sacrifice of individual interests to the greater needs of the whole. Thus, the people, conceived of as a homogeneous body (especially when set against their rulers), became the great determining factor in whether a republic lived or died. The most essential prerequisite for good government was the maintenance of virtue, and those factors that might weaken this were corrupt and unrepublican; they had to be purged before they destroyed the good society.

This recent understanding of republicanism—which has been instrumental in prompting new research, in revising traditional interpretations, and in reopening old questions—is most generally associated with the scholarship of Caroline Robbins, Trevor Colbourn, Bernard Bailyn, and Gordon Wood. Their work, however, represents the culmination of decades of intensive research by a great many scholars.[1] Only upon an examination of the etiology of the republican synthesis can we realize the full impact of Douglass Adair's life and work—the importance of his efforts as author, editor, critic, and provocateur to the emergence of an understanding of American republicanism.

When Adair moved to the College of William and Mary in 1943 he began a decade and a half of work that contributed, either directly through his own research or indirectly through that of others whom he inspired, to a greater comprehension of the role of ideas in early American political history. Such an understanding—vital to achieving a full perception of republicanism—constituted an important shift away from the prevailing historiography of the day. Progressive historians, viewing social action as a clash of interests (usually eco-

---

1. For a fuller discussion of this research see Robert E. Shalhope, "Toward a Republican Synthesis: The Emergence of an Understanding of Republicanism in American Historiography," *William and Mary Quarterly*, 3d Ser., XXIX (1972), 49–80.

nomic) disguised by a thin veneer of principles, reduced ideas to weapons in a *guerre de plume* and obscured their creative role in society.

In a two-part essay, "The Authorship of the Disputed Federalist Papers," Adair not only presented an outstanding example of the historian's craft but provided insights into the minds of several of the Founding Fathers.[2] By studying the research done by James Madison and Alexander Hamilton previous to the Constitutional Convention, Adair revealed the dependence of these men upon political philosophy in the writing of the Constitution. James Madison emerged as one particularly given to employing ideas in a creative manner rather than as a propagandist. Thus in this early essay Adair expressed in embryonic form ideas that he would later fully amplify.[3]

During the next two years (1945–1946) Adair expanded his discussion of Madison and, with the aid of his newly emerging frame of reference, presented fresh insights regarding Thomas Jefferson. In an introduction to Madison's autobiography Adair called attention to that statesman's constant attempt to regulate his politics in strict accord with " 'the purity of . . . republican principles.' "[4] Feeling that the autobiography illuminated Madison's conception of the relation-

---

2. *Ibid.*, I (1944), 97–122, 235–264 (reprinted in this volume). Twenty years after the appearance of this essay, a computer study employing Bayes's theorem proved conclusively what Adair had claimed through the use of manuscript sources and an insightful intelligence. Frederick Mosteller and David L. Wallace, *Inference and Disputed Authorship: The Federalist* (Reading, Mass., 1964). For other striking examples of Adair's skill in such historical detective work, see "The Mystery of the Horn Papers" and "The Jefferson Scandals," also printed in this volume.

3. In view of the fact that one of the major theses of this essay is Adair's ability to suggest new ideas to be followed by other historians, it is interesting to note that in this essay and in his review essay "The New Thomas Jefferson," *WMQ*, 3d Ser., III (1946), 123–133 (reprinted below), Adair revealed the manner in which acceptance or rejection of Madison and Jefferson depended upon the historical moment. Merrill Peterson employed this method in his imaginative study *The Jefferson Image in the American Mind* (New York, 1960).

4. Douglass Adair, ed., "James Madison's Autobiography," *WMQ*, 3d Ser., II (1945), 191–209. The quotation appears on 194.

ship between economic interests and politics, Adair questioned both
the prevailing habit among scholars of reading into the tenth *Federalist* the dogmas of Karl Marx and also the further assumption that
economic motives lay behind the creation of the Constitution. Such
a belief supported the thesis that the "more perfect union" emanated
solely from "the selfish economic appetites of American capitalists,
land speculators, and holders of depreciated government bonds." As
an antidote to this "crudely materialistic view," Adair suggested that
future editions of *The Federalist* should note Madison's statement
in the autobiographical memoir concerning the " 'strict rules' " he
personally adhered to in " 'pecuniary matters.' " This would demonstrate that Madison, the chief architect of the Constitution, early
resolved " 'never to deal in public property, land, debts or money,
whilst a member of a [political] body whose proceedings might influence these transactions.' "

Believing the autobiography suggested an approach to Madison's
political philosophy previously ignored by historians, Adair maintained that the memoir afforded striking evidence that Madison, "by
deliberate choice," lived his entire life in an atmosphere of books
and study. Ever the scholar, he always believed that "academic"
learning provided essential guidance to the practicing statesman.
Adair believed the autobiography conclusively revealed Madison to
be "an intellectual, a theorist, a political philosopher" who studied the
past to prepare himself for each assignment he faced as a republican
statesman. Adair then brought out his most provocative insight:
"Only by relating Madison's thought to the great western tradition
of political philosophy, will it be possible to define his service as
chief theorist of the American Constitution."[5]

Pursuing this same mode of thought in an essay published in *The
Lives of Eighteen from Princeton* (1946), Adair observed how politics
for Madison was "rather a science than a business" and noted in a

5. *Ibid.,* 195–196.

general manner the influence Francis Hutcheson, David Hume, and Adam Smith exerted upon the young Virginian.[6] He reiterated the point that for Madison theory and experience went hand in hand and noted that at the Constitutional Convention Madison "transcended the impossible by inventing a completely new type of federal state, which while solidly resting on majority rule at the same time provided adequate safeguards for the rights of minority groups. From his reading and experience he evolved an original theory of republican federalism differing completely from the principles of any of the historic confederations." Adair emphasized that Madison's work at the convention institutionalized his previously developed theory and proved to be "the greatest triumph in practical application of the Enlightenment's ideal of scientific political research."[7]

In a review essay also written in 1946, "The New Thomas Jefferson," Adair further explored his thesis that late eighteenth-century American leaders made extensive use of European ideas in a New World environment. After gently chiding the authors under review for suggesting the Virginian was "a unique superman, mastering and adding to all fields of knowledge," Adair pointed to the necessity of showing in detail Jefferson's actual contributions to the accumulated knowledge of his own age before making any final assessment.[8] Adair believed historians in fact knew very little about the Virginian's ideas in relation to the total civilization of which he was a part. Instead "American historians for fifty years have bayed down the false scent laid by Turner and have viewed Jefferson as a peculiarly

6. Willard Thorp, ed., *The Lives of Eighteen from Princeton* (Princeton, N.J., 1946), 142. The essay is reprinted below.

7. *Ibid.*, 151.

8. *WMQ*, 3d Ser., III (1946), 123–133 (reprinted below). The quotation appears on 131. Well aware that Jefferson's increasing popularity might result in uncritical scholarship, Adair observed in another review that "there is a saying among publishers that any book about Lincoln, doctors, or dogs will sell enough copies to justify the cost of printing it. Apparently we have now entered a period when books about Thomas Jefferson can be added to that list." *Ibid.*, IV (1947), 112–113.

American product of his 'frontier' environment." As a result "few students have analyzed the agreements and divergences between Jefferson's theories and statements and those of his European contemporaries." Adair considered it impossible at that time "to go through Jefferson's writings on any topic and to say with assurance, here Jefferson is breaking new ground, here he is making his own original contribution, and here he is merely repeating the borrowed idea of someone else." In a prophetic remark Adair suggested that twenty years hence scholars might well dismiss Jefferson's observations on various subjects as "the superlative product of an intellectual middleman, whose literary skill made him an ideal popularizer of other people's thoughts." Once again tying his conclusions to his own intellectual quest, Adair stated that "until all of Jefferson's ideas and projects are carefully examined against the background of contemporary European developments, and until his theories are appraised as part of the great tradition of Western social thought, we will be unable to take the true measure of the man."[9]

Adair constantly remained alert to relevant sources in Western social thought in order to bring them to the attention of the scholarly community. His review of Zera Fink's *The Classical Republicans* (1945) did just that by noting the dependence of the Revolutionary generation in America upon the ideas of the political philosophers examined by Fink—James Harrington, Henry Neville, Walter Moyle, Jonathan Swift, and Algernon Sidney. For this reason he felt that Fink's book could be read with "especial profit" by scholars interested in the intellectual background of the American Revolution. Adair believed that no one reading Fink's book, which dealt with only "one part of the intellectual background of modern republicanism," could "fail to be aware of the complex influences playing upon the founders of the American republic"; he concluded with a call for additional

9. "The New Thomas Jefferson," *ibid.*, III (1946), 132–133.

studies of libertarian thought, which he knew would be necessary before historians could "accurately trace the genesis and development of our modern democracy."[10]

Although writing a favorable review, Adair clearly realized something that had escaped Fink. The republican ideas explicated in his book did not die with Algernon Sidney in 1683; instead they were carried on and amplified by left-wing English libertarians. Adair fostered this perception through his support of the publications of Caroline Robbins. As early as her essay on Sidney in 1947, Robbins maintained that "the debt . . . of America to the men who failed to impose their ideas on England in 1689, has not yet been properly assessed."[11] While it would be years before other scholars took up this insight, Robbins made an important early contribution by initiating a move toward understanding English libertarian thought and indicating its influence in America. As editor of the *William and Mary Quarterly* Adair furthered this development by commissioning essays dealing with the libertarian persuasion and by publishing additional essays by Robbins that laid the basis for her vitally important *The Eighteenth-Century Commonwealthman.*[12] This book explicated clearly the radical English thought that played such a large role in American Revolutionary republicanism.

10. Zera S. Fink, *The Classical Republicans: An Essay in the Recovery of a Pattern of Thought in Seventeenth Century England* (Evanston, Ill., 1945); the review appeared *WMQ*, 3d Ser., III (1946), 610–612.

11. "Algernon Sidney's *Discourses Concerning Government*: Textbook of Revolution," *WMQ*, 3d Ser., IV (1947), 267–296. The quotation appears on 273.

12. See Robbins's "The Strenuous Whig, Thomas Hollis of Lincoln's Inn," *ibid.*, VII (1950), 406–453; "'When It Is That Colonies May Turn Independent': An Analysis of the Environment and Politics of Francis Hutcheson (1694–1746)," *ibid.*, XI (1954), 214–251; and *The Eighteenth-Century Commonwealthman: Studies in the Transmission, Development, and Circumstance of English Liberal Thought from the Restoration of Charles II until the War with the Thirteen Colonies* (Cambridge, Mass., 1959). For an excellent analysis of Adair's contribution as editor of the *Quarterly* see Keith B. Berwick, "A Peculiar Monument: The Third Series of the *William and Mary Quarterly*," *WMQ*, 3d Ser., XXI (1964), 3–17.

In 1951, in "The Tenth Federalist Revisited," Adair drew together his own previous research and thoughts regarding James Madison. Historians directing their efforts to American Revolutionary thought received considerable assistance from this essay, which maintained that the work of Charles A. Beard and other Progressive historians had cast a shadow over the study of the Constitution—and by implication over all of early American history—by minimizing the importance of ideas and ideological factors. Adair demonstrated far more completely and convincingly than he had done previously (and perhaps more than anyone had before) that political ideas and philosophies were central to the writing of both the tenth *Federalist* and the Constitution. Further, he contended that Madison's tenth *Federalist* was "eighteenth-century political theory directed to an eighteenth-century problem; and it is one of the great achievements of that intellectual movement that later ages have christened 'Jeffersonian democracy.' "[13] Adair's essay assumes importance not only because it expertly delineated an aspect of eighteenth-century American thought but because it represented a major step in shifting attention toward ideological factors in the creation of the Constitution and in the understanding of early American society.[14]

In the three years subsequent to the publication of this essay, Adair showed both his own awareness of the sources essential to an understanding of the eighteenth-century American mind and his ability to disseminate imaginative leads to fellow historians in order to bring that understanding closer to fruition. The latter constituted a hallmark of his scholarship throughout his career.

Reviewing E. Millicent Sowerby's *The Catalogue of the Library*

13. WMQ, 3d Ser., VIII (1951), 48–67 (reprinted below). The quotation appears on 67.

14. Recent research relative to ideology indicates that it should no longer be considered as simply a rhetorical shield to further crass interests. Ideology is employed in this essay in the manner seen in Clifford Geertz, "Ideology as a Cultural System," in David E. Apter, ed., *Ideology and Discontent* (New York, 1964), 47–76.

of Thomas Jefferson, Adair explored Jefferson's dependence upon books and maintained that the Virginian's books "offer scholars one unsurpassed approach to the innermost citadel of his personality— an approach that reveals significant traits of his character both as private citizen and public man." Jefferson's libraries, Adair said, "are the hyphen in the phrase now commonly used to describe him as the young republic's most spectacular 'scholar-statesman.'" Observing that Jefferson early began a systematic collection of books to further his studies, Adair acclaimed Sowerby's *Catalogue* as "a major event in the field of Jefferson studies." He considered it "a marvelous guide to the intellectual world of Jefferson—a world which a few earlier scholars have glimpsed but have hardly yet begun to map— a key to the whole circle of late eighteenth-century politics, science, and arts." More important, "since Jefferson's power as a thinker did not depend on originality, it is a key which will serve wonderfully well, if used intelligently, to open up for inspection the common pattern of libertarian ideas, in all fields of knowledge, prevailing on both sides of the Atlantic during Jefferson's lifetime."[15] In an earlier essay Adair himself noted Jefferson's intense interest in the Stuart period of English history and hinted broadly that he was particularly drawn to the "Whig" conception of that period.[16]

The review predicted that Sowerby's work would serve as a starting point "in the immediate future of a larger number of fruitful studies of Jefferson and his age. . . ."[17] Adair could not have been more prophetic; his student Trevor Colbourn—making full analyses of the

15. *WMQ,* 3d Ser., XI (1954), 637–641 (reprinted below). The quotation appears on 637–638.

16. "Rumbold's Dying Speech, 1685, and Jefferson's Last Words on Democracy, 1826," *ibid.,* IX (1952), 521–531 (reprinted below). Indeed, as early as his essay on the authorship of *The Federalist* Adair noted Madison's familiarity with the work of James Burgh—perhaps the most influential of all the libertarians in America. *Ibid.,* I (1944), 260–261 (reprinted below).

17. *Ibid.,* XI (1954), 638.

libraries of various eighteenth-century American leaders—revealed the impact of Whig history upon Americans in perceptive essays dealing with Thomas Jefferson and John Dickinson. Colbourn then brought together his research in his important *Lamp of Experience* (1965)—a book that documented the influence of libertarian thought upon Jefferson throughout his life.[18]

Previous to this review Adair wrote for the *Quarterly* a short introductory essay to a collection of British cartoons dealing with the Stamp Act. Once again, in a seemingly insignificant essay he revealed his capacity for penetrating into the transatlantic flow of ideas. Claiming that a careful study of the cartoons showed "a certain feature of the Stamp Act controversy, as it developed, that later historians have tended to forget or write off as of minor importance because scholarly research so soon revealed it to be the most arrant propaganda and the most arrant nonsense," Adair called attention to the link of the American Revolutionary cause with that of John Wilkes. He considered the cartoons to be "graphic signposts pointing to a major historical study, as yet unwritten, on the background of the American Revolution. . . ." Continuing, Adair contended that "the Wilkite thesis, that coercion in the Colonies was the complement to a ministerial and royal scheme to subvert Liberty in the Motherland through 'corruption' of Parliament, carried increasing conviction in Boston, Philadelphia, Charleston, and Williamsburg, as the conflict of the 1760's continued into the early 1770's." Twelve years later this strand of thought—greatly amplified and brilliantly executed—formed the core of Bernard Bailyn's introduction to his *Pamphlets of the American Revolution* and, subsequently, of Bailyn's *Ideological Origins of the American Revolution*, the essential book to be read

18. See Colbourn's "Thomas Jefferson's Use of the Past," *ibid.*, XV (1958), 56–70; "John Dickinson, Historical Revolutionary," *Pennsylvania Magazine of History and Biography*, LXXXII (1959), 271–292; and *The Lamp of Experience: Whig History and the Intellectual Origins of the American Revolution* (Chapel Hill, N.C., 1965). Both Caroline Robbins and Trevor Colbourn reveal their personal relationship with Adair in their essays in this volume.

for an understanding of the eighteenth-century political mind in America.[19]

In the mid-1950s Adair wrote two essays that further developed his ideas regarding the importance of historical precedent in the creative process of writing the Constitution. "'Experience Must Be Our Only Guide': History, Democratic Theory, and the United States Constitution" offered additional impressive evidence that those who wrote the Constitution spent much time researching their positions and that the ideas they offered in the Constitutional Convention reflected that research.[20] Thus, the Constitution represented an attempt to forge a workable government based on the experience of history. In this paper Adair dealt primarily with the pessimistic and deterministic views of John Adams and Alexander Hamilton, but in a brilliant essay published several years later that focused on James Madison, Adair analyzed a more optimistic and unique plan of government. " 'That Politics May Be Reduced to a Science': David Hume, James Madison, and the Tenth Federalist" (1957) demonstrated that ideological rather than economic motives impelled Madison and, by implication, the other Federalists. Adair contended that Madison's use of history in the Constitutional Convention did not represent "mere rhetorical-historical window dressing, concealing substantially greedy motives of class and property," and analyzed Madison's intellectual struggle with Montesquieu, showing how, drawing upon David Hume, he worked to fashion a republican form of government that encompassed the entire nation. In his tenth *Federalist* Madison

19. "The Stamp Act in Contemporary English Cartoons," *WMQ*, 3d Ser., X (1953), 538–542. The quotation appears on 538–539. *The Ideological Origins of the American Revolution* (Cambridge, Mass., 1967) is an expanded version of the introduction, "The Transforming Radicalism of the American Revolution," in Bailyn, ed., *Pamphlets of the American Revolution, 1750–1765* (Cambridge, Mass., 1965).

20. Later published in Ray Allen Billington, ed., *The Reinterpretation of Early American History: Essays in Honor of John Edwin Pomfret* (San Marino, Calif., 1966), 129–148, this essay was first an address delivered by Adair at a meeting of the American Historical Association in 1955. It is reprinted in this volume.

turned Montesquieu on his head by showing that stability—that most precious commodity in a republican government—could be achieved in a large geographic area by checking factions against each other within a vitalized federalism.[21]

It still remained to be explained why Madison felt the need for a vitalized federalism. To show that he thought as a political scientist and not as a class-conscious elitist did not explain why he thought as he did. Nonetheless, Adair's article represented an important step toward a republican synthesis, because it established Madison's concern for republicanism and showed that he reasoned within this context. What was still lacking was a sophisticated understanding of the context; republicanism was yet to be clearly defined as something other than simply a form of government. It was still not perceived as a pervasive political ideology. The publication of books by Robbins, Bailyn, and Wood over the next decade accomplished this; their work provided access into the mind of late eighteenth-century America through a full explication of republicanism.[22]

This understanding of republicanism has prompted recent studies taking the new synthesis as a starting point. At the time of his death Adair himself had begun an approach that still requires fuller development. In his essay "Fame and the Founding Fathers" (1967), Adair argued that "the greatest and the most effective leaders of 1787—no angels they, but passionately selfish and self-interested men—were giants in part because the Revolution had led them to redefine their notions of interest and had given them, through the concept of fame, a personal stake in creating a national system dedi-

21. *Huntington Library Quarterly,* XX (1956–1957), 343–360 (reprinted below). The quotation appears on 347.

22. Adair felt such an interest in getting this new perspective before the scholarly community that he wrote a letter to the editor of the *American Historical Review* in response to the review of Robbins's book that appeared in that journal. In his letter Adair pointed out the worth of an understanding of libertarian thought to those interested in the American Revolution. *American Historical Review,* LXV (1959–1960), 1048–1051.

cated to liberty, to justice, and to the general welfare." Continuing, he observed that "the love of fame, and the belief that creating a viable republican state would win them fame, is part of the explanation of the élan, the tremendous energy, the dedicated and brilliantly effective political maneuvers by which the small minority of American leaders who were nationalists kidnapped the movement to reform the Articles, wrote what they conceived to be a more perfect union, and then managed to get it ratified by the reluctant representatives of an apathetic populace."[23]

This insight should lead historians to a more careful analysis of the goals set for the United States by late eighteenth-century leaders. Joseph Charles's statement that "the fundamental issue of the 1790's was no other than what form of government and what type of society were to be produced in this country" becomes even more meaningful when viewed in this new context.[24] A careful study of the concept of fame held by various American leaders and of their drive for fame—to be gained through analysis of the society and form of government they hoped to construct—could lead to a sharper insight into these men and greater discrimination in judging them, in place of the blurred understanding achieved by lumping diverse figures into amorphous blocs labeled "Federalist" and "Republican."[25]

An understanding of republicanism can contribute more than sim-

23. Edmund P. Willis, ed., *Fame and the Founding Fathers* (Bethleham, Pa., 1967), 27–52 (reprinted below). The quotation is on 49.

24. *The Origins of the American Party System: Three Essays* (Chapel Hill, N.C., 1956), 6.

25. In his essay on the authorship of *The Federalist* (reprinted below), Adair recognized the beginning of a distinction in the approach to government and society between Madison and Hamilton even prior to the Constitutional Convention. *WMQ*, 3d Ser., I (1944), 241–242, 259. Despite his own anti-Hamiltonian bias, Adair's essays on Hamilton did stimulate a new approach to that statesman's life. See especially his "A Note on Certain of Hamilton's Pseudonyms," *ibid.*, XII (1955), 282–297. This essay foreshadowed Gerald Stourzh's impressive reinterpretation, *Alexander Hamilton and the Idea of Republican Government* (Stanford, Calif., 1970).

ply added sophistication to eighteenth-century intellectual history. Through study of the ideology's vital link to social forces in early America, the historian can gain insight into the dynamics of economic and religious as well as social and political life in late eighteenth- and early nineteenth-century America. Research by social scientists indicates that there is a dynamic relationship between language and the milieu from which it emanates. Gordon Wood's essay on rhetoric and reality reveals the need for study of the social environment that gives rise to a particular ideology—in this instance republicanism.[26] Thus, a new thrust directed toward social history is needed to broaden knowledge of early American politics and early American culture in general.

Fully realizing that ideas do not exist in a vacuum, Adair probed the social history of eighteenth-century Virginia throughout his career. As in his intellectual studies, several of his insights into social history were later developed by fellow historians. In an editorial introduction to Robert Munford's play *The Candidates*, Adair uncovered several interesting phenomena. By identifying Virginia as a deferential society—an idea later expanded by J. R. Pole and a concept that underlies the work of Bailyn and Wood—Adair revealed a paradox in Virginia society.[27] Because Virginia was a deferential society, that colony's aristocratic leadership could support a radical type of eighteenth-century republicanism. A similar paradox—although related to slavery—would later find brilliant application by Edmund

26. "Rhetoric and Reality in the American Revolution," *WMQ*, 3d Ser., XXIII (1966), 3–32.

27. Jay B. Hubbell and Douglass Adair, "Robert Munford's *The Candidates*," *ibid.*, V (1948), 217–257. Implicit in this essay and explicit in "The New Thomas Jefferson," *WMQ*, 3d Ser., III (1946), 123–133, and a later book review, *ibid.*, XVI (1959), 589–593, was Adair's understanding that such terms as *democratic, liberal, aristocratic,* and *conservative* must be understood in their eighteenth-century context. This is basic to Pole's important essay "Historians and the Problem of Early American Democracy," *AHR*, LXVII (1961–1962), 626–646. In his "Rhetoric and Reality," *WMQ*, 3d Ser., XXIII (1966), 3–32, Wood also employs Munford's play, but to illustrate the uneasiness within the aristocracy rather than its firm hold on Virginia society.

Morgan in his 1971 presidential address to the Organization of American Historians.[28]

While the idea of deference has been carefully analyzed, several other ideas found in Adair's work have not. In his essay on James Madison and in an introduction to the autobiography of Devereux Jarratt, Adair noted an aspect of eighteenth-century Virginia society well worth investigation. In both pieces Adair represented Virginia to be a society that neither admired nor fostered a literary or an intellectual life as an end in itself. He observed that "higher learning and literary culture were valued in Virginia, but this was because the higher learning was an upper-class monopoly; and it was valued chiefly as a sign of class superiority and as a conspicuous badge of prestige." In consequence colonial Virginia constituted a terribly frustrating environment for her native intellectuals, "and a major effort of will was required even by such privileged upper-class intellectuals as Jefferson to resist the powerful social pressure toward philistinism and dilettantism." Adair believed that none of the aristocracy's potential thinkers—including "a James Madison who transcended his environment, or a John Page who fell victim to it—had to fight so hard for their intellectual salvation as Jarratt."[29] There are suggestions to be developed here. The dynamics of a society that exerts a stifling influence on low-status individuals and requires a great effort by the upper class to avoid intellectual stultification requires examination. This is especially true given the direction Southern society took as it moved into the later antebellum period and found itself locked in a sectional struggle with the North. Was a latent anti-intellectualism and a tendency toward mindless conformity already present? Does late antebellum society simply reflect its earlier antecedents? Study of antebellum America could profit greatly from questions arising from Adair's succinct observations.

28. The address appeared as "Slavery and Freedom: The American Paradox," *Journal of American History*, LIX (1972), 5–29.

29. "The Autobiography of the Reverend Devereux Jarratt, 1732–1763," *WMQ*, 3d Ser., IX (1952), 346–393. The quotation appears on 347.

In a review of a biography of Patrick Henry, Adair raised additional intriguing questions. He felt that the author under review might have focused on Henry's famous speeches and asked such questions as "why Henry's treasonable statements of 1763 were acceptable to his lower-class audience in Hanover while the same sort of demagogy tried in 1765 in Williamsburg was unacceptable to an upper-class audience." He further believed that "analytical questions should be directed to Henry's ambition and an attempt should be made to evaluate his competitive drives in terms of eighteenth-century Virginia standards of success."[30] Here Adair clearly foreshadowed his own attempt to deal with the concept of fame.

The Patrick Henry review elicited a bitter personal attack upon Adair's demand for an "inner view" of history.[31] However, Adair's quest for an "inner view"—which now appears to be developing through the integration of the efforts of social and intellectual historians—emanated from a mind constantly questioning easy answers and probing difficult problems, sometimes working out solutions but more often than not raising provocative questions to be dealt with by others. For this reason an assessment of Adair's place in American scholarship based solely upon his own finished work cannot do full justice to the man and to his unforgettable services to a profession that prospers only through the free exchange of ideas.

---

30. Adair's review of *Patrick Henry: Patriot in the Making* (Philadelphia and New York, 1957), the first volume of Robert Douthat Meade's two-volume biography, appeared *ibid.*, XVI (1959), 589–593. The quotation is on 592.

31. *WMQ*, 3d Ser., XVII (1960), 283–286.

I

ARTICLES
AND
ESSAYS

❧ 1 ❧

FAME AND THE
FOUNDING FATHERS

"Fame and the Founding Fathers" had a curious history of its own that is informative about Douglass Adair's approach to writing history. There is reason to believe that it was in 1964 that he first gave serious thought to the quest for fame as a motivating force. Certainly he referred to such an approach long before the spring of 1965, when he spectacularly unveiled what many scholars believe to be his most intriguing and successful disquisition. The occasion was the Kansas City meeting of the Organization of American Historians, and for Douglass it was a particularly special occasion since he knew his banker-brother would be in the audience. Consequently he was determined to mount an oratorical tour de force and show his skeptical sibling just how exciting intellectual history could be. The meeting room was crowded, hot, humid, and unairconditioned. But no one left until the bitter end. Adair did what he intended. He gave the performance of his life; seemingly inspired, he communicated directly with his audience, apparently referring only to rough notes as he developed his theme. There is some doubt that he had a paper to read, and certainly his commentator, Robert E. Brown, had no paper on which to base a reaction.

In later correspondence with Brown, Adair remarked that he should have had John Schutz on the platform with him, since they had worked in partner-

SOURCE: Reprinted by permission of Moravian College from Edmund P. Willis, ed., *Fame and the Founding Fathers* (Bethlehem, Pa., 1967), 27–52.

3

ship for three years on the Rush-Adams papers, which disclosed "a sort of pathology of 'the love of fame.' " Adair also took this occasion to observe that it was Gerald Stourzh who first noted the significance of Hamilton's discussion of fame in *Federalist* Number 72.

During the ensuing year Adair reconsidered and refined his thoughts on "Fame," knowing he was committed to a paper for the March Conference on Early American History at Moravian College. His focus on Forrest McDonald's *E Pluribus Unum* (1965) reflected a reading of that recent publication, as well as an acknowledgment of McDonald's presence at the same conference to give a paper on "The Completion of the Continental Union, 1789–1792." Listeners to Adair's presentation of "Fame" were disappointed: he did not keep to his text, he seemed unduly self-absorbed and reflective. But the printed version that follows represents a significant reconsideration of Adair's earlier thinking. It also constitutes the last historical testament of Douglass Adair and, in the view of some, his most perceptive.

1

MY TOPIC this evening is Fame—"Fame and the Founding Fathers." It might be subtitled: "Who were *our* HEROES' Heroes?" or, "The effect of the Revolution in transforming the ambitions and life goals of some of the Revolutionaries."

You can instantly divine from my use of the words "life goals" that I will be throughout discussing implicitly the ambitions and motives of some at least of the Founding Fathers, and this means inevitably that I will be dealing with a topic, "self-interest," that the late great Charles Beard and his young follower Forrest McDonald have written about so cogently. So in the last part of my talk, I want explicitly to give two cheers—but only two cheers—for McDonald's study *E Pluribus Unum* and to criticize its restricted definition of the term "self-interest."

Now, I have no doubt, national sentiment being what it is, that we have a trained-in tendency to exaggerate the stature and virtues of the Revolutionary generation, the group of men, chiefly born between 1730 and 1760, who led Americans down the road to Independence in 1776, fought the war through to victory, and created a stable national union with the Constitution of 1787. Nevertheless any generation that could produce a John Adams, a Hamilton, a Dickinson, a Rutledge, and the galaxy of great Virginians, must be set down as a remarkable one, for this or any other country.

In some ways the most remarkable aspect of their rise on the American political horizon was the tiny population pool out of which they emerged. If twentieth-century nationalism invites us to magnify, perhaps, their stature, it also encourages us to forget how few there were in the America of 1776, how small the nation that bred this generation of founders.

According to the census of 1790, even if one counts all the slaves and women and children, the total population of the United States was but 3,600,000 souls. The Nigerian Republic which achieved independence in 1960 had ten times that population; Cuba and the Arab Republic of Iraq today are both twice as large as our Republic in 1790. Los Angeles County in 1966 has more people than the whole of the United States that elected Washington president. The total population of the Union when the Constitution was ratified was slightly more than the present population of *Alabama;* slightly less than that of *Wisconsin;* it was a little larger than *Minnesota* today; somewhat less than the current population of *Georgia.* Kansas today has a larger population than the total combined population in the eighteenth century of *all* New England, *plus* New York and New Jersey, *plus* Pennsylvania, *plus* North Carolina and Georgia. Virginia in 1790, the largest of the states, contained just over seven hundred thousand people, if one counts the slaves as well as free inhabitants; but this state, which produced Washington, Mason, Henry, Jefferson, Madison, Marshall, had a total white population, including women and children, of about four hundred thousand souls. This is much smaller in number than such modern spawning grounds of political genius as the Wilkes-Barre metropolitan area or Phoenix, Arizona.

Why this unexpected explosion of talent? How can we account for this amazing concentration of political ability in this generation born into a tiny nation on the fringe of the Atlantic? It is so astonishing, it seems so lacking in antecedent causes that Professor McDonald, contemplating the writing and ratification of the Constitution, uses the word "miracle"—which my dictionary tells me is an "event due to some supernatural agency." This implies that the birth of the Republic was at least a little like the famous virgin birth reported in the New Testament.

Contemporaries, some men of 1776, some members of the Revolutionary generation, were as struck by the phenomenon as we are, but they, as befits an age that was skeptical of direct divine intervention in human affairs, spoke in terms of secular cause and effect. David Ramsay, who served in the Continental army and was a delegate from South Carolina to the Continental Congress, puzzled over the problem in his *History of the American Revolution,* published in 1789. The "Revolution," he says, "called forth many virtues and gave occasion for the display of abilities which, but for that event, would have been lost to the world. . . . In the years 1775 and 1776, the country being suddenly thrown into a situation that *needed* the ability of all its sons . . . a vast expansion of the human mind speedily followed. . . . It seemed as if the war not only required but *created* talents. Men whose minds were warmed with the love of liberty . . . spoke, wrote, and acted, with an energy far surpassing all expectations, which could be reasonably founded on their previous acquirements."[1]

But Ramsay noted, too, that the Revolution evoked, along with patriotism, self-sacrifice, and splendid performance in defense of liberty, a sordid picture of many Americans trying selfishly to cash in

---

1. "Great occasions call forth, and in a manner create, great and unknown ability as we have lately seen in the history of the American Revolution." Joseph Priestley, *Letters to the Right Honourable Edmund Burke, occasioned by his Reflections on the Revolution in France* (Birmingham, 1791).

on the crisis, treating the war as an excuse to get rich quick, to scramble for place and profit.[2] I don't think, then, that we can merely rest on Toynbee's formula of challenge and response as an adequate explanation. The challenge of our Revolution, to quote Alexander Hamilton, exhibited "human nature" in its "blackest colors" as well as "its brightest."

So we must seek some additional element, more specific than challenge and response, some shared stimulus that operated in common on the leading statesmen of the Revolution, whether they came from New England or the South—some factor which sets them apart from the cheap-jack politicians, summer soldiers, and sunshine patriots of their own day, and also from the run-of-the-mill politicians of ours.

Here I think an observation by de Tocqueville about American ambitions is helpful in our inquiry. "The *first* thing which strikes a traveller in the United States," de Tocqueville says, "is the drive of ambition," the democratic urge to better oneself that feverishly stimulates an "innumerable multitude" of the Americans. The *second* striking feature of American character, however, the Frenchman thought, was

the *rarity* of *lofty* ambition to be observed in the midst of the universally ambitious stir of society. No Americans are devoid of a yearning desire to rise; but hardly any appear to entertain hopes of *great* magnitude, or to pursue very *lofty* aims. All are constantly seeking to acquire property, power, reputation; few contemplate these things on a great scale. . . . Ambitious men in democracies are [little] . . . engrossed . . . with the interests and judgments of posterity; the present moment alone engages and absorbs

2. "Behind the facade of slogans about the rights . . . of man, different colonies had supported the revolution in pursuit of different goals, all local and few highminded. . . . Intrigue and factional strife in Congress were common, and men of all factions embezzled public funds, profiteered in procuring army supplies, and speculated on the basis of secret information." Forrest McDonald, *E Pluribus Unum: The Formation of the American Republic, 1776–1790* (Boston, 1965), 9–10, 12.

them. They are more apt to complete a number of undertakings with
rapidity, than to raise lasting monuments of their achievements; and they
care much more for success than for fame.

The most significant feature of de Tocqueville's observation lies
not only in the fact that it applies to most twentieth-century Americans but also that it applies to the great generation of founders
themselves before the Revolution. Listen to John Adams on the low
aims of New Englanders, the trivial ambitions of his contemporaries
before 1776. "When I was young," he told Jefferson in 1813, "the
Summum Bonum in Massachusetts was to be worth ten thousand
pounds Sterling, ride in a Chariot, be a Colonel of a Regiment of
Militia and hold a seat in his Majesty's Council. No Man's Imagination aspired to anything higher beneath the skies."

The young George Washington, as portrayed by Freeman and
Knollenberg—a rather unattractive youth in many ways—exempli-
fies with slight southern differences variations on this provincial
theme. Instead of a sterling balance, Washington lusted after land.
Driven ceaselessly by ambition, he was also obsessed with his "honor"
and reputation; but he set his sights low—thought in terms of success,
not fame—his "Summum Bonum" was to obtain a colonel's commission in the British regular army.

Hear Jefferson speak of his youthful ambitions and the small-scale
models he set for himself to copy. "I had the good fortune to become
acquainted very early with some characters of *very* high standing
and to feel the incessant wish that I could even become what they
were. Under temptations and difficulties I would ask myself what
would Dr. Small, Mr. Wythe, Peyton Randolph do in this situation?
What course in it will insure me their approbation?" His "Summum
Bonum" of ambition was to model himself on a provincial schoolteacher, a provincial lawyer, and to try to be like a "very" high-
placed member of His Majesty's Council in the colony of Virginia.

So far as I am aware, there are only two of the great generation who we know set themselves very "lofty aims" (in the de Tocqueville sense) before the Revolution. One is the oldest of the major leaders, Benjamin Franklin, who as a young man wrote down among the rules by which he tried to govern his behavior: "Imitate Jesus and Socrates." And, as we know, when he had won a comfortable income, he retired from business to become a full-time philosopher, teacher, and community servant, hoping thus—and succeeding at it—to build himself a "lasting monument." Franklin is the only American Revolutionary to have won world fame before 1776. The other who aimed high is among the youngest of the Fathers, Alexander Hamilton. By the time he was fourteen he had taken General Wolfe as his model and his idol; and trapped, as he felt it, in the "groveling" status of a merchant's clerk, Hamilton was fantasizing as early as 1769 about winning immortal glory, even at the cost of his life, as Wolfe had done on the Plains of Abraham.

It is the conflict with the mother country itself that, as Ramsay notes, "creates" the characters of the leaders we celebrate. The Founding Fathers, in a very true sense, are thus children of the Revolution, men who are transformed in the process of making it.

Before 1776, Ramsay recalled, American legislators made laws "about *yoking hogs, branding cattle* or *marking rice.*" After 1776 these same men were "called upon to determine on the issues of peace and war, treaties and negotiations with foreign states, and other subjects interesting to the . . . liberty, sovereignty and independence of a wide extended empire." And the evidence, I think, is conclusive that one aspect of the "expansion of the human mind" which Ramsay noted as occurring in this context is a transformation of the life goals the greatest leaders set for themselves, a redefinition in their own minds of their ambitions and the choice of new heroes to model themselves on. As the War for Independence enlarges the provincial stage upon which they act their roles to that of a world theater, the greatest of the great generation develop an almost obsessive desire for fame. They become fantastically concerned with posterity's judgment of their behavior. And since they are concerned with the image that will remain in the world's eye, "that love of fame which is the ruling passion of the noblest minds," to quote Hamilton, becomes a spur and a goad that urges some of them to act with a nobleness and greatness that their earlier careers had hardly hinted at.

Of course they were patriots, of course they were proud to serve their country in her need, but Washington, Adams, Jefferson, and Madison were not entirely disinterested. The pursuit of fame, they had been taught, was a way of transforming egotism and self-aggrandizing impulses into public service; they had been taught that public service nobly (and selfishly) performed was the surest way to build "lasting monuments" and earn the perpetual remembrance of posterity.

Listen again to Hamilton, who like Franklin and Jefferson and Madison, and unlike Washington or John Adams, seems never to have really cared about getting rich, and who died almost a bankrupt: "The desire for reward is one of the strongest incentives for human conduct." But there are rewards and rewards; and the different rewards, the different ends men strive for, control to a degree the means they employ to win their ends. The specific reward striven for thus affects behavior. It is my argument that the lust for the psychic reward of fame, honor, glory, after 1776 becomes a key ingredient in the behavior of Washington and his greatest contemporaries.

2

Is NOT this merely stating a truism? Isn't this merely saying that all men like to be praised? And does the desire to be praised, admired, and thought well of really set this Revolutionary generation apart from modern politicians, college teachers, or contemporary businessmen? It is obvious from the title of this paper that I do think it makes a difference; that the desire for sovereign honor, the passion for fame, in the eighteenth century, is a special variety of praise sought from a particular audience, and it is different both in degree and kind from the desire of approval that animates most twentieth-century Americans.

Today the word *fame*, the concept of "the love of fame" as "a ruling passion" has for us but a faint and tattered remnant of its eighteenth-century meaning. "Honor" in the traditional sense is used hardly at all now, and the word *fame* has been vulgarized and democratized. For example, in a recent issue of *Look* magazine (March 9, 1965) an interview with Richard Burton and Liz Taylor entitled "King and Queen" quotes Burton's pronouncement: "Fame you get accustomed to, but if it ever takes possession of you, then . . . you're in . . . trouble"—implying that an actor gets stuck-up and offends his fans if he assumes his popularity is permanent—if he tries to build an "enduring monument." This application of a noble word to the ephemeral bubble-like reputation of a Welsh actor and his wife would have astonished George Washington and his contemporaries. Clearly Burton and the *Look* editors, who solemnly print his comments on "the fame" of Liz and Dick as a serious statement, define fame as a synonym for great mass popularity—the approval and acclaim of a populace—the judgment, to quote Milton, of "a herd confused; a miscellaneous rabble, who extol things vulgar." Popularity,[3] in the view of the eighteenth century, was really the small change—the copper coinage—of true fame of golden glory; they would mock Burton's complacency with Goldsmith's couplet: "Of praise a mere glutton he swallowed what came, and the puff of a dunce, he mistook it for fame."

There is too little time this evening to explore the eighteenth-century concept of *fame* and its cognates *glory* and *honor* except in

3. "POPULACE. The vulgar; the multitude. . . .
POPULAR. Vulgar; plebian. Suitable to the common people; familiar, not critical. . . .
POPULARITY. Gracious among the people. . . . Representation suited to vulgar conception; what affects the vulgar.
POPULARLY. In a popular manner; so as to please the crowd." Samuel Johnson's *Dictionary of the English Language . . .* (London, 1756).

the most superficial way. It is clear, however, from even the most cursory check of the literature of Europe from the age of the Renaissance to the nineteenth century, that these words indicate values and interests that fascinated successive generations of moralists, artists, preachers, politicians, playwrights, soldiers, and poets. There are books written on the subject; fame is analyzed by Machiavelli and Montaigne, by Bacon, Hobbes, Bolingbroke, Mandeville, Adam Smith, and literally hundreds of other writers. Shakespeare's trilogy of plays on Henry IV and Henry V deals explicitly with the pursuit of honor and the ethical and moral pitfalls along the way. Addison and Steele, in the *Spectator,* and countless other journalists comment, criticize, and compare the different types of honor and different kinds of fame. Pope in 1711 will compose a five-hundred-line poem called the *Temple of Fame,* and later in the century Edward Young will take twenty-five hundred lines and seven books to describe the *Love of Fame, the Universal Passion.* This summary merely scratches at the surface.

Most of us in common speech today use the words *honor, glory,* and *fame* as if their meanings were exactly interchangeable. The three words, although they all share the common ingredient of *praise* and *blame,* although they all assume some independent audience that judges and assesses behavior in order to award praise or blame, each differ very significantly as to *who* that audience is and *when* the praise or blame is awarded.

Glory, in its core meaning, is an attribute of God and, strictly speaking, of God alone. God is not famous; nor is Jesus designated as "the honorable," though a devout Christian writing on honor (Robert Ashley, c. 1596) can speak of "the Godhead itselfe" as "the well-springe and fountayne of all honour." The concept of *glory* assumes that He is always watching men (and sparrows) and that those men who, conscious that God's eye is continually on them, behave with such piety and goodness in rendering homage to Him, will shine with reflections of His glory. Saints, through their divinity acquired by their love of God and through their actions pleasing to God, diffuse His glory among mankind. Halos, aureoles, nimbuses (as Dr. Johnson's *Dictionary* notes) are called "glories" and are iconographic symbols in Christian art of those who in their lives glorify God and shine in the reflected light of His glory.

The concept of *honor*, like the concept of glory, is both the goal of character formation and an instrument of social control, building into the heart and mind of an individual a powerful personal sense of socially expected conduct, a pattern of behavior calculated to win praise from his contemporaries who are his social equals or superiors. For a particular person in a particular culture a sense of honor—a sense of due self-esteem, of proper pride, of dignity appropriate to his station—acts like conscience for a practicing Christian.[4] Like conscience it is capable of inspiring in some men and women systematized and regularized conduct that is noble, magnanimous, and admirable.

However, as an eminent seventeenth-century English divine, John Rogers, noted, *honor* differs from conscience because it is rooted in its intense "regard to the censure of the world" at a particular time and in a given place. *Honor* thus is inevitably conservative and is linked with the morale of the status quo. It is elitist, for small male in-groups, traditionally those "that are free, well-born, well-bred," who (by implication) alone possess that "instinct and spur . . . called honour." Thus the concept of *honor* in a social sense is narrow, technical, exclusive. As T. V. Smith comments, a code of *honor*, even at its best, is ethically reactionary.[5] *Honor* all too easily becomes an adjunct of the unequal distribution of power and privilege in a historic society; it attaches itself to *status by ascription*.

4. "Honor's the moral conscience of the great." William D'Avenant, *Gondibert: an heroick poem* (London, 1651).

5. See *Honor* and (cross-references) in the *Encyclopedia of the Social Sciences* by the late T. V. Smith, philosopher, poet, and politician. And also note the definitions (which fill a folio page) of Johnson's *Dictionary*.

When Jefferson, in 1785, urged his young nephew Peter Carr if ever he was tempted to do a dishonorable act, "tho' it can never be known but to yourself, ask yourself how you would act if all the world were looking at you, and act accordingly," he advocated a pattern of manners which we today can admire only in part, for the Virginia gentleman's code of 1785—which was Carr's world—judged women to be intellectual inferiors and accepted chattel slavery as a proper and necessary institution.

Honor thus is primarily a private ethic that links a person's identity with social stratification or occupational specialization. It is an ethic of competition, of combat, of struggle for eminence and distinction; and therefore *honor* is traditionally antithetical to the Christian demands of humility, abnegation, altruism.[6] "One notes little organic unity between codes of honor and norms of social welfare," T. V. Smith observes.

Fame, in contrast to honor, is more public, more inclusive, and looks to the largest possible human audience, horizontally in space and vertically in time. Fame is "celebrity; renown" (Dr. Johnson); it is the action or behavior of a "great man," who stands out, who towers above his fellows in some spectacular way. To be famous or renowned means to be widely spoken of by a man's contemporaries and also to act in such a way that posterity also remembers his name and his actions. The desire for fame is thus a dynamic element in the historical process; it rejects the static complacent urge in the human heart to merely *be* and invites a strenuous effort to *become*— to become a person and force in history larger than the ordinary. The love of fame encourages a man to make history, to leave the mark of his deeds and his ideals on the world; it incites a man to refuse to be the victim of events and to become an "event-making" personality—a being never to be forgotten by those later generations that will be born into a world his actions helped to shape.

6. See Arthur Livingston on the *Gentleman* in *Encyclopedia of the Social Sciences*.

It is this dynamism—one could almost say demonic quality—in the desire for fame that leads classical authors and their seventeenth- and eighteenth-century commentators to use the metaphor of the "spur," or the "goad," when *fame* is discussed.[7] *Glory*, at least in strict Protestant thought, is a *gift* through the grace of God; *honor* can be inherited, and as the duke of Wellington is supposed to have said about the Order of the Garter, there need be "no damned nonsense about merit" involved, but *fame* has to be earned. *Fame* can never be a gift; it cannot be inherited; it must be won by a person who imposes his will, his ideas, for good or ill, upon history in such a way that he will always be remembered.

Notice there is an ambiguity in the love of fame as "a ruling passion." If it is a passion, a lust, a desire that takes possession of one, it can produce actions on occasion that are memorable because of their superlative wickedness or their vice. If a person, frantic at the threat of death and oblivion, determines to become famous at any cost, he may act as Herostratus, the man who burned down the Temple of Diana at Ephesus in order to immortalize himself. Fame thus may be morally neutral. A man may stand out in his time and after because he is a brilliant and forceful scoundrel. Plutarch's *Lives of the Noble Greeks and Romans* offers standing proof that preeminence and fame may be divorced from private virtue or public good.

The great tradition of Fame, however, is neither ethically blind nor morally neutral. The audience that men who desire Fame are incited to act before is the audience of the wise and the good in the

---

7. "The love of fame puts spurs to the mind." Ovid; "The desire of glory clings even to the best men longer than any other passion." Tacitus, speaking of Helvidius Priscus; "The desire for fame tempts even noble minds." St. Augustine; "The man who spends his life without winning fame leaves such mark of himself on earth as smoke in air or foam on water." Dante; "Contempt of fame begets contempt of virtue." Ben Jonson; "Fame is the spur that the clear spirit doth raise (that last infirmity of noble minds), To scorn delights and live laborous days." Milton; "Fame and rest are utter opposites." Steele; "Who pants for glory finds but short repose." Pope; "Passion for fame; a passion which is the instinct of all great souls." Burke.

future—that part of posterity that can discriminate between virtue and vice—that audience that can recognize egotism transmuted gloriously into public service. The love of fame is a noble passion because it can transform ambition and self-interest into dedicated effort for the community, because it can spur individuals to spend themselves to provide for the common defense, or to promote the general welfare, and even on occasion to establish justice in a world where justice is extremely rare.

It is clear, I think, that the desire for fame is primarily the desire for immortality. Fame defeats that threat of oblivion with which Death confronts every man. In our age, when medical knowledge has lengthened the span of life and somewhat banished the fear of Death to the fringes of consciousness, we forget what an omnipresent specter it was even two hundred years ago. In England at the beginning of the eighteenth century, of every hundred babies born alive, thirty-six died before the age of six, twenty-four more before the age of sixteen, and fifteen more before the age of twenty-six. Thus only a quarter of the population survived to reach full maturity. In mid-eighteenth-century America (—rich, healthy America!), Franklin would actually celebrate the fact that only half of American children died before coming of age. So we must remember that the ever-present consciousness of Death stood in the forefront of our ancestors' minds in the eighteenth century; we must recognize the hope of fame like the hope of Christian immortality is a mode for dealing with proud Death and conquering him.

Carl Becker saw this connection and wrote mockingly and ironically of it in his somewhat perverse little classic, *The Heavenly City of the Eighteenth-Century Philosophers.* Becker notes Diderot's statement that "posterity is for the philosopher, what the other world is for the religious man." Becker then links this eighteenth-century concern with posterity's opinion to the idea of progress and presents the paradoxical argument that the idea of fame as a mode of immortality is merely a metamorphosis of medieval Christian values. In fact, the tradition of fame and honor that was most significant to the American

Revolutionaries (and the French, too, for that matter) predates Christianity itself.[8] It is classical in its origin, and educated men of the Enlightenment were drilled and educated in it at college, not at church; from the Renaissance, with its "revival" of classic values, it parallels and competes with the Christian tradition. Not that the two don't intermingle and overlap often in the eighteenth century. See, for example, Franklin's setting up as models to be imitated "Jesus and Socrates"; and see, too, the climactic third act of the most popular English play of the century, Addison's *Cato*, for its mingling of Christian and pagan dreams of immortality. However, the point that must be made is that the classical tradition of fame usually has nothing in it of progress or future perfectibility of man. What it does have, looking backward, is a pantheon of models that an eighteenth-century individual was invited to copy and emulate if he would win secular glory and immortality.

Just as the medieval Christian was urged by Thomas à Kempis to the *Imitation of Christ* and was offered in the Bible models of piety, so in the classical tradition Plutarch's *Lives of the Noble Greeks and Romans* offered examples of heroism and secular virtue—standing, in Plutarch's words, as "a sort of looking glass" in which a man "may see how to adjust and adorn . . . [his] own life.[9]

3

THE AMERICAN REVOLUTIONARIES found in Plutarch not merely a generalized image of glory, but one very specific and concrete

8. "Honor and dishonor are the matters with which the high-minded man is especially concerned." Aristotle, *Ethics*, iv (c. 340 B.C.), and Cicero, *De Officiis*, Book II, 30*ff*, especially, written 40 years before the birth of Christ.

9. Plutarch's opening paragraphs of the *Life of Timoleon*. As Moses Hadas notes in his *Ancilla to Classical Reading* (New York, 1954), 310, Plutarch "has indubitably had more European readers than any other pagan Greek and has been the greatest single channel for communicating to Europe a general sense of the men and manners of antiquity." Cf. Jonathan Swift to Stella, 1727: "In points of honor to by try'd / All passions must be laid aside: / Ask no advice but think alone; / Suppose the question not your own. / How shall I act? is not the case; / But how would Brutus in my place? / In such a cause would Cato bleed? / And how would Socrates proceed?"

type of fame that became most meaningful to the greatest of our Revolutionary leaders after 1776. This is a tradition of fame almost completely forgotten in twentieth-century America; it is a pattern Plutarch offers—a model he provides—of the great LAWGIVER and the FOUNDER OF A COMMONWEALTH. Perhaps the easiest way to rediscover it is to listen to a dialogue—to recreate a dramatic scene that occurred in Philadelphia, April 11, 1791.

President Washington, who was away from Philadelphia on his tour of the southern states that spring, had asked Hamilton and the other cabinet members to consult with each other if any urgent business developed that "required despatch." One such occasion did arise and Jefferson invited John Adams, the vice-president, and Hamilton, secretary of the Treasury, to dine with him in his lodgings, to confer on the problem. "After the cloth was removed," Jefferson reports, "and our question agreed and dismissed, conversation began on other matters. . . . The room being hung around with a collection of the portraits of remarkable men, among them those of Bacon, Newton, and Locke. Hamilton asked me who they were. I told him they were my *trinity* of the *three greatest men* the world had ever produced, naming them [Bacon, Newton, and Locke]. He [Hamilton] paused for some time. 'The greatest man' he said, 'that ever lived, was Julius Caesar.' "[10]

This dramatic confrontation between the mature Hamilton and the mature Jefferson is significant *not* because of the conclusion that Jefferson drew from it: that Hamilton in 1791 was a secret enemy of our republican Constitution, which as secretary of the Treasury he had sworn to uphold, or that Hamilton was already working to overthrow the Republic and to establish himself as a Caesar, but because it allows us to discover both Jefferson and Hamilton revealing a shared commitment to fame in its maximum glory.

The most explicit and revealing gloss on this profoundly revealing

10. Jefferson to Benjamin Rush, Monticello, Jan. 16, 1811.

scene can be found in the writings of that same Sir Francis Bacon, the first of Jefferson's trinity, whose picture Jefferson carried with him wherever he went much as a devout Roman Catholic maintains a shrine with images and pictures in his home.

In Bacon's *Essays*—a Renaissance equivalent of Dale Carnegie's success manual showing how to win powerful friends and influence the top people in a fiercely competitive hierarchical society—Bacon notes that "praise is the reflection of virtue; but it is as the glass . . . which giveth the reflection. If it be from the common people, it is commonly false and naught; for the common people understand not many excellent virtues. The lowest virtues draw praise from them; the middle virtues work in them astonishment or admiration; but of the highest virtues they have no sense of perceiving at all." However, "if persons of quality and judgment concur," the "judgment of these persons of quality is like unto a sweet ointment . . . and will not easily away." The "winning of Honour is but the revealing of a man's virtue and worth. . . ."

And then Bacon offered a five-stage classification of the highest, the ultimate in fame and honor—a ladder of glory—that guaranteed immortal remembrance to those men great and forceful enough to win to the top levels.

The lowest or fifth stage of Bacon's pyramid of "sovereign honor" is allocated to those rulers of states who are called *"patres patriae, fathers of their country; which reign justly, and make the times good wherein they live."*[11] And Bacon named examples. More famous, and hence "in fourth place," are *"propugnatores imperii, champions of the empire; such as in honorable wars enlarge their territories or make noble defence against invaders."* Ranked above them, in third place from the very top, stand *"salvatores imperii, saviors of empire,*

11. It should be apparent that the title accorded Washington as the "Father of his Country" was not a title invented de novo by his grateful countrymen. Compare the memorial tablet placed over the tomb of the Corsican patriot and rebel Paoli in Westminster Abbey, which designates him as "the father of his country."

such as compound the long miseries of civil war, or deliver their country from the servitude of strangers or tyrants; as Augustus Caesar . . . King Henry the Seventh of England, King Henry the Fourth of France." In second place, marshaled on the rarified level just below the top rank of sovereign honor and fame stand "the *legislatores*, the great law givers, who are also called *perpetui principes* or perpetual rulers, because they govern by their ordinances after they are gone; such were Lycurgus, Solon, Justinian." Finally at the ultimate peak of honor and fame, "in the first place are *conditores imperiorum*, FOUNDERS OF STATES AND COMMONWEALTHS; such as were Romulus, Cyrus, Ottoman," and significantly, "Julius Caesar."[12]

Hamilton's statement, then, in the spring of 1791, that he considered Caesar "the greatest man that ever lived" did not necessarily carry the sinister undertones that Jefferson would impute to the statement twenty years later. In 1791 the French Revolution was still in its honeymoon state; all the great powers of the Atlantic community were at peace; and neither Jefferson nor Hamilton that April night could foresee the outbreak of war between England and France in 1793, which would so profoundly affect the politics of the United States and which would give Hamilton the chance to contemplate the use of an American army, raised in 1798 in the quasi war with France, as a weapon of domestic politics directed against Jefferson and his party. In 1791 Napoleon, still unknown to history, had not yet begun his bloody march toward world empire

---

12. For Machiavelli's comparable pyramid of fame, see *Discorsi*, chap. 10, entitled "In Proportion as the Founders of a Republic or Monarchy are entitled to Praise, So do the founders of Tyranny deserve execration": "Of all men who have been eulogized, those deserve it most who have been the authors and founders of religions; next come such as have established republics or kingdoms. After these the most celebrated are those who have commanded armies, and have extended the possessions of their kingdom or country. To these may be added literary men, but, as these are of different kinds, they are celebrated according to their respective degrees of excellence. All others—and their number is infinite—receive such share of praise as pertains to the exercise of their arts and professions.

"On the contrary, those are doomed to infamy and universal execration who have destroyed religions, who have overturned republics and kingdoms. . . ."

that reached its climax in 1811 and gave a new and contemporary meaning to Caesarism. In 1791 Dr. Rush himself, who shuddered appropriately in 1811 at Jefferson's anecdote of Hamilton's admiration of Caesar, had casually set down in a letter to Jeremy Belknap his admiration of Caesar's greatness, "perhaps" (so Rush wrote) "unequalled in the history of mankind."[13]

But when Hamilton named Caesar as the greatest of men, did he think of him as the immortal "founder of a commonwealth"? It is surely not enough merely to show that Bacon, and perhaps others, thought of the divine Julius thus; what is needed is specific evidence to prove that Hamilton viewed the great Roman so, that Hamilton's admiration of Caesar was married in his mind to the problems and opportunities facing the leaders of the American Revolution as *conditores imperiorum.*

Listen to Alexander Hamilton speak in 1778, thirteen years before his dialogue with Jefferson. In a pamphlet, significantly signed with the pseudonym Publius, it was the first time, but not the last, that Hamilton would identify himself with this famous figure from Plutarch—he wrote:

The station of a member of Congress is the most illustrious and important of any I am able to conceive. He is to be regarded not only as a LEGISLATOR, but as a FOUNDER OF AN EMPIRE. "A man of virtue and ability, dignified with so precious a trust, would rejoice that fortune had given him birth at a time and placed him in circumstances so favorable for promoting human happiness. He would esteem it not more the duty than the privilege and ornament of his office to do good to all mankind. From this commanding eminence he would look down with contempt upon every mean or interested pursuit."

Hamilton undoubtedly thought of Caesar—identified himself with the Caesar who was the "founder of a commonwealth." Hamilton believed himself to be one who through the grace of fortune was

13. Rush to Jeremy Belknap, Apr. 5, 1791, L. H. Butterfield, ed., *Letters of Benjamin Rush* (Princeton, N.J., 1951), I, 579.

destined to establish an American empire that could promote the happiness of the human race and at the same time reward Alexander Hamilton with fame and immortality. Gerald Stourzh is entirely correct when he argues that this statement over the signature of Publius in 1778 is the most revealing probably that the mature Hamilton ever wrote, showing his "own conception of his life work and the ultimate goal of his ambition."[14]

But what of Jefferson's competing category of immortal fame? Where in the eighteenth century do Bacon, Newton, and Locke stand in relation to Caesar, the soldier-legislator *conditor imperiorum?* Again, it is Sir Francis Bacon who provides the clue. In his *Advancement of Learning,* published eight years after he had placed Romulus and Caesar at the very pinnacle of fame, Bacon offered a second thought and an even higher category of greatness by adding a sixth rank superior even to "founders of empires and commonwealths." Bacon in 1605 argued that the greatest glory should be awarded to those philosophers—we would call them "scientists"—and inventors who had employed "the Divine gift of Reason to the use and benefit of mankind." Such men exemplified the ultimate combination of the qualities of "action and contemplation," of thought and deed, that "dignify and exalt" human nature. In contrast, Bacon's earlier hierarchy of fame had chiefly honored men of action—soldiers and statesmen, some of whom had been worshipped after their death as demigods. Caesar, for example, and most of the later Roman emperors had been voted divine honors by the Roman Senate, which had

14. The Hamilton quotation can best be studied in Harold C. Syrett and Jacob E. Cooke, eds., *The Papers of Alexander Hamilton* (New York, 1961–), I, 580. Gerald Stourzh was the first scholar to call attention to the significance of this passage (unpubl. paper delivered at the American Historical Association meeting in New York, Dec. 30, 1957), in allowing us to recognize Hamilton's demonic passion for fame. The context of Hamilton's statement is also a significant comment on those who would overemphasize the role of avarice in the establishment of the Constitution—the Publius essays of 1778 pour contempt and scorn on Samuel Chase, member of Congress from Maryland, who was using his office, and the inside information it gave him, to engross the supply of flour before the French expeditionary forces arrived, in order to corruptly enrich himself and his partners.

decreed temples in their honor and added them as lesser deities to the pantheon of *dii majores*. Bacon's later and highest category of immortal fame looked to these major gods of classical civilization. "Deification," Bacon noted, "was the highest honor among the heathens; that is to obtain veneration, as a god was the supreme respect which man could pay to man." But the political "honors" distributed by antiquity to such as Caesar "by a formal act of the State" were "inferior" to the "voluntary, internal assent and acknowledgement" that was accorded by the ancients to "inventors, and authors of new arts or discoveries for the service of human life, [who] were ever advanced among the [greater] gods as in the case of Ceres, Bacchus, Mercury, Apollo and others." Clearly, in Bacon's mind, as he reconsidered the problem, the "human honors" by senatorial vote were "inferior" to this fame "heroical and divine" because "founders of states, lawgivers, extirpers of tyrants, fathers of the people, and other eminent persons in civil merit were honoured but with the [lesser] titles of heroes or demigods, such as Hercules, Theseus, Minos, Romulus, etc." This distinction between the lesser and greater fame, between "demi-gods" and "major gods," in Bacon's view was made "with great justice and judgment, for the merits of the former [statesmen and soldiers] were generally confined within the circle of one age or nation, [and] are but the fruitful showers which serve only for a season and a small extent, while the others [the philosopher-inventors] are like the benefits of the sun, permanent and universal." Moreover, the deeds of legislators and generals are "mixed with strife and contention," while the gifts to mankind of the scientist-philosophers have the "true character of the Divine presence, as coming without tumult and noise."[15]

Thanks to Frank E. Manuel's fascinating monograph analyzing

15. The casting of constitution makers and founders of empires in the role of demigods explains Jefferson's designation of the members of the Philadelphia Convention of 1787 as a convention of "demi-gods," a term which has puzzled some modern scholars who think Jefferson must have spoken thus "with tongue in cheek." Richard M. Gummere, *The American Colonial Mind and the Classical Tradition: Essays in Comparative Culture* (Cambridge, Mass., 1963), 174.

eighteenth-century ideas about the nature of the pagan gods, we are able the better to comprehend what Bacon's thesis implied when he drew the distinction between the different degrees of immortal fame resulting from the classical distinction between the greater gods and demigods.[16] To the man of the Renaissance like Bacon, and to later neoclassic writers educated in the Christian tradition, the pagan gods presented one great logical puzzle. How could the noble Greeks of the age of Socrates, and the illustrious Romans of Virgil's and Livy's time, have rationally worshipped the pluralistic medley of gods and godlings that made up the pagan pantheon? It was unthinkable to damn the great men of classic times as superstitious fools or the ignorant dupes of priests, yet they had built temples to Zeus-Jupiter and Poseidan-Neptune, to Demeter-Ceres, Pomona and Bacchus. Thus by Christian definition they bowed down before idols and graven images. Was there a solution to this intellectual dilemma?

The resolution of this paradox, facing the Christian who admired the ancients, was provided by a Hellenistic theory about the origins of the pagan gods.[17] Jupiter-Ammon, Vulcan, Mercury, Aesculapius were actually great men, so the theory held—"inventors and authors of new arts and discoveries for the service of mankind"—whose contribution to humanity was so transcendent that they were worshipped as gods by a grateful superstitious people in the dim early ages of prehistory.[18] It seemed completely plausible, for if human

16. Frank E. Manuel, *The Eighteenth Century Confronts the Gods* (Cambridge, Mass., 1959).

17. The technical name for this theory is *Euhemerism;* it ascribed the origins of pagan religion to a historical apotheosis of some once-living hero or king. See *ibid.,* chap. 3, pt. 2, especially.

18. For a classical attempt to harmonize the Egyptian, Grecian, Babylonian, and Roman pantheons, and so assimilate the Egyptian Osiris, the Greek Zeus, and the Roman Jupiter into one dimly seen historic inventor of agriculture in prehistoric times, see *The History of Diodorus Siculus* (London, 1653); for an 18th-century scholarly restatement, see Abbe Goguet's three-volume work, *The Origin of Laws, Arts, and Sciences* . . . (London, 1761), which President Witherspoon recommended to Princeton students like James Madison. For an assimilation of Norse mythology to this theme, see Alexander Pope's *The Temple of Fame: A Vision* (London, 1715),

heroes like Alexander and Caesar had been voted shrines and temples in historic times,[19] would not Dionysus-Bacchus, the inventor of viniculture, or Zeus-Osiris-Jupiter, the inventor of agriculture, also have been worshipped in earlier ages? Nor were eighteenth-century Protestant critics of the Catholic calendar of saints, like the scholar Mosheim, or the reformer Tom Paine, reluctant to draw the conclusion that "honors paid to the [early Christian] martyrs were gradually assimilated . . . to the worship which the pagans had in former times paid to their gods."[20]

This at least is implied in Sir Francis Bacon's argument in his *Advancement of Learning*. Since the ancients made the distinction between the categories of *dii majores* and *dii minorum gentium*, between gods and demigods, fame in modern times, Bacon thought, should make the same distinction. Modern philosophers-scientists-inventors who gave such great service to humanity ought to be more highly honored by posterity than even great Legislators and Founders of Commonwealths.

Since Bacon's own ruling passion was the desire for fame (as his last will and testament reveals), he would have been happy to have known that his own name had been accorded this highest category of divine honor by Voltaire hardly a century after his death. Voltaire in 1734, ten years before Jefferson was born,[21] had reported a debate on "the trite and frivolous question . . . who was the greatest man,

---

where Odin-Wodin is viewed as the great inventor of the Runic alphabet and "the great Legislator and Hero of the Goths" (Pope's notes).

19. Lily Ross Taylor, *The Divinity of the Roman Emperor* (Middletown, Conn., 1931); L. R. Farnell, *Greek Hero Cults and Ideas of Immortality* (Oxford, 1921).

20. J. L. Mosheim, *Institutes of Ecclesiastical History* (Helmsted, 1755), Pt. II, chap. 3, 2. Cf. Thomas Paine's *The Age of Reason; being an investigation of true and fabulous theology* (London, 1794–1795): "The Christian Church sprung out of the tail of heathen mythology. . . . Mary succeeded . . . Diana . . . ; the deification of heroes changed into the canonization of saints. . . ." The classic statement in English of this idea can be seen in Conyers Middleton, *A Letter from Rome, shewing an exact conformity between Popery and Paganism* (London, 1729).

21. *Lettres sur les Anglais* (London, 1734).

Caesar, Alexander, Tamerlane, Cromwell, etc." The Frenchman, the most consummate publicist of the Age of Reason, had then offered his judgment that "politicians and conquerors . . . were generally so many illustrious wicked men." In contrast and echoing Bacon himself, he declared that "supreme honour should be given to those men, who command not by arms," but by "the force of truth"—and the greatest of these in modern times, according to Voltaire, are: Bacon, Newton, and Locke.[22] Publicized thus by Voltaire, this trinity would become the tutelary deities of eighteenth-century liberalism, enshrined in Diderot's *Encyclopedia* and other works, where knowledge, as in Jefferson's own library, was classified according to Bacon's categories of memory (history), reason (philosophy), and imagination (the fine arts).

The 1791 dialogue between Jefferson and Hamilton on the different categories of greatness then is a debate that, rooted in the neoclassical tradition, contrasts the relative merits of "antique" fame, won by men of action and praised by Hamilton, and "modern" scientific fame, won by men of thought and praised by Jefferson. The categories of *thought* versus action are not mutually exclusive, of course; but the different vote for "greatest" by the New Yorker and the Virginian does sharply reflect differences in temperament and values between the two party leaders, while at the same time it also reveals a similarity of ambition that each share: for glory, which both men lusted after— immortal fame at the very highest level. Moreover, both the Virginian and the New Yorker could view himself, thanks to the opportunity provided by the Revolution, as "the founder of an American empire,"

22. Somewhat earlier Pierre Bayle in his famous *Dictionaire historique et critique* (Rotterdam, 1697), had discussed the same problem in his essay on Pythagoras, "the first of the ancient sages who took the name of Philosopher." Bayle, echoing Cicero, divides mankind into these categories: those who seek money; those who hunt after glory; and, the most commendable, those who diligently study nature, who are called "lovers of wisdom, that is philosophers," then stressing the polarity between those who seek glory through the arts of war and the arts of peace, he awards his vote of true glory to the latter.

although the role of one was by choice "scientist/legislator" and the other by his choice "soldier/legislator."

Here then is evidence of the effect of the Revolution on two of the men who made it. Here in this exchange of 1791 we can see what an enormous "expansion of the minds" of Hamilton and Jefferson had taken place since 1776. Hamilton, who had as an adolescent identified with General James Wolfe, a mere "champion of empire," now thinks of his opportunities and life goals in terms of Julius Caesar, legislator and the founder of an empire, admitted by all to be one of the very greatest men to ever live. Jefferson, who as a teenager had taken as his model a provincial schoolteacher and a pedantically intellectual provincial lawyer, now identified his role as a founder-legislator of the Republic with the scientific tradition of Bacon, Newton, and Locke—the divinely great philosophers. As is well known, Jefferson's final judgment on his own career was inscribed on his tombstone. He ordered: "On the face of the obelisk the following inscription and *not a word* more:

Here was buried

Thomas Jefferson

Author of the Declaration of American Independence,

Of the Statute of Virginia for Religious Freedom,

And Father of the University of Virginia.

because by these, as testimonials that I have lived, I wish most to be remembered." This is Jefferson's letter to posterity, self-consciously planned in its somewhat ostentatious simplicity, which has, as he correctly foresaw, gained him more fame than an inscription detailing the long list of his political offices. Jefferson's gravestone is thus a final reminder of how seriously he took Bacon's hierarchy of fame set forth in the *Advancement of Learning* and its promise of immortality to scientist-legislators.[23]

23. Jefferson's self-conscious and slightly fake modesty regarding his tombstone invites the ironic recitation of Edward Young's lines from the *Love of Fame, the*

If there were time tonight I would like to explore with you the story of John Adams's passion for fame, which, thanks to his revealing *Diary* and self-justifying autobiographical writings, can be charted with more exactitude than that of any of his major contemporaries. In Adams's case we can actually watch Ramsay's "expansion" of the American provincial mind taking place as "Yankee John" acts his role before an ever more significant and wider audience between 1766 and 1800. Then, after his repudiation by the electorate in the presidential election of 1800, we can see his lust for fame soured into anguish and envy since he fears that his great contemporaries, Franklin, Washington, Jefferson, and Hamilton have unfairly robbed him of the honor that is rightfully his.[24] But the mature Adams, certainly in part because of his love of fame, is a more noble figure than the young pettifogger of Braintree, and even in the bitter later

---

Universal Passion . . . (London, 1728): "The Love of Praise, howe'er concealed by Art; / Reigns more or less, and glows in every Heart; / The proud to gain it, Toils on Toils endure, / The modest shun it but to make it sure."

It should be noted that Jefferson's acceptance of Bacon's formulation that the scientist-inventor deserves a higher need of fame than the founders of common-wealths and legislators, while representing a respectable intellectual position, is nonetheless a minority opinion in the 18th century. See for example Adam Smith's contrary view in his *Theory of Moral Sentiments* (London, 1759) : "The greatest and noblest of all characters is . . . the reformer and legislator of a great state . . . [who] by the wisdom of his institutions, secure[s] the internal tranquility and happiness of his fellow citizens for many succeeding generations." And compare David Hume's comment in his essay "Of Parties in General": "Of all men that distinguish them-selves by memorable achievements the first place of honor seems due to LEGISLATORS and FOUNDERS OF STATES, who transmit a system of laws and institutions to secure the peace, happiness and liberty of future generations. . . . I must, therefore, presume to differ from Lord Bacon in this particular, and must regard antiquity as somewhat unjust in its distribution of honors, when it made gods of all the inventors of useful arts, such as Ceres, Bacchus, Aesculapius; and dignified legislators . . . only with the appelation of demigods. . . ."

24. John Schutz and I have edited the revealing exchange of letters between Adams and Rush from 1805 to 1813 where this theme of glory unfairly withheld provides the plot of the correspondence. *The Spur of Fame: Dialogues of John Adams and Benjamin Rush, 1805–1813* (San Marino, Calif., 1966).

years he saw no reason to repudiate the statement he made to Richard Henry Lee in 1777: "You and I, my dear friend, have been sent into life at a time when the greatest lawgivers of antiquity would have wished to live. How few of the human race have ever enjoyed an opportunity of making election of government . . . for themselves or their children."

If there were time tonight I would like also to say something more in greater specific detail about the Plutarchian model of the Great Lawgivers, the demigods of the Grecian and Roman republics— Lycurgus and Solon, Numa and Publius. As most of you are aware, the image of the Legislator who could establish the perfect constitution haunted the minds of leading political thinkers from the time of Machiavelli to Hume; Harrington, Bolingbroke, Montesquieu, Rousseau, all specifically associate their writings with the idea of the perfect commonwealth created by great lawgivers. And it is obvious if one notes the pseudonym signed to *The Federalist* papers and reads carefully Madison's *Federalist* 38, that in 1787 Hamilton and Madison self-consciously identify their labors with the role of the classical Lawgivers and Legislators. One can argue, too, that the curious literary form of *The Federalist* itself, so poorly designed in many ways for polemical effectiveness in 1787–1788, grew out of the desire to tell the truth about the formation of the Constitution in a way that posterity—or at least the educated part—could understand and acclaim. Finally, in this connection, it should be noted that modern historians can chiefly evaluate the motives and ideas of the fifty-five men who attended the Philadelphia Convention of 1787 because Madison took and preserved such complete and careful notes of the debates. If Jefferson's tombstone is his letter to posterity and a deliberate bid for immortal fame, so Madison's *Notes*, not printed until after his death, are his bid for us to recognize him as an American Lycurgus, an American Publius; the record of the secret debates in Convention in Madison's letter to posterity staking out his claim to secular immortality as "father of the Constitution."

4

IN THIS classical and neoclassical tradition of fame that I have been describing, the historian has a very special role to play. This role is perhaps best presented in the words of Tacitus, words which Jefferson would echo in 1813 (to William Duane, April 4, 1813). Tacitus wrote: "This I hold to be the chief duty and office of the historian, to judge the actions of men, to the end that the good and the worthy may meet with the reward due to eminent virtue, and that pernicious citizens may be deterred by the condemnation that waits on evil deeds at the tribunal of posterity." As can be seen in this secular tradition of fame, the historian is required to assume the same ultimate task that the Christian tradition allots to Christ—the function of the last judgment. The historian is invited both to praise virtuous behavior that deserves immortal remembrance and to damn infamous actions.

It is in the context of Tacitus' opinion about the double responsibility of the historian that I want to conclude my talk with two cheers, but only two cheers, for Forrest McDonald's recent outstanding study, *E Pluribus Unum*. My first cheer is given for the way that his twenty thousand hours of research has validated the thesis of the late Charles Beard that the men who wrote the Constitution and the men who opposed it were "not angels" (Madison, *Federalist* 51). McDonald shows with a complete persuasiveness that at issue during the Critical Period, running like a dirty thread through the warp of state politics and the woof of national politics, was the desire on the part of many leading American politicians to enrich themselves by both legitimate and illegitimate manipulation of political power. This emphasis on the importance of economic interest, it seems to me, was the very great contribution that Beard's book of 1913 made to our understanding. Beard was the historian who taught our profession to remember that not all of the Founding Fathers were demigods, that like a substantial number of politicians throughout our history, for many of them the ruling passion was the love of power to obtain money. As de Tocqueville observed, they worshipped at the altar of the bitch-goddess, Success, not in the Temple of Fame.

Since our profession is so beholden to Beard as a great teacher, it has distressed me that it has become the style in the last twenty-five years to focus only on the errors that any bright young students now can find in Beard's early work. One of the features of our graduate programs in history is the necessity of training of our students to emulate Oedipus. If they are to be taught to be critical, they must be taught not only to understand but to "see through" their intellectual and professional "fathers." Since Beard was the greatest "intellectual father" of all students of the Constitution for a whole generation, it was inevitable that, as the passage of time and more penetrating research revealed features of the Critical Period that Beard had ignored or misunderstood, his work would be the target for drastic attack. I submit that this attack has now gone too far; a book like Robert Brown's throws out the baby with the bath water. We should remember, obeying Tacitus' injunction, the great virtue of Beard's formulation when first made, and we should honor Beard's contribution as well as criticize his errors. Since Forrest McDonald has in his recent book revived and again given validation to the Beard approach, I say hurrah for him.

My second cheer is for the way in which McDonald has shown, as no historian before, how economic appetites and greed in *state* politics between 1783 and 1787 threatened to destroy the fragile Union of the Articles. McDonald gives chapter and verse proof of Madison's charge in *Federalist* 62 of the unjust and unreasonable advantages that "sagacious" and "enterprising" political insiders took over "the industrious and uninformed mass of the people." The picture that McDonald presents of the financial shenanigans of the dominant political factions in Rhode Island, New York, and Pennsylvania explains why Madison would decry "a state of things in which it may be said with some truth that laws are made for the *few* and not for the *many*." As one reads McDonald's book, one has the sense of eavesdropping on a group of slippery modern legislators at Albany or Boston or Sacramento, who have let their hair down after the third bourbon and are talking informally about "boodle legislation" and who got what, how, and when. In many ways then the McDonald book gives a far more sweeping and a far more sophisticated picture of the dynamic interrelationships of avarice and American politics than Beard's simple-minded view that economic appetites in 1787 could be divided into two major categories of capitalist and agrarian. In this, McDonald correctly sees what Madison said in 1787—that the multiplicities of economic interests and greeds in the United States were as important, if not more important, than the dual conflict that Beard celebrated. And so my second cheer is for the original new light that McDonald throws on the economic context in which both the Antifederalists and the Federalists operated before the writing of the Constitution. Like Beard earlier, he has put every scholar in the field in his debt.

My reservation about McDonald's fine study, the reason I am unwilling to give *three* cheers for the book as a work of scholarship and as a balanced judgment of the Critical Period, is the narrowness with which he defines the word *self-interest*. Here, too, he parallels the work of the younger Beard. In *E Pluribus Unum* the story of the framing of our Constitution becomes almost entirely wheeling and dealing on the state and national level for economic benefits.[25]

25. This is not completely fair to McDonald. His usual "reductionism" of politics to economic determinants of behavior does recognize that given the long cold winters of New Hampshire, and "an ignorant breed of men incongruously characterized by lethargy and volatility, . . . all men save the most industrious stayed indoors making their wives pregnant, and praying to a Fundamentalist, Calvinist God to make it warmer; . . . when spring finally broke, all men save the most industrious got fiercely drunk and made other men's wives pregnant." *E Pluribus Unum*, 113–114. This would seem to accept Bayle's theory that along with avarice and the drive for domination, sexual aggressiveness is one of the key determinants of political behavior. But McDonald nowhere follows up this interesting insight into the role of climate and sex, and this reader feels his characterization of New Hampshire is more designed to shock his more genteel colleagues than to seriously enlighten them.

This is why I find the book a failure in an artistic sense, why McDonald himself, perhaps unconsciously, admits on his last page that the body of his two hundred preceding pages of text does not lead up to, or prepare one for, his conclusion. The writing and ratification of the Constitution he calls a "miracle," and in terms of the politics that he has described in such vivid detail previously, there is no other adequate explanation.

He approves of the Constitution that was framed in 1787, because it made Americans "politically one nation." He praises it as a political system adequate to govern us, the American people—"of all the world's peoples the most materialistic and most vulgar and least disciplined." He even recognizes the stature of the leading framers— "there were giants in the earth in those days, and they spoke in the name of the nation, and the people followed them." But nowhere in his study has he found one of the "giants" interested in political justice, the *common* defense (unless British bayonets were at his throat!), the *general* welfare, or the liberties of posterity. One could fairly deduce from McDonald's text that he thinks the Preamble of that Constitution he so obviously admires is no more than a "facade of slogans."

It has been the argument of my paper that the greatest and the most effective leaders of 1787—no angels they, but passionately selfish and self-interested men—were giants in part because the Revolution had led them to redefine their notions of interest and had given them, through the concept of fame, a personal stake in creating a national system dedicated to liberty, to justice, and to the general welfare.

The "love of fame the ruling passion of the noblest minds" thus transmuted the leaden desire for self-aggrandizement and personal reward into a golden concern for public service and the promotion of the commonwealth as the means to gain glory. The desire for fame operated thus as constant goad in the political behavior of the mature Washington, of Adams, of Jefferson, Hamilton, and Madison.

If one can accept a passion for secular immortality as a possible ingredient of a person's definition of his interest, one need not account for the writing of the Constitution in terms of "a miracle" or a phenomenon outside of human nature.

The love of fame, and the belief that creating a viable republican state would win them fame, is part of the explanation of the élan, the tremendous energy, the dedicated and brilliantly effective political maneuvers by which the small minority of American leaders who were nationalists kidnapped the movement to reform the Articles, wrote what they conceived to be a more perfect union, and then managed to get it ratified by the reluctant representatives of an apathetic populace.

Here is a paradox perhaps: that you and I—no giants politically ourselves, merely an average group of college teachers, because we make up that *audience of posterity* whose approval the leading framers were so anxious to gain—you and I, unborn in 1787, nevertheless played our part even then as an invisible audience that spurred some of the Fathers to nobility and political greatness.

It has been said that history itself is a dialogue in the present with the past about the future. These men drunk with the hope of fame looked to the classic past for models to emulate, as they made history in 1787, in order to win our applause—the praise that only we their posterity could grant.

EPILOGUE

MAY I here leave my prepared paper and say informally a few sentences in conclusion. As I read over what I had written flying east from Claremont, I had the sinking feeling that all I had done was to elaborately underline the obvious, to belabor a truth that you and I as historians know as the most elementary fact of our professional life. I have argued that the audience that men set themselves to perform for governs and controls to a large extent the nature and quality of their performance. All of us, as practicing historians, are terribly conscious of just this truth: different audiences, different behavior! As professional historians we have our *three* audiences before which we act to gain prestige and praise. I think the cliché about "publish or perish," with its element of half-truth, points directly at the problem raised by the different standards evoked by two of our different audiences. The cliché does recognize that it is quite possible, on occasion, to impress and win the applause of semieducated adolescents by lecturing with what one can only call the low arts of pedagogical showmanship—the tricks of shallow and superficial display. It has therefore been a firm convention of the historian's guild that popularity with undergraduates is not enough *by itself* to give the highest status to the teacher—the undergraduate audience, it has been judged, is not one that will always and inevitably call forth the most virtuous performance of a historian. It is because our writings will be judged by the audience of our peers, it is because this informed audience will expect and demand more from us before it accords praise, that the need for publication has been so emphasized in our profession. And, if you look into your own hearts, can any of you doubt that the thought of being judged by learned colleagues does not usually spur you to more carefulness, more concentrated effort, more laborious days than preparing a lecture for beginning students?

Finally, of course, there is the third audience that the greatest of our profession have foremost in their minds. I think, for example, of Lawrence Gipson's great and monumental work on the British Empire; of Allan Nevins's *Ordeal of the Union;* I think of Julian Boyd's concern to edit the Jefferson papers in such a way that his work will never have to be done again. And one could name others of our profession who thus judge themselves, not by the standard of the average monographs that can win current promotion, but measure themselves and their efforts by the yardstick of the greatest histories that have been written in the past, hoping thus to build enduring literary monuments that will be read and praised by posterity.

It is this urge to model oneself on the very greatest, to emulate the best, that provides the spur that sets this creative minority apart. Who can doubt that this obsessive concern with the judgment of posterity was not one of the ingredients that made the late John Kennedy something more than just another Irish politician from Boston. Who can doubt that it was his concern with his fame—his concern with the judgment of posterity—that made him respond, as Arthur Schlesinger has told us, to those lovely lines of Stephen Spender's poem:

> I think continually of those who are truly great . . .
> The names of those who in their lives fought for life,
> Who wore at their hearts the fire's center.
> Born of the sun they travelled a short while towards the sun,
> And left the vivid air signed with their honor.

THE AUTHORSHIP OF THE
DISPUTED FEDERALIST PAPERS

Douglass Adair's fascination with *The Federalist* was perhaps only equaled by his enthusiasm for literary detective work (as confirmed by *The Horn Papers* collaboration and his later work on the *Annual Register*). In this major two-part article, Adair happily combined both interests. He also revealed his early preference for Madison—a disposition he gradually overcame. Jacob E. Cooke in his edition of *The Federalist* (Middletown, Conn., 1961) pays tribute to Adair's study as a brilliant summary of the century-old controversy in which the authorship of the disputed *Federalist* essays was assigned on the basis of their political philosophy. Cooke does not find Adair's arguments totally persuasive (as with *Federalist* Number 56), but substantially accepts his suggestions on authorship. In fact Adair's essays deserve fresh currency for their superb exploration of the political thought of Hamilton, Jay, and Madison; the question of which *Federalist* papers each wrote was an inviting occasion for that task.

I

IN 1886 HENRY CABOT LODGE noted that "the authorship of certain numbers of the 'Federalist' has fairly reached the dignity of

SOURCE: Reprinted from the *William and Mary Quarterly*, 3d Ser., I (1944), 97–122, 235–264.

a well-established historical controversy." For three-quarters of a century preceding Lodge's pronouncement adherents of Alexander Hamilton and of James Madison had periodically disputed as to which of these distinguished coauthors had contributed certain of the individual essays to that famous exegesis of the United States Constitution. With all the research in American constitutional history since Lodge wrote, the problem still remains unsolved. When Edward Mead Earle in 1937 brought out the most recent edition of *The Federalist,* he marked twelve essays as still awaiting positive proof of authorship.[1] The disagreement has been from the beginning an American cause célèbre, a mystery quite as intriguing as the authorship of Junius and one far more worthy of scholarly attention.

1

THE OBSCURITY surrounding the *Federalist* authorship has not been for lack of historical evidence on the subject, but from overabundance of contradictory evidence. The eighty-five essays which make up *The Federalist* were first published anonymously in the New York newspapers during the fall of 1787 and the spring of 1788 in order to convince the inhabitants of that state of the advantages to be obtained by ratifying the new Constitution. The idea of laying down this propaganda barrage on the still undecided minds of New Yorkers belonged to Alexander Hamilton, already at thirty an experienced pamphleteer. He called to his aid John Jay and James Madison. Jay's knowledge of foreign affairs and his experience as a diplomat made him a most useful ally in expounding the necessity of a stronger union to counteract the "dangers from foreign force and influence."

---

1. Edward Mead Earle, ed., *The Federalist: A Commentary on the Constitution of the United States* . . . (Washington, D.C., 1937), Sesquicentennial edition issued by the Modern Library. Earle refers "students who wish to pursue the investigation further" to Bourne's and Ford's 40-year-old articles: Edward Gaylord Bourne, "The Authorship of The Federalist," *American Historical Review,* II (1896–1897), 444–460; Paul Leicester Ford, "The Authorship of The Federalist," *ibid.,* 675–682; Bourne, *Essays in Historical Criticism* (New Haven, Conn., 1913), chaps. 2, 3. He detours

Madison too had a unique and specialized knowledge to contribute to Hamilton's project.

For while both Hamilton and Jay were strongly in favor of the proposed national government as necessary for the obvious ills of the Confederation, neither of them was as well equipped as Madison to justify and elaborate many of the unexpected provisions that the Convention had written into the new Constitution. Jay had not been at the Philadelphia meeting at all. Hamilton himself had attended only the opening and closing sessions. Since he had been absent during over a third of the Convention, he had only hearsay knowledge of the revealing debates of July and early August when the basic federal structure of the new government was hammered out on the anvil of compromise. Madison, on the other hand, had been present at every session. Moreover, he had taken careful notes of the proceedings, which preserved in usable form all the arguments pro and con for every clause that the Fathers had included in the final instrument. The Virginian's unique knowledge of the complex document, accordingly, could be used most satisfactorily to enrich the arguments of *The Federalist*. Nor was the illusion disturbed that the anonymous writer, "Publius," was a single author; for like Hamilton and Jay, Madison was a master of that Addisonian prose style which had all but standardized the tone of eighteenth-century essays.

The series of essays which Hamilton, Jay, and Madison produced over the name of Publius for the newspapers proved popular from the beginning. It appeared to the cooperating authors worthwhile therefore to publish the collected series as a book, to be used in promoting ratification in other states besides New York. This was done in the spring of 1788, when a two-volume edition of *The Federalist* was offered to the public. Anonymity was still preserved, even in this more permanent format; the unknown Publius took the

---

the difficulty of the conflicting claims of Madison and Hamilton by "assigning joint authorship in each case of the slightest doubt." p. xxii.

credit for all eight-five essays. In spite of this, the identity of the three authors was not an especially well-kept secret. Almost at once close friends of the trio, partly on the basis of hints from the authors themselves, partly from internal evidence, commenced marking the separate papers in their private copies with the names of specific authors.[2] And in 1792 the first French edition ended all pretense of collective anonymity by proclaiming on its title page that *The Federalist* had been written by "Mm Hamilton, Maddisson E Gay, citoyens de l'Etat de New York."

The appearance of a foreign edition of *The Federalist* also signified that the vehicle of propaganda hurriedly issued five years before had qualities that set it apart from ephemeral pamphlet literature. In the United States also during that same period political developments conspired to keep *The Federalist* in the public mind. Madison and Hamilton had become political enemies, and each stood as champion of mutually exclusive interpretations of the Constitution they had both cooperated in getting ratified. Under the circumstances the exposition of the Constitution presented by Publius in 1787–1788 was a pawn in the game of power as the Hamiltonians and the newly organized "republican" opposition led by Madison and Jefferson struggled to control the national government. Both sides inevitably appealed to Publius to justify their position. A second American edition issued in 1799 found a ready market. This continued public demand for *The Federalist* led the enterprising New York printer George F. Hopkins to undertake a new edition in 1802. He approached Hamilton through mutual friends—"two respectable professional gentlemen"—but discovered a certain disinclination on Hamilton's part to see a new publication of the essays.

---

2. Madison to Jefferson, Aug. 10, 1788, [William C. Rives and Philip R. Fendall, eds.,] *Letters and Other Writings of James Madison* (Philadelphia, 1865), I, 408, hereafter cited as *Letters of Madison*. See the reply, Jefferson to Madison, Nov. 18, 1788, Andrew A. Lipscomb and Albert Ellery Bergh, eds., *The Writings of Thomas Jefferson* (Washington, D.C., 1903–1904), VII, 183.

As Hopkins reported in 1847 to Hamilton's son, "Your father, it appeared, did not regard the work with much partiality; but nevertheless, consented to its publication on condition that it should undergo a careful revision by one of the gentlemen, above alluded to." On one point, however, Hamilton was adamant: no list of authors should be published. Hopkins had expected—and even advertised in his prospectus of the edition—that "the name of the writer should be prefixed to each number; but this, as I was told, met with your father's decided disapprobation."[3] Thus, when the edition of 1802 came out, although everyone knew that Publius was three men, and although everyone knew who these three men were, the share that each had borne in the work still remained, so far as the general public was concerned, a well-kept secret.

This strange reluctance of Hamilton in 1802 to allow *The Federalist* papers to be divided among the three authors, an aspect of the controversy hitherto ignored by historians, offers a clue to the mystery surrounding the authorship. Why did Hamilton bridle at the innocent request of Hopkins for a list of authors? Anonymity was desirable in 1787–1788 when *The Federalist* was written, but why did Hamilton consider it so necessary in 1802? This curious hesitation of Hamilton's to advance his claims is understandable only when it is recalled that some of his essays written in 1787–1788 did not square with certain constitutional theories that he had come to espouse publicly after 1790. *The Federalist*, it should be remembered, was not a scholarly commentary on the meaning of an established Constitution; it contained special pleading designed to secure ratification for a Constitu-

3. John C. Hamilton, ed., *The Federalist: A Commentary on the Constitution of the United States* . . . (New York, 1864), I, xcii. It was at Hamilton's request that his "Letters of Pacificus" were included with *The Federalist* in 1802. Apparently he was more "partial" to them than his "Publius" at the time; for Hopkins reports that "he [A. H.] remarked to me, that 'some of his friends had pronounced them to be his best performance.' " Madison felt it was somewhat unscrupulous of Hamilton to include this later polemic with *The Federalist* and thus trade on the latter's prestige. See *Letters of Madison*, III, 58.

tion still untested. After the government was in operation, both Hamilton and Madison lived to regret theories and interpretations they had advanced in 1787–1788 under the name of Publius.

Opponents of the Constitution in 1787, with their continual harping on the argument that the new national government would destroy the state governments, led Hamilton, for example, to promote a reassuring constitutional theory which he was later to deny. In his heart he hoped that their fears would be realized; and when he was in power he did his best to consolidate the central government at no matter what cost to the states. To lull the suspicions of his opponents in 1787, however, he had insisted in *Federalist* 28 that "the State governments would in all possible contingencies, afford complete security against invasions of the public liberty by the national authority"; and in Number 26 he had specifically cast the "State legislatures" in this role of "guardian" of the public liberty "against the encroachments of the general government."[4] Once the government was established, his own inclinations and the exigencies of party politics combined to make Hamilton repudiate the idea of preserving strong state governments and combat it with every means at his disposal.[5] In fact his whole public life centered around weakening the political power of the individual states.

Unfortunately for his plans the party of the opposition had been quick to seize upon this very theory of state guardianship as a device to attack Hamilton's policies, and in 1798 the doctrine was used to justify the Virginia and Kentucky Resolutions in a manner which Hamilton considered threatening to the stability of the Union. Thus

4. As guardians, the state legislatures, Hamilton prophesied in *Federalist* 26, would be always ready "to *sound the alarm* to the people and not only be the *voice*, but if necessary the *arm*, of their discontent."

5. When the legislature of Virginia in 1790 remonstrated against the assumption of state debts, Hamilton wrote to Chief Justice Jay: "This is the first symptom of a spirit which must either be killed or will kill the Constitution. . . . Ought not the collective weight of the different parts of the government be employed in exploding principles which they contain?"

for the New Yorker to lay public claim to certain of his *Federalist* essays in 1802 would have been both personally embarrassing and politically inexpedient. Hopkins's innocent request for a list of authors was loaded with unsuspected political dynamite and thereby earned for the startled printer a sharp refusal. No statesman likes to eat his own words; Alexander Hamilton was decidedly not "partial" to putting a new propaganda weapon in the hands of his enemies. As long as he was actively concerned in politics it was most desirable to keep the authors of *The Federalist* decently hidden under the mask of Publius.

Hamilton, moreover, was aware that Madison was no more anxious than he to publicize the division of all the essays among the authors. For Madison had also advanced an interpretation of the Constitution before ratification that he was bitterly to regret when he saw how the government actually worked under Hamilton's executive leadership. In *Federalist* 44, explaining the "necessary and proper" clause, the Virginian had argued that "no axiom is more clearly established in law, or in reason, that wherever the end is required, the means are authorized; wherever a general power to do a thing is given, every particular power necessary for doing it is included."

Madison strongly regretted these words when Hamilton used them to justify the creation of the National Bank and then used the Bank both to break down the separation of powers between Congress and the executive and to weaken the division of authority between the states and the national government. In rebuttal to his own axiom in Number 44 he then developed the "strict construction" theory that Jefferson relied on to prove the Bank unconstitutional.

It is accordingly very probable that Madison hoped no publication of *Federalist* authors would be made until all the authors had died. The Virginian had early remarked on the advisability of such a procedure with his notes on the secret debates in the Philadelphia Convention: "Posthumous publication as to others as well as myself may be most delicate, and most useful also. . . . As no personal or party views can then be imputed, they will be read with less of personal or party feeling."[6] The conditions favoring anonymity here were comparable to those surrounding *The Federalist*.

2

IT WAS Hamilton's duel with Burr that precipitated the open designation of the *Federalist* authors. Premonitions of death spurred the New Yorker hurriedly to set all of his affairs in order. Among the matters that Hamilton, so typically a man of the eighteenth century, could not ignore was the judgment that posterity would make of his political career as spokesman for union and interpreter of the United States Constitution. His signature on certain controversial essays, while inconvenient during his life, might well add to his fame if issued posthumously. And so Hamilton stopped by the law office of Egbert Benson two days before his fatal meeting with Burr and ostentatiously concealed in his friend's book case a slip of paper in his own handwriting listing by number the authors of the various essays in *The Federalist*.[7] After his tragic death the memorandum was discovered as he had planned; nor were well-wishers loath to undertake the commemorative task of making certain his greatness was recognized. In 1810, on the basis of this dramatically planted list, a new edition of *The Federalist* appeared—the first to attribute specific essays to individual authors. In this edition of 1810, however, *The Federalist* suffered a sea change: it was not published as a separate and independent work. It was issued as the second and third volumes of the collected "Works of Hamilton."[8] *The Federalist*, this publication implied, had not only been the original conception of a single man; it was for all practical purposes the creation of one individual.

6. *Letters of Madison*, III, 549. Cf. *ibid.*, 228, 243.

7. It read as follows: "Nos. 2, 3, 4, 5, 54, by J. Nos. 10, 14, 37, to 48 inclusive, M. Nos. 18, 19, 20, M. & H. jointly. All the others by H." See J. C. Hamilton, ed., *The Federalist*, I, xcvi, for the fullest account of the hiding and discovery of this list.

8. It was printed by Williams and Whiting in New York City.

For, on the basis of the Benson list, Hamilton was credited with writing sixty-three out of the total of eighty-five essays signed Publius. If the Benson list was accurate, James Madison and John Jay could hardly be dignified with the title of coauthors of *The Federalist*; at most they were incidental helpers who had contributed a small wing to the massive intellectual structure designed and built by Alexander Hamilton.

When Henry Cabot Lodge in 1886, following the earlier precedent, reissued *The Federalist* as an integral part of Hamilton's writings, he advanced as one of his reasons the fact that Madison did not immediately contradict Hamilton's extensive claims as soon as the Benson list was published. This failure of Madison's to enter at once into a literary controversy with the dead man's family and devoted friends Lodge considered "a very serious matter"[9]—so serious, in fact, that it cast doubt on the creditability of Madison's counterclaims made after a lapse of several years. James Madison's interests and energies were deeply absorbed at this period and for some time thereafter in the snarled foreign relations that exploded into war in 1812. Even assuming he had read that number of the *Portfolio* with Hamilton's list, he might well have relegated the whole unpleasant business to the back of his mind for the duration. President Madison was well aware that while he was in office every opposition newspaper would have seized on the dispute and exploited it heavily for partisan purposes. Delaying his challenge of Hamilton's claims until after he had retired to private life saved him from this type of political attack.[10]

9. Henry Cabot Lodge, ed., *The Federalist: A Commentary on the Constitution of the United States* . . . (New York, 1886), xxxi. Lodge even insists that Madison ought to have rushed forward in 1807 when the Benson list was first published in a New York newspaper, the *Portfolio*. He assumes that Madison knew of the *Portfolio* paragraph, without having any proof that he did. Neither Lodge nor Ford show that the item was copied by other newspapers or attracted any particular attention.

10. His silence nevertheless did not save him from the embarrassment attendant upon the appearance of his name signed to Number 44. John Marshall used Madison's "axiom" only slightly paraphrased to explode the Madisonian strict-construction theory in *M'Culloch* v. *Maryland* in 1819. To place himself or others in this position

When, however, the Benson list later received wide publicity after its appearance in the biography of Hamilton in Joseph Delaplaine's *Repository of the Lives and Portraits of Distinguished Americans*,[11] Madison indicated clearly that his temporary silence could by no means be construed as assent. For the publication of the Hamilton list in Delaplaine's *Repository* almost immediately transformed the question of the authorship of *The Federalist* into a heated public controversy.

The first challenge of the Benson list on behalf of James Madison[12] came from one of his friends signing himself "Corrector," who printed in the *National Intelligencer* (April 18, 1817) a list he claimed Madison had given him several years earlier. This list assigned to Madison twenty-nine numbers of *The Federalist* instead of fourteen. A second defender, likewise anonymous, produced a slightly different Madison list, laying claim to thirty of the essays, in the *Washington Gazette* for December 15, 1817. Presumably this friend of Madison's had also had his information for some time. These independent challenges, however, were but tokens of the renewed and indignant concern over the authorship of *The Federalist* stirred up among Madison's intimate friends by the Delaplaine biography and the Benson list contained in it.

Not until 1818, when Jacob Gideon published his edition of *The Federalist*, did the Virginian launch his formal counterattack. It was a typically Madisonian rebuttal—deliberate, cautious, but thorough. Madison had lent his own copy of *The Federalist*, with the names of the authors at the head of each essay, to the printer; he had also made certain minor revisions in those numbers which he claimed as

of inconsistency was the very thing Madison had hoped to avoid by his plan of posthumous publication. For Madison's unhappiness over the M'Culloch decision, see Madison to Judge Spencer Roane, Sept. 2, 1819, *Letters of Madison*, III, 143.

11. Published at Philadelphia and issued serially from 1813 to 1818.

12. It was first publicly called "inaccurate" in the life of Jay published in Delaplaine's 1815 volume. The manuscript for *Federalist* 64 (not 54 as Hamilton had written) has been found among Jay's papers with the other numbers he had written.

his own. Gideon's edition, carefully checked and formally issued, represented therefore Madison's official pronouncement on his contribution to the writing of *The Federalist*.[13]

James Madison's correction of Hamilton's claims in the Benson list was as nonprovocative as positive contradiction could be. The Virginian said nothing of motives; he did not attribute the New Yorker's mistakes either to malice, enmity, or ambition. The misstatements in the Benson list, he suggested, were due only to the "fallibility of memory"; although the proportion of errors appeared exceedingly large, this was "owing doubtless to the hurry in which the memorandum was made out." Madison, however, after careful consideration and in the face of the dead man's claims, was prepared to take oath that he himself had written twenty-nine of the essays instead of the fourteen attributed to him by Hamilton. He had written Numbers 49 to 58 inclusive, and Numbers 62 and 63—all claimed by the New Yorker; he had also written Numbers 18, 19, and 20 (claimed by Hamilton as a joint product), merely incorporating in these three essays a small amount of supplementary material that Hamilton had gathered on the same subject. Madison thus laid claim to authorship of nearly 40 percent of *The Federalist*—a far more respectable proportion than the 20-odd percent attributed to him by Hamilton. Implicit in Gideon's edition of *The Federalist* was a mild demand that Madison henceforth be acknowledged as a full coauthor of the work, without any effort to detract from Hamilton's deserved honor as originator of the scheme and leading contributor.

To Madison's contemporaries this carefully considered rebuttal was undoubtedly convincing. Indeed it was so generally accepted that when the Virginian died in 1836 he must have believed that his

13. "The true distribution of the numbers of the *Federalist* among the three writers is ... the Edition ... of Gideon. It was furnished to him by me, with a perfect knowledge of its accuracy, as it related to myself, and a full confidence in its equal accuracy as it relates to the two others." A Madison memorandum deposited in the Liberty of Congress entitled "The Federalist," quoted in J. C. Hamilton, ed., *The Federalist*, I, c.

share in *The Federalist,* as set forth in Gideon's edition, was established beyond question. And so it was until the Civil War. Ten
American editions of Publius' essays were printed between 1818 and
1857, and each of them followed the Gideon division of authors.[14]
During this interval no edition accepted the Hamilton claims as
authentic. Nor was such a policy unnatural. The circumstances surrounding the "discovery" of the Benson list made it all too clear that
is was written by Hamilton in a moment of greatest agitation and
haste. It contained at least one undeniable slip of the pen in giving
the authorship of 54 rather than 64 to Jay. It seemed highly probable
that a similar slip of the pen set down "37 to 48 inclusive, by M."
instead of 37 to 58.[15] Likewise, Hamilton's failure to note down the
two isolated numbers, 62 and 63, named by Madison as his own
work, could be a very natural omission for a preoccupied and hurried
man to make, all the more so since he had produced all the last
twenty-one essays in a solid block. What Madison termed Hamilton's
"lumping" method of division would thus normally lead to this sort
of error.

Madison's formal statement, in contrast, was not compromised by
haste or characterized by uncertainty. He knew that his claims would
be closely scrutinized and that his veracity would be called into
question if he made the slightest error, since he was deliberately
contradicting Hamilton; he therefore of necessity gave time and
thought to his statements. On its face, accordingly, Madison's carefully considered claim was more worthy of belief, merely as historical
evidence, than the tragically evoked Benson list. This fact, added to
Madison's reputation for prudent carefulness, and his all but pedantic

---

14. For the bibliography of *The Federalist* up to 1886 see Lodge's edition.
15. Hamilton's son, in dealing with the error of his father in setting down "54"
for "64," terms it a natural mistake and calls attention to the roman numbering of
the essays: "Bringing Roman numerals into Arabic, an erroneous glance of the eye,
and either a slip or blur of the pen, might easily pervert a figure." J. C. Hamilton,
ed., *The Federalist,* I, cv.

rectitude,[16] carried to most contemporary observers the overwhelming conviction that he had established his position against Hamilton as author of the disputed numbers of *The Federalist*.

3

AT THIS POINT a curious aspect of the *Federalist* controversy may be noted, quite distinct from the scholarly worth of the competing lists offered by the two principals. This is the clear-cut rhythm of acceptance and rejection by historical writers of the respective claims of the Virginian and the New Yorker, in successive periods of American history. For a period of forty years Madison was generally conceded to have discredited the Benson list; then during the succeeding half-century this list was again restored to favor. This alternating sequence of belief and disbelief that marks the controversy is directly correlated with the seesaw of prestige between these two interpreters of the Constitution, depending upon whether agrarian or capitalistic interests were politically dominant in the country.

The Virginian's renown as statesman and constitutional sage was at its peak with historians and the general public up to the Civil War, over a period of years when Hamilton's fame was undeservedly minimized. During this pre-Sumter era it was generally believed that Madison's word as to which essays he had composed could be subject to no doubt whatsoever. From the end of the Civil War to the beginning of the first World War the contestants' roles were reversed: Madison's political reputation sank low, while Hamilton's rose to great heights; and it was in this later period that the Benson list, generally repudiated during the preceding forty years, achieved a new persuasiveness among writers and students of history.

This complementary rise and fall of Madison's and Hamilton's political reputations resulted from the nineteenth century's use of

16. As a trivial but characteristic example: when a member of Congress, Madison even refused to accept free government stationery. See Edward McNall Burns, *James Madison: Philosopher of the Constitution* (New Brunswick, N.J., 1938), 26.

the Constitution, first, as a symbol of agrarian democracy, later as a symbol of financial capitalism. The Constitution of 1787 established in the United States a novel compound of oligarchic and quasi-democratic elements. The Federalist party, led by Hamilton, steadily emphasized the aristocratic features of the Constitution; but the Republicans, led by Jefferson and Madison, came in time to stress its democratic aspects almost exclusively. By 1815 the Jeffersonian view of the Constitution as an expression of agrarian democracy had achieved legal and popular sanction among the American people,[17] and by 1828 this view had enlarged into the radically democratic theory of the Jackson "revolution."

As the Constitution was extolled more and more as an instrument of frontier individualism, and of leveling democracy, it became increasingly difficult to assimilate the figure of Alexander Hamilton in the *mythos* that clustered about the origins of the document. The New Yorker's uncompromising stand in favor of a moneyed aristocracy and a hierarchial society was anathema to a generation of democratic enthusiasts that was creating its heroes in the image of Old Hickory and Tippecanoe. Even the memory of Hamilton's passion for union was compromised by his admiration of England and by the semitreasonable record of his party during the War of 1812. During the pre–Civil War decades, then, as the Constitution came to reflect exclusively agrarian democracy, Alexander Hamilton's historical connection with the document tended to become ever hazier in the public mind.[18] Only when America became industrialized after

17. So complete was the popular acceptance of the Jeffersonian view that the young aristocrat de Tocqueville, who was welcomed in Federalist circles, noted that even those who were "galled by its continuance" were generally heard to "laud the delights of a republican government, and the advantage of democratic institutions when they are in public." Alexis de Tocqueville, *Democracy in America*, 3d ed. (New York, 1839), chap. 10, 175.

18. See the lament of George Ticknor Curtis that Hamilton "is less well known to the nation at the present day than most of the leading statesmen of the Revolution." *History of the Origin, Formation and Adoption of the Constitution of the United*

1865 could the Constitution be reanalyzed, and Hamilton restored to favor as an "authority" on its "ultimate meanings." Before this could happen all his pronouncements concerning the Constitution—including his *Federalist* claims—were subject to subtle deflation in an intellectual atmosphere that automatically cast James Madison in the role of leading constitutional champion.

Madison's career was in itself an integral part of this liberal rereading of the Constitution; his political activities and Jefferson's had poured the new meaning into classic phrases that allowed the charter to mold American political behavior and thinking into agrarian shape. During the last part of his life the Virginian forged the intellectual link between the diluted democracy of 1787 and the radical democracy of 1828. His name was inseparable from the two great bywords of Constitutional symbolism: union and liberty; and to the public mind he was the understudy of both the great leaders who personified these values: Washington and Jefferson.

Madison had taken a leading part in the Philadelphia Convention; he had worked valiantly for ratification; and when the new government was organized he had served as President Washington's legislative aid and confidant in the House of Representatives. Madison's name indubitably stood for union. On the other hand, he had participated in the fight against the Federalist party's unpopular fiscal program and the Alien and Sedition Laws; he had written the federal Bill of Rights, and he had led in the creation of a loyal opposition under the Constitution. If Madison's name stood for union, it stood equally with Jefferson's for liberty. Madison's public life could thus be dramatized as a long struggle to establish "liberty and union . . . one and indivisible."

States, with Notices of Its Principal Framers (New York, 1854–1858), I, 406. Curtis's work has been termed the "classic" Federalist history of the Constitution. It is significant that although Curtis considered Madison a lesser statesman than Hamilton, who "towered above all his compeers," he accepted Madison's division of *Federalist* authors as valid. See *ibid.*, I, 418n.

The intimate association in the pre–Civil War era of James Madison's name with the cult of the Constitution was strengthened by his unusual longevity. The Virginian outlived all of his great contemporaries. For many years before his death he was the sole survivor of the Philadelphia Convention, and as the only living participant in that momentous event he acquired added prestige as constitutional sage and oracle.[19] Publicists, politicians, and historians beat a path to Montpelier during his last years, seeking eyewitness anecdotes of those hallowed days when the mighty dead led by Washington had new-modeled a free government for the American people. Thus Madison by the end of his life had assumed the character of a holy national relic, tangibly representing in that later age the austere and classic republicanism of the nation's genesis.

Even in his death, Madison was credited by his contemporaries with having elicited from heaven a miraculous sign of divine approval of his life's work as constitutional spokesman. Just as Jefferson's and John Adams's deaths on July 4, 1826, were taken to manifest the Diety's personal interest in the anniversary of the Declaration of Independence, so Madison's passing on June 28, 1836, was discovered to have put God's imprimatur on the Constitution. John Quincy Adams noted mystically that June 28 was "the anniversary of the day on which the Convention of Virginia in 1788 had affixed the seal of James Madison as the father of the Constitution of the United States, when his earthly part sank without a struggle into the grave, and a spirit, bright as the seraphim that surround the throne of Omnipotence, ascended to the bosom of his God."[20]

19. By 1830 Madison was being forced to deny that he had written the majority of the Publius essays. "You have erred in stating that I wrote the greatest parts of the Federalist; a greater number of the papers were written by Col. Hamilton, as will be seen by . . . Gideon." To Edward Everett, Oct. 7, 1830, *Letters of Madison*, IV, 116.

20. Quoted in Sydney Howard Gay, *James Madison* (Boston, 1884), 2. Gay in two witty pages was happy to prove that J. Q. Adams was wrong in believing God was interested in identifying Madison with the Constitution; for as he pointed out, Virginia actually ratified on June 25, 1788.

This attitude of reverence for James Madison continued to exist for more than two decades after his death, sanctifying even the most insignificant of his dicta concerning the writing and ratification of the Constitution with an aura of transcendent truth. Then the shells fired from the Confederate guns at Charleston in April 1861 demolished his political reputation almost as effectively as they wrecked the brick casements of Fort Sumter. For when the four years of bloody civil war had ended, the re-United States had a new pattern of economic life and a new political party with a novel scheme of historical values. Almost at once publicists and historians began the development of a new cult of the Constitution which necessitated a reinterpretation and deflation of Madison's contribution to the writing and ratification of that document.

Even while the Civil War was still in progress, a forecast had been made of the Virginian's decline in fame as constitutional statesman. Hamilton's son had already for years made a career of vindicating his father's memory; his edition of *The Federalist* published in 1864 was merely his final effort along these lines. Exploiting the mood of the times, in his introductory essay on the writing of *The Federalist* the younger Hamilton stressed the note of his father's passion for union; likewise too he traced back to the Revolutionary period Southern—especially Virginian—arrogance and secession sentiment. "By almost all historical writers, under the enthrallment which the slave power seemed to have imposed upon the mind of this country, the precedence in this great movement [toward union] has been ascribed to Virginia. . . . This precedence unquestionably belongs to New York."[21] In claiming all of the controverted *Federalist* essays for his father, and denying them to the Virginia slaveholder, Hamilton, Jr., conceived of himself as purifying the ideal of nationalism itself from the taint of Southern disunion.

In the new nation, reconstituted after Appomattox and politically

21. J. C. Hamilton, ed., *The Federalist*, I, xxxiv. See also *ibid.*, I, xv, xvi, xxv, xxvii, xxxvi, xl, xlii, xliii, lxxx*ff*.

dominated by a Republican party solicitous of the interests of finance and industry, the memory of the Jeffersonians drooped and withered. Jefferson's own name, saved from complete eclipse by its association with the Declaration of Independence, was gradually to be refurbished by a slowly reviving Democratic party that kept him as its patron saint.[22] Madison's reputation lacked these compensating aids. From Appomattox to the turn of the century the historic figure of James Madison, like Hamilton's in the earlier period, became more and more separated from a vigorously developing new cult of the Constitution, which sought through a neo-Federalist interpretation of history to give a traditional sanction to the Republican party's politics of capitalistic acquisition.

The fate of Madison's reputation during the period when early American history was being rewritten in post-Appomattox terms is clearly seen in his biography written by S. H. Gay in 1884. Gay's life of Madison was not merely the "accredited" biography of the Virginian for the postwar generation, it was the only complete biography of Madison published before 1902.[23] And though Gay was hostile to his subject "personally, to his party, his state, and his section," as A. E. Smith notes, this biography was accepted as a scholarly production even in the circle of professional historians.[24] Gay found it quite impossible to forgive Madison for leading the

22. For the record of the ups and downs of Jefferson's reputation, see Dixon Wecter's *The Hero in America: A Chronicle of Hero-Worship* (New York, 1941), chap. 7, "Thomas Jefferson, the Gentle Radical," especially 173*ff*.

23. Gaillard Hunt, *The Life of James Madison* (New York, 1902), was actually the first critical biography of Madison to be published. William C. Rives's ponderous and solemn *History of the Life and Times of James Madison* (Boston, 1859–1868) in three volumes represents the culmination of the pietistic prewar view of Madison as father of the Constitution. The work is really a history of the early republican period, built about Madison's career up to 1796, rather than a biography, and though Rives was a conscientious and intelligent historian, his stress on Madison's compact theory of the Constitution (which was completely anachronistic after Appomattox) tended to harm rather than help his subject's reputation in the postwar years.

24. Gay was an able journalist and amateur historian of impeccable Federalist background. He had been associated in early life with the extreme abolitionists and

opposition to Hamilton, for being a Virginian, and for helping to organize the Democratic—i.e. the secessionist, party. "Had he [Madison] been born in a free State ... his place in the history of his country would have been higher. The better part of his life was before he became a party leader." Madison could not be presented by Gay as an outright enemy of American nationalism and foe of the Constitution; but the victory of Jefferson and the defeat of the Federalists in the campaign of 1800, Gay argued, escaped being a fatal disaster for the country only because "the principles and the policy of Federalism survived the party organization." The Democratic party, which Madison had helped to found, was of service to the country, Gay insisted, only in so far as "that party adopted Federal measures. It was in accordance with the early principles of Federalism that the Republic was defended and saved in the war of 1860–65; it was the principles of the Democratic state-rights party, administered by a slave-holding oligarchy that made that war inevitable."[25] Gay's political tract, mislabeled as the standard biography of Madison, was both a symptom of the Virginian's dwindling prestige as constitutional interpreter and a strong factor in his neglect after 1865.

Gay and most of the other Americans of his generation, emotionally shell-shocked by the ordeal of the Southern war, found it psychologically impossible to identify Madison with the idea of union symbolized by the "preserved" and "reconstructed" Constitution.[26] Gay

---

had served as an active agent in the "underground railroad." The author of Gay's sketch in the *Dictionary of American Biography* calls his biography of Madison, somewhat incongruously, "a severe though sympathetic study from the Federalist point of view."

25. Gay, *James Madison*, 173–174.

26. See his attacks on Madison as "a Virginian before he was a Unionist," *ibid.*, 187, and cf. 4, 5, 239. See the discussion of Madison's and Jefferson's relation to the Virginia and Kentucky Resolutions and the doctrines therein set forth, "held by nullifiers and secessionists as their covenant of faith," *ibid.*, 243. See also the discussion of Madison as a slaveholder, *ibid.*, 333.

even challenged Madison's right to be called "the father of the Constitution." He conceded that Madison provided most of the ideas in
the Virginia Plan and had done well to take notes on the debates in
the Convention. But as Gay saw it, Madison never properly understood either the character of the new nation or the kind of government
that had been secured by the Constitution; "Nor till he had been
dead near thirty years was it to be determined what union under
the Constitution really meant. . . ."[27] It gives some indication of how
far Madison's figure had been separated from the Constitution during
this period that Gay's book was hailed by a reviewer in Godkin's
Nation as deserving "the highest praise."

As Madison's political name went under a cloud, Hamilton's shone
ever brighter, and inevitably this reversal of prestige affected the
two men's *Federalist* claims. J. C. Hamilton's filiopietism, his superficial use of internal evidence, and his unconcealed personal dislike of
Madison had mitigated against his early attempt to establish his
father's authorship of all of the disputed essays. Perhaps, too, in
1864 the time was still not ripe for a wholesale revision of the
Madison list that had stood unchallenged during forty years. But
two decades later, by the time Henry Cabot Lodge issued his new
edition of Hamilton's *Works*, the New Yorker's superiority could
be proclaimed without fear of contradiction. Hamilton's reputation,
Lodge believed, had risen phoenix-like from "almost complete
eclipse," because "after the Civil War . . . the American people, purged
by a great ordeal of fire . . . awoke to a full realization . . . of the

27. *Ibid.*, 89. Gay's conclusion and summing up of Madison's character ignore
his creative part in establishing the Constitution and deprecate his fame as president.
"It is our amiable weakness . . . that all our geese are swans, or rather eagles; that
we are apt to mistake notoriety for reputation; that it is the popular belief . . . that
he who . . . has reached a distinguished position, is . . . a great and good man. This
is not less true . . . of Mr. Madison than of some other men who have been Presidents." *Ibid.*, 326. Cf. "His title to fame rests, with the multitude, upon the fact
that he was one of the earliest Presidents of the Republic." *Ibid.*, 328.

meaning and the power of the nation they had built up."[28] Given this new awareness, Lodge felt that the rediscovery of Hamilton's greatness was inevitable. He noted the many ways by which fiction and biography had made Hamilton's "luminous" figure known to the popular mind; while history, too, had vindicated his economic theories until now their soundness was "silently accepted."[29] In other words, between 1861 and 1902 a political enthusiasm had developed in which any statement from the great Federalist leader was sacrosanct, and the Benson list was accordingly reconsidered in this light.

4

AS THE NEW PROPHET of the Benson list, Henry Cabot Lodge met with a success out of all proportion to the weight of the evidence he submitted in its favor. Examined by scholarly standards, or indeed by the light of common sense, he is found guilty of self-contradiction, distortion of his data, and sins of documentary omission, all of which further illustrate the curious way in which even a scholar's integrity may be swept into strong currents of popular sentiment. Only the burgeoning strength of the pro-Hamilton intellectual current can explain why the weakness of Lodge's case for the New Yorker was not at once detected.

The publication of Lodge's 1886 edition of *The Federalist* marks a turning point in the controversy. From that day to the present the division of authors has continued frozen in the indecisive, yet strongly biased, form instituted by the Massachusetts scholar. When this edition was republished in 1902, Lodge made no alterations, disregarding the valuable evidence unearthed from Madison manuscripts by E. G. Bourne; and the three editions of *The Federalist*, by

28. Henry Cabot Lodge, ed., *The Works of Alexander Hamilton,* 2d ed. (New York, 1904), I, iv–v. Lodge reissued *The Federalist* both in the *Works* and as a separate volume.

29. *Ibid.,* I, vi.

Ford, Ashley, and Earle, simply followed Lodge's policy of placing the names of both Hamilton and Madison beneath all twelve of the questionable essays. But Lodge's impartiality with the signatures, and in certain editorial statements,[30] is only a gesture. He is convinced that "the balance is strongly in Hamilton's favor," and the arguments he presents for this belief are remarkable examples of scholarly method betrayed by prejudice.

Lodge offers three reasons for tilting the balance "strongly in Hamilton's favor." For one thing, he finds it "a very serious matter" that Madison neglected to challenge the Benson list as soon as it appeared.[31] There were political reasons, already considered, why Madison did not care publicly to assert authorship of specific essays while holding office; but Lodge does not even admit into his testimony the fact that Hamilton, too, had earlier expressed "decided disapprobation" of naming the authors for each essay.

The second point that Lodge brings against Madison was for making an appeal to internal evidence. "This," Lodge asserted, "would not have been done probably by a man who had no doubt in his own mind as to the essays, and it certainly would not be the course of any one who had contemporary memoranda to guide and assure him."[32] In making this curious deduction, Lodge conveniently ignores several statements of Madison's that the Gideon list was not written from memory,[33] that the inaccuracy of Hamilton's memory could be

30. Before Lodge begins his discussion of the disputed essays, he concedes that regarding the authorship of at least ten he "felt that the probabilities were in favor of Madison." Lodge, ed., *The Federalist*, xxxiii.

31. *Ibid.*, xxxi.

32. *Ibid.*

33. Lodge cites Madison's letter to J. K. Paulding, Apr. 1831, and insinuates that Madison had depended only upon internal evidence to support his case. An examination of this letter shows, on the contrary, that Madison's appeal to internal evidence was supplementary to and followed an unambiguous statement that he did not write from memory. He stated that his Gideon list, "if erroneous, could not be ascribed to a lapse of memory" but to a "lack of veracity," for it was "communicated by me at an early date to a particular friend, and finally to Mr. Gideon." *Letters of Madison*, IV, 176.

proven, "independent of any internal evidence," and that he, Madison, had made his list "at a time and under circumstances" when he would have had no reason or excuse for a "slip of the memory or attention."[34] For Lodge to overlook these positive statements from Madison's own pen, while condemning him on a shaky deduction, proves how psychologically difficult it was for him to do the Virginian justice in the pro-Hamilton atmosphere of the 1880s.

Having established by specious argument and neglect of evidence that Madison's lists were compiled from memory, Lodge in the next breath confesses that Hamilton's lists, too, were doubtless made from memory. He then attempts to prove Madison's memory inferior to Hamilton's by a mathematical demonstration perhaps unparalleled in historical scholarship.

To place beside the Benson memorandum—the "best Hamilton list" as Lodge calls it—there were available two lists personally vouched for by Madison. One, the Rush list, is in his handwriting; the other, the Gideon, was publicly affirmed by Madison. These two lists agree in every important detail.[35] Incredibly enough, Lodge equates in value with these firsthand data two newspaper lists of

34. In 1819 Robert Walsh wrote Madison mentioning internal evidence favoring his claim as against the Benson list; the Virginian emphatically replied: "I take the liberty of remarking, independent of any internal evidence that may be discernible, the inaccuracy of Mr. Hamilton's memory" is proved by his handling of Numbers 54 and 64. He further explained to Walsh that "if I have any interest in proving the fallibility of Mr. Hamilton's memory, it is not that the authorship in question is of itself a point deserving the solicitude of either of the parties; but because I had, at the request of a confidential friend or two, communicated a list of the numbers in that publication, with the names of the writers annexed, at a time and under the circumstances depriving me of a plea for so great a mistake in a slip of the memory or attention." Mar. 2, 1819, *ibid.*, III, 126.

35. The only variation between the Rush list and the Gideon edition is a footnote to Number 18 in the latter by Madison explaining why he claimed sole authorship of Numbers 18, 19, and 20 as against the Benson list's claim of Hamilton's joint authorship. In the Rush copy he simply marked these essays as his own without comment or justifying explanation. Thus the only two lists that we can be sure accurately represent Madison's own personal statements agree exactly with each other in the division of the essays.

1817, both published anonymously. Since these two dubious lists purporting to exhibit material "furnished by Madison," or copied from him at some time, do not strictly agree either with each other or with the Rush-Gideon figures, Lodge totals all variations among the four, serious and trivial alike, to give to "the Madison lists" a sum of twelve errors in memory regarding six numbers of *The Federalist*.

The process by which Lodge now shows Hamilton's memory, and hence, his claim, to be more accurate than Madison's, is a triumph of loyalty. He simply dismisses all Hamiltonian tabulations which do not agree with the Benson list. Included in the favored lists is one dictated by Hamilton to his son,[36] Hamilton's copy of *The Federalist*, with authorship "said to be designated in his own handwriting," and two other marked copies belonging to personal friends of Hamilton's.[37] In all of these lists, Hamilton claims Number 64, attributed to Jay by Madison and later found among Jay's manuscripts. In still another list made by Chancellor Kent and revised, so Kent said, by Hamilton himself, Number 64 is restored to its rightful owner, Jay. Yet this Kent list is disqualified from taking part in Lodge's statistical tally because it disagrees in other particulars from the Benson list by giving credit to Madison for two of the disputed essays.[38] By failing to count the variation of this Kent table and also those of the

36. Lodge, ed., *The Federalist*, xxvi. In 1802–1803 Hamilton dictated to his son a list sent to his nephew that agreed with the Benson memo.

37. *Ibid.*, xxvii. Lodge put in evidence as authoritative lists the divisions of authors found in the copies of *The Federalist* owned by Fisher Ames and his own ancestor George Cabot. They both corresponded to the Benson memo, but since Lodge confesses that Cabot's list was probably copied from the 1810 edition, its value would appear nil. There is no way of dating the Ames list or discovering whether he too copied it from the Benson memo.

38. Kent reported that in 1802 Hamilton had given him a list of the authors and that Hamilton then attributed 64 to Jay and attributed 49 and 53 to Madison. Lodge comments that these variations from the Benson list are "peculiar." He resolutely refuses to consider them as Hamilton errors; since the chancellor "corrected his list in later years . . . the changes as to 49 and 53 seem to lose significance, especially as they are two of . . . the disputed numbers, and these . . . all coming

Washington list (a document which was Lodge's only piece of "new" evidence),[39] Lodge was able to contrast with Madison's twelve errors in six numbers, a happy score for Hamilton of only two errors in two numbers. Lodge concludes with éclat, "Tried therefore by the list of admitted errors, Hamilton's authority is shown to be six times as good as that of Madison."[40]

It is symptomatic of the pro-Hamilton fever of the 1880s that for ten years no historian challenged either Lodge's unscholarly devices or his conclusions. Then almost by accident Edward Gaylord Bourne stumbled into the *Federalist* controversy. Bourne had no particular interest in Hamilton, Madison, or *The Federalist*. In 1896, however, in preparing a paper to be read before the American Historical Association on "The Use of History made by the Framers of the Constitution," he carefully examined both the elaborate historical memoranda

---

consecutively, must on any reasonable theory be assigned to one or the other of the authors in a block." *Ibid.*, xxx. Lodge does not indicate that Kent, an intimate friend of Hamilton's who had originally accepted as correct his division of the authors, later came to accept Madison's. Sometime after 1817 he pasted a copy of the *Washington Gazette* list on the flyleaf of his copy of *The Federalist*, opposite the list Hamilton had given him in 1802, and wrote under it: "Memr. I have no doubt Mr. Jay wrote 64 on the Treaty Power. He made a speech on that subject in the N.Y. Convention, and I am told he says he wrote it. I suspect, therefore, from the internal Ev[idence] the above to be the correct list and not the one on the opposite page."

39. Lodge had discovered in Washington's copy of *The Federalist* a tabulation of authors in the general's handwriting that he felt "both from its date [1798–1799] and the character of its author, seems to me to tell very strongly against Madison." Lodge, ed., *The Federalist*, xxxiv. The list contained four errors of the type Lodge so carefully scored against Madison: Jay's name was added as third coauthor to 18, 19, and 20, and Hamilton was given 48, never attributed to him in any other list. Lodge notices these "curious variations" from the Benson memo, but does not consider them errors. "The striking and important fact" of this Washington division was that it "agrees in the main with the Benson list, and assigns the twelve disputed numbers unhesitatingly to Hamilton." *Ibid.*, xxviii. Cf. Lodge's reason for dismissing the Kent list as insignificant because two of the disputed numbers were given to the Virginian. Poor Madison was caught here in a heads-I-win, tails-you-lose squeeze by the Massachusetts scholar.

40. *Ibid.*, xxxi.

prepared by Madison on ancient and modern confederations and Numbers 18, 19, and 20 of *The Federalist,* where Madison's research reappeared in literary form.[41] Thus by easy stages, Bourne was led to examine the internal evidence of authorship in those three numbers which Madison had claimed in the Rush list (these three were also attributed to him by one newspaper correspondent; another gave him 18 and 19 but falsely added 17 and 21). Lodge claimed that Madison had "conceded" these as "joint" products in the Gideon edition. He had then used the concession to total up eight errors against Madison for forgetfulness. Bourne found Lodge's method deplorable and in the *American Historical Review* accused him of "studied disparagement" of the Virginian and of "unfairly discrediting Madison's testimony as compared with that of Hamilton."[42]

Bourne pointed out that in spite of Lodge's statement to the contrary, the Gideon list did not admit Hamilton to be joint author of 18, 19, and 20.[43] He further demonstrated by internal evidence that Madison was accurate in calling these numbers his own, since they were only slightly revised reproductions of his preconvention notes. As Madison had cited in these memoranda the books from which he

41. *Annual Report of the American Historical Association,* I (Washington, D.C., 1897), 226

42. Bourne, "Authorship of The Federalist," *AHR,* II (1896–1897), 444.

43. In the Gideon edition Madison's name alone is given as author. However, Madison in a footnote to Number 18 explained why Hamilton had claimed joint authorship: "The subject of this and the following numbers happened to be taken up by both Mr. Hamilton and Mr. Madison. What had been prepared by Mr. Hamilton, who had entered more briefly into the subject, was left to Mr. Madison, on its appearing that the latter was engaged upon it, with larger materials, and with a view to a more precise delineation, and from the pen of the latter the several papers went to press." Madison also repeated this explanation to George Bancroft, when the latter was writing his *History of the Formation of the Constitution* (Boston, 1882), II, 337. "It is possible," Madison said, "though not recollected, that something in the draught [i.e. Hamilton's] may have been incorporated into the numbers as printed. But it was certainly not of a nature or amount to affect the impression left on the mind of J. M., from whose pen the numbers went to the press that the numbers were of the class written by him." An examination of Madison's "Notes" proves he was justified in claiming sole authorship.

had drawn his material, Bourne was able to check further on the source of the ideas and information presented in the three essays. His conclusion was that in Number 20, for example, Madison had drawn so heavily on Temple's *Observations of the United Nether-lands* that Sir William had a "far stronger" claim than Hamilton "to be recognized as joint author." The case of Numbers 18 and 19 was similar. Madison had certainly written all of the essays himself, including in revised form only a small amount of pertinent information submitted by Hamilton from his rather sketchy research on the same subject.[44]

Bourne was sufficiently encouraged by the light shed from internal evidence upon the authorship of Numbers 18, 19, and 20 to apply the same test to the twelve disputed essays. Though the amount of relevant material that he discovered varied considerably from essay to essay, his results were most rewarding. On page after page of these numbers Bourne found sentences and whole paragraphs that could be matched almost exactly by selections from Madison's letters and historical studies, written before *The Federalist* was composed. The historian then argued, after having printed these identical samples in long parallel columns, that Madison's claim to be the writer of these twelve essays stood on nearly as good ground as Jay's claim to Number 64. "Jay's authorship of No. 64 was finally established by finding a draft of the essay in his papers. It will hardly be denied that a considerable part of Nos. 62 and 63 has been found in Madison's writings. The evidence in regard to Nos. 51 and 53 is also convincing; and that in the case of Nos. 49 and 50 is confirmatory."[45] All the evidence that Bourne discovered operated to increase his confidence in

44. Bourne, "Authorship of The Federalist," *AHR*, II (1896–1897), 455. In Number 20, two paragraphs out of 24 incorporated Hamilton material.

45. *Ibid.*, 459. An examination of Bourne's monograph shows that he did not exaggerate when he claimed that a substantial portion of the disputed essays actually duplicated Madison's pre-Convention writings. If Bourne had carefully checked the Debates in the Convention he could have discovered even more confirmatory material.

the accuracy and honesty of Madison's claim. He concluded therefore that the Gideon list gave an exact statement of *Federalist* authorship.

Lodge's essay with its specious pro-Hamilton conclusion had been in print ten full years before it was openly questioned. Bourne's careful study favoring Madison was angrily challenged by Paul Leicester Ford within three months of its publication.[46] Moreover the personal tone of Ford's reply to Bourne indicated that any writer tending to diminish the luminous greatness of Hamilton would be charged in certain historical quarters with the crime of lese majesty.[47]

Bourne had presented a quantity of new evidence to verify the accuracy of the Gideon list. Ford's answer to this valuable new material was first to deny that Bourne's internal evidence was relevant, next to repeat certain of Lodge's exploded arguments, and finally to make an inconsistent use of pro-Hamilton internal evidence which he did consider to be in point. Ford's conclusion, needless to say, paralleled the Lodge conclusion of 1886: that the Benson list gave the most nearly accurate division of the *Federalist* authors.

Among the echoes of Lodge in Ford's essay is the old suspicion concerning Madison's delay in answering the Benson list. Lodge's disproved hypothesis that Madison wrote his list from memory was also revived by Ford despite Bourne's citation of chapter and verse indicating the contrary. Having rested his case partially on a paraphrase of Lodge's old theories, Ford offers as his own contribution

46. Ford, "Authorship of The Federalist," *ibid.*, II (1896–1897), 675–682. Ford had been interested in *The Federalist* for some time, having produced a bibliography of *The Federalist* in 1886, the same year in which he issued his *Bibliotheca Hamiltoniana: A List of Books Written by, or Relating to, Alexander Hamilton* (New York, 1886).

47. Ford's article exhibits a shortness of temper somewhat out of place in an objective historical study. Bourne had used parallel quotations from the disputed numbers and the Virginian's writings to prove Madison's authorship. Why, then, did he not go on, asked Ford with labored sarcasm, "to prove that 'Publius' wrote *Esprit des Lois*" by quoting the paraphrase of Montesquieu in *The Federalist*? Ford, "Authorship of The Federalist," *AHR*, II (1896–1897), 676n.

certain arguments based on internal evidence, although he had dismissed Bourne's careful presentation of like material as "unsafe."

Ford's polemic started with the major premise that "Hamilton . . . as the originator of the series intended to take the laboring oar" in the writing of *The Federalist*. He then made the large leap to the minor premise that Madison was therefore only permitted to write as Publius when Hamilton was too busy to do it himself. In fact, Ford asserted, even when the Virginian took up his pen to defend the Constitution he had helped to create, Hamilton outlined his material for him and "guided" his efforts.[48] From this point it was but a short step to Ford's conclusion that if Hamilton knew anything at all about a topic he would not have allowed Madison to write on it. This was the expressed syllogism upon which Ford based his attack on Bourne.

"In Nos. 53, 54, and 56," Ford pointed out, "are paragraphs discussing taxation, the militia, the slavery compromise in the convention, or about which subjects Hamilton had familiarized himself with, and which he had made his own topics in his earlier essays."[49] This

---

48. The hypothesis that Hamilton, who had taken little active part in drafting the Constitution, would have to tell Madison, who was the leading author of it, how to defend and explain the document seems rather curious. Ford brought forward as evidence to establish this startling deduction a syllabus found among Hamilton's papers, which all Hamilton editors, before and since Ford wrote, have listed as the outline of a Convention speech. Ford rearranges the topics of this syllabus, notes that it treats of certain of the subjects that Madison wrote on in essays 37*ff*—the parallel is far from exact—and confidently asserts that it is "the preliminary outline of *The Federalist* from the point at which Hamilton was interrupted in his composition by his legal and political operations, and it was presumably drawn up as a guide for Madison in his continuance of the task." *Ibid.*, 677.

49. Ford made no attempt to show, as Bourne had done in presenting his internal evidence, that any of the paragraphs in question could be duplicated in the New Yorker's earlier writings; the fact that the topics were Hamilton's "own" seemed to him sufficient proof. In regard to Number 54, however, he does point out that Hamilton followed the essay's arguments later in the New York convention. He also categorically states that the idea of property representation defended in Number 54 was directly contrary to Madison's views, thus betraying his ignorance of Madison's political theories.

was proof enough for Ford that Hamilton had written the three numbers. He discovered equally convincing evidence in essays 52, 56, 57, 58, and 63. Here, the clues were "citations of examples in English history, like references being numerous in many of Hamilton's essays."[50] This was sufficient to convince Ford that all five of the numbers belonged to the New Yorker. To clinch the point that the scholarly Madison knew too little English history to have made such "citations," Ford pointed with a flourish to the pre-Convention research of the Virginian.[51] Nowhere in Madison's "Notes," Ford exclaimed, was any mention made of England! He refrained, however, from citing the full title of Madison's historical study, which would have explained why discussion of the British monarchy was naturally omitted. The exact title of Madison's "Notes" was "Notes of Ancient and Modern *Confederacies.*"[52]

These were not the only bits of evidence that Ford's diligent scholarship turned up for Hamilton. His sharp eye discovered many similar examples. The merits of his evidence, however, can best be weighed by balancing it against the data put forward by the disinterested Bourne. Certainly a comparison of the two scholars' work in this instance demonstrates Ford's determined partiality for Hamilton, better than his proven ability in fields of research where his emotional commitments were less strong.

Although Ford's assiduous efforts denied Madison any knowledge about taxation, the militia, the slavery compromise in the Convention, or about English history, he finally grants Madison three of the disputed numbers. Arguing a "disjointedness of connection" and

50. *Ibid.*, 681.

51. Ford acknowledged in a footnote that the presumably ignorant Madison "boned" up on English history in preparing supplementary notes for the Virginia convention. This, Ford believed, primarily demonstrated that Hamilton had been a good teacher and guide for the Virginian. Madison, he states, turned to the study of British precedents only "after *The Federalist* [i.e., Hamilton] had called his attention to the value of the material." *Ibid.*, 681.

52. Italics mine.

change of style between essays 46 and 47, and between 51 and 52, Ford reasoned that essays 47 to 51 inclusive must have been written by a single author. Ford felt, moreover, that essays 48 to 51 were written "from the historical and theoretical" standpoint, while all the rest of *The Federalist* (including the nine other disputed numbers) was the work of a writer "prone to take the practical rather than the theoretical view of things."[53] After this dubious appeal to internal evidence, "it appears," he says, "that Madison probably wrote Nos. 49 to 51, and Hamilton Nos. 52 to 58 and Nos. 62 and 63." Even after this closing note of scholarly objectivity[54] Ford still followed the precedent of Lodge in placing Hamilton's name first on all twelve of the disputed essays.

The wheel had made a full turn. The Benson list after being discredited for longer than half a century had now been revived as an authority as good as the Gideon list, if not superior to it. This

53. Ford, "Authorship of The Federalist," *AHR*, II (1896–1897), 680. It is hard to find more "historical and theoretical" essays than Numbers 62 and 63 anywhere in *The Federalist*. There is, furthermore, a break of continuity between Numbers 58 and 59 which is reknit with Number 62; but Ford ignores this.

54. Ford was not quite so generous to Madison as his concluding remark would appear. To balance the "probable" three essays given to the Virginian, he gave to Hamilton as "possible" Numbers 47 and 48, which the New Yorker himself had never claimed in any list. The reason Ford felt these two essays could no longer be "positively ascribed" to the Virginian was their homogeneity with the three disputed essays. Even more important than this, in Ford's estimation, was the fact that John Taylor of Caroline had attributed all essays after Number 46 to Hamilton when he wrote his *New Views of the Constitution of the United States* (Washington, D.C., 1823). Ford notes: "Yet though he [Taylor] was the friend and correspondent of Madison, and though his book was well-known to the latter, neither publicly nor privately, so far as is known did he correct Taylor's conclusion." *Ibid.*, 680n. The truth of the matter is that Taylor had been Madison's bitter enemy since before 1808, when with the Tertium Quid faction in Virginia he had tried to block Madison's election as president. Furthermore, *New Views* itself was considered by Madison to carry unfair "imputations" against him. *Letters of Madison*, IV, 209. Since Ford knew little about Madison's public or private character and writings, it was but natural for him to make this mistake. It is less understandable, even excusing his ignorance, that the Gideon edition was not accepted by him as a "public" correction of Taylor's preposterous error.

had happened in spite of the fact that Ford himself confessed that the Benson memorandum was "probably" inaccurate regarding Numbers 49, 50, and 51, as well as 54 and 64. This had happened in spite of the fact that neither Lodge nor Ford had been able to prove an instance in which the Gideon list positively erred. All of their assumptions about Madison's bad "memory," all of their a priori deductions, all of their queerly woven tissue of evidence had not produced a specific case to show Madison's official list was definitely mistaken in its claim to a single essay. Under the circumstances, the reestablishment of the Benson memo as trustworthy must be considered one of the most amazing literary coups on record.

There can be no question that the Hamiltonians had achieved a triumph by reopening the controversy over the disputed numbers. Bourne, of course, replied to Ford and easily scored many critical points against him.[55] But Ford thereafter blandly ignored Bourne and in 1898 reissued his same essay as the introduction to a new edition of *The Federalist*. Lodge's study, also unchanged, went into a second edition in 1902. At best Bourne's effort was in the nature of a rearguard action, insuring only that Madison's name be kept on the disputed essays, even though in second place.[56]

---

55. *AHR*, II (1896–1897), 682–685. Bourne's reply was printed as a postscript to Ford's article. Though short it adequately refuted Ford's contentions.

56. The only modern edition that gives all of the disputed numbers to Hamilton without qualification is the World's Great Classics edition, first issued by the Colonial Press in 1901 and still available in a cheap reprint. [See essay 13 for Adair's views on more recent editions of *The Federalist*.—Ed.] However, the usual marking of the 12 disputed numbers, followed by W. J. Ashley in the Everyman's Library edition of 1911 and by Earle in the Modern Library edition of 1937, became "Hamilton or Madison." It has also become traditional since Lodge's edition to mark Numbers 18, 19, and 20 "Hamilton and Madison," though there is not the slightest justification for this except the unwarranted assumption that in every case of the slightest doubt Hamilton is the major and Madison the minor contributor. The New Yorker himself in the Benson list marked these "Nos. 18, 19, 20, M. & H. jointly." Bourne proves that the notation of the Gideon edition is accurate: the essays should be marked simply "Madison," with a footnote explaining the Virginian's use of a small amount of Hamilton's data in writing them.

By 1900 it looked as if the prophecy made by Lodge in 1882 would be fulfilled: "There has been some controversy as to the proportionate share of these eminent men in this undertaking, but the discussion is of little moment. . . . To posterity 'Publius' will always be Hamilton."[57] The political prestige of Hamilton, the prophet of capitalism, has now over a period of sixty years vitiated the strong external evidence pointing to Madison's authorship. The same pro-Hamilton bias has likewise discouraged the examination of internal evidence, even more sharply revealing. It will be the task of another paper to show through the use of such material that Publius spoke with a Virginia accent in the controversial essays and that James Madison undoubtedly wrote every number he claimed in the Gideon list.

II

1

It was early in May 1788 that Alexander Hamilton penned the last paragraph of the eighty-fifth number of *The Federalist*. As climax and conclusion of the essay he wrote: "A nation without a national government, is, in my view, an awful spectacle. The establishment of a Constitution in time of profound peace, by the voluntary consent of a whole people, is a prodigy, to the completion of which I look forward with trembling anxiety." With another sentence or two added, and the signature of Publius, Hamilton's literary task was done. Number 85 was ready for the printer. More important, with its completion, the whole of *The Federalist* was finished.

In less than a month *Federalist* 85 with the forty-eight preceding essays had been printed together and bound in book form.[58] Immedi-

---

57. Henry Cabot Lodge, *Alexander Hamilton* (Boston, 1882), 68.
58. The first volume of *The Federalist* containing Numbers 1 through 36 had been issued as a book in March.

ately, during the first week in June, "forty of the common copies and twelve of the finer ones" were sent off in haste to Virginia, where Hamilton's coauthor, Madison, was impatient for them.[59] The Virginia ratifying convention was just assembling; and when the volumes arrived at Richmond they were carefully divided among the members of the pro-Constitution party to serve as a debater's handbook in organizing the defense of the new government. Another batch of copies was similarly distributed in New York, where the ratifying convention had been called for June 17. And there, too, advocates of the Constitution practically memorized the persuasive reasoning of Publius in preparation for the oratorical battle that impended. In both the Virginia and New York conventions, these strategically placed copies of *The Federalist* were to provide the most potent arguments by which the friends of the Constitution could vindicate its adoption. At both Richmond and Poughkeepsie the writings of Publius, served up hot in debate, played an important part in getting the new government ratified.[60]

It was only then, after Virginia and New York had been added as the tenth and eleventh "pillars . . . of the Federal temple," that the secrecy surrounding the authorship of *The Federalist* was little by little dispelled. While ratification was still in doubt the identity of

59. "The number of the volumes of the Federalist which you desired have been forwarded, as well the second as the first, to the care of Governor Randolph." Hamilton to Madison, June 8, 1788, Lodge, ed., *Works of Hamilton*, IX, 434. The number of copies that Madison had requested is established in Hamilton's letter of May 19, 1788, informing Madison that the 52 copies of Volume I had been sent. *Ibid.*, 431.

60. *The Federalist*'s propaganda value, as first published in the newspapers, should not be overrated; the essays probably influenced few votes among the general electorate. In the Virginia and New York conventions, however, the bound volumes were enormously valuable. The pro-Constitution party in both states was eager for a clause-by-clause discussion of the proposed government. Under this procedure, with Publius' systematic analysis of the document at hand, the Constitutionalist leaders were able to arrange the order of debate beforehand, to coach specific speakers to talk on the various parts of the Constitution, and generally to organize and manage its defense in a systematic way. For an enlightening discussion of the disciplined tactics of the Virginia Constitutionalists, see Albert J. Beveridge, *The Life of John Marshall* (Boston, 1916), I, 367ff, especially 370, 374, 379, 392.

Publius had been carefully concealed. Hamilton, Jay, and Madison were all agreed that the effect of Publius' writings would be augmented if the names of the actual authors remained unknown.[61] There is, moreover, plentiful evidence to show how strictly they maintained their anonymity during the whole ten months preceding New York's formal acceptance of the Constitution.

Hamilton, during this period, so far as his published correspondence shows, revealed his share in the writing of *The Federalist* only to Washington. Even in this special instance, however, Hamilton did not directly admit his authorship. He merely sent the general the earliest of the Publius essays, stating that it was the first of a projected series, and allowed Washington to draw his own conclusions about the author's identity.[62] Madison in his correspondence with Washington was only slightly less cautious. In November he wrote the general from New York asking if *The Federalist* could be reprinted in some Virginia newspaper. "I will not conceal *from you*," he wrote, underlining his words to show the exceptional nature of his disclosure, "that I am likely to have such a *degree* of connection with the publication here as to afford a restraint of delicacy from interesting myself in the republication elsewhere. You will recognize one of the pens concerned in the task. There are three in the whole."[63] Madison

61. The use of pseudonyms in political writings was standard 18th-century practice. It was especially advisable, however, in the case of *The Federalist*. Madison had little personal prestige in New York, where, in fact, as a Virginian he was viewed as a "foreigner." The same was true of Jay's and Hamilton's positions in the Old Dominion.

62. "The enclosed is the first number of a series of papers to be written in its [the Constitution's] defense." Hamilton to Washington, Oct. 30, 1787, Lodge, ed., *Works of Hamilton*, IX, 425.

63. Madison to Washington, Nov. 18, 1787, Gaillard Hunt, ed., *The Writings of James Madison* (New York, 1900–1910), V, 55. Washington sent these papers to David Stuart, who found a printer for them in Richmond; the general, however, carefully concealed the authors' identity from Stuart. John C. Fitzpatrick, ed., *The Writings of George Washington from the Original Manuscript Sources, 1745–1799* (Washington, D.C., 1931–1944), XXIX, 324. Washington himself, in spite of Madison's and Hamilton's hints, was unable to guess who the third author was, for on Feb. 5, 1788, he wrote Henry Knox asking, "Pray, if it is not a secret, who is the author or authors of Publius?" *Ibid.*, 401.

was equally circumspect when he partially lifted the veil of secrecy for Edmund Randolph. In December he sent him newspapers containing certain of the essays with the promise of more to follow. Concerning Publius he wrote: "You will probably discover marks of different pens. I am not at liberty to give you any other key, than that I am in myself for a few numbers & that one besides myself was a member of the Convention."[64]

Even in the letters relating to *The Federalist* that passed between Hamilton and Madison after the latter had left New York for Virginia great care was taken to maintain anonymity. No names were mentioned in discussing the work, and Hamilton deliberately spoke as though Publius were some third and unknown person. "I send you the *Federalist* . . . to the conclusion of the commentary on the Executive Branches," he wrote Madison in April. "If our suspicions of the author be right, he must be too much engaged to make a rapid progress in what remain. The Court of Chancery and a Circuit Court are now sitting."[65] This habit of secrecy, so strictly cultivated by the authors, hung on even after ratification had been secured. When on August 10, 1788, Madison wrote Jefferson in Paris informing him that the new government was now assured of a fair trial, he remarked on the copy of *The Federalist* sent to Jefferson by a mutual friend. He also felt safe at this time in confiding to Jefferson the names of all three authors. Madison still was careful, however, to send this information in cypher, although it was then nearly a month after New York's ratification.[66] So strict were the precautions maintained

64. Madison to Edmund Randolph, Dec. 2, 1787, Hunt, ed., *Writings of Madison,* V, 61.

65. Hamilton to Madison, Apr. 3, 1788, Lodge, ed., *Works of Hamilton,* IX, 427. Cf. Hamilton's letter to Madison, May 19, 1788, telling him that "the printer announces the second volume in a day or two. . . . He informs that the Judicial Department—Trial by Jury—Bill of Rights, etc., is discussed in some additional papers which have not yet appeared in the Gazettes." *Ibid.,* 431.

66. "Col. Carrington tells me [he] has sent you the first volume of the federalist, and adds the 2d by this conveyance. I believe I never have yet *mentioned to you that publication. It was undertaken last fall by Jay, Hamilton, and myself. The*

by the three authors of *The Federalist* throughout the whole period while ratification hung in the balance that, of all the hundreds of people who read the Publius essays in 1787–1788, there were probably not a dozen individuals who definitely could state that Hamilton, Madison, and Jay had written them.

This aura of secrecy surrounding the authorship of *The Federalist* indirectly played its part in producing the controversy between the admirers of Hamilton and Madison over the exact share of the two men in its composition. The most intimate friends and political allies of the three authors knew that they had collectively produced the work; but even this select inner group had no exact way of knowing which parts each had written. Nor were they especially concerned in 1788–1789 to solve the riddle. For with ratification secured, the writings of Publius temporarily became unimportant as the problems incident to the organization of the new government pressed for immediate solution. When the identity of Publius again became politically interesting, Hamilton and Madison were open enemies. Later, with the appearance of the contradictory authors' lists it was natural for prejudiced supporters of the Virginian and the New Yorker to make the question of authorship a personal issue between the two men. This spirit of partisanship has tainted the *Federalist* controversy ever since, and most probably will continue to do so as long as scholars focus their entire attention upon Hamilton's claims in the Benson memo and Madison's counterclaims set forth in the Gideon list.

Fortunately it is not necessary to depend on any list in distributing the majority of *The Federalist* essays among the three authors. Even if Hamilton, Madison, and Jay had never given a written or spoken hint as to which numbers each had written, there would still be enough evidence available to make it possible to assign most of the

---

proposal came from the two former. The execution was thrown, by the sickness of Jay, mostly on the two others." Madison to Jefferson, Aug. 10, 1788, Hunt, ed., *Writings of Madison*, V, 246. All words italicized were in cypher.

eighty-five numbers of Publius to the different individuals who wrote them. And when Hamilton's and Madison's several statements of authorship are used in conjunction with this evidence, strangely ignored for three-quarters of a century, it becomes entirely unnecessary to mark the writer of a single number as uncertain.

Jay's contribution to *The Federalist* was the most easily ascertained, and it was determined in spite of contradictions among the various lists. For the manuscripts of Jay's five essays (Numbers 2, 3, 4, 5, and 64) were preserved among his papers. This fact has been sufficient to establish his share in the project, notwithstanding Hamilton's claim that he had written 64 and that Jay had written 54. It is safe to say that even the discovery of several additional lists would not change Jay's accredited portion, thus independently established.

It is more difficult to sort out Hamilton's and Madison's exact contribution to *The Federalist* than it is to determine Jay's. Nevertheless, no matter how carefully Madison and Hamilton sought for secrecy in writing *The Federalist*, no matter how carefully they tried to submerge their real personalities in that of the fictitious Publius, the lens of time magnifies for the historian many individual traces which in their haste they left behind them. Some of this evidence can be found in their papers; other data less concrete but just as positive exist in the imprint, on all they wrote, of their opposed method and direction of thought. The very speed with which *The Federalist* had to be written guaranteed that the writing of both men would reveal sharp differences which they had no time to level off into perfect editorial unity.

For the rate at which *The Federalist* was written and published was hardly short of phenomenal. According to tradition, Hamilton wrote the first essay some time after the middle of October, while traveling down the Hudson in a sloop from Albany to New York. It appeared on October 27, 1787, in the *Independent Advertiser*. Number 85, the last essay, was written in May 1788 and on May 28 appeared with its forty-nine immediate predecessors in book form.

In the six months' period between October 1787 and May 1788 Hamilton and Madison had written for publication approximately 175,000 words.[67] This is an astonishing feat simply from the quantitative standard; yet the papers signed by Publius consisted of closely reasoned political analysis. It is even more noteworthy when it is recalled that Madison and Hamilton could produce *The Federalist* only in their spare time. Each man was engaged in other activities which could not be set aside. Madison was one of the Virginia representatives in the Continental Congress, while Hamilton had his extensive law practice to maintain; and both men were committed to keeping up a heavy political correspondence with pro-Constitutional leaders throughout the country. Nevertheless, from October through March *The Federalist* papers were written at an average rate of nearly a thousand words a day.

Many years later James Madison was still to recall the strain and hurry of this period when the printer's deadline perpetually hung over the composition of *The Federalist*. And in recalling the tension incident to writing as Publius he reveals one obvious clue to the division of his own from Hamilton's numbers: "The haste with which many of the papers were penned in order to get through the subject whilst the Constitution was before the public, and to comply with the arrangement, by which the printer was to keep his paper open for four numbers every week,[68] was such that the performance must have borne a very different aspect without the aid of historical and other notes which had been used in the Convention. . . . It frequently happened, that, whilst the printer was putting into type parts of a number, the following parts were under the pen and to be furnished in time for the press."[69] Here in the "historical studies" and in the

---

67. Jay's total contribution was approximately 7,500 words.

68. New York newspapers in which *The Federalist* first appeared were published twice a week. At first only one *Federalist* essay was printed per issue, but commencing with Numbers 8 and 9 they appeared two at a time, twice a week.

69. From an unpublished memorandum entitled "The Federalist" drawn up by Madison after he retired from the presidency, quoted in J. C. Hamilton, ed., *The*

"notes" for Convention speeches by both men are to be found in
embryonic form dozens of the papers published later under the shared
pseudonym of Publius. These "studies," as well as the Convention
speeches of the two men (which have been in print for nearly a
century), serve as a sure guide to the authorship of many of the
anonymously issued essays.

The breakneck speed at which *The Federalist* was written provides
another valuable aid for the latter-day historians who would distinguish Madison's share of the papers from that of Hamilton. It is
clear that the haste of composition and publication forced the two
main authors to work independently of each other. Hamilton wrote
his essays alone, and they were published as he had written them.
Madison's papers went straight from his pen to the press without
any editing by Hamilton. As Madison explained to Jefferson when
disclosing his part in the enterprise, "Though carried on in concert,
the writers are not mutually answerable for all the ideas of each
other, there being seldom time for even a perusal of the pieces by
any but the writer before they were wanted at the press, and sometimes hardly by the writer himself."[70] As a result each of the essays
is pure Hamilton or pure Madison; none of the essays in *The Federalist* was composed as a joint product. Inevitably each bears in unadulterated form the mark of its author's habitual modes of expression,
pet phrases, and characteristic political ideas.

Inevitably, too, the essays written by Madison are not completely
fused in a logical or a literary sense with those written by Hamilton.
The New Yorker, a literary craftsman of the highest order, was well
aware of this lack of unity and roughness in the various sections of
The Federalist. When in March 1788 he wrote the preface for the

---

Federalist, I, lxxxvi, note. This memorandum was found by J. C. Hamilton when
he examined the Madison papers in the Department of State about the middle of
the last century. Lodge searched for it unsuccessfully in the 1880s, however, and
reported that it had disappeared.

70. Madison to Jefferson, Aug. 10, 1788, Hunt, ed., *Writings of Madison*, V,
246. This statement was written in cypher.

first volume of the work he was careful to apologize for it. "The particular circumstances under which these papers have been written, have rendered it impracticable to avoid violations of method and repetitions of ideas which cannot but displease a critical reader." Although the "critical reader" may have disapproved in 1787–1788, this same "impracticability" of editing any of the essays or of imposing a uniform style and strictly logical organization upon Publius was a blessing for the twentieth-century scholar who would separate Madison's contribution from Hamilton's. For it puts in the hands of the historian a key to unlock the mystery of *The Federalist* and concomitantly points the way to a deeper insight into the meaning of the Constitution itself.

These leads provided by Hamilton and Madison, as they discussed their problems of publication, have too long been passed over in the confusion of the contradictory lists. Madison and Hamilton carried to the Philadelphia Convention markedly divergent plans for the formation of the new union. In the Convention they espoused sharply differing theories of government, and these they defended with historical arguments which, again, show what very separate roads the two men took in their studies and reading. These theoretical disagreements between Madison and Hamilton, as will be seen, did not end with the writing of the Constitution. Each man valued the document for different reasons, and each hoped it would function in a different way when it began operations. In the meantime, both men yet agreed that it should be ratified and laid aside all differences in order to bring this about. *The Federalist* is the fruit of that cooperation; but it will not be hard to demonstrate that the two statesmen's radical divergence on what constituted good government gave Publius truly a split personality; so that he speaks now in the voice of the Virginian and again in the unmistakable accents of the New Yorker. These opposing views, which later were to make the men political enemies, can accordingly be used as the surest index to tell whether Madison or Hamilton is responsible for the several disputed *Federalist* essays.

Let us first, therefore, consider Hamilton's preliminary plan for the series and the procedure he proposed to follow in getting Publius written. We shall then consider how that plan was carried out in the actual production of the work. Against this background of knowledge, never before treated adequately by historians, it will be possible in the last section of this study to view the controversial numbers themselves in a manner that will clearly indicate their true author.

2

WHEN ALEXANDER HAMILTON and James Madison left Philadelphia at the close of the Convention in September, neither man was aware that they soon would cooperate in writing a commentary defending the new Constitution. The first public reaction to the proposed government, in New York as well as in most of the other states, showed strong approval of the Convention's work. As late as the middle of October, therefore, Hamilton was able to write Washington informing him that "the new Constitution is as popular in this city as it is possible for anything to be, and the prospect thus far is favorable to it throughout the state." Hamilton was aware even then, however, that opposition was forming, for he added, "But there is no saying what turn things may take when the full flood of official influence is let loose against it."[71] Governor Clinton had not committed himself at that time, but the newspaper attacks of his "confidential friends" seemed ominous. By the end of October, Clinton was openly opposing the new government, with the result that Hamilton had feared. Another letter, accordingly, was dispatched to Washington on October 30, informing him of the unhappy turn of affairs. "The constitution proposed has in this state warm friends and warm enemies. The first impressions everywhere are in its favor,

---

71. Hamilton to Washington, Oct. 1787, Lodge, ed., *Works of Hamilton,* IX, 425. This letter is undated, but it was written before Oct. 15.

but the artillery of its opponents makes some impression. The event cannot yet be foreseen."[72]

It was this belated shift in public opinion and the steadily mounting attacks of the Constitution's foes that convinced Hamilton of the need for a counterbarrage of propaganda. He and John Jay decided therefore to undertake the task of vindicating the Constitution to the New York electorate. This decision was almost immediately translated into action. For in his letter of October 30 to Washington, Hamilton enclosed an essay which he described as "the first number of a series of papers to be written in its [the Constitution's] defence." This paper, which had appeared in the *Independent Journal* just three days earlier, was the first *Federalist* essay.

This first number of *The Federalist* furnishes several significant clues to the contemplated scope of the series and the author's plan of composition. It contained a prospectus of the major topics to be discussed, which makes it clear that from the first Hamilton and Jay intended *The Federalist* to be a scholarly and thorough exposition of the Constitution. Inevitably the series would be long and detailed, for Hamilton, under his nom de plume, promised to treat, point by point: the need for union; the inadequacy of the Confederation as a bond of union; the necessity of a powerful national government if the union was to be preserved; the conformity of the proposed Constitution to the true principles of republicanism; and a comparative analysis of the new government and the state government of New York. Lastly, Publius was prepared to prove that adoption of the Constitution would give "additional security" to liberty and property.[73] This project of political education outlined by Hamilton

72. Hamilton to Washington, Oct. 30, 1787, *ibid.*, 425.
73. "I propose in a series of papers to discuss the following interesting particulars:—*The utility of the UNION to your political prosperity*—*The insufficiency of the present Confederation to preserve that Union*—*The necessity of a government at least equally energetic with the one proposed, to the attainment of this object*—*The conformity of the proposed Constitution to the true principles of republican government*—*Its analogy to your own State constitution*—and lastly, *The additional*

in *Federalist* 1 was certainly ambitious. It was an undertaking that would severely tax the capacities of the most brilliant publicist, for it had to be completed before the New York ratifying convention met.

Several factors, unmentioned by Hamilton in his prospectus and unsuspected by his newspaper audience, were to facilitate the composition of *The Federalist*. The enterprise might well have proved impracticable if Publius had not possessed certain unacknowledged advantages. In the first place Hamilton himself had already worked out in detailed outline a substantial percentage of the essays he had contracted to write for *The Federalist*. The first two topics to be discussed by Publius were: "The utility of the Union" and "The insufficiency of the present Confederation." A glance at Hamilton's Convention syllabus shows that he had covered exactly those subjects in the opening pages of his famous speech of June 18.[74] Hamilton, therefore, had a quantity of material recently used at Philadelphia which he could present again in New York. Indeed, every essay that he wrote at the beginning of *The Federalist* on the necessity for a stronger union repeated the ideas, theories, and historical examples that he had already used at the Convention.[75]

The fact that Hamilton already had systematically organized many of his ideas clearly influenced his decision to embark on the arduous task of writing *The Federalist*. He knew the business would be exacting

---

security *which its adoptation will afford to the preservation of that species of government, to liberty and to property.*

"In the progress of this discussion, I shall endeavor to give a satisfactory answer to all the objections which shall have made their appearance, that may have any claim to your attention." *Federalist* Number 1.

74. The section of *The Federalist* labeled "The insufficiency of the present Confederation" is outlined in Hamilton's syllabus under III, "I—Objections of the present confederation." Max Farrand, ed., *The Records of the Federal Convention of 1787* (New Haven, Conn., 1911), I, 304. The first section of *The Federalist* on "The utility of the Union" is outlined in the syllabus under VI, E–H (*ibid.*, 306–308); in both the syllabus and *The Federalist* the main thrust of the argument on this topic is toward the dangers of disunion.

75. Numbers 1 through 22 of *The Federalist* deal with the "utility of union" and the "insufficiency of the Confederation."

and difficult, requiring time and energy that could ill be spared from his other activities. However, the use of his Convention syllabus and the incorporation of his prepared material in the new work would considerably ease the burden of composition. Therefore Hamilton, speaking as "Publius" in *Federalist 1*, was willing to promise his New York readers a lengthy commentary on the proposed government. He knew, though they did not, that a sizable portion of the projected study would require little additional labor on his part. If this had not been so, as Madison was to confess later, *The Federalist* could not have been written in time to be effective propaganda for the Constitution.

There was another circumstance that Alexander Hamilton counted on to facilitate the production of *The Federalist*. From the beginning the work was planned as a cooperative enterprise. The anonymous mask of Publius was calculated to permit several authors to share in the composition in order to speed its completion. As it turned out Hamilton was forced to write a major part of *The Federalist* by himself, but this was not his choice or his original expectation. At least three other writers were asked to participate in the undertaking. Jay was a partner in the scheme from the beginning and actually produced the first bloc of published essays—Numbers 2 through 5. Madison began to lend a hand in November; and at that time, he reports, William Duer was expected to share the burden of authorship.[76] Gouverneur Morris also testifies that he too "was warmly pressed by Hamilton to assist in writing *The Federalist*."[77]

The evidence of Hamilton's desire for collaborators is overwhelm-

76. "The undertaking was proposed by Alexander Hamilton to James Madison with a request to join him and Mr. Jay in carrying it into effect. William Duer was also included in the original plan; and wrote two or more papers, which though intelligent and sprightly, were not continued, nor did they make a part of the printed collection." Madison's memorandum entitled "The Federalist," quoted in J. C. Hamilton, ed., *The Federalist*, I, lxxxv, note. Duer's three essays, signed "Philo-Publius," are included as an appendix in J. C. Hamilton's edition of *The Federalist*. They are undistinguished in style and thought, despite Madison's praise.

77. "I was warmly pressed by Hamilton to assist in writing The Federalist, which I declined." Morris to W. H. Wells, Feb. 24, 1815, Jared Sparks, ed., *The Life of Gouverneur Morris* . . . (Boston, 1832), III, 339.

ing; nevertheless a contrary opinion advanced by P. L. Ford is still widely accepted by historians. Ford, in discussing Madison's share in *The Federalist*, argues that "Hamilton held by far the readier pen, and as originator of the series undoubtedly intended to take the laboring oar."[78] According to this theory Hamilton, eager for the glory of sole authorship, grudgingly accepted assistance only when he was too busy to write *The Federalist* by himself. Ford's hypothesis ignores the fact that Jay's papers were written and published when Hamilton was least pressed for time. More important still, this theory, enunciated in 1897 after Publius had been accepted as a great political classic, misconstrues the purpose of *The Federalist*. In 1787–1788 Hamilton, Madison, and Jay were not conscious of producing a "classic," nor were they concerned about future literary fame. *The Federalist* was at bottom an electioneering pamphlet written to persuade contemporary New Yorkers to vote right. When *The Federalist* was being written its hard-pressed authors considered it a necessary but wearing chore.

Consequently Hamilton was delighted to have Jay do the initial essays on "the dangers from foreign force and fraud." Not only did this allow Hamilton to save his strength for other topics, but it also produced a stronger argument. For Jay's knowledge of foreign affairs surpassed even Hamilton's. In like manner, he showed no hesitation in assigning Madison the task of discussing the historical weaknesses of ancient and modern confederations in Numbers 18, 19, and 20. Although the New Yorker had prepared some material on the subject, Madison's more thorough studies and more comprehensive knowledge made him the logical author for this section. Hamilton, therefore, turned over his comparatively sketchy notes to the Virginian; and it was from Madison's pen that these essays went to the printer.[79]

78. Ford, "Authorship of The Federalist," *AHR*, II (1896–1897), 677.
79. See Madison's footnote to Number 18 published in Gideon's edition: "The subject of this and the following numbers happened to be taken up by both Mr. Hamilton and Mr. Madison. What had been prepared by Mr. Hamilton, who had entered

There can be little doubt that this purely pragmatic approach characterized Hamilton's attitude toward *The Federalist* from beginning to end. He was determined that the series should be effective propaganda, and this entailed rapid publication. To guarantee a speedy flow of essays Hamilton counted upon using his Convention material and upon finding willing collaborators. The aid of these coauthors would allow a functional division of labor, by which their special knowledge and particular skills would supplement his own facile pen and fortify Publius' argumentative appeal.

Keeping these factors in mind let us now examine the actual writing of the essays to see if Hamilton's original plan of composition throws any light upon the authorship of the disputed numbers.

3

THE FIRST and introductory number of *The Federalist* appeared on the New York newsstands Saturday, October 27, 1787. John Jay was already working on his essays dealing with foreign affairs, as they were published during the following two weeks.[80] In the meantime, according to the prearranged plan, Hamilton was preparing his quota of papers on "the utility of the Union"; added to Jay's they would keep the printer supplied with material past the end of November. Hamilton's first group of essays, Numbers 6 through 9, discussed "the dangers . . . which will in all probability flow from dissensions between the States themselves, and from domestic factions and convulsions"; for, as he explained to his readers, if the states remained joined in a mere "partial" confederacy, they would inevitably have "frequent and violent contests with each other."[81] To write this series

---

more briefly into the subject, was left to Mr. Madison, on its appearing that the latter was engaged upon it, with larger materials, and with a view to a more precise delineation, and from the pen of the latter the several papers went to press."

80. Number 2 appeared Wednesday, Oct. 31; Number 3 on Sat., Nov. 3; Number 4 on Nov. 7; and Number 5 on Nov. 10.

81. *Federalist 6.*

of essays with its prophecy of interstate and class war Hamilton relied on his Convention syllabus.[82]

At the same time that these early essays were appearing Hamilton was searching for other collaborators. Morris, however, refused his request for help; and though Duer acceded to it, the papers he produced were too poor to use. It was only then, sometime toward the middle of November, that Hamilton turned to Madison.[83] It was fortunate for Hamilton's plan that the Virginian agreed to participate, since Jay's aid was soon to be lost. Jay was desperately sick before the end of November; and as late as the following February the excruciating pains he suffered prevented any continuous writing.[84] Consequently after November Jay would contribute but one more

82. Hamilton's syllabus, VI–H, reads: "Leage Offensive & Defensive &c.—particular Govs. might exert themselves &c.—But liable to usual Vicissi[tudes]—Internal Peace affected—Proximity of Situation—natural enemies—Partial confederacies from unequal extent—Power inspires ambition—Weakness begets jealousy—Western Territory—Obj: Genius of republics pacific—Answer—Jealousy of commerce as well as jealousy of power begets war—Sparta Athens Thebes Rome Carthage Venice Hanseatic Leage England as many Popular as Royal Wars—Lewis the 14th *Austria Bourbon* William & Anne—wars depend on triffling circumstances everywhere—Dutchess of Malboroughs Glove—Foreign Conquest—Dismemberment—Poland—Foreign Influence—Distractions set afloat Vicious humour—Standing armies by dissensions—Domestic Factions—Montesquieu." Farrand, ed., *Records*, I, 307–308. *Federalist 6* covers the topics through "Dutchess of Malboroughs Glove"; *Federalist 7* runs through "Vicious humour"; the rise of "Standing armies" in a disunited America is discussed in *Federalist 8*; while "Factions" form the theme of *Federalist 9*, which concludes with a long quotation on the subject from Montesquieu's *Spirit of the Laws*, Book IX, chap. 1.

83. Madison was not taken into the *Federalist* partnership until after the middle of the month, for during the week of Nov. 12 he traveled to Philadelphia and considered going on from there to Virginia; see letter to Randolph of Nov. 18, Hunt, ed., *Writings of Madison*, V, 56. The fact that Hamilton did not ask Madison to take a part in the enterprise earlier throws an interesting light on the relationship of the two men. Their personal tastes, amusements, habits of life, and political ideas were poles apart; at no period except while *The Federalist* was being written were they intimate. It was natural, when *The Federalist* was first projected, for Hamilton to call on Jay, Morris, and Duer, who were close friends and political allies, for their aid. He seems to have approached Madison only as a last resort when the others had failed him.

84. Frank Monaghan, *John Jay* (New York, 1935), 290.

essay to Publius. With the exception of Number 64—dealing with Jay's specialty, the Senate's treaty power—every *Federalist* essay after Number 5 had to be written either by Hamilton or Madison.

Hamilton's loss of Jay's assistance was more than counterbalanced by the aid gained from James Madison. The Virginian, while not quite as fluent a propagandist as Hamilton, was a political pamphleteer of distinction. Furthermore he had unique qualifications for writing as Publius. No man in America knew as much about the specific clauses of the new Constitution as Madison; no man in all the world had studied so thoroughly the general problems of federalism.[85] Furthermore Madison, like Hamilton, had organized and clarified his ideas on paper; the extensive manuscript materials he had at hand could speedily be reworked as essays for *The Federalist*.[86] Moreover, although he and Hamilton subscribed to differing political theories and viewed the Constitution from opposite angles, this divergence promised to be an advantage that would increase Publius' persuasiveness. When the two men touched on the same topic their papers would supplement each other instead of presenting repetitious arguments. These facts all combined to make James Madison's alliance with Alexander Hamilton to write *The Federalist* one of the most fruitful examples of collaboration in the history of political literature.

Madison began his actual contributions to Publius almost as soon as he agreed to help. His first paper, Number 10, appeared on November 24. It was inserted among Hamilton's group of essays on the utility of union and actually dealt with a topic the New Yorker had

85. Madison was the first thorough and systematic student of the history of federal government. By 1784, when the Confederation was already showing its inadequacies, he had commenced building up a library on the subject that became the most comprehensive private collection on the topic of 18th-century America, if not in the world; see Edward Gaylord Bourne, "Madison's Studies in the History of Federal Government," in *Essays in Historical Criticism*, 165–169.

86. Madison's definite promise of aid allowed Hamilton to double the speed of newspaper publication. Beginning on Nov. 21 the essays were published at the rate of two per issue, twice a week instead of one per issue every Wednesday and Saturday.

just discussed in Number 9: the danger of the class struggle in republican governments.[87] Like so many of Publius' essays, no list of authors is required to prove that Madison wrote it. We can trace the development of Number 10 from its first rough form in Madison's "Notes on the Confederacy" through its appearance in his Convention speech of June 6 and in his letter to Jefferson of October 24, 1787, until it finally made its appearance in polished style in *The Federalist*.[88] Madison's only other contribution to the first part of Publius was Number 14, which in a sense was a continuation of Number 10.[89]

The second major division of *The Federalist*, the commentary on "the insufficiency of the present Confederation to the preservation of the Union," commences with Number 15. In this section of the work Hamilton again was prepared to take "the laboring oar," since his syllabus would furnish him ample materials for it. Madison, however, was to write three of the essays, for his careful research on the subject made him more competent than Hamilton to compare the "vices" of the Confederation with the weaknesses of other historic

87. It is characteristic of the different outlook of the two men that Hamilton in Number 9 advocates the new union because it will make it easier to suppress with military force such outbreaks as Shays's Rebellion, while Madison in Number 10 argues that union will prevent the recurrence of any such outbreaks. Hamilton prized the union as an instrument guaranteeing that the rich would win every class struggle; Madison hoped that union would prevent class war from being declared in America.

88. "Notes on the Confederacy," written in Apr. 1787 and subtitled "Vices of the Political System of the U. States," is published in *Letters of Madison*, I, 320–328. The part that was rewritten as *Federalist* 10 appears as Sec. 11, 325–328; for the relevant part of his letter to Jefferson of Oct. 24, 1787, see *ibid.*, 350–353. For Madison's speech of June 6, see Farrand, ed., *Records*, I, 134–136.

89. *Federalist* 10 argues that a large republic will "break and control the violence of faction," while *Federalist* 14 sets out to prove that, contrary to contemporary theory, it is possible to extend a federal republic "over a large region." Numbers 10 and 14 are obvious interpolations in Hamilton's series. Material for Numbers 11, 12, and 13 is to be found in Hamilton's syllabus as follows: *Federalist* 11— Syllabus VI, I, beginning "Foreign Nations . . . Would reduce us to a passive Commerce," and ending "Fleet"; *Federalist* 12—Recapitulation III, paragraph beginning "And the revenues"; and *Federalist* 13—Recapitulation III, paragraph beginning "Expense admits of this answer." Farrand, ed., *Records*, I, 308, 311.

confederacies. Thus, after Hamilton in *Federalist* 15, 16, and 17 had developed the theme that no national government could endure unless it had jurisdiction over the individuals in the states rather than over the states in their corporate capacities,[90] Madison took up his pen again. In Numbers 18, 19, and 20 he enforced Hamilton's arguments by an appeal to the history of the Amphictyonic Council, the Achaean League, the Holy Roman Empire, the Swiss Confederation, and the United Netherlands. Madison in writing these essays merely had to turn to his elaborate research memorandum entitled, "Notes of Ancient and Modern Confederacies."[91]

With the publication of *Federalist* 22 on Saturday, December 15,

---

90. *Federalist* 15, 16, 17, 21, and 22 are paralleled in the syllabus under II, I, "Objections to the Present Confederation." *Ibid.*, 304. Other parts of the syllabus, however, were drawn upon to develop the arguments in certain of the essays. For example, cf. C, V (*ibid.*, 306) passage commencing "*Coertion* of laws *Coertion* of arms" with the 11th paragraph of *Federalist* 15 on the need for a sanction either "by the COERCION of the magistracy, or by the COERCION of arms." And cf. B, I (*ibid.*, 305), "Distance has a physical effect on mens minds," with the discussion in *Federalist* 17.

91. It is printed in *Letters of Madison*, I, 293–315, with the historical references exactly given. It is possible to compare Madison's treatment of this topic not only with Hamilton's rough outline but also with a finished and complete essay he had written on the same subject. For Hamilton's treatment of historic confederacies in his Convention speech merely duplicated the arguments he had written for *The Continentalist* in 1781. It is instructive to compare Madison's careful and scholarly use of history in his essays with Hamilton's, as it reveals clearly the different personal qualities of the two men. The New Yorker was not scholarly in his approach to politics; his use of history was that of a propagandist citing examples from the past in order to make a debater's point rather than to establish historical truth. Madison's treatment of Greek confederations was based on widely gathered material from all the available authorities, carefully cross-checked and qualified before being synthesized into a rich and suggestive study. Hamilton's research consisted in superficially extracting bits of a speech of Demosthenes and a hasty reading of Plutarch. This is not to say that on topics in which he was interested the New Yorker could not write brilliantly and profoundly. On the problem of war and republicanism treated in *Federalist* 6 his thought is mature and suggestive. But Hamilton was not really interested in the problems of federalism, and even on subjects like war and finance to which his mind was congenial his approach was less that of the scholar in politics than of the brilliant publicist. *The Continentalist*, III, is printed in J. C. Hamilton, ed., *The Federalist*, I, cxlii; cf. Hamilton's outline of this *Continentalist* essay in his syllabus, VI, E, F, G, Farrand, ed., *Records*, I, 307.

the second formal section of the work was completed. Publius, as he had promised in his first essay, had treated the need for union and the weakness of the Confederation; now came the more difficult task of discussing "the necessity of a Constitution, at least equally energetic with the one proposed," and an analysis of that Constitution itself. At this point Hamilton and Madison agreed to apply the principle of division of labor to the major topics of *The Federalist*, instead of continuing to divide up individual essays in each part. Hamilton would now write all of the essays under the third head, while Madison would commence immediately upon the following section, "the conformity of the proposed Constitution to the true principles of republican government."

This division of chapters between the two men was entirely logical. Hamilton took the subject that he was most interested in and most competent to deal with, while Madison chose the topic he was most anxious to write about. So as the New Yorker in Numbers 23 through 35[92] insisted that the new government must have unlimited power to raise money and organize the national defense, Madison was busy writing to show that these great powers were so controlled under the Constitution that they could never threaten liberty.

Hamilton's series of fourteen papers on the vital need for an energetic state ended with Number 36, published on January 8, 1788. On January 11, Madison commenced explaining how the Convention had combined "energy in government, with the inviolable attention due to liberty and to the republican form."[93] In this division of the work so peculiarly suited to his talents he had occasion not only to develop the federal principles of the Constitution, but also to discuss in his own characteristic vein the various questions which lie at the

92. One suspects that Hamilton was especially eager to write these essays on the tax power and the war power because it gave him a chance to construe them liberally, thus preparing the way for the "invigoration" and "energizing" of the Constitution after it went into effect by "broad interpretation."

93. *Federalist* 37.

foundation of free government itself. And although twelve of the twenty-four essays he wrote in this section have been claimed for Hamilton, an examination of the papers themselves shows they were indubitably written by the Virginian.

Madison's first two essays were devoted to the difficulties faced by the Convention in guaranteeing both the security of the few and the liberty of the many.[94] Madison's thoughts on the relationship of liberty and authority are still worthy of study, for it was a problem which had been his chief concern since he had entered politics. In Number 39 he established the republican character of the Constitution by stressing the ultimate responsibility of the government to the majority of the people. This he followed in the next essay with a brilliant analysis of the compound aspects of the proposed system with its mixed national and federal features.[95] Next, in a block of six papers, Madison applied the yardstick of federalism to the powers vested in the national government and to the restraints imposed on the states; he was anxious to show that the states would always remain as a bulwark of liberty against national encroachments.[96] The last of this group of papers, *Federalist* 46, was published January 29.[97] The Virginian, having reviewed "the general mass of power" allotted to the proposed government, then intended, as the climax of his series, to write on "the particular structure of this government,

94. "Energy in government is essential to that security against external and internal danger, and to that prompt and salutary execution of the laws, which enter into the very definition of good government. Stability in government is essential to national character.... On comparing, however, these valuable ingredients with the vital principles of liberty, we must perceive at once the difficulty of mingling them in their due proportions." *Ibid.*

95. *Federalist* 40.

96. *Federalist* Numbers 41, 42, 43, 44, 45, and 46. The first four of these essays deal with the question of divided powers; the last two with the states' capacities to halt "the ambitious encroachments of the federal government."

97. This group of papers provided the justification for the Virginia-Kentucky Resolutions of 1798, just as Hamilton's series, 23*ff*, foreshadowed the doctrine of "broad construction."

and the distribution of this mass of power among its constituent parts."[98]

Numbers 47, 48, 49, 50, and 51 of *The Federalist* analyze the purpose of the separation of powers in the Constitution and the functions of the different departments of government: legislative, executive, and judicial.[99] The series of essays is a carefully wrought unit, culminating in Number 51 with an explanation of how, in "the compound republic of America," the power surrendered by the people is first divided between the states and the nation and then the portion allotted to the latter is "subdivided among distinct and separate departments."[100] *In Federalist* 10 Madison had prophesied that a functional balance of many economic and social interests would favor liberty in a large republic; in *Federalist* 46 he had shown how the mixture of powers vested in the states and nation would work to the same end. Now in Number 51 the Virginian characteristically applied his theory of balance to the interdepartmental organization of the new state.

Federalist 51 was published February 8, and by that time Madison was writing under extreme pressure. The letters he had recently received from Virginia all urged him to return home at once. The election of delegates to the ratifying convention was scheduled for early March, and Madison's friends feared he would lose the ballot if he did not return immediately. The tone of these letters became increasingly insistent as time went on. In early December, Henry Lee had merely pointed out that, "It becomes you to return in time to secure your election";[101] before the end of the month his neighbor

98. *Federalist* 47.

99. All the essays that Madison wrote after 48, except 54, were claimed by Hamilton. Number 54 was erroneously assigned to Jay, who had actually written 64.

100. *Federalist* 51.

101. Henry Lee to Madison, Dec. 7, 1787, Hunt, ed., *Writings of Madison*, V, 71n.

Lawrence Taliaferro was "earnestly" begging that he set out in good time;[102] and by January, when Madison still showed no signs of leaving New York, the letters of his friend William Moore began to exhibit almost hysterical urgency. "You know the disadvantage [he wrote] of being absent at elections. . . . I must therefore entreat and conjure you—nay command you if it were in my power—to be here in February, or the first of March next. Pray don't disappoint the wishes of your friends, and many others, who are wavering on the Constitution, and anxiously awaiting for an explanation from you. In short, they want your sentiments *from your own mouth*, which, they say, will convince them of the necessity of adopting it. I repeat again, come."[103] Madison's knowledge that his continuance in New York was imperiling his chance of election in Virginia must have given him many uneasy moments throughout February. Nevertheless he determined to stay on, writing as Publius, until the last possible moment. He calculated his time exactly, setting out for Virginia on March 4, and arrived home just one day before the poll.[104] His appearance, although belated, was enough to insure his election.

Madison's decision to stay in New York through February and risk his election in Virginia allowed him to analyze the structure of Congress for *The Federalist*. While Hamilton was mainly interested in the executive and the judiciary, the Virginian had always been

102. Lawrence Taliaferro to Madison, Dec. 16, 1787, *ibid.*

103. Col. William Moore to Madison, written sometime in Jan., quoted in Rives, *Life and Times of Madison*, II, 549. Cf. the letter from Madison's father of Jan. 30, 1788, warning him that if he were not home "early in March" he would be "shut . . . out of the Convention." Hunt, ed., *Writings of Madison*, V, 105n.

104. If one accepts the hypothesis that Madison stopped writing as Publius after Number 48, which was published Feb. 1, there is no explanation of his risky policy of staying in New York until Mar. 4. For it was a risk to allow himself only one day to spare before the election. It should be remembered that a 300-mile winter trip in 18th-century America was an enterprise fraught with the possibility of delaying accidents.

concerned with the correct organization of the legislature. Seven
papers were therefore devoted to the House of Representatives.[105] In
them Madison discussed: the qualifications of the electors and the
elected; the term of office; the ratio of representation; the total size
of the House; its alleged tendency to represent the rich rather than
the whole people; and finally the system of increasing the size of
the House as the country grew. Then to round out his discussion of
Congress, Madison composed two long papers on the Senate, Numbers 62 and 63. These two final essays were much more carefully
written than his preceding seven papers on the House of Representatives,[106] for in preparing them Madison had the benefit of a long
research memorandum he had drawn up on the senates of Sparta,
of Carthage, and of Rome.[107]

Madison had continued writing until the last possible minute. He
left New York on March 4, 1788, and his final essay on Publius
appeared on the newsstands almost simultaneously with his departure
for Virginia.[108]

105. Numbers 52, 53, 54, 55, 56, 57, 58. The style and organization of these
papers show how hurriedly they were written. This would be characteristic of a
tired man trying to finish up a job rather than of a fresh author commencing on a
new series.

106. Between Madison's last essay on the House (Number 58) and his first essay
on the Senate (Number 62), Hamilton wrote three essays on the congressional
control of elections. They are an obvious interpolation and do not logically belong
with a section devoted solely to the House of Representatives. However, the breathing space allowed Madison may account for the literary excellence of his last pair
of essays in comparison with those he had written just previously.

107. The historical material in this memorandum is drawn from Aristotle, Cicero,
Polybius, Conyers Middleton's *The History of the Life of Marcus Tullius Cicero*
(London, 1741), Edward Gibbon's *The History of the Decline and Fall of the Roman
Empire* (London, 1776–1788), and an encyclopedia of comparative politics, edited
by Fortuné Barthélemy de Félice in 1778, which Madison cites under its secondary
title, *Le Code de l'Humanité*. This memo is printed in *Letters of Madison*, I, 394–
398.

108. It is significant that in this first part of *The Federalist* the division of labor
between Hamilton and Madison was exactly even in terms of quantity. When
Number 63 was published each man had written exactly 29 essays. It was Madison's

4

THE DISPUTED NUMBERS of *The Federalist* claimed by both Hamilton and Madison are Numbers 49 through 58 and Numbers 62 and 63; they appeared in the newspapers during the month of February and the first week of March 1788. The evidence we have already considered makes it extremely probable that these essays were actually written by Madison. They were part of the division of *The Federalist* assigned to the Virginian according to Hamilton's own plan for the work. If Madison was not writing as Publius during February his delay in leaving New York is inexplicable. Assuredly too Hamilton had no desire or reason to do these papers if Madison's pen was available for the task. The New Yorker was well aware that from the date of Madison's departure he would be forced to carry *The Federalist* alone; he could not have relished any extra work added to an already excessive burden. Recognition of these factors strengthens Madison's claim to the papers; it is the appeal to internal evidence, however, that decisively establishes the Virginian's right to them.

The first three of the disputed essays are Numbers 49, 50, and 51. They form the last part of a continuous discussion complete in itself, commencing with Number 47, dealing with the separation of powers in the Constitution. Madison's claim to the first pair of papers in this unit has never been seriously disputed. The evidence that he also wrote *Federalist* 51 is too strong to deny, for the political theory contained in Number 51 can be positively identified as Madison's very own. It is the novel theory of the Virginian, developed before he went to Philadelphia, explained by him on the floor of the Convention, and again enunciated in *Federalist* 10. This disputed paper not only contains this theory, which was Madison's most profound contribution to political thought, but also uses that theory specifically

---

departure for Virginia which forced Hamilton against his will to pull the "laboring oar" alone in the last part of Publius.

to demolish Hamilton's pet plan for a "high toned" government. An examination, therefore, of Madison's pre-Convention writings in conjunction with Hamilton's syllabus, which expounds the New Yorker's theory of state, gives us both a positive and negative check on the author of *Federalist* 51.

It has long been recognized that Alexander Hamilton arrived at the Philadelphia Convention with a scheme of government modeled after the British monarchy.[109] Hamilton's disillusion with the working of the Confederation and his fear of democracy, especially after Shays's Rebellion, had convinced him that it would be almost impossible to set up a stable republic in a country as large as the United States.[110] As he informed the Convention, any society in which political power was vested in the hands of all the people would be continually torn by the class struggles of the rich and the poor.[111]

Hamilton's remedy for this class war was the Hobbesian expedient

---

109. "In his private opinion he had no scruple in declaring . . . that the British Govt. was the best in the world: and that he doubted whether anything short of it would do in America." Madison's notes of Hamilton's speech of June 18, Farrand, ed., *Records*, I, 288. Cf. the version of this statement in Robert Yates's notes of the speech, *ibid.*, I, 299*ff*, and Hamilton's own syllabus, *ibid.*, I, 308. To get the full flavor and force of Hamilton's appeal to the Convention it is necessary to read all the reports of his speech printed in Farrand along with his syllabus; since it lasted nearly five hours the various reporters each tended to omit certain details.

110. "This view of the subject almost led him to despair that a Republican Govt. could be established over so great an extent." *Ibid.*, 288, Cf. *ibid.*, 299; syllabus, *ibid.*, 305.

111. "Society naturally divides itself into two political divisions—the *few* and the *many*, who have distinct interests.

"If government in the hands of the *few*, they will tyrannize over the many.

"If [in] the hands of the many, they will tyrannize over the few." Hamilton's syllabus, *ibid.*, 308. This was the traditional 18th-century formula for describing the class struggle. As Yates's notes make clear, Hamilton was primarily concerned with the tyranny of the many: "All communities divide themselves into the few and the many. The first are the rich and well born, the other the mass of the people. The voice of the people has been said to be the voice of God; . . . it is not true in fact. The people are turbulent and changing; they seldom judge or determine right. Give therefore to the first class a distinct permanent share in the government." *Ibid.*, 299.

of setting up a Leviathan state to impose order upon the American people from above. Hamilton was sure that the only alternative to social anarchy was the establishment of a consolidated government capable of maintaining itself independently of the people's will.

He proposed to the Convention, therefore, that they copy the British constitution as closely as possible. In the first place he advocated the creation of a senate that would correspond to the House of Lords and represent the wealthy few. Recognizing the impossibility of making this upper house hereditary, Hamilton nevertheless hoped to give it strength and power by electing his senators for life. In this way, as he told the Convention, it would have "a permanent will," be irresponsible to the electorate as a whole, and be capable of blocking the attacks of the multitudinous poor upon "the rich and well born."[112] The chief "organ" of Hamilton's "strong souled" government,[113] however, was not its senate but its elective king. As Hamilton insisted in Philadelphia nothing less would check "the amazing violence & turbulence of the democratic spirit."[114] This "republican" monarch, like the senate, would be elected for life; he would have power to veto all national legislation, and the prerogative of appointing the governors of all the states, which would thus, under Hamilton's scheme, be reduced to administrative satrapies of the national government. Finally he hoped this elective king would be given control of the patronage in order to bribe the legislature and insure a steady administration.[115] His study of England had convinced him that this

112. "The aristocracy ought to be entirely separated; their power should be permanent. . . . They should be so circumstanced that they can have no interest in a change—as to have an effectual weight in the constitution. . . . 'Tis essential there should be a permanent will in a community." Hamilton's syllabus, *ibid.*, 308.

113. "The general government must . . . not only have a strong soul, but *strong organs* by which that soul is to operate." *Ibid.*, 308.

114. "This check is a monarch." *Ibid.*, 309. The remark on the "violence" of democracy is to be found in Madison's notes, *ibid.*, 389.

115. "Effect of British government.—A Vigorous execution of the laws—and a vigorous defence of the people, will result.—Better chance for a good administration.—It is said a republican government does not admit a vigorous execution.—It

"corruption"—to use the eighteenth-century word—was required for a stable government. "Take mankind in general, they are vicious—their passions may be operated on. We have been taught to reprobate the danger of influence in the British government, without duly reflecting how far it was necessary to support a good government. We have taken up many ideas upon trust. . . . Take mankind as they are, and what are they governed by? Their passions . . . and it ever will be the duty of a wise government to avail itself of those passions, in order to make them subservient to the public good—for these ever induce us to action."[116]

This "strong souled" government copied after England's was Hamilton's ideal for America. Only by the establishment of a state which institutionalized in its very organs a "will" independent of the people could the class struggle be allayed in the United States.[117] When the Convention turned Hamilton's scheme down in favor of the more democratic and responsible government outlined in the Virginia Plan, he was bitterly disappointed. In July he left the Convention and returned to Philadelphia only for the last sessions. When he signed the Constitution he admitted that "no man's ideas were more remote from the plan than his were known to be." He further confessed that his signature was given only because the choice was between "anarchy and Convulsion on one side, and the chance of good to be expected from the plan on the other."[118]

It was in this same spirit of disdain, only partially concealed, that Hamilton wrote as Publius. He was never reconciled to the Constitution's "weaknesses" as long as he lived. Even while he was

---

is therefore bad; for the goodness of government consists in a vigorous execution." Hamilton's syllabus, *ibid.*, 310.

116. Speech of June 22 on clause prohibiting congressmen from holding government jobs during their tenure of office, reported by Yates, *ibid.*, 381. Madison's notes for this debate are incomplete though they report on the gist of this speech; cf. *ibid.*, 376.

117. "The principle chiefly intended to be established is this—that there must be a permanent *will*." Hamilton's syllabus, *ibid.*, 310.

118. Sept. 17, *ibid.*, II, 645–646.

preparing to write *The Federalist* he drew up a private memorandum in which he prophesied its failure unless additional power could be squeezed out of its clauses by interpretation.[119] When appointed secretary of the Treasury under Washington, all of his actions were directed to strengthening the "frail and worthless fabric" by administrative action. Moreover Hamilton felt so strongly about the need for an overruling, irresponsible, and unlimited government that it showed through even in his *Federalist* essays, in spite of his attempt to conceal his opinions in order to achieve ratification. *Federalist 9* indicates clearly that he expected a continual use of military force would be required to keep the rebellious poor in their place. In this essay the union is advocated because it will permit the use of troops raised in one section of the country to stamp out revolts in other districts, an expedient resorted to by Hamilton during the Whiskey Rebellion. Essays 23 and 30 mirror his belief that no government could endure without unlimited fiscal and military power and fore-shadow his doctrine of "liberal construction," which was later invoked to justify the National Bank.[120] Hamilton's discussion of the executive in *Federalist 71* reveals his dearest hope that the president would develop an "independent will." And his analysis of the powers of the Supreme Court in Number 78 was in time to provide an enduring sanction for the development of an independent and irresponsible judiciary. It is necessary to hold Hamilton's scheme of government and the qualities he valued in a constitution clearly in view if one would understand the political theory of the disputed *Federalist 51*. For this essay of Publius' is leveled directly against Hamilton's theory of state and proposes Madison's republican alternative to it.

James Madison carried to the Convention a plan that was the exact opposite of Hamilton's. In fact the theory he advocated at Philadelphia

119. This memorandum entitled "Impressions as to the New Constitution" is printed in Lodge, ed., *Works of Hamilton*, I, 420–424.

120. The Bank, as Madison was to later charge, provided a device for the executive to "influence" and "corrupt" the legislature, thus detouring the separation of powers in the Constitution.

and in his *Federalist* essays was developed as a republican substitute for the New Yorker's "high toned" scheme of state. Madison was convinced that the class struggle would be ameliorated in America by establishing a limited federal government that would make functional use of the vast size of the country and the existence of the states as active political organisms. He argued in his "Notes on the Confederacy," in his Convention speeches, and again in *Federalist* 10 that if an extended republic was set up including a multiplicity of economic, geographic, social, religious, and sectional interests, these interests, by checking each other, would prevent American society from being divided into the clashing armies of the rich and the poor. Thus if no interstate proletariat could become organized on purely economic lines, the property of the rich would be safe even though the mass of the people held political power. Madison's solution for the class struggle was not to set up an absolute and irresponsible state to regiment society from above; he was never willing to sacrifice liberty to gain security. He wished to multiply the deposits of political power in the state itself sufficiently to break down the sole dualism of rich and poor and thus to guarantee both liberty and security. This, as he stated in *Federalist* 10, would provide "a republican remedy for the diseases most incident to republican government."

It is possible to trace the development of Madison's novel theory from its first appearance in April 1787 until its appearance in *Federalist* 51.[121] It is also possible to show where Madison derived the raw material of hints and ideas that he synthesized into this original doctrine.[122] Limitations of space, however, forbid such a study here.

---

121. The simplest procedure for comparing the basic statements of Madison's theory is to use Edward Gaylord Bourne's article on "The Authorship of The Federalist," *AHR*, II (1896–1897), 449–451. Bourne set up all the early statements of Madison's doctrine with parallel quotations from *Federalist* 51. He did not consider the theory in relation to Hamilton's ideas.

122. I have done this in my unpublished thesis on "The Intellectual Origins of Jeffersonian Democracy: Republicanism, the Class Struggle, and the Virtuous Farmer," which is deposited in the Yale University Library.

It is sufficient for our purpose merely to quote from *Federalist* 51 and then to refer back to Hamilton's syllabus. This by itself will show that the New Yorker did not write the essay in dispute.

Madison commenced the statement of his theory in *Federalist* 51 with an acknowledgment that the "have nots" in any society are extremely likely to attack the "haves," for like Hamilton the Virginian believed class struggle to be inseparable from politics. "It is of great importance in a republic not only to guard the society against the oppression of its rulers, but to guard one part of the society against the injustice of the other. Different interests necessarily exist in different classes of citizens. If a majority be united by a common interest the rights of the minority will be insecure." Then referring pointedly to Hamilton's favorite theory he continued,

There are but two methods of providing against this evil: the one by creating a will in the community independent of the majority—that is of the society itself; the other, by comprehending in the society so many separate descriptions of citizens as will render an unjust combination of a majority of the whole very improbable, if not impracticable. . . . In a free government the security for civil rights must be the same as that for religious rights. It consists in the one case in the multiplicity of interests, and in the other of the multiplicity of sects. The degree of security in both cases will depend on the number of interests and sects; and this may be presumed to depend on the extent of country and number of people comprehended under the same government.

Madison, it is clear, had emancipated himself from the sterile dualistic view of society that was so common in the eighteenth century and that so obsessed Hamilton. Madison was one of the pioneers of "pluralism" in political thought. Where Hamilton saw the corporate spirit of the several states as poisonous to the union, Madison was aware that the preservation of the state governments could serve the cause of both liberty and union. Finally the vastness of the United States which Hamilton considered as the prime excuse for autocracy was recognized by Madison as the surest preservative of liberty.[123] To assert after reading this passage that Alexander Hamilton wrote *Federalist* 51 is to imply, first, that he was a magician in mimicking Madison's very words and tone of voice and, in the second place, that he was the most disingenuous hypocrite that ever wrote on politics. No unprejudiced or informed historian would accept for an instant this latter charge against Hamilton.[124]

If *Federalist* 51 is accepted as definitely written by Madison, there can be no question that he also wrote Numbers 49 and 50, for these essays are the middle section of a unified group, commencing with 47, obviously penned by the same hand. Moreover, Professor Bourne has revealed that there is enough internal evidence to attribute both of these papers unhesitantly to Madison, even without the unit test.[125] In like manner, Bourne's array of parallel quotations from Numbers 52, 53, and 56 and his discussion of 54 may be referred to as adequate

123. Hamilton was in the Convention on June 6 when Madison first explained his theory. His criticism scratched down at the time shows him highly skeptical of its validity. [In the quote from *Federalist* 51 the phrase "the number of interests . . . depend on" was dropped in typesetting the original *Quarterly* article.—Ed.]

124. Gouverneur Morris, Hamilton's dearest friend, claims his greatest failing was lack of hypocrisy. "One marked trait of the General's character was the pertinacious adherence to opinions he had once formed. . . . [He] was of all men the most indiscreet. He knew that a limited monarchy, even if established, could not preserve itself in this country. . . . And he very well knew that no monarchy whatever could be established but by the mob. But although General Hamilton knew these things . . . he never failed on every occasion to advocate the excellence of, and avow his attachment to, monarchial government. By this course he not only cut off all chance of rising into office, but singularly promoted the views of his opponents, who with the fondness for wealth and power which he had not, affected a love of the people, which he had and they had not." Morris to Robert Walsh, Feb. 15, 1811, Sparks, *Life of Morris,* II, 260–262.

125. Bourne, "Authorship of The Federalist," *AHR,* II (1896–1897), 448–449. It is in regard to Numbers 49 and 50 that Hamilton's son, who was determined to prove that his father had written all the disputed essays, ruefully confessed, "As this [49] and the following number [50] relate to a topic as to which no similar project had ever come under Hamilton's view, no analogy was to be expected in his writings." J. C. Hamilton, ed., *The Federalist,* I, cxi.

confirmation of Madison's claim to these essays also.[126] It is worthwhile noting, however, that the citation in essay 56 of James Burgh's *Political Disquisitions*, to which Bourne calls attention, is far stronger evidence of Madison's authorship than he realized. As Bourne shows, we know Madison was reading Burgh just at the time these papers were written, for *Political Disquisitions* was quoted in his "Additional Memorandum for the Convention of Virginia."[127] What Bourne did not suspect was that the character of Burgh's book made it extremely unlikely that Hamilton would quote it as an authority in Publius. For *Political Disquisitions* was the most famous contemporary exposé of the "corruption" of the British Parliament—that same corruption which Hamilton had praised as a prime virtue of the English system. It is significant too that the passage in Number 56 which cites Burgh speaks of the "monitory lessons" to be learned from British history.[128] The author who wrote this essay, and who speaks of "the vicious ingredients in the parliamentary constitution" of Great Britain in Number 52,[129] could hardly be called an ardent admirer of the British constitution.

The evidence of Madison's authorship of this group of papers,

126. Bourne, "Authorship of The Federalist," *AHR*, II (1896–1897), 451–453.

127. *Letters of Madison*, I, 392n. Burgh is cited in the memo in regard to the union between England and Scotland.

128. As Bourne points out, "monitory" is a favorite word of Madison's; see his citations of Madison's continual repetition of it, in "Authorship of The Federalist," *AHR*, II (1896–1897), 454. Note also Madison's statement in the Convention on June 28, that "experience is an instructive monitor," an example that Bourne overlooked. Farrand, ed., *Records*, I, 448. The "monitory lesson" that Publius learned from Burgh was that half of the 558 members of Parliament were elected in the rotten-borough system by a mere 5,723 voters. It is also notorious, Publius continued, "That they are more . . . the . . . instruments of the executive magistrate than the guardians and advocates of popular rights." He had just pointed out in Number 55 that under the Constitution no such horrible situation could develop in America because no congressman was eligible to hold a second office.

129. Cf. Madison's Convention speech of June 29 where he speaks of "reproaches & evils which have resulted from the vicious representation in G[reat] B[ritain]." Farrand, ed., *Records*, I, 464.

commencing with 52 and running through 58, is certainly not as obvious as the evidence in Numbers 51, 62, and 63.[130] If each parallel idea, pet phrase, or characteristic theory in every one of the essays was considered by itself it would not decisively tip the balance in the Virginian's favor. It is the cumulative weight of all these bits and scraps taken in conjunction with the striking data in 51, 62, and 63 that positively confirms Madison's right to the twelve disputed papers. All of the evidence points in the same direction; each example proportionately strengthens the Virginian's claim and weakens that of the New Yorker.

It can be confidently asserted that the authorship of the controversial *Federalist* essays no longer presents a riddle to be solved. The very positiveness of this decision, however, raises an important new question. If we can see clearly today that Hamilton did not write *Federalist* 63 or 51, for example, how could the New Yorker possibly claim them as his own in 1802? The indisputable evidence which assures us that these are Madison's papers should have plainly told Hamilton that he did not write them.

On this point no positive answer can be given; our best hypothesis will always remain a guess. It is highly probable however that Alexander Hamilton drew up his list of authors without bothering to again read over the individual essays he so carelessly divided. There is certainly very suggestive evidence to support this conclusion. We know that while Madison personally corrected all of his papers for the

130. It was in regard to the two latter essays that Bourne remarked: "Jay's authorship of No. 64 was finally established by finding a draft of the essay in his papers. It will hardly be denied that a considerable part of Nos. 62 and 63 has been found in Madison's writings." "Authorship of The Federalist," *AHR*, II (1896–1897), 459. Nor does Bourne exaggerate, for it required five full pages of the *AHR* to contain his parallel citations from these papers on the Senate and Madison's earlier treatments of the same subject, *ibid.*, 454–459; cf. especially Madison's Convention speech on the Senate, June 26, Farrand, ed., *Records*, I, 421, and *Federalist* 62; *Federalist* 63 on the Senates of ancient republics and "Additional Memorandum for the Convention of Virginia," in Hunt, ed., *Writings of Madison*, I, 394–398.

Gideon edition of 1818,[131] Hamilton refused to do this for Hopkins's edition of 1802. Hopkins himself reported to Hamilton's son, "Your father . . . did not regard the work with much partiality; but, nevertheless consented to its republication on condition that it should undergo a careful revision by one [of his friends]. . . . Having performed his duty, he put the volumes into the hands of your father, who examined the numerous corrections, most of which he sanctioned, and the work was then put to press."[132] Apparently Hamilton was not interested in Publius in 1802. Hopkins also informs us that Hamilton at that time considered *The Federalist* as outmoded and was considering the publication of a new treatise on politics to supersede Publius.[133] Hopkins further reports that Hamilton insisted on the republication of his "Letters of Pacificus" in the 1802 edition of *The Federalist*: "He remarked to me, at the time; that 'some of his friends had pronounced them to be his best performance.' "[134]

This depreciatory attitude of Hamilton's toward *The Federalist* in 1802 clearly illustrates his characteristic approach to all his writings. As Felix Gilbert points out, Hamilton was not an "intellectual" like Madison or Jefferson. Although he was an omnivorous reader and a brilliant writer he simply did not take political theory seriously as theory. Nor was he interested in ideas as such. His political theorizing was always used as a means to some practical end; the ideas he advocated were always counters to be manipulated for some specific

131. We also know that Madison did not divide the essays in a lump when satisfying his friends' curiosity as to the authors. In Richard Rush's copy of *The Federalist*, for instance, he went through the entire work marking each separate essay he claimed with the initials "J. M." J. C. Hamilton, ed., *The Federalist*, I, ci, note.

132. *Ibid.*, xcii.

133. See the comment in J. C. Hamilton's peculiar style: "Mr. Hopkins relates; when Hamilton hesitated his consent to republication, that he remarked to him, 'Heretofore I have given the people *milk*; hereafter I will give them *meat*;' words indicating his formed purpose—to write a treatise on government." *Ibid.*, ciii.

134. *Ibid.*, xcii.

purpose. Hamilton was intensely proud of Pacificus, not because it was better written than Publius, but because, pragmatically speaking, it had worked to keep the United States neutral in 1793 and could still be used for the same purpose in 1802. The new pamphlet he contemplated writing in 1802 seemed more important to him than *The Federalist* because it would work toward some positive goal that he had in mind at that time. Publius, ten years after publication, merely bored him, for Hamilton took little pride in past literary achievements. Only on the basis of some such hypothesis can we explain Hamilton's peculiar view of *The Federalist* in the last years of his life.[135]

This instrumental approach to Publius would account for the cavalier and offhand fashion in which Hamilton drew up his list of authors. Since he did not really care about the papers once they were written he was not concerned to do a careful job in assigning authorship. The continual nagging of his curious friends, however, finally led him to draw up a list of *Federalist* authors, which he pasted in his own copy of the work. His claims were never checked against the papers themselves; therefore included in the list were essays by Jay and Madison. Since Hamilton's master list was erroneous, every other list by him would naturally be in error, for his inertia led him to copy it several times just as it stood. It was one of these exact copies of the faulty original that Hamilton left in Benson's office the day before his duel with Burr.

Hamilton's claim that he wrote twelve of Madison's essays resulted from indifference rather than from a desire to be known as the main author of *The Federalist*. His monumental disinterest in the whole matter made him an unconscious thief. This, at least, is the only hypothesis that squares with all the facts which we know.

135. Madison, in contrast, very proud of his share in *The Federalist*, drew up a memorandum, now lost, on its composition and got Jefferson to require it as a text in politics at the University of Virginia. Madison was an intellectual par excellence; one feels very strongly that he often valued theory for theory's sake and thought almost inevitably in terms of interrelated systems of ideas.

The supreme paradox of *The Federalist* controversy lies in the fact that it resulted from an equal mixture of apathy and passion—from a combination of inertia and aggressive partisanship. It was Hamilton's indifference towards Publius, ten years after it had been written, that produced the original error; he simply did not take time to reread the essays before drawing up his list because they had ceased to be important to him. Many years later Hamilton's authorship of *The Federalist* was considered his most brilliant achievement by his son, by Lodge, and by Ford. In attempting to prove that he alone was Publius, that he had written three-fourths of *The Federalist* by himself, they were exhibiting Hamilton as the symbolic father of the Constitution. Consequently these Hamiltonian editors gave full rein to prejudice and spurred on their hero-worship in overriding Madison's long-established claims to his essays. The participation of Lodge and Ford in the controversy finally turned it into an aggressive and violent exhibition of literary imperialism.[136] On the foundation of Hamilton's apathetic error they passionately proceeded to build their elaborate structure of specious scholarship as a monument to a man who did not in the least care to be remembered as Publius.

136. Ashley and Earle in preparing their later editions of *The Federalist* were not primarily concerned with the problem of authorship and naturally followed the procedure, which seemed fair on its face, of assigning the disputed essays to either Hamilton or Madison. These editors were quite disinterested in attempting to hold an even balance between the conflicting claims of the two men, nor did they suspect that the system of double signature was demonstrably unfair to Madison.

❧ 3 ❧
THE TENTH FEDERALIST
REVISITED

Adair's absorption with James Madison's *Federalist* Number 10 went back
to his graduate school days at Yale. In his doctoral dissertation, "The Intellectual Origins of Jeffersonian Democracy: Republicanism, the Class Struggle,
and the Virtuous Farmer" (which still deserves publication), Adair devoted
substantial attention to the tenth *Federalist* (see pages 220–271). Adopting
the basic organization he had followed in his dissertation, Adair conceived
of a two-part article that would resemble in plan his treatment of "The
Authorship of the Disputed Federalist Papers"—that is, he would first attend
to the historiography of his topic and then make his own special contribution.
This essay, the first of the two projected sections, appeared in the *William
and Mary Quarterly* in January 1951.

As can happen so often, there were distractions and demands that delayed
the delivery of the promised second part of "The Tenth Federalist Revisited."
Readers of the *Quarterly* looked in vain for "the last half of this discussion"
(see p. 131). When Adair did complete part two he was at Claremont
and already a habitué of the Huntington Library. A Conference on Early
American History was planned at the Huntington for February 1957, and
Adair offered his essay. And so, in August 1957, part two appeared in
the *Huntington Library Quarterly* under the title " 'That Politics May Be

SOURCE: Reprinted from the *William and Mary Quarterly*, 3d Ser., VIII (1951), 48–67.

Reduced to a Science': David Hume, James Madison, and the Tenth Federalist." The two essays deserve to be read in tandem—as Adair intended.

ALTHOUGH JAMES MADISON wrote the tenth *Federalist* in 1787, it was not until 1913, 125 years later, that Charles A. Beard made this particular essay famous for students of the United States Constitution. Before Beard published *An Economic Interpretation of the Constitution*, practically no commentator on *The Federalist* or the Constitution, none of the biographers of Madison, had emphasized *Federalist* 10 as of special importance for understanding our "more perfect union"; after Beard's book appeared the tenth *Federalist* became the essay most often quoted to explain the philosophy of the Fathers and thus the "ultimate meaning" of the United States Constitution itself.

A sampling of the evidence for this generalization not only makes clear Beard's role in generating this latter-day fame for Madison's essay but also shows the peculiar twist that the historian gave to that fame—a twist, a perspective, an interpretation that still governs to a remarkable degree the contemporary view of *Federalist* 10, Madison, and the Constitution.

To note this fact is to acknowledge the special greatness of Charles Beard as a scholar and to recognize the long shadow that his *Economic Interpretation* still casts over a crucial area of the American thought about the past. Nor is the word "shadow" inexact; for although Beard's research threw a brilliant beam of light on certain facets of the Constitution, his aim was selective, and by highlighting special features of the document he thereby cast others into deep obscurity. Judged in terms of its effect on the thought of a whole generation, Beard's famous book is certainly the most significant piece of modern scholarship on the Constitution of 1787.[1] It was

1. A survey of the textbooks used today in college courses on United States history shows the powerful influence still exerted by Beard's monograph of 1913. Perhaps the most succinct statement of the questions posed by Beard and still debatable can be seen in the Amherst readings in "Problems in American Civiliza-

also, when it appeared in 1913, the most important party tract of the Progressive Era that used scholarship as a weapon for twentieth-century politics.

The fact that Madison's tenth *Federalist* was first widely publicized in this way and at this time in a monograph with a very special modern bias has had a curious aftereffect. The peculiar anachronisms of the Beardian school have effectively diverted attention from what are, prima facie, the most obvious questions to ask about Madison's exercise in political theory: what did the theory of *Federalist* 10 mean in 1787 when the Virginian enunciated it? What function did Madison's abstract theoretical speculations serve in the creation of the Constitution?

It will be the aim of the first section of this study to show, by describing the intellectual climate in which Charles Beard "discov-

---

tion," Earl Latham, ed., *The Declaration of Independence and the Constitution* (New York, 1949), vi: "What was it the Founding Fathers did in Philadelphia in 1787? Were they selfless patriots bent upon establishing a new and enduring form of government that would save the fruits of successful Revolution which were threatened by the inadequacies of the confederation government? Or were they self-seekers bent instead upon protecting the material advantage of the propertied class at the expense of the political rights of the many? Did the Constitution of 1787 reaffirm or reject the doctrine of the Declaration of Independence?"

Since historians, even in writing textbooks, do not always express their position with complete clarity and precision, it is difficult to fit their writings into completely exclusive neat categories on this point. Certainly the volumes of Billington, Loewenberg, and Bockunier, Chitwood and Owsley, Faulkner, Harlow, Hicks, and Hockett state or imply that the Constitution rejected the doctrines of the Declaration. Most of these texts also imply or state with differing degrees of emphasis that the Fathers were intent on protecting the property of the few at the expense of the political rights of the many. All of them absolve the Fathers of being entirely motivated by desire "to line their own pockets" (Harlow's words), but seemingly subscribe to Chitwood and Owsley's belief that it is "impossible" to say exactly "to what extent the framers were influenced by these selfish motives." The texts of Dumond, Rae and Mahoney, and Wellborn argue that the Fathers undoubtedly were patriots intent on saving the fruits of the Revolution and that the Constitution was a consummation of the Declaration. Craven and Johnson, Morison and Commager, Saville and Barck, Wakefield and Lefler call them patriots but leave the relation of the Constitution to the Declaration unclear.

ered" *Federalist* 10, why the historian was only slightly concerned with Madison's theory as theory, but found in the Virginian's essay one element—the doctrine of class struggle—which, lifted out of context, served admirably the political causes of 1913 dear to Beard's heart. We shall see, as a result, that Beard was led to argue persuasively, but falsely, that Madison's *Federalist* theory expounded the doctrine that theories are unimportant in politics.

It will be the aim of the second half of this study to show by tracing the development of Madison's theory as he thought it out in the spring of 1787, before the Philadelphia Convention met and a year and a half before *Federalist* 10 was written, that Madison subscribed to no such naïve doctrine. Furthermore it will then be shown that Madison's theory as abstract speculative thought played a significant role in the writing and ratification of the United States Constitution.

DURING THE NINETEENTH CENTURY the tenth *Federalist* was generally ignored by commentators; nor is the reason difficult to discover, for it is a truism apparent to everyone who has reflected on American history that every generation sees mirrored in the Constitution its own deepest political interests. When James Madison died in 1836—just one year before the fiftieth anniversary of the Philadelphia Convention—the burning political issues of that day centered on the powers and structure of the federal Union and its relation to the state governments. In this atmosphere the *Federalist* essays which seemed of most importance were those that dealt with the powers of Congress; the relationship between the president, the Congress, the judiciary; and increasingly as the year 1860 drew closer, the rights of the states to nullify or otherwise protect themselves against obnoxious legislation. The tenth *Federalist* was not directly in point in the fierce debates that raged over these issues before the Civil War; so although thousands of Americans must have read the essay while seeking to obtain light on the meaning of the Constitution, practically no one in this era publicly signaled it out for especial praise or comment.

The editors of the twelve editions of the *Federalist* published between 1818 and 1860 ignored Number 10, but indicated by reprinting Madison's Helvidius essays and Hamilton's Pacificus as an appendix to Publius, that Publius' most important topics related to the "strict" or "liberal" interpretation of the Constitution's powers.[2] The most able foreign interpreter of American democracy, de Tocqueville, describing *The Federalist* as an "excellent book, which ought to be familiar to the statesmen of all countries," specifically referred to more than fifty of the essays, but Madison's tenth was not among them.[3] The two chief historians of the formation of the Constitution who were read during this generation, Hildreth and Curtis, in like manner silently bypassed the essay.[4] Not even the stylistic pains that Madison took with *Federalist* 10 gained the paper inclusion in Griswold's famous anthology of *The Prose Writers of America;* Madison was indeed represented, but it was *Federalist* 37 that Griswold chose to show the Virginian as a literary artist.[5]

It is true that the two pre–Civil War biographies of Madison do mention *Federalist* 10, but the casualness of the reference is perhaps the most convincing proof that during the first half of the nineteenth century this essay was taken for granted and held to be of less

2. The editions of *The Federalist* printed before the Civil War are listed in Henry Cabot Lodge, ed., *The Federalist: A Commentary on the Constitution of the United States* ... (New York, 1886), I, xxxv–xlii. The Gideon edition of 1818 set the precedent, followed by almost every early editor, of including the Pacificus and Helvidius essays.

3. Alexis de Tocqueville, *Democracy in America*, 4th ed. (New York, 1841), I, 115–145 *passim*. For quotation, see 119n.

4. Richard Hildreth ignores *The Federalist*, but George Ticknor Curtis, *History of the Origin, Formation and Adoption of the Constitution of the United States, with Notices of Its Principal Framers* (New York, 1854–1858), speaks of the work in some detail. See I, 417–418.

5. Rufus Wilmot Griswold, [ed.], *The Prose Writers of America. With a Survey of the History, Condition, and Prospects of American Literature* (New York, 1847).

immediate significance than other of the Virginian's commentaries on the Constitution. The first of these biographies, written in 1836 by John Quincy Adams—who here first baptized Madison "the father of the Constitution"[6]—discusses at some length the writing of all *The Federalist*, but Adams's analysis stresses lack of unity to be seen in Hamilton's and Madison's joint enterprise. "In examining closely the points selected by these two great co-operators . . . and their course of argument . . . it is not difficult to perceive that diversity of genius and character which afterwards separated them. . . ." Adams then offers as an example *Federalist* Numbers 9 and 10, where "the advantages of a confederated republic . . . to control [faction] . . . are insisted upon with equal energy in both—but the ninth number, written by Hamilton, draws its principal illustrations from the history of the Grecian Republics; while the tenth, written by Madison, searches for the disease and its remedies in the nature and faculties of MAN."[7] Adams, however, did not bother to elaborate on his praise or quote from Number 10; with manifest destiny looming on the political horizon he turned his attention and most of his space to

6. John Quincy Adams, "Eulogy on James Madison," in *The Lives of James Madison and James Monroe, Fourth and Fifth Presidents of the United States* (Buffalo, 1851). This sketch was delivered in a condensed form as a speech at Boston, Sept. 27, 1836; printed the same year, it was widely circulated. Adams did an immense amount of research in preparing it, and it still stands as an able, but dated, short biography. Adams's bestowal of the title of "father of the Constitution" on Madison was due largely to the recognition of the Virginian's great role in 1787–1788, but the use of the title was not divorced from Adams's strategy in using Madison's authority in the biography to belabor as constitutional heresies Jefferson's Kentucky Resolution of 1798 and the South Carolina nullification theories of 1831. Adams, who believed Madison to be "a greater and far more estimable man" than Jefferson, expected his treatment of the Alien and Sedition Acts to cause controversy since Madison's "party friends" considered his conduct of 1798–1799 "perhaps the greatest of his merits and services." Adams also expected attacks from idolators of Jefferson because of the "very explicit terms" in which he played Madison's theories off against Jefferson; see Charles Francis Adams, ed., *Memoirs of John Quincy Adams, Comprising Portions of His Diary from 1795 to 1848* (Philadelphia, 1874–1877), IX, 305–310.

7. Adams, "Eulogy," *Lives of Madison and Monroe*, 42.

discussion and gloss of Number 14, dealing with the maximum extent of territory that can be ruled by a republican government, "a question" which he felt in 1836 was of "transcendant interest, and of fearful portent to the people of the Union," who were even then eyeing the "alluring spoils" of Canada and Mexico.

Even more negative is the treatment of Madison's second biographer, William C. Rives. In his outline of all of the Virginian's essays, he cursorily praises Number 10 in one sentence for its "power of analysis" and its "abstract reasoning," and then devotes fifteen pages (with lengthy quotation) to *Federalists* 37–51, "that division of the work," according to Rives, "which was . . . peculiarly his [Madison's] own."[8] Moreover, if Rives's biography had carried Madison's career past 1796 he would probably have indicated that, with Adams, he felt Madison's most significant commentary on the Constitution was not any of the *Federalist* essays. For Adams, by allotment of space in his biography, showed clearly that he thought Madison's most crucial comment on the more perfect union lay in his exegesis of the Tenth Amendment in the Virginia Resolutions of 1798–1799— those Resolutions which figured so prominently in the nullification crisis of the 1830s and which were featured in every Democratic party platform from 1852 to 1860.

Madison was still "father" of the Constitution after Appomattox, for such tags once rooted in the textbooks seem impossible to eradicate; but he was a parent treated with increasing disrespect—a parent to be apologized for—by the most authoritative commentators who wrote on *The Federalist* and the Constitution between the Civil War and the end of the nineteenth century. The most widely read biography of the Virginian written during this period, Gay's, treated him with contempt and scorn; Henry Adams, in the great history of Madison's administration, etched his portrait of the president with

8. William C. Rives, *History of the Life and Times of James Madison* (Boston, 1859–1868), II, 487*ff.*

the acid of irony.[9] Henry Cabot Lodge, P. L. Ford, and Goodwin Smith in the process of editing *The Federalist* stole—the word is exact—twelve of the essays written by Madison and attributed them to Hamilton, who all these editors agreed was the greatest of the Founding Fathers.[10] It was no wonder, then, that in 1900, when a poll was taken by the promoters of the newly founded American Hall of Fame to determine which of our dead statesmen were worthy of enshrinement there, Madison ignobly failed to qualify.[11] By 1900 the Virginian's "fatherhood" of the Constitution was being explained by sophisticated historical experts as an accidental phenomenon. Madison's skill as a stenographer in reporting the Convention debates had misled the vulgar into attributing to him the paternity of the Constitution—so ran the argument—but this skill of a reporter was not to be compared with the truly great political genius that Hamilton exhibited at Philadelphia.[12]

One of the greatest triumphs of Charles Beard in 1913, thus, was

9. Sydney Howard Gay, *James Madison* (Boston, 1884); Henry Adams, *History of the United States during the Administrations of Jefferson and Madison* (New York, 1890–1891).

10. The Lodge, Ford, and Goodwin Smith editions of *The Federalist* appeared respectively in 1886, 1898, and 1901. For a discussion of the devices by which 15 numbers by Madison were stolen and allocated to Hamilton, see Douglass Adair, "The Authorship of the Disputed Federalist Papers," *WMQ*, 3d Ser., I (1944), 94–122 [Pt. I of essay 2 above].

11. The anonymous author of the sketch of Madison in John Howard Brown, ed., *Lamb's Biographical Dictionary of the United States* (Boston, 1900–1903), comments on the Hall of Fame vote and on the shameful neglect at that time of Madison's grave at Montpelier.

12. Worthington Chauncey Ford, "Alexander Hamilton's Notes in the Federal Convention of 1787," *American Historical Review*, X (1904–1905), 97. Ford, contrasting the forceful personality of Hamilton with the negative character of the Virginian, notes that "Madison's studies had produced almost a colorless attitude of mind, in which his learning threatened to neutralize his energy. . . . His influence in the convention was small in spite of the many times he took part in the debates, and it was exerted rather through others than through himself. This attitude made him the best possible recorder of the debates as he was in a receptive frame of mind . . . ready to study what others had to propose."

to reestablish Madison's reputation as a major statesman of the Convention rather than as its mere "reporter." Beard's magnification of Madison, however, was essentially a by-product of the strategy in *An Economic Interpretation* of using the tenth *Federalist* as a bomb to shatter the post-Appomattox interpretation of the Constitution—Alexander Hamilton's "Constitution"—which was proclaimed by conservatives and utilized by them in the party battles of the turn of the century.

The story of the historical revisionism which from the 1870s until the Progressive Era had devalued Madison's role in the creation of the Constitution while glorifying Alexander Hamilton's is too complicated to be told here in any detail. It is enough to note that the ruling groups in the new nation that emerged from the Civil War—a nation with its new pattern of industry, its deification of the businessman and the banker as the country's most valuable citizens—found the traditional agrarian interpretation of the Constitution—an interpretation personified by Madison and Jefferson and dominant from 1800 to 1860—politically and emotionally unsatisfactory.

The symbolic figure of Alexander Hamilton and a neo-Hamiltonian Constitutional philosophy, in contrast, suited the emotional needs and the political interests of the most potent social classes of America's Gilded Age. It was Hamilton's "Report on Manufactures" that with prophetic insight had first painted the vision of a powerful and rich industrialized nation—a vision that this generation of Americans, aided by tariffs and railroad subsidies, was turning into an actuality. To an age that applauded Carnegie's "gospel of wealth" and merged Darwinian biology with Spencerian sociology to justify the new rich as the most "fit" and the "best," Hamilton's eighteenth-century glorification of men of property as those best fitted to rule the state also seemed inspired social thinking. Finally Hamilton's pro-English orientation—his desire that the American Constitution approach the British in form and function, and above all his bitter denunciation of the French Revolution and "Gallic democracy"—appeared wholly admirable in an era when the bloody work of the Paris Commune of 1871 seemed to prove once again the lesson of Robespierre's "Reign of Terror": pure majority-rule democracy—the Rousseauistic "tyranny of numbers"—inevitably would end in social anarchy and open class war.

It was this proletarian threat to the status quo—still small in the United States but nevertheless a recognized danger after the great railroad strikes of the seventies and the Haymarket Riot of 1886— that gave added emotional appeal to the message preached by such historians as von Holst, Henry Cabot Lodge, John Bach MacMaster, Paul Leicester Ford, Theodore Roosevelt, William Graham Sumner, and dozens of lesser scholars and publicists: the greatest glory of the American system established by the Constitution was its political and economic conservatism. The *ethos* of this document, thanks to the "racial" wisdom of Hamilton and other of the Fathers, exemplified "the Anglo-Saxon" love of order, respect for the sacredness of property, and recognition that the only true liberty was the liberty of minority groups to be protected in their rights against the envy and malice of tyrannical majorities. This was the theme of von Holst's ponderous volumes.[13] This was the point of Gladstone's famous praise of the Constitution as "the most wonderful work ever struck off at a given time by the hand and purpose of man" and his comparison of the document with the British constitution.[14] In spite of the fact, Gladstone says, in spite of the fact that the American Constitution is an *artificial* creation, written in the age of a priori theory, of Rousseau and Tom Paine, of Voltaire and Jefferson, it has created a

---

13. [Hermann Edward] von Holst, *The Constitutional and Political History of the United States* (Chicago, 1877–1892); see esp. I, chap. 2, "The Worship of the Constitution, and its Real Character."

14. W. E. Gladstone, "Kin Beyond the Sea," *North American Review*, CXXVII (1878), 179–212. The famous quotation sentence can be found on p. 185, but the whole essay should be read, with its distinction between Anglo-American "ordered liberty" and the "autocracy" of Russia and France, and its warning to Americans in the concluding paragraph against "the proposal to tamper with the true monetary creed which the Tempter lately presented to the nation in the Silver Bill."

political society as stable, and orderly, and *natural* as that established by the English constitution, "which has proceeded from the womb and long gestation of progressive history."

In this climate of opinion, in which top American scholars vied with the most distinguished foreign commentators to sing the glories of the Constitution as an instrument of conservatism, even statesmen and students whose inherited allegiance was to Jefferson's and Madison's Democratic party echoed the philosophy of neo-Hamiltonianism. Grover Cleveland, the only Democrat to be president during the last half of the nineteenth century, in a speech made during the Centennial Celebration of the Constitution at Philadelphia, September 16, 1887, called for "business men" to participate more actively "in political affairs" and thus directly to help the nation follow policies that would advance prosperity. This counsel, Cleveland recognized, "might be considered at first a departure that would cause a diminution in personal profit," but the example of 1787 showed the reverse was true: the Constitution—"a triumph of patriotism over selfishness"—indicated that if the Fathers by public service sacrificed the quick cash rewards of private business their eventual repayment came from a sound government under which business and, consequently, all lesser interests flourished magnificently.[15] Hamilton's ghost could applaud such a sentiment; and it could applaud equally the remark, two years later, of a still unknown young Democrat named Woodrow Wilson: "Ever since I have had independent judgements of my own," said Wilson, Virginia-born, Georgia-raised, and educated at Madison's and Jefferson's colleges, "I have been a Federalist."[16]

15. Hampton L. Carson, ed., *History of the Celebration of the One Hundredth Anniversary of the Promulgation of the Constitution of the United States* (Philadelphia, 1889), I, 375. For the sporadic comments on anarchism that periodically appeared during the celebration see the speech of John A. Kasson, the president of the Centennial Committee, and the remarks of the French consul at Philadelphia, M. Voission, on the celebration, *ibid.*, 323, 447.

16. Letter to Albert Bushnell Hart, June 3, 1889, quoted in Arthur S. Link, *Wilson: The Road to the White House* (Princeton, N.J., 1947), 22.

It is necessary to remember this almost unanimous chorus of voices during the 1870s and 1880s, hymning the sacred conservatism of the Constitution, in order to evaluate the originality of Charles Beard's study of 1913. Clearly when Beard then called the "Fathers" conservative he was stating no novel doctrine; nor was there originality in his exhibiting Alexander Hamilton as "the colossal genius of the new system."[17] The shock quality of Beard's study of 1913 arose from two things; first, the shift in the political climate of opinion between 1887 and 1913 had turned the adjective "conservative" from a word of praise to one of censure; and, second, Beard was vastly original in offering, explicitly and by innuendo, historical evidence on the *motives* for the Fathers' conservatism. In short, Beard told a generation that gloried in calling itself "progressive" why the Constitution was the antithesis of progressivism.

The beginning of this major shift away from political conservatism, so evident by 1913, was first conspicuous during the great depression of 1893, at which time the pocket-slapping complacency that characterized the 1887 Centennial Celebration of the Constitution had evaporated, not to reappear in America until the Coolidge "normalcy" of the 1920s. Agrarian unrest in the South and West exploded into Populism; in the great industrial centers of the country an unprecedented number of strikes were marked with scenes of terrorism, violence, and class war reminiscent of the Paris Commune. Cleveland's invitation to businessmen to take a more active part in running the government (applauded generally in 1887 as an appeal to men of virtue and probity) now took on a sinister sound in circles listening

17. Charles A. Beard, *An Economic Interpretation of the Constitution of the United States* (New York, 1913), 100. Obviously, in reacting against certain features of the standpat Republican interpretation of the Constitution, Beard did not react against all of them. Most conspicuously he emphasized even more than Lodge *et al.* Alexander Hamilton's role at Philadelphia. Indeed in the key chapter, "The Economic Interests of the Members of the Convention," in which Beard proves that the Fathers were not "disinterested," approximately one-fifth of the discussion is concerned solely with Hamilton and the Hamilton connection.

to Tom Watson denounce the "Vampires of Wall Street" or reading Henry Demerest Lloyd's *Wealth v. Commonwealth*. As the economic disaster deepened and became more and more catastrophic, fear and hatred manifested themselves at every level of American society as the poor made the acquaintance of starvation and the rich shuddered to think what the starving might do.

Then from the 1895 spring term of the Supreme Court issued the three famous decisions on the sugar monopoly, on the Pullman strike injunction, and on the income tax, which cast the Constitution and Alexander Hamilton's *Federalist* 78, justifying judicial review, squarely into the very storm center of contemporary politics. The Court, the Constitution, and the writings of Publius were to stay there until the entrance of the United States in World War I diverted public attention from domestic reform.

The Debs and the Sugar Trust decisions seemed to outraged radicals and reformers to indicate that the Constitution, as interpreted by the Supreme Court, established a double standard of justice between labor and capital. The income tax decision appeared even more portentous. No matter if an overwhelming majority of the American people wished their representatives in Congress to tax the overgrown income of the wealthy, the words of the Founding Fathers inscribed in the Constitution forbade it; so said the Court. The economic expediency of an income tax, its justification as an equitable levy, all the arguments from public policy, were irrelevant weighed against those ghostly phrases of 1787.[18] Inevitably the justices were subjected

18. For a fascinating contemporary report of Joseph H. Choate's oral argument before the Court attacking the constitutionality of the income tax, see David Graham Phillips's news story written for the New York *World*, printed in Edward Sandford Martin, *The Life of Joseph Hodges Choate* . . . (New York, 1920), 7–15. See especially Phillips's conclusion: Choate "paid small attention to the arguments from public policy, from political economy with which his adversaries dealt so admirably. He kept close to the Constitution, and addressed himself to the interpreting of constitutional principles. And when he sat down everyone there present felt that . . . the income tax had had its worst blow."

to what the historian of the Court describes as "violent criticism" and "bitter attack."[19]

This constitutional crisis of 1895 and the years following, like the similar crises touched off by the Dred Scott opinion and the Court's overruling of New Deal legislation in 1936, produced two different reactions among critics of the decisions. There were some who accepted the Court's edicts as bad policy, but good constitutional law; others cried they were bad policy and bad law. In the first group was Debs himself, who spent his jail term reading socialist literature and came to the conclusion that his conviction did represent capitalist justice—the only kind of justice available under a capitalist constitution—and that the whole system should be revolutionized. By 1912 nearly a million Americans followed Debs to the polls and gave him their votes for president. Far more numerous, however, was the group who insisted that the Court had "usurped" power not granted it under the Constitution in order to twist that document's phrases to annul the intent of Congress and the wishes of the American people. This was the position taken by the Democratic platform in 1896; this was the semiofficial position of the Bull Moose party that rallied behind Theodore Roosevelt in 1912. And in the years between 1895 and 1912 hundreds of scholars, publicists, and politicians explored American constitutional history, reread *The Federalist*, and disputed over the intentions of the Founding Fathers in order either to justify demands for reform or to fortify the conservative position whose strongest inner citadel was the United States Constitution, as interpreted by Chief Justice Fuller's Court.[20] Charles Beard's *An*

19. Charles Warren, *The Supreme Court in United States History*, rev. ed. (Boston, 1937), II, 701–702. For Beard's contemporary criticism of the Court's policy from 1877 to 1914, see his *Contemporary American History* (New York, 1914), 6–7, 13–19, 54–84, 219–220, 313–314; for his sardonic comments on the Debs and income-tax cases, see 152–161.

20. A short but representative bibliography of the attacks on the Court from 1895 to 1912 can be found in the references listed in Warren's footnotes, *Supreme Court*, II, 703, 713, 743.

Economic Interpretation of the Constitution, published in 1913, was
the climactic product of the left wing of "progressive" scholarship—
a work whose artful selectivity dealt with those particular features
of the Constitution which were most distressing to the American
radicals of the first decade of the twentieth century.

Beard, before addressing himself to the meaning of the Constitution as a whole, had first explored the possibility that the Supreme
Court of his day was "usurping" power not granted by the Fathers
in overruling congressional legislation and thwarting the will of the
people. His researches convinced him that there was no usurpation,
that a majority of the Fathers approved of "judicial control," of
majority will, and that the antidemocratic principle of judicial su-
premacy was in harmony with the whole spirit of the Constitution.[21]
As Beard was to argue in *An Economic Interpretation,* "the keystone"
of the whole constitutional structure of 1787 was the Court, whose
position allowed it to use "the sanctity and mystery of the law" to
"foil" democracy. It was thus historically impossible, in Beard's
words, to give "the color of legality, so highly prized by revolutionaries as well as by apostles of law and order," to any movement
"designed to strip the court of their political function."

What course was then open to radicals and reformers? Their project
for making over America into a land where social justice prevailed

21. Beard's study in its earliest form appeared in the *Political Science Quarterly,*
XXVII (1912), 1–35, with the title "The Supreme Court—Usurper or Grantee."
The quotation is in the lead paragraph. The study was also published as a book in
expanded detail the same year, *The Supreme Court and the Constitution* (New
York, 1912). For evidence of Beard's view that "judicial control" was essentially
and inevitably antidemocratic, see the way he uses the approval of the doctrine as
the yardstick to measure the liberal or reactionary complexion of members of the
Convention in *An Economic Interpretation:* Gunning Bedford of Delaware—of all
people—and R. D. Spaight of North Carolina can by "inference" (the word is
Beard's) be called democrats because they disapproved "judicial control" (pp. 191,
214), while George Wythe is set down as conservative on the bare evidence that
he was a "warm advocate" of the doctrine (p. 216), and James Wilson, although
"he took a democratic view on several matters" in the Convention, is flatly denied
the title of "democrat" for the same reason (pp. 215–216).

was denied even the color of legality, not by a usurping court, but by the sacred words of the Constitution of 1787. Beard's answer in *An Economic Interpretation* was to expose the nature of that Constitution, to unmask its hidden features in order to show that it deserved no veneration, no respect, and should carry no authority to democratic Americans of the twentieth century. Indeed, by what amounted to a stroke of tactical genius, Beard divined that the most devastating attack on the Court of 1913, the most powerful thrust against the whole conservative political position, could be made by a "purely historical" study.[22] This approach would exclude explicit discussion of contemporary issues in order to strip "the sanctity and mystery" from that venerable Constitution on which the Court and the old guard were standing pat.[23]

The contemporary reform issues that were agitating the progressives were, of course, all treated in Beard's book by indirection—the theme of social justice, the unholy and corrupt alliance of business and politics that made economic injustice a regular feature of the American system, and, at greatest length, the sabotage of majority rule by a conspiracy of predatory minority groups concealing their operations behind the rhetorical false face of "We, the people." After Beard had had his say it became extremely difficult for even the

22. For a sketch of Beard's early political orientation by a student-disciple who became a close friend, see Matthew Josephson, "Charles A. Beard: A Memoir," *Virginia Quarterly Review,* XXV (1949), 593–595. For a brilliant analysis of Beard's political values as they are revealed in *The Development of Modern Europe: An Introduction to the Study of Current History* (Boston, 1907–1908), written with James Harvey Robinson, and in his *Contemporary American History* (1914), see Morton G. White, *Social Thought in America: The Revolt against Formalism* (New York, 1949), 32–58.

23. Beard's book ostentatiously masquerades throughout as a dull monograph whose findings will be of interest only to professional scholars. See, for example, the preface statement of the modest aim of the work as merely "designed to suggest new lines of historical research" and to encourage "a few of this generation of scholars . . . to turn away from barren 'political' history." Note how in his summary Beard speaks of the importance "for political science" of the conclusions warranted by "this long and arid survey."

most naïve conservatives to glorify the Constitution in quite the manner of Paul Leicester Ford in 1898, who in the introduction to his edition of *The Federalist* congratulated the American people on their great good luck that their "federal compact was the first deliberate attempt and assent of a majority to tie its own hands."

This same indirection conditioned the use to which Beard put James Madison and the tenth *Federalist*. All the evidence we have—and it will remain incomplete until we have an adequate biography of Charles Beard—indicates that the historian discovered Madison a good deal later than he discovered Karl Marx.[24] Certainly Beard's use of the concept of "economic determinism" in his famous study of 1913 is in many ways more Marxian than Madisonian. In fact, when Beard paraphrases from *Federalist* 10 what he calls Madison's "masterly statement of the theory," his method is to quote one passage of that essay incompletely; to change subtly, but decisively, a key element in Madison's theory into Marxian terms; and then to buttress this misstatement of Madison's "economic determinism" with a footnote which is almost a verbatim transcription of a paragraph by Engels.[25]

24. Matthew Josephson reports that Beard first read the Communist Manifesto while at DePauw College, 1895–1898, at a time when the future historian, deeply stirred by the free-silver campaign, was defending as a college debater the federal income tax and labor's right to organize. His postgraduate work in England, where he helped found Ruskin College, the first labor college at Oxford, threw Beard into close contact with young Socialist intelligentsia as well as English trade-union leaders. Certainly by 1907 when Beard published, with Robinson, *Development of Modern Europe,* he was familiar with the theories of Marx, which are adequately covered in that volume. Josephson reports that Beard described himself as "almost-a-socialist." If my reading of Beard's *Contemporary American History* is correct, the immediate program of reform that he desired to see carried through was the advancement of "direct democracy" (p. 284*ff*) by preferential primaries, the initiative, referendum, and recall, as a first step in what he and Robinson had called in 1908 the "war on poverty."

25. The section of *Federalist* 10 omitted in both Beard's paraphrases is the elaborate catalogue of noneconomic factions; the misstatement of Madison's theory is the denial of Madison's explicit point that "opinions concerning government"

Apparently Beard's use of Madison's tenth *Federalist* was, in part at least, a matter of political strategy—a device, quite self-consciously adopted, of wrapping himself in the American flag as he muckraked the motives of the Founding Fathers and, by implication, pointed to the Constitution as an instrument of class exploitation. My economic interpretation, Beard claimed, "is based upon the political science of James Madison, the father of the Constitution and later President of the Union he had done so much to create. . . . Those who are inclined to repudiate the hypothesis of economic determinism as a European importation [i.e. Marxism] must therefore revise their views on learning that one of the earliest and certainly one of the clearest statements of it came from a profound student of politics who sat in the convention that framed our fundamental law."[26]

It would be possible to show in detail how this special version of "economic determinism," created by Beard's grafting of Marx on Madison, colored the general conclusions reached in *An Economic Interpretation of the Constitution*. For the purposes of this paper, however, it is more important to note the ambiguous effect of Beard's book on Madison's reputation. Clearly, Beard's acclaim of *Federalist* 10, his praise of this essay's "master theory" of the Constitution publicized the essay and its author spectacularly among American

can be causes of "violent conflicts," which becomes in Beard's restatement: "The theories of government which men entertain are emotional reactions to their property interests." *Economic Interpretation*, 157, 15–16. The footnote quotation from Seligman's *Economic Interpretation of History* quoted by Beard (p. 15) is as Morton White points out verbatim from Engels. For White's acute discussion of the hybrid nature of Beard's "determinism" see *Social Thought in America*, 119–127.

26. Beard, *Economic Interpretation*, 14–16. I myself doubt very much if Beard was ever a thoroughgoing Marxist in his analysis; certainly his books were reformist rather than revolutionary in their mood. In effect then his stress on "economic determinism" and "the class struggle" was to call attention to legislation that would give disadvantaged groups in American society (women, Negroes, labor, etc.) more political power and consequently more favorable legislative treatment. It should be noted further that the connotations of the term "Marxist" are different in 1913 and 1951.

historians. Scholars, following Beard's lead, almost all came to subscribe, with varying degrees of enthusiasm, to an economic interpretation of history during the 1920s and 1930s.[27] In this period, particularly after 1930, the tenth *Federalist* became the most frequently
quoted and most regularly anthologized essay of Publius.[28]

But what of Madison himself, the "master theorist" of 1787?
Perhaps the most equivocal feature of Beard's latter-day revival of
Madison's fame lies in the fact that the historian's major thesis about
the Constitution can be taken to imply that "theory" played little
or no part in the creation of the federal Union. The Fathers, as
pictured by Beard, were "practical" men who, knowing exactly what
they wanted in the way of concrete economic privileges, were willing
to stage a "coup d'etat" to gain their ends.[29] Collectively they were
exhibited as being adepts in the use of force, fraud, and false propaganda.[30] Beard gives no hint, however, that political theory played

27. Henry Steele Commager, *The American Mind: An Interpretation of American Thought and Character since the 1880's* (New Haven, Conn., 1950), chap. 13,
makes this point in his account of the transition in the style and content of historical
writing that came in America after the 1890s. Commager also suggests reasons for
the popularity of an economic interpretation during the 1920s in his estimate of
Beard's mushrooming influence during that decade. *Ibid.*, 307.

28. Many of the pre-Beard anthologies and "libraries of American literature"
made no mention of Madison or *The Federalist*. Among those that do, including
the collections edited by E. C. Stedman, E. C. Alderman, J. C. Harris, and W. P.
Trent, *Federalist* essays by Madison are printed but never Number 10. Even as late
as 1918 the author of the essay on the political writings of the critical period published
in *The Cambridge History of American Literature* dismisses all of Madison's Publius
essays as written under the influence of Hamilton (I, 148). In amusing contrast, 30
years later when *Federalist* 10 had been printed and reprinted, Bernard Smith,
anthologizing documents for *The Democratic Spirit: A Collection of American
Writings from the Earliest Times to the Present Day* (New York, 1941), almost
apologizes for not reprinting *Federalist* 10 but for substituting an essay of Madison's
on religious liberty—a "phase" of Madison's thinking "not widely enough known."

29. Beard, *Economic Interpretation*, 62–63.

30. *Ibid.*, chap. 8, "The Process of Ratification." For fraud in Massachusetts see
the heavy irony—"they are all—all honorable men"—with which King, Gorham,
and Strong are treated (p. 228); for force in Pennsylvania see pp. 231–232; for false
propaganda see Beard's explicit linking of "exaggeration of danger" characteristic
of contemporary tariff propaganda with the federalist talk of commercial depression

any consequential role in creating the Constitution; speculation there was in plenty in the Convention, but it was land and debt speculation, not speculative thought.[31] Indeed, if it is possible to determine an individual's political motives by cataloguing his property, the irrelevance of theory should be apparent. It was thus easy to deduce from Beard's study—though he did not himself go on to make that deduction—that Madison's "master theory" merely revealed him as a writer who was indiscreet enough to reveal in the tenth *Federalist* the grinning death's head of economic exploitation concealed behind the decorous and misleading phrases of the Constitution. Certainly, this was the deduction made by Vernon Louis Parrington, Beard's most distinguished and influential disciple.

Parrington, in the fragment of autobiography entitled "A Chapter in American Liberalism," telling of the intellectual influences which shaped his early thinking, describes the explosive impact of Beard's volume.[32] First, he remembers, had come the muckrakers—Steffens, Russell, Tarbell, Myers, and Sinclair—blazing across the political sky like "the tail of a comet," indoctrinating Parrington and his fellow progressives "in the elementary principles of political realism," revealing the "hidden cess pool . . . fouling American life, . . . not one cess pool but many, under every city hall and beneath every state capitol—dug secretly by politicians in the pay of respectable business men." During this first period of education, Parrington reports, he hoped in vain that "a democratic electorate would speedily democratize" America. But the muckraking died off, and as the reform move-

---

in 1787 (p. 41); and finally the hypothesis tentatively advanced (pp. 47–48) that the "critical period" was "but a phantom of the imagination produced by some undoubted evils which could have been remedied without a political revolution."

31. In Beard's *Economic Interpretation*, 189–190, it is significant that Beard does not speak of political theories of the members of the Convention but describes what he calls their "doctrines."

32. Parrington's fragment of autobiography is printed as an addendum to Vol. III of *Main Currents in American Thought* (New York, 1927–1930), 401–403; all quotations in this paragraph are from this fragment.

ment entered its second stage, Parrington and his fellow liberals passed from political to economic programs. In Parrington's judgment "Professor Beard's notable study, *An Economic Interpretation of the Constitution* (1913), was the greatest intellectual achievement" of this second phase.[33] Beard's book offered "a discovery that struck home like a submarine torpedo—the discovery that the drift toward plutocracy was not a drift away from the spirit of the Constitution, but an inevitable unfolding from its premises; that instead of having been conceived by the Fathers as a democratic instrument, it had been conceived in a spirit designedly hostile to democracy; that it was in fact, a carefully formulated expression of eighteenth-century property consciousness, erected as a defense against the democratic spirit that had got out of hand during the Revolution. . . ." This, Parrington learned from Beard, was the secret of the continual frustration of American democracy—"the source of the weakness of the democratic principle in governmental practice." America had never been a democracy, Parrington believed, "for the sufficient reason that too many handicaps had been imposed upon the majority will. The democratic principle had been bound with withes like Sampson and had become a play thing for the Philistines. From the beginning . . . democracy and property had been at odds. . . ." Moreover "in this ceaseless struggle between the man and the dollar, between democracy and property the reasons for the persistent triumph of property" could be found in the provisions of that Constitution which James Madison had fathered.

Converted to "realism" by the dazzling light that Beard had thrown on the nature of the Constitution, Parrington labored for twenty years to document the never-ending struggle "between the man and

33. The other piece of scholarly writing on the Constitution praised by Parrington, but rated below Beard, is J. Allen Smith, *The Spirit of American Government. A Study of the Constitution: Its Origin, Influence and Relation to Democracy* (New York, 1907). *Main Currents* was dedicated to Smith, whose book is one of the earliest scholarly tracts during this period to contrast the "reactionary" Constitution with the "democratic" Declaration.

the dollar" throughout American history. Taking as the positive liberal pole of American experience Jefferson's Declaration of Independence—"it seemed incredible that honest men [before Beard] could have erred so greatly in confusing the Constitution and the Declaration"—Parrington set up in sharp contrast the Constitution as the negative pole of black reaction; and in his great *Main Currents in American Thought* he showed how all American history from colonial times to his own day had vibrated between the doctrines of these two documents.[34]

Parrington's discussion of Madison the theorist and author of *Federalist* 10 in *Main Currents in American Thought* illustrates the dilemma of a conscientious scholar carrying to a logical conclusion the half-hints, the deliberate ambiguities left unresolved by Beard. Parrington, of course, could not evade the problem as his master had done, for *Main Currents* was intellectual history. But Parrington's conclusion, oddly enough, while giving lip service to Madison as "a profound political thinker," resolutely denied that *Federalist* 10 represented original or profound thought, or even accurate political observation.

The tone of Parrington's estimate of Madison is set by the first sentence of the chapter—"The Great Debate"—in which he analyzes the creation of the Constitution.[35] "When one considers the bulk of the commentary that has grown up about the Constitution," the historian notes, "it is surprising how little abstract political speculation accompanied its makeup and adoption. . . . It was the work of able lawyers and men of affairs confronting a definite situation, rather than of political philosophers; and it was accompanied by none of that searching examination of fundamental rights and principles

---

34. This contrast was not a unique phenomenon of the Progressive era, but is the normal product of every major and prolonged constitutional crisis in American history, namely 1793*ff*, 1854*ff*, 1935*ff*.

35. Parrington, *Main Currents*, I, 279–291. All the quotations from Parrington that follow are taken from this chapter.

which made the earlier Puritan and later French debate—so rich in creative speculation."

In Parrington's view it was unfortunate that in 1787 the seventeenth-century doctrines of the "Commonwealth Levelers"—manhood suffrage and annual parliaments—were "buried too deep under Tory obloquy to be resurrected" and "French democratic theory still awaited the rise of Jacobinism to clarify its principles." Consequently "the authorities bandied to and fro in the great debate" were such conservative English theorists as Hobbes, Locke, Harrington, Milton, Sidney, Halifax, Hume, and Blackstone, and a handful of Continental writers, Machiavelli, Vattel, Pufendorf, and Montesquieu.[36] Every one of these authorities "either distrusted or violently condemned democracy, yet they provided the major body of theory made use of by the Federalists." Actually, Parrington argued, the antidemocratic nature of these authorities relied on by the Fathers was relatively unimportant in the first debate at Philadelphia, where "in the privacy of the convention the speakers were free to express interests openly acknowledged." Indeed "in elaborating a system of checks and balances the members of the convention were influenced by the practical considerations of economic determinism more than by the theories of Montesquieu." But in the second debate—the debate over ratification in 1788—when the case for the Constitution was argued "before the generality of voters without doors," the lack of the democratic theory which would have been available after the French Revolution put the opponents of the Constitution at a great disadvantage. It was in this theoretical vacuum (Parrington felt) that the sophistries of Madison's *Federalist* 10 proved so harmful to the democratic cause.

Parrington was frank to admit that despite the fame of *The Federal-*

36. It should be noticed that although Parrington as an intellectual historian is presumably aware of the great differences between the theories of Locke and Hobbes, for example, and the practical consequences of those theoretical differences in politics, he is content to lump crudely the whole group together in the simple and misleading category "anti-democratic."

ist he could not value it as a truly great classic of political theory. In substance it was "the work of able lawyers, with whom was joined a notable political thinker," but, "designed as a frankly partizan argument," it is "in very large part . . . of interest only to students of early constitutional practice." Yet the one essay of Publius that Parrington bothers to quote and analyze is "the remarkable tenth number, which compresses within a few pages pretty much the whole Federalist theory of political science."

In Parrington's analysis of this "remarkable" essay he finds three aspects of Madison's argument worth comment: the Virginian's theory of faction, his explanation of the cause of faction, and the false conclusions that Parrington feels Madison drew in favor of minority rule. No theory, Parrington believes, "is more representative of the time than the theory of faction" which served the purpose in 1787 of "a first line of defense thrown up against the advancing democratic movement" by giving political parties an evil name. In 1787, Parrington argues, "in a world moving inevitably towards manhood suffrage, a sharp alignment of parties with definite platforms was greatly feared by the minority, for the organization of the rank and file of the voters must end in majority control. An honest appeal to the people was the last thing desired by the Federalists, and the democratic machinery of recalls and referendums and rotation in office, which had developed during the war, was stigmatized as factional devices which in the end must destroy good government." As a good progressive democrat Parrington could be contemptuous of such biased and faulty reasoning.

Madison, in the historian's view, was more intelligent in tracing "political parties to economic sources." The Virginian, however, was not original or unusually perspicacious in this insight, which was apparent to "the greater political thinkers of the past"; nor was he original or even logical in deducing from this premise the need for "a republican rather than a democratic form of government." In this conclusion, Parrington felt sure, Madison was merely "adapting to

his purpose the views of Milton and other seventeenth century republicans" whose fear of the people led them to attempt "to manacle
the native libertie of mankinde." Then in a summary that practically
stripped from the father of the Constitution all pretensions to profundity Parrington dismissed the theory of *Federalist* 10 with the remark,
"It has long since become a commonplace of political observation
that the minority and not the majority is the more dangerous to the
common well-being, for it is the minority that most frequently uses
government to its own ends."[37]

The surprising feature of Parrington's analysis of Madison as a
thinker is not the derogatory conclusions reached—these, indeed,
were implicit in any analysis that followed Beard's hints to a logical
end or that allowed the Progressive Era's value judgments on political
and economic democracy to be smuggled into the discussion—but the
fact that in the forty years since Beard first publicized the *Federalist* 10
and in the twenty years since Parrington's feeble attempt at dissec-
tion, no scholar has examined directly *all* the theoretical elements
of the essay or studied the part played by the theories during the
whole period of constitutional creation. In regard to this second point
it should be noted that the closely knit parts of *Federalist* 10 were
not, as Parrington assumes, hastily worked up by Madison after the
Convention was over, merely as an argument for ratification. All
the ideas, the whole thesis of the essay we know as *Federalist* 10,
had been systematically worked out as part of a research project by
the Virginian immediately before the Philadelphia meeting. What
was Madison's purpose in this? What place did he think a complicated
piece of speculative political philosophy would have in a Convention

---

37. Entirely logical from Parrington's point of view was the final argument that
Richard Henry Lee's anti-Constitution pamphlet, *Letters from the Federal Farmer*,
was superior to *The Federalist* as political analysis and "in its frank and disinterested
examination" of the Constitution. One of the curious, but not entirely logical,
results of the progressives' attack on the Constitution as "anti-democratic" was the
tendency to label anyone who opposed the Constitution a great democrat; see, for
example, Beard on Luther Martin, Parrington on Patrick Henry.

of hardheaded "practical" men? And finally what of the separate but related themes of Madison's essay? Beard and his followers fixed on Madison's discussion of property and faction, calling it a theory of "economic determinism." How did Madison envision the relation of economic factions with those that he is careful to distinguish as growing out of noneconomic roots? What of the essay's obvious preoccupation with "justice"?

These are not merely hypothetical questions that have remained unanswered because they are unanswerable. Because of the special cast of Madison's personality, because of the special school of political philosophy to which he gave his intellectual allegiance, he has left ample evidence which makes it possible to trace the development of his theory from its "first shoots"—the phrase is Madison's own— until its final flowering in the tenth *Federalist*. In the process of studying the evolution of Madison's ideas it will become apparent that it is highly anachronistic to tag his theory "antidemocratic" in the nineteenth- or twentieth-century meaning of the term. Madison's tenth *Federalist* is eighteenth-century political theory directed to an eighteenth-century problem; and it is one of the great creative achievements of that intellectual movement that later ages have christened "Jeffersonian democracy."

To these points will be addressed the last half of this discussion.

⚹ 4 ⚹

"THAT POLITICS MAY BE
REDUCED TO A SCIENCE"

David Hume, James Madison,
and the Tenth Federalist

The introductory note to the preceding essay, "The Tenth Federalist Revisited," explains the background of this article. The two were originally planned as a pair, similar to the two parts of "The Authorship of the Disputed Federalist Papers."

IN JUNE 1783, the War for American Independence being ended, General Washington addressed his once-famous circular letter to the state governors with the hopeful prophecy that if the Union of the states could be preserved, the future of the Republic would be both glorious and happy. "The foundation of our Empire was not laid in the gloomy age of Ignorance and Superstition," Washington pointed out, "but at an Epocha when the rights of mankind were better understood and more clearly defined, than at any former period; the researches of the human mind after social happiness, have been carried to a great extent, the treasures of knowledge, acquired by the labours of Philosophers, Sages, and Legislators, through a long

SOURCE: Reprinted by permission from the *Huntington Library Quarterly*, XX (1957), 343–360.

succession of years, are laid open for our use, and their collected wisdom may be happily applied in the Establishment of our forms of Government. .... At this auspicious period, the United States came into existence as a Nation, and if their Citizens should not be completely free and happy, the fault will be intirely their own."

The optimism of General Washington's statement is manifest; the reasons he advances for this optimism, however, seem to modern Americans a century and a half later both odd and naïve, if not slightly un-American. For Washington here argues in favor of "the Progress of the Human Mind." Knowledge gradually acquired through "researches of the human mind" about the nature of man and government—knowledge which "the gloomy age of Ignorance and Superstition" did not have—gives Americans in 1783 the power to new-model their forms of government according to the precepts of wisdom and reason. The "Philosopher" as Sage and Legislator, General Washington hopes, will preside over the creation and reform of American political institutions.

"Philosopher" as written here by Washington was a word with hopeful and good connotations. But this was 1783. In 1789 the French Revolution began; by 1792 "philosophy" was being equated with the guillotine, atheism, the Reign of Terror. Thereafter "philosopher" would be a smear word, connoting a fuzzy-minded and dangerous social theorist—one of those impractical Utopians whose foolish attempts to reform society according to a rational plan created the anarchy and social disaster of the Terror. Before his death in 1799 Washington himself came to distrust and fear the political activities of philosophers. And in time it would become fashionable among both French conservatives and among all patriotic Americans to stress the sinister new implications of the word "philosophy" added after 1789 and to credit the French philosophers with transforming the French Revolution into a "bad" revolution in contrast to the "good" nonphilosophical American Revolution. But this ethical transformation of the word still lay in the future in 1783. Then "philosophy" and "philosopher" were still terms evoking optimism and hopes of the high tide of Enlightenment on both sides of the Atlantic.

Dr. Johnson in his *Dictionary* helps us understand why Washington had such high regard for philosophy as our War for Independence ended. "Philosophy," according to the lexicographer, was "knowledge natural or moral"; it was "hypothesis or system upon which natural effects are explained." "To philosophize," or "play the philosopher," was "to search into nature; to enquire into the causes of effects." The synonym of "Philosophy" in 1783 then was "Science"; the synonym of "Philosopher" would be our modern word (not coined until 1840) "Scientist," "a man deep in knowledge, either moral or natural."

Bacon, Newton, and Locke were the famed trinity of representative great philosophers for Americans and all educated inhabitants of Western Europe in 1783. Francis Bacon, the earliest prophet of philosophy as a program for the advancement of learning, had preached that "Knowledge is Power" and that Truth discovered by Reason through observation and free inquiry is as certain and as readily adapted to promote the happiness of human life as Truth communicated to mankind through God's direct revelation. Isaac Newton, "the first luminary in this bright constellation," had demonstrated that Reason indeed could discover the laws of physical Nature and of Nature's God, while John Locke's researches into psychology and human understanding had definitely channeled inquiry toward the discovery of the immutable and universal laws of Human Nature. By the middle of the eighteenth century a multitude of researchers in all the countries of Europe were seeking, in Newtonian style, to advance the bounds of knowledge in politics, economics, law, and sociology. By the middle of the century the French judge and philosophe Montesquieu had produced a compendium of the behavioral sciences, cutting across all these fields in his famous study of *The Spirit of the Laws*.

However, Washington's assurance that already scientific knowledge about government had accumulated to such an extent that it could be immediately applied to the uses of "Legislators" pointed less toward France than toward Scotland. There, especially in the Scottish universities, had been developed the chief centers of eighteenth-century social science research and publication in all the world. The names of Francis Hutcheson, David Hume, Adam Smith, Thomas Reid, Lord Kames, Adam Ferguson, the most prominent of the Scottish philosophers, were internationally famous. In America the treatises of these Scots, dealing with history, ethics, politics, economics, psychology, and jurisprudence in terms of "system upon which natural effects are explained," had become the standard textbooks of the colleges of the late colonial period. At Princeton, at William and Mary, at Pennsylvania, at Yale, at King's, and at Harvard, the young men who rode off to war in 1776 had been trained in the texts of Scottish social science.

The Scottish system, as it had been gradually elaborated in the works of a whole generation of researchers, rested on one basic assumption, had developed its own special method, and kept to a consistent aim. The assumption was "that there is a great uniformity among the actions of men, in all nations and ages, and that human nature remains still the same, in its principles and operations. The same motives always produce the same actions; the same events follow from the same causes. . . . Would you know the sentiments, inclinations, and course of life of the Greeks and Romans? Study well the temper and actions of the French and English . . . "—thus David Hume, presenting the basis of a science of human behavior. The method of eighteenth-century social science followed from this primary assumption—it was historical-comparative synthesis. Again Hume: "Mankind are so much the same, in all times and places, that history informs us of nothing new or strange in this particular. Its chief use is only to discover the constant and universal principles of human nature, by showing men in all varieties and situations, and furnishing us with materials from which we may form our observations and become acquainted with the regular springs of human action and behavior."[1] Finally, the aim of studying man's behavior in its comparative-historical manifestations was for the purpose of prediction—philosophy would aid the legislator in making correct policy decisions. Comparative-historical studies of man in society would allow the discovery of the constant and universal principle of human nature, which, in turn, would allow at least some safe predictions about the effects of legislation "almost as general and certain . . . as any which the mathematical sciences will afford us." "Politics" (and again the words are Hume's) to some degree "may be reduced to a science."

By thus translating the abstract generalizations about "philosophy" in Washington's letter of 1783 into the concrete and particular type of philosophy to which he referred, the issue is brought into new focus more congenial to our modern understanding. On reviewing the specific body of philosophical theory and writing with which Washington and his American contemporaries were familiar, we immediately remember that "the collected wisdom" of at least some of the Scottish academic philosophers was applied to American legislation during the nineteenth century. It is obvious, for example, that

---

1. David Hume, "Of Liberty and Necessity," in *An Enquiry concerning Human Understanding* (London, 1748). An examination of the social theory of the Scottish school is to be found in Gladys Bryson, *Man and Society: The Scottish Inquiry of the Eighteenth Century* (Princeton, N.J., 1945). Miss Bryson seems unaware both of the position held by Scottish social science in the curriculum of the American colleges after 1750—Princeton, for example, where nine members of the Constitutional Convention of 1787 graduated, was a provincial carbon copy, under President Witherspoon, of Edinburgh—and of its influence on the Revolutionary generation. For a brilliant analysis of Francis Hutcheson's ideas and his part in setting the tone and direction of Scottish research, as well as the transatlantic flow of ideas between Scotland and the American colonies in the 18th century, with a persuasive explanation of why the Scots specialized in social science formulations that were peculiarly congenial to the American Revolutionary elite, see Caroline Robbins, " 'When It Is That Colonies May Turn Independent': An Analysis of the Environment and Politics of Francis Hutcheson (1694–1746)," *William and Mary Quarterly*, 3d Ser., XI (1954), 214–251.

the "scientific predictions," based on historical analysis, contained in Professor Adam Smith's *An Inquiry into the Nature and Causes of the Wealth of Nations* (London, 1776), concerning the role of free enterprise and economic productivity, were of prime significance in shaping the relations of the state with the American business community, especially after 1828. Washington's expectations of 1783 were thus accurate in the long-run view.[2]

It is the purpose of this paper, however, to show that Washington's immediate expectations of the creative role of "philosophy" in American politics were also accurate in the period in which he wrote. It is thus the larger inference of the following essay that "philosophy," or "the science of politics" (as defined above), was integral to the whole discussion of the necessity for a *more* perfect Union that resulted in the creation of the American Constitution of 1787.

It can be shown, though not in this short paper, that the use of history in the debates both in the Philadelphia Convention and in the state ratifying conventions is not mere rhetorical-historical window dressing, concealing substantially greedy motives of class and property. The speakers were making a genuinely "scientific" attempt to discover the "constant and universal principles" of any republican government in regard to liberty, justice, and stability.

In this perspective the three hundred pages of comparative-historical research in John Adams's *Defence of the Constitutions of the United States* (1787), and the five-hour closely argued historical analysis in Alexander Hamilton's Convention speech of June 18, 1787, were both "scientific" efforts to relate the current difficulties of the thirteen American republics to the universal tendencies of republicanism in all nations and in all ages. History, scientifically

2. The theoretical and prophetic nature of Adam Smith's classic when it was published in 1776 is today largely ignored by other scholars and spokesmen for the modern American business community. In 1776, however, Smith could only theorize from scattered historical precedents as to how a projective free enterprise system might work, because nowhere in his mercantilist world was a free enterprise system of the sort he described on paper actually operating.

considered, thus helped *define* both the nature of the crisis of 1787 for these leaders and their audience, and also determined in large part the "reforms" that, it could be predicted, would end the crisis. To both Adams and Hamilton history proved (so they believed) that sooner or later the American people would have to return to a system of mixed or limited monarchy—so great was the size of the country, so diverse were the interests to be reconciled that no other system could be adequate in securing both liberty and justice. In like manner Patrick Henry's prediction, June 9, 1788, in the Virginia ratifying convention, "that one government [i.e., the proposed constitution] cannot reign over so extensive a country as this is, without absolute despotism" was grounded upon a "political axiom" scientifically confirmed, so he believed, by history.

The most creative and philosophical disciple of the Scottish school of science and politics in the Philadelphia Convention was James Madison. His effectiveness as an advocate of a new constitution, and of the particular constitution that was drawn up in Philadelphia in 1787, was certainly based in large part on his personal experience in public life and his personal knowledge of the conditions of America in 1787. But Madison's greatness as a statesman rests in part on his ability quite deliberately to set his limited personal experience in the context of the experience of men in other ages and times, thus giving extra reaches of insight to his political formulations.

His most amazing political prophecy, formally published in the tenth *Federalist*, was that the size of the United States and its variety of interests could be made a guarantee of stability and justice under the new constitution. When Madison made this prophecy the accepted opinion among all sophisticated politicians was exactly the opposite. It is the purpose of the following detailed analysis to show Madison, the scholar-statesman, evolving his novel theory, and not only using the behavioral science techniques of the eighteenth century, but turning to the writings of David Hume himself for some of the suggestions concerning an extended republic.

It was David Hume's speculations on the "Idea of a Perfect Commonwealth," first published in 1752, that most stimulated James Madison's thought on factions.[3] In this essay Hume disclaimed any attempt to substitute a political utopia for "the common botched and inaccurate governments" which seemed to serve imperfect men so well. Nevertheless, he argued, the idea of a perfect commonwealth "is surely the most worthy curiosity of any the wit of man can possibly devise. And who knows, if this controversy were fixed by the universal consent of the wise and learned, but, in some future age, an opportunity might be afforded of reducing the theory to practice, either by a dissolution of some old government, or by the combination of men to form a new one, in some distant part of the world." At the very end of Hume's essay was a discussion that could not help being of interest to Madison. For here the Scot casually demolished the Montesquieu small-republic theory; and it was this part of his essay, contained in a single page, that was to serve Madison in new-modeling a "botched" Confederation "in a distant part of the world" (I, 480–481, 492).

Hume concluded his "Idea of a Perfect Commonwealth" with some observations on "the falsehood of the common opinion, that no large state, such as France or Great Britain, could ever be modelled into a commonwealth, but that such a form of government can only take place in a city or small territory." The opposite seemed to be true, decided Hume. "Though it is more difficult to form a republican government in an extensive country than in a city; there is more facility, when once it is formed, of preserving it steady and uniform, without tumult and faction."

3. David Hume, *Essays, Moral, Political, and Literary* (London, [1875]). Madison apparently used the 1758 edition, which was the most complete printed during the Scot's lifetime, and which gathered up into two volumes what he conceived of as the final revised version of his thoughts on the topics treated. Earlier versions of certain of the essays had been printed in 1742, 1748, and 1752; there are numerous modern editions of the 1758 printing. All page references to Hume in this article are to the 1875 edition.

The formidable problem of first unifying the outlying and various segments of a big area had thrown Montesquieu and like-minded theorists off the track, Hume believed. "It is not easy, for the distant parts of a large state to combine in any plan of free government, but they easily conspire in the esteem and reverence for a single person, who, by means of this popular favour, may seize the power, and forcing the more obstinate to submit, may establish a monarchical government" (I, 492). Historically, therefore, it is the great leader who has been the symbol and engine of unity in empire building. His characteristic ability to evoke loyalty has made him in the past a mechanism both of solidarity and of exploitation. His leadership enables diverse peoples to work for a common end, but because of the power temptations inherent in his strategic position he usually ends as an absolute monarch.

And yet, Hume argued, this last step is not a rigid social law as Montesquieu would have it. There was always the possibility that some modern leader with the wisdom and ancient virtue of a Solon or of a Lycurgus would suppress his personal ambition and found a free state in a large territory "to secure the peace, happiness, and liberty of future generations" ("Of Parties in General," I, 127). In 1776—the year Hume died—a provincial notable named George Washington was starting on the career that was to justify Hume's penetrating analysis of the unifying role of the great man in a large and variegated empire. Hume would have exulted at the discovery that his deductive leap into the future with a scientific prediction was correct: all great men who consolidated empires did not necessarily desire crowns.

Having disposed of the reason why monarchies had usually been set up in big empires and why it still was a matter of free will rather than necessity, Hume then turned to the problem of the easily founded and unstable small republic. In contrast to the large state, "a city readily concurs in the same notions of government, the natural equality of property favours liberty,[4] and the nearness of habitation enables the citizens mutually to assist each other. Even under absolute princes, the subordinate government of cities is commonly republican. . . . But these same circumstances, which facilitate the erection of commonwealths in cities, render their constitution more frail and uncertain. Democracies are turbulent. For however the people may be separated or divided into small parties, either in their votes or elections; their near habitation in a city will always make the force of popular tides and currents very sensible. Aristocracies are better adapted for peace and order, and accordingly were most admired by ancient writers; but they are jealous and oppressive" (I, 492). Here, of course, was the ancient dilemma that Madison knew so well, restated by Hume. In the city where wealth and poverty existed in close proximity, the poor, if given the vote, might very well try to use the power of the government to expropriate the opulent, while the rich, ever a self-conscious minority in a republican state, were constantly driven by fear of danger, even when no danger existed in fact, to take aggressive and oppressive measures to head off the slightest threat to their power, position, and property.

It was Hume's next two sentences that must have electrified Madison as he read them: "In a large government, which is modelled with masterly skill, there is compass and room enough to refine the democracy, from the lower people, who may be admitted into the first elections or first concoction of the commonwealth, to the higher magistrates, who direct all the movements. At the same time, the parts are so distant and remote, that it is very difficult, either by

4. Hume seems to be referring to the development in cities of a specialized product, trade, or industrial skill that gives the small area an equal interest in a specific type of economic activity. All the inhabitants of Sheffield from the lowly artisan to the wealthiest manufacturer had an interest in the iron industry; every dweller in Liverpool had a stake in the prosperity of the slave trade. It was this regional unity of occupation that Hume was speaking of, not equality of income from the occupation, as is shown by the latter part of his analysis.

intrigue, prejudice, or passion, to hurry them into any measures against the public interest" (I, 492). Hume's analysis here had turned the small-territory republic theory upside down: *if* a free state could once be established in a large area, it would be stable and safe from the effects of faction. Madison had found the answer to Montesquieu. He had also found in embryonic form his own theory of the extended federal republic.

Madison could not but feel that the "political aphorisms" which David Hume scattered so lavishly in his essays were worthy of his careful study. He reexamined the sketch of Hume's perfect common-wealth: "a form of government, to which," Hume claimed, "I cannot in theory discover any considerable objection." Hume suggested that Great Britain and Ireland—"or any territory of equal extent"—be divided into a hundred counties, and that each county in turn be divided into one hundred parishes, making in all ten thousand minor districts in the state. The twenty-pound freeholders and five-hun-dred-pound householders in each parish were to elect annually a repre-sentative for the parish. The hundred parish representatives in each county would then elect out of themselves one "senator" and ten county "magistrates." There would thus be in "the whole common-wealth, 100 senators, 1100 [*sic*] county magistrates, and 10,000 . . . representatives." Hume would then have vested in the senators the executive power: "the power of peace and war, of giving orders to gen-erals, admirals, and ambassadors, and, in short all the prerogatives of a British King, except his negative" (I, 482–483). The county magistrates were to have the legislative power: but they were never to assemble as a single legislative body. They were to convene in their own counties, and each county was to have one vote; and although they could initiate legislation, Hume expected the senators normally to make policy. The ten thousand parish representatives were to have the right to a referen-dum when the other two orders in the state disagreed.

It was all very complicated and cumbersome, but Hume thought that it would allow a government to be based on the consent of the "people" and at the same time obviate the danger of factions. He stated the "political aphorism" which explained his complex system: "The lower sort of people and small proprietors are good judges enough of one not very distant from them in rank or habitation; and therefore, in their parochial meetings, will probably chuse the best, or nearly the best representative: But they are wholly unfit for county meetings, and for electing into the higher offices of the republic. Their ignorance gives the grandees an opportunity of deceiving them."[5] This carefully graded hierarchy of officials therefore carried the system of indirect elections to a logical conclusion.

Madison quite easily traced out the origin of Hume's scheme. He found it in the essay entitled "Of the First Principles of Government." Hume had been led to his idea of fragmentizing election districts by his reading of Roman history and his contemplation of the historically verified evils incident to the direct participation of every citizen in democratical governments. The Scotsman had little use for "a pure republic," that is to say, a direct democracy. "For though the people, collected in a body like the Roman tribes, be quite unfit for government, yet when dispersed in small bodies, they are more susceptible both of reason and order; the force of popular currents and tides is, in a great measure, broken; and the public interest may be pursued with some method and constancy" (I, 113). Hence, Hume's careful attempts to keep the citizens with the suffrage operating in thousands of artificially created electoral districts. And as Madison thought over Hume's theoretic system, he must suddenly have seen that in this

5. *Essays*, I, 487. Hume elaborated his system in great detail, working out a judiciary system, the methods of organizing and controlling the militia, etc. The Scot incidentally acknowledged that his thought and theories on the subject owed much to James Harrington's *The common-wealth of Oceana* (London, 1656), "the only valuable model of a [perfect] commonwealth that has yet been offered to the public." For Hume thought that Sir Thomas More's *Utopia* and Plato's *Republic* with all other utopian blueprints were worthless. "All plans of government, which suppose great reformation in the manners of mankind," he noted, "are plainly imaginary." *Essays*, I, 481.

instance the troublesome corporate aggressiveness of the thirteen American states could be used to good purpose. There already existed in the United States local governing units to break the force of popular currents. There was no need to invent an artificial system of counties in America. The states themselves could serve as the chief pillars and supports of a new constitution in a large-area commonwealth.

Here in Hume's *Essays* lay the germ for Madison's theory of the extended republic. It is interesting to see how he took these scattered and incomplete fragments and built them into an intellectual and theoretical structure of his own. Madison's first full statement of this hypothesis appeared in his "Notes on the Confederacy" written in April 1787, eight months before the final version of it was published as the tenth *Federalist*.[6] Starting with the proposition that "in republican Government, the majority, however composed, ultimately give the law," Madison then asks what is to restrain an interested majority from unjust violations of the minority's rights? Three motives might be claimed to meliorate the selfishness of the majority: first, "prudent regard for their own good, as involved in the general ... good"; second, "respect for character"; and finally, religious scruples.[7] After examining each in its turn Madison concludes that they are but a frail bulwark against a ruthless party.

In his discussion of the insufficiency of "respect for character" as a curb on faction, Madison again leans heavily upon Hume. The Scot had stated paradoxically that it is "a just *political* maxim *that every man must be supposed a knave:* Though at the same time, it appears somewhat strange, that a maxim should be true in *politics*, which is

6. *Federalist* 10 appeared in the *New-York Packet*, Nov. 23, 1787. There are thus three versions of Madison's theoretic formulation of how a properly organized republic in a large area, incorporating within its jurisdiction a multiplicity of interests, will sterilize the class conflict of the rich versus the poor: (1) the "Notes" of Apr. 1787; (2) speeches in the Convention during June 1787; and (3) the final polished and elaborated form, in *The Federalist*, Nov. 1787.

7. [William C. Rives and Philip R. Fendall, eds.], *Letters and Other Writings of James Madison* (Philadelphia, 1867), I, 325–326, hereafter cited as *Letters of Madison*.

false in *fact* . . . men are generally more honest in their private than in their public capacity, and will go greater lengths to serve a party, than when their own private interest is alone concerned. Honour is a great check upon mankind: But where a considerable body of men act together, this check is, in a great measure, removed; since a man is sure to be approved of by his own party . . . and he soon learns to despise the clamours of adversaries."[8] This argument, confirmed by his own experience, seemed to Madison too just and pointed not to use, so under "Respect for character" he set down: "However strong this motive may be in individuals, it is considered as very insufficient to restrain them from injustice. In a multitude its efficacy is diminished in proportion to the number which is to share the praise or the blame. Besides, as it has reference to public opinion, which, within a particular society, is the opinion of the majority, the standard is fixed by those whose conduct is to be measured by it."[9] The young Virginian readily found a concrete example in Rhode Island, where honor had proved to be no check on factious behavior. In a letter to Jefferson explaining the theory of the new constitution, Madison was to repeat his category of inefficacious motives,[10] but in formally presenting his theory to the world in the letters of Publius he deliberately excluded it.[11] There was a certain disadvantage in making derogatory remarks to a majority that must be persuaded to adopt your arguments.

In April 1787, however, when Madison was writing down his first

8. "Of the Independency of Parliament," *Essays*, I, 118–119.

9. *Letters of Madison*, I, 326.

10. To Thomas Jefferson, Oct. 24, 1787, *ibid.*, 352.

11. In Madison's earliest presentation of his thesis certain other elements indicating his debt to Hume appear that have vanished in *The Federalist*. In the "Notes on the Confederacy" the phrase "notorious factions and oppressions which take place in corporate towns" (*ibid.*, 327) recalls the original starting point of Hume's analysis in the "Perfect Commonwealth." Also the phraseology of the sentence: "The society becomes broken into a greater variety of interests . . . which check each other" (*ibid.*) varied in the letter to Jefferson to: "In a large society, the people are broken into so many interests" (*ibid.*, 352), is probably a parallel of Hume's "The force of popular currents and tides is, in a great measure, broken." ("First Principles of Governments," *Essays*, I, 113.)

thoughts on the advantage of an extended government, he had still not completely thought through and integrated Hume's system of indirect elections with his own ideas. The Virginian, nevertheless, had not dismissed the subject from his thoughts. He had taken a subsidiary element of Hume's "Perfect Commonwealth" argument and developed it as the primary factor in his own theorem; but he was also to include Hume's major technique of indirect election as a minor device in the constitution he proposed for the new American state. As the last paragraph of "Notes on the Confederacy" there appears a long sentence that on its surface has little organic relation to Madison's preceding two-page discussion of how "an extensive Republic meliorates the administration of a small Republic": "An auxiliary desideratum for the melioration of the Republican form is such a process of elections as will most certainly extract from the mass of the society the purest and noblest characters which it contains; such as will at once feel most strongly the proper motives to pursue the end of their appointment, and be most capable to devise the proper means of attaining it."[12] This final sentence, with its abrupt departure in thought, would be hard to explain were it not for the juxtaposition in Hume of the material on large area and indirect election.

When Madison presented his thesis to the electorate in the tenth *Federalist* as justification for a more perfect union, Hume's *Essays* were to offer one final service. Hume had written a scientific analysis on "Parties in General" as well as on the "Parties of Great Britain." In the first of these essays he took the position independently arrived at by Madison concerning the great variety of factions likely to agitate a republican state. The Virginian, with his characteristic scholarly thoroughness, therefore turned to Hume again when it came time to parade his arguments in full dress. Hume had made his major contribution to Madison's political philosophy before the Philadelphia Convention. Now he was to help in the final polishing and elaboration of the theory for purposes of public persuasion in print.

12. *Letters of Madison*, I, 328.

Madison had no capacity for slavish imitation; but a borrowed word, a sentence lifted almost in its entirety from the other's essay, and, above all, the exactly parallel march of ideas in Hume's "Parties" and Madison's *Federalist* 10 show how congenial he found the Scot's way of thinking and how invaluable Hume was in the final crystallizing of Madison's own convictions. "Men have such a propensity to divide into personal factions," wrote Hume, "that the smallest appearance of real difference will produce them" (I, 128). And the Virginian takes up the thread to spin his more elaborate web: "So strong is this propensity of mankind to fall into mutual animosities, that where no substantial occasion presents itself, the most frivolous and fanciful distinctions have been sufficient to kindle their unfriendly passions and excite their most violent conflicts."[13] Hume, in his parallel passage, presents copious examples. He cites the rivalry of the blues and the greens at Constantinople and recalls the feud between two tribes in Rome, the Pollia and the Papiria, that lasted three hundred years after everyone had forgotten the original cause of the quarrel. "If mankind had not a strong propensity to such divisions, the indifference of the rest of the community must have suppressed this foolish animosity [of the two tribes], that had not any aliment of new benefits and injuries. . . ." (I, 128–129). The fine Latinity of the word "aliment"[14] apparently caught in some crevice of Madison's mind, soon to reappear in his statement, "Liberty is to faction what air is to fire, an aliment, without which it instantly expires."[15]

13. Max Beloff, ed., *The Federalist: or, The New Constitution* . . . (Oxford and New York, 1948), Number 10, 43. Hereafter page references to *The Federalist* will be to this edition.

14. L. *alimentum*, fr. *alere* to nourish. Food; nutriment; hence, sustenance, means of support.—SYN. see PABULUM. This word is not a common one in 18th-century political literature. Outside of *The Federalist* and Hume's *Essay* I have run across it only in Bacon's works. To the man of the 18th century even the cognate forms "alimentary" (canal) and "alimony," so familiar to us in common speech, were still highly technical terms of medicine and law.

15. *Federalist* 10, 42. Cf. Hume's remarks: "In despotic governments, indeed, factions often do not appear; but they are not the less real; or rather, they are more real and more pernicious, upon that very account. The distinct orders of men, nobles

So far as his writings show, he never used the word again; but in this year of 1787 his head was full of such words and ideas culled from David Hume.

WHEN ONE EXAMINES these two papers in which Hume and Madison summed up the eighteenth century's most profound thought on party, it becomes increasingly clear that the young American used the earlier work in preparing a survey on faction through the ages to introduce his own discussion of faction in America. Hume's work was admirably adapted to this purpose. It was philosophical and scientific in the best tradition of the Enlightenment. The facile damnation of faction had been a commonplace in English politics for a hundred years, as Whig and Tory vociferously sought to fasten the label on each other. But the Scot, very little interested as a partisan and very much so as a social scientist, treated the subject therefore in psychological, intellectual, and socioeconomic terms. Throughout all history, he discovered, mankind has been divided into factions based either on personal loyalty to some leader or upon some "sentiment or interest" common to the group as a unit. This latter type he called a "Real" as distinguished from the "Personal" faction. Finally he subdivided the "real factions" into parties based on "interest," upon "principle," or upon "affection." Hume spent well over five pages dissecting these three types; but Madison, while determined to be inclusive, had not the space to go into such minute analysis.

---

and people, soldiers and merchants, have all a distinct interest; but the more powerful oppresses the weaker with impunity and without resistance; which begets a seeming tranquility in such governments." *Essays*, I, 130. Also, see Hume's comparison of faction to "weeds . . . which grow most plentifully in the richest soil; and though absolute governments be not wholly free from them, it must be confessed, that they rise more easily, and propagate themselves faster in free governments, where they always infect the legislature itself, which alone could be able, by the steady application of rewards and punishments, to eradicate them," and notice Madison's "The regulation of these various and interfering interests forms the principal task of modern legislation, and involves the spirit of party and faction in the necessary and ordinary operations of the government." *Ibid.*, 127–128; *Federalist* 10, 43.

Besides, he was more intent now on developing the cure than on describing the malady. He therefore consolidated Hume's two-page treatment of "personal" factions and his long discussion of parties based on "principle and affection" into a single sentence. The tenth *Federalist* reads: "A zeal for different opinions concerning religion, concerning government, and many other points, as well of speculation as of practice;[16] an attachment to different leaders ambitiously contending for pre-eminence and power;[17] or to persons of other descriptions whose fortunes have been interesting to the human passions,[18]

16. This clause of Madison's refers to Hume's "parties from *principle,* especially abstract speculative principle," in the discussion of which he includes "different political principles" and "principles of priestly government . . . which has . . . been the poison of human society, and the source of the most inveterate factions." Hume, in keeping with his reputation as the great skeptic, feels that while the congregations of persecuting sects must be called "factions of principle," the priests, who are "the prime movers" in religious parties, are factions out of "interest." The word "speculation" that appears in Madison is rendered twice as "speculative" in Hume. *Essays,* I, 130–132.

17. Here is Hume's "Personal" faction, "founded on personal friendship or animosity among such as compose the contending parties." Hume instances the Colonesi and Orsini of modern Rome, the Neri and Bianchi of Florence, the rivalry between the Pollia and Papiria of ancient Rome, and the confused mass of shifting alliances that marked the struggle between Guelfs and Ghibellines. *Ibid.,* 128–129.

18. This phrase, which is quite obscure in the context, making a separate category of a type of party apparently just covered under "contending leaders," refers to the loyal bitter-end Jacobites of 18th-century England. These sentimental irreconcilables of the Squire Western ilk made up Hume's "party from *affection.*" Hume explains: "By parties from affection, I understand those which are founded on the different attachments of men towards particular families and persons, whom they desire to rule over them. These factions are often very violent [Hume was writing only three years before Bonnie Prince Charlie and the clans had frightened all England in 1745]; though, I must own, it may seem unaccountable, that men should attach themselves so strongly to persons, with whom they are no wise acquainted, whom perhaps they never saw, and from whom they never received, nor can ever hope for any favour." *Ibid.,* 133.

The fact that Madison includes this category in his paper satisfies me that, when he came to write the tenth *Federalist* for publication, he referred directly to Hume's volume as he reworked his introduction into its final polished form. One can account for the other similarities in the discussion of faction as a result of Madison's careful reading of Hume's works and his retentive memory. But the inclusion of this "party from affection" in the Virginian's final scheme where its ambiguity indeed detracts

have, in turn, divided mankind into parties, inflamed them with mutual animosity, and rendered them much more disposed to vex and oppress each other than to co-operate for their common good."[19] It is hard to conceive of a more perfect example of the concentration of idea and meaning than Madison achieved in this famous sentence.

It is noteworthy that while James Madison compressed the greater part of Hume's essay on factions into a single sentence, he greatly expanded the quick sketch of the faction from "interest" buried in the middle of the philosopher's analysis. This reference, in Madison's hands, became the climax of his treatment and is the basis of his reputation in some circles as the progenitor of the theory of economic determinism. Hume had written that factions from interest "are the most reasonable, and the most excusable. When two orders of men, such as the nobles and people, have a distinct authority in a government, not very accurately balanced and modelled, they naturally follow a distinct interest; nor can we reasonably expect a different conduct, considering that degree of selfishness implanted in human nature. It requires great skill in a legislator to prevent such parties; and many philosophers are of opinion, that this secret, like the *grand elixir,* or *perpetual motion,* may amuse men in theory, but can never possibly be reduced to practice" (I, 130). With this uncomfortable thought Hume dismissed the subject of economic factions as he fell into the congenial task of sticking sharp intellectual pins into priestly parties and bigots who fought over abstract political principles.

Madison, on the contrary, was not satisfied with this cursory treatment. He had his own ideas about the importance of economic forces. All that Hume had to say of personal parties, of parties of

---

from the force of the argument, puts a strain on the belief that it resulted from memory alone. This odd fourth classification, which on its face is redundant, probably was included because Hume's book was open on the table beside him, and because James Madison would leave no historical stone unturned in his effort to make a definitive scientific summary.

19. *Federalist* 10, 42, 43.

principle, and of parties of attachment was but a prologue to the Virginian's discussion of "the various and unequal distribution of property" throughout recorded history. "Those who hold, and those who are without property, have ever formed distinct interests in society. Those who are creditors, and those who are debtors, fall under a like discrimination. A landed interest, a manufacturing interest, a mercantile interest, a moneyed interest, with many lesser interests, grow up of necessity in civilized nations, and divide them into different classes actuated by different sentiments and views."[20] Here was the pivot of Madison's analysis. Here in this multiplicity of economic factions was "the grand elixir" that transformed the ancient doctrine of the rich against the poor into a situation that a skillful American legislator might model into equilibrium. Compound various economic interests of a large territory with a federal system of thirteen semisovereign political units, establish a scheme of indirect elections which will functionally bind the extensive area into a unit while "refining" the voice of the people, and you will have a stable republican state.

This was the glad news that James Madison carried to Philadelphia. This was the theory which he claimed had made obsolete the necessity for the "mixed government" advocated by Hamilton and Adams. This was the message he gave to the world in the first *Federalist* paper he composed. His own scientific reading of history, ancient and modern, his experience with religious factions in Virginia, and above all his knowledge of the scientific axiom regarding man and society in the works of David Hume, ablest British philosopher of his age, had served him and his country well. "Of all men, that distinguish themselves by memorable achievements, the first place of honour seems due to Legislators and founders of states, who transmit a system of laws and institutions to secure the peace, happiness, and liberty of future generations" (I, 127).

20. *Ibid.*, 43.

⚇ 5 ⚇

"EXPERIENCE MUST BE OUR ONLY GUIDE"

History, Democratic Theory, and the United States Constitution

When Ray Billington secretly planned his festschrift for John Pomfret (on his retirement from the directorship of the Huntington Library), it was inevitable that he would ask Douglass Adair to contribute. As president of the College of William and Mary, Pomfret had been among the first to recognize Adair's talents; theirs was the lasting friendship of scholars. But Adair was in poor health in the spring of 1966, and there was some question whether he would be able to complete the essay originally intended. The editor of the present memorial collection must take some responsibility for what followed. I recalled a superb paper that Adair had given at a session of the American Historical Association convention in 1955. In fact we had participated jointly in a program in which I treated "The Historical Optimism of Thomas Jefferson"* and Adair examined "The Historical Pessimism of Alexander Hamilton." Gerald Stourzh and Dumas Malone were also on the panel. I found my original copy of Adair's unpublished paper and

SOURCE: Reprinted by permission from Ray Allen Billington, ed., *The Reinterpretation of Early American History: Essays in Honor of John Edwin Pomfret* (San Marino, Calif., 1966), 129–148.

*Later published as "Thomas Jefferson's Use of the Past," *William and Mary Quarterly*, 3d Ser., XV (1958), 56–70.

submitted it to Ray Billington for his consideration. It was promptly accepted, subject to Adair's agreement—which was immediate. He was able to make some revisions, and the result was one of his best-received essays, a study that is in point of chronology and subject a bridge between "The Tenth Federalist Revisited" and "Fame and the Founding Fathers."

"THE HISTORY OF GREECE," John Adams wrote in 1786, "should be to our countrymen what is called in many families on the Continent, a *boudoir*, an octagonal apartment in a house, with a full-length mirror on every side, and another in the ceiling. The use of it is, when any of the young ladies, or young gentlemen if you will, are at any time a little out of humour, they may retire to a place where, in whatever direction they turn their eyes, they see their own faces and figures multiplied without end. By thus beholding their own beautiful persons, and seeing, at the same time, the deformity brought upon them by their anger, they may recover their tempers and their charms together."[1]

Adams's injunction that his countrymen should study the history of ancient Greece in order to amend their political behavior suggests two points for our consideration. First, John Adams assumed without question that history did offer lessons and precepts which statesmen could use in solving immediate problems. Second, Adams urged the study of the classical Greek republics as the particular history especially relevant, most full of useful lessons and precepts for Americans in 1787.

Adams, as is well known, practiced what he preached. Working at high speed between October 1786 and January 1787, in time stolen from his duties as United States minister to Great Britain, he composed his *Defence of the Constitutions of the United States*, a three-hundred-page book exhibiting for his countrymen the lessons of

1. John Adams, *A Defence of the Constitutions of the United States of America . . .* (1787), in Charles Francis Adams, ed., *The Works of John Adams, Second President of the United States . . .* (Boston, 1850–1856), IV, 469.

history. And though he included material from all periods of Western civilization, a large part of his data was collected from the classical republics of antiquity.

Nor did his American audience who read Adams's work in the weeks immediately prior to the meeting of the Philadelphia Convention deny his assumptions or purposes in urging them to study the lessons of Greek history. Benjamin Rush, for example, reporting to the Reverend Richard Price in England on the attitude of the Pennsylvania delegation to the Convention, gave Adams's study the highest praise. "Mr. Adams' book," he wrote, "has diffused such excellent principles among us that there is little doubt of our adopting a vigorous and compounded federal legislature. Our illustrious Minister in this gift to his country has done us more service than if he had obtained alliances for us with all the nations of Europe."[2]

Do Adams and Rush in their view on the utility of history for the constitutional reforms of 1787 represent the typical attitude of the members of the Convention? Did the fifty-five men gathered to create a more perfect union consciously turn to past history for lessons and precepts that were generalized into theories about the correct organization of the new government? Did lessons from the antique past, applied to their present situation, concretely affect their actions at Philadelphia? The evidence is overwhelming that they did, although the weight of modern commentary on the Constitution either ignores the Fathers' conscious and deliberate use of history and theory or denies that it played any important part in their deliberations.

Max Farrand, for example, after years of study of the debates in the Convention concluded that the members were anything but historically oriented. Almost all had served (Farrand noted) in the Continental Congress and had tried to govern under the impotent Articles of Confederation. There is little of importance in the Consti-

2. To Richard Price, Philadelphia, June 2, 1787, Lyman H. Butterfield, ed., *Letters of Benjamin Rush* (Princeton, N.J., 1951), I, 418.

tution (Farrand felt) that did not arise from the effort to correct specific defects of the Confederation.

Robert L. Schuyler, an able and careful student of the Constitution, goes even further in denying the Convention's dependence upon history:

The Fathers were practical men. They lived at a time when a decent respect for the proprieties of political discussion required at least occasional reference to Locke and Montesquieu . . . but . . . such excursions into political philosophy as were made are to be regarded rather as purple patches than as integral parts of the proceedings. The scholarly Madison had gone extensively into the subject of Greek federalism . . . but it was his experience in public life and his wide knowledge of the conditions of his day, not his classical lucubrations that bore fruit at Philadelphia. . . . The debate . . . did not proceed along the theoretical lines. John Dickinson expressed the prevailing point of view when he said in the Convention: "Experience must be our only guide. Reason may mislead us."[3]

Dickinson's statement on August 13, "Experience must be our only guide," does indeed express the mood of the delegates; no word was used more often; time after time "experience" was appealed to as the clinching argument for a controverted opinion. But "experience," as used in the Convention, more often than not referred to the precepts of history. This is Dickinson's sense of the word when he warned the Convention that "reason" might mislead. "It was not reason," Dickinson continued, "that discovered the singular and admirable mechanism of the English Constitution . . . [or the] mode of trial by jury. Accidents probably produced these discoveries, and experience has given a sanction to them." And then Dickinson, turning to James Wilson and Madison, who had argued that vesting the power to initiate revenue bills exclusively in the lower house of the legislature had proved "pregnant with altercation in every [American]

3. Robert Livingston Schuyler, *The Constitution of the United States: An Historical Survey of Its Formation* (New York, 1923), 90–91.

State where the [revolutionary] Constitution had established it," denied that the short "experience" of the American states carried as weighty a sanction as the long historic "experience" of the English House of Commons. "Shall we oppose to this long [English] experience," Dickinson asked, "the short experience of 11 years which we had ourselves, on this subject."[4] Dickinson's words actually point to the fact that theories grounded in historical research are indeed integral parts of the debate on the Constitution.

For Dickinson is not alone in using "experience" in this dual fashion to refer both to political wisdom gained by participation in events and wisdom gained by studying past events. Franklin and Madison, Butler and Mason, Wilson and Hamilton all appeal to historical "experience" in exactly the same way. "Experience shows" or "history proves" are expressions that are used interchangeably throughout the Convention by members from all sections of the United States.[5] Pure reason not verified by history might be a false

4. Max Farrand, ed., *Records of the Federal Convention of 1787* (New Haven, Conn., 1911–1937), II, under date of Aug. 13, 1787. Unless otherwise noted, quotations from the Debates are from Madison's "Notes." Dickinson, in noting that the English constitution was not the result of "reason" but of "accident," is referring to the commonly held belief in the 18th century that the most successful republican constitutions of antiquity had almost without exception been drafted single-handed by a semidivine legislator at one creative moment in time: Moses, Lycurgus, Minos, Zaleueus. For a discussion of this tradition see *Federalist* 38. The two striking exceptions of constitutions not born in the brain of one great lawgiver were the English constitution and the Roman. On the latter see Machiavelli's statement in *Discourses on Livy* (which Adams quotes in his *Defence*): "Though that city [Rome] had not a Lycurgus to model its constitution at first . . . yet so many were the accidents which happened in the contests betwixt the patricians and the plebians, that chance effected what the lawgiver had not provided for." C. F. Adams, ed., *Works of Adams*, IV, 419.

5. Farrand, ed., *Records*: Franklin, Sept. 7, "Experience shewed"; Mason, June 4, "Experience, the best of all tests"; Hamilton, June 18, "Theory is in this case fully confirmed by experience"; Madison, June 28, "Experience . . . that instinctive monitor"; Butler, June 22 (Yates), "We have no way of judging of mankind but by experience. Look at the history of Great Britain. . . ." H. Trevor Colbourn uses a quotation from Patrick Henry's 1765 oration, "The Lamp of Experience," as the title of his able and suggestive study of the way in which historical interpretation helped transform a three-penny tax on molasses and a two-penny tax on tea into revolutionary constitutional principles that Americans would die to defend. H.

guide; the mass of mankind might indeed be the slave of passion and unreason, but the fifty-five men who gathered at Philadelphia in 1787 labored in the faith of the Enlightenment that experience-as-history provided "the least fallible guide of human opinions,"[6] that historical experience is "the oracle of truth, and where its responses are unequivocal they ought to be conclusive and sacred."[7]

Schuyler's insistence that the Fathers were "practical men" who abhorred theory associates him with a standard theme of American anti-intellectualism that honors unsystematic "practicality" and distrusts systematic theoretical thought. His argument, undoubtedly too, reflects nineteenth-century theories of "progress-evolution" that assume the quantitative lapse in time between 400 B.C. and 1787 A.D. a priori makes the earlier period irrelevant for understanding a modern and different age. And, of course, what came to be called "sound history" after 1880, when the discipline came to roost in academic groves, is quite different itself from the "history" that eighteenth-century statesmen found most significant and useful. Modern historians have tended to insist that the unique and the particular is the essence of "real history"; in contrast the eighteenth-century historian was most concerned and put the highest value on what was universal and constant through time.

Eighteenth-century historians believed

that there is a great uniformity among the actions of men, in all nations and ages, and that human nature remains still the same, in its principles and operations. The same motives always produce the same actions; the same events follow from the same causes. Ambition, avarice, self-love, vanity, friendship, generosity, public spirit; these passions, mixed in various degrees, and distributed through society, have been from the beginning of the world, and still are the source of all the actions and enterprizes, which

---

Trevor Colbourn, *The Lamp of Experience: Whig History and the Intellectual Origins of the American Revolution* (Chapel Hill, N.C., 1965).

6. Alexander Hamilton, *Federalist* 6.

7. James Madison, *Federalist* 20.

have ever been observed among mankind. Would you know the sentiments, inclinations, and course of life of the Greeks and Romans? Study well the temper and actions of the French and English.

Thus David Hume, distinguished eighteenth-century historian and philosopher.[8]

The method of eighteenth-century history for those who would gain political wisdom from it followed from this primary assumption—it was historical-comparative synthesis. Again Hume speaks:

Mankind are so much the same, in all times and places, that history informs us of nothing new or strange, in this particular. *Its chief use is only to discover the constant and universal principles of human nature,* by showing men in all varieties of circumstances and situations, and furnishing us with materials, from which we may form our observations and become acquainted with the regular springs of human action and behavior. These records . . . are so many collections of experiments, by which the politician or moral philosopher fixes the principles of his science, in the same manner as the physician or natural philosopher becomes acquainted with the nature of plants, minerals, and other external objects, by the experiments which he forms concerning them.

John Adams would echo Hume's argument and use the identical metaphor in the preface to his *Defence.* "The systems of legislators are experiments made on human life, and manners, society and government. Zoroaster, Confucius, Mithras, Odin, Thor, Mohamet, Lycurgus, Solon, Romulus and a thousand others may be compared to philosophers making experiments on the elements." Adams was too discreet to list his own name with the Great Legislators of the

---

8. David Hume, one of the most penetrating intellects of the age and famed as a great contemporary historian, used "experience" in the same fashion as Dickinson, Madison *et al.* and offered analytic proof to show why the two kinds of experience together might provide the highest measure of practical wisdom. See Hume's *Enquiry concerning Human Understanding* (London, 1748), Sec. VIII, "Of Liberty and Necessity," from which this and the following quotations are taken.

past, but in his own mind, we know from his *Diary* and letters to his wife, he identified himself with Moses, Lycurgus, and Solon as the Lawgiver of his state, Massachusetts, whose republican constitution, based on his study of history, he had written almost single-handedly in October 1779. Now eight years later his *Defence* both justified the form of government he had prepared for his own state and "fixed the principles"—to use Hume's words—of the science of government that ought to be followed in modeling a more perfect union of the states. Adams's book, in complete accord with eighteenth-century canons, was a comparative-historical survey of constitutions reaching back to Minos, Lycurgus, and Solon.

History proved, Adams felt sure, "that there can be no free government without a democratical branch in the constitution." But he was equally sure that "democracy, simple democracy, never had a patron among men of letters." Rousseau, indeed, had argued, as Adams pointed out, that "a society of Gods would govern themselves democratically," but this is really an ironic admission by "the eloquent philosopher of Geneva that it is not practicable to govern *Men* in this way." For very short periods of time pure democracy had existed in antiquity, but "from the frightful pictures of a democratical city, drawn by the masterly pencils of ancient philosophers and historians, it may be conjectured that such governments existed in Greece and Italy . . . [only] for short spaces of time."[9] Such is the nature of pure democracy, or simple democracy, that this form of government carries in its very constitution, infirmities and vices that doom it to speedy disaster. Adams agreed completely with Jonathan Swift's pronouncement that if the populace of a country actually attempted to rule and establish a government by the people they would soon become their "own dupe, a mere underworker and a purchaser in trust for some single tyrant whose state and power they advance to their own

9. The following quotations, unless otherwise noted, are all from the preface to Adams's *Defence*, in C. F. Adams, ed., *Works of Adams*, IV, 283–298, and chap. 1 of "Democratic Republics," *ibid.*, IV, 303–327.

ruin, with as blind an instinct as those worms that die with weaving magnificent habits for beings of a superior order to their own." It was not surprising then to Adams that when he surveyed contemporary Europe he found no functioning democracy. Indeed, governments that had even the slightest "democratical mixture" in their constitutions "are annihilated all over Europe, except on a barren rock, a paltry fen, an inaccessible mountain, or an impenetrable forest." The one great exception outside of the American states where a democratic element was part of the constitution was Britain, the great monarchical or regal republic. And as Adams contemplated the English constitution, he felt it to be "the most stupendous fabric of human invention. . . . Not the formation of languages, not the whole art of navigation and shipbuilding does more honor to the human understanding than this system of government."[10]

The problem for Americans in 1787 was to recognize the principles exemplified in Britain, Adams thought, and to frame governments to give the people "a legal, constitutional" *share* in the process of government—it should operate through representation; there should be a balance in the legislature of lower house and upper house; and there should be a total separation of the executive from the legislative power, and of the judicial from both. Above all, if the popular principles of government were to be preserved in America it was necessary to maintain an independent and powerful executive: "If there is one certain truth to be collected from the history of all ages, it is this; that the people's rights and liberties, and the democratical mixture in a constitution, can never be preserved without a strong executive, or, in other words, without separating the executive from the legislative power. If the executive power . . . is left in the hands either of an aristocratical or democratical assembly, it will corrupt the legislature as necessarily as rust corrupts iron, or as arsenic poisons the human body; and when the legislature is corrupted, the people are undone."

10. Quoted in Adams's *Defence, ibid.,* IV, 388.

And then John Adams took on the role of scientific prophet. If Americans learned the lessons that history taught, their properly limited democratic constitutions would last for ages. Only long in the future when "the present states become . . . rich, powerful, and luxurious, as well as numerous, [will] their . . . good sense . . . dictate to them what to do; they may [then] make transitions to a nearer resemblance of the British constitution," and presumably make their first magistrates and their senators hereditary.

But note the ambiguity which underlies Adams's historical thinking. Science, whether political or natural, traditionally has implied determinism—scientific prediction is possible only because what was, is and ever shall be. Reason thus might be free to discover the fixed pattern of social phenomena, but the phenomena themselves follow a predestined course of development. The seventeenth-century reason of Isaac Newton discovered the laws of the solar system, but no man could change those laws or the pattern of the planets' orbits; Karl Marx might in the nineteenth century discover the scientific laws of economic institutions, but no man could reform them or change the pattern in which the feudal economy inevitably degenerated into bourgeois economy, which in its turn worked inexorably toward its predetermined and proletarian end.

In the same fashion Adams's scientific reading of history committed him and his contemporaries in varying degrees of rigidity to a species of *political determinism*. History showed, so they believed, that there were only three basic types of government: monarchy, aristocracy, and democracy, or government of the one, the few, or the many. Moreover history showed, so they believed, that each of these three types when once established had particular and terrible defects—"mortal diseases," Madison was to call these defects—that made each pure type quickly degenerate: every monarchy tended to degenerate into a tyranny. Every aristocracy, or government of the few, by its very nature, was predestined to evolve into a corrupt and unjust oligarchy. And the democratic form, as past experience proved, inevitably worked toward anarchy, class conflict, and social disorder of such virulence that it normally ended in dictatorship.[11]

On this deterministic theory of a uniform and constant human nature, inevitably operating inside a fixed pattern of limited political forms, producing a predictable series of evil political results, John Adams based his invitation to Americans to study the classical republics. This assumption of determinism explains the constant and reiterated appeal to Greek and Roman "experience," both during the Philadelphia Convention and in the state ratifying conventions. At the beginning of the Revolution, Adams had invited his rebellious compatriots to study English history, for from 1765 to 1776 the immediate and pressing questions of practical politics related to the vices and corruption of the English monarchy.[12] But after 1776, at which time Americans committed their political destinies to thirteen democratic frames of government loosely joined in a confederation, English monarchical history became temporarily less relevant to American problems. The American states of 1776 in gambling on democratic republics stood alone in the political world. Nowhere in contemporary Europe or Asia could Americans turn for reassuring precedents showing functioning republican government. So, increasingly from 1776 to 1787, as Americans learned in practice the difficulties of making republican systems work, the leaders among the Revolutionary gen-

11. The classification of the three pure forms of government with their corrupt counterparts is a legacy from Greek political theory first stated by Herodotus (c. 495–425 B.C.), which reached its most penetrating and comprehensive statement in Aristotle's (384–322 B.C.) *Politics*. It was Polybius (201–120 B.C.), however, who first froze the earlier flexible analysis into a doctrinaire theory of cyclical change in Book VI of his *History*. This classical theory was "rediscovered" and popularized by various Renaissance thinkers, among them Machiavelli. It became important in English history in the 17th century when republican thinkers like Harrington, Milton, and Sidney became converts. See Zera S. Fink, *The Classical Republicans: An Essay in the Recovery of a Pattern of Thought in Seventeenth Century England* (Evanston, Ill., 1945). Adams's *Defence* reprints Polybius, in C. F. Adams, ed., *Works of Adams*, IV, 435ff.

12. Adams, *A Dissertation on the Canon and Feudal Law* (1765), in C. F. Adams, ed., *Works of Adams*, III, 464–465.

eration turned for counsel to classical history. They were *obliged* to study Greece and Rome if they would gain "experimental" wisdom on the dangers and potentialities of the republican form. Only in classical history could they observe the long-range predictable tendencies of those very "vices" of their democratic confederacy that they were now enduring day by day.

It was these frightening lessons from classical history added to their own present difficulties under the Confederation that produced the total dimension of the crisis of 1787.[13] Standing, as it were, in John Adams's hall of magic mirrors where past and present merged in a succession of terrifying images, the Founding Fathers could not conceal from themselves that republicanism in America might already be doomed. Was it indeed possible to maintain stable republican government in any of the thirteen American states? And even if some of the state units could maintain republicanism, could union be maintained in a republican confederation?

The answer of history to both of these questions seemed to be an emphatic no. As Alexander Hamilton reminded the Convention on June 18 and later reminded the country speaking as Publius,

It is impossible to read the history of the petty Republics of Greece and Italy without feeling sensations of horror and disgust at the distractions

13. American historians have praised one scholarly research memorandum that Madison prepared for use at Philadelphia. This is his study, running to 8 printed pages, entitled "Notes on the Confederacy:—April 1787. Vices of the Political System of the United States," in [William C. Rives and Philip R. Fendall, eds.], *Letters and Other Writings of James Madison* (Philadelphia, 1867), I, 293–328, hereafter cited as *Letters of Madison.* Historians in contrast have generally ignored the 22-page historical research memorandum, "Notes of Ancient and Modern Confederacies, Preparatory to the Federal Convention of 1787," *ibid.,* I, 293–315, which Madison rated of equal weight in reaching the conclusions that he voiced at Philadelphia. These two memos which provided the theoretical foundation for the Virginia Plan and hence for the completed Constitution are the most strikingly successful examples of the Enlightenment ideal of a rational attempt to reduce politics to a science put into practice. See my essay, "'That Politics May Be Reduced to a Science': David Hume, James Madison, and the Tenth *Federalist*," *Huntington Library Quarterly,* XX (1957), 343–360 [reprinted as essay 4 above].

with which they were continually agitated, and at the rapid succession of revolutions, by which they were kept in a state of perpetual vibration between the extremes of tyranny and anarchy. If they exhibit occasional calms, these only serve as shortlived contrasts to the furious storms that are to succeed. If now and then intervals of felicity open themselves to view, we behold them with a mixture of regret, arising from the reflection, that the pleasing scenes before us are soon to be overwhelmed by the tempestuous waves of sedition and party rage.[14]

Hamilton along with Madison, Adams, Jefferson, and every educated eighteenth-century statesman thus knew from history that the mortal disease of democratical republics was and always would be the class struggle that had eventually destroyed every republican state in history.[15] And *now* with the "desperate debtor" Daniel Shays, an American Catiline—an American Alcibiades—proving only ten years after Independence, the class struggle was raising monitory death's-heads among the barely united republican states of America. If potential class war was implicit in every republic, so too did war characterize the interstate relations of adjacent republics. The only union that proved adequate to unite Athens and Sparta, Thebes and Corinth in one functioning peaceful whole was the monarchical power of Philip of Macedon; Rome, after conquering her neighbor city-states, it is true, had maintained republican liberty for a relatively long period, in spite of internal conflict of plebes and patricians, but when the empire increased in extent, when her geographical boundaries were enlarged, Roman liberty died and an emperor displaced the Senate as the center of Roman authority. In 1787 the

14. Hamilton, *Federalist 9*.

15. Maj. William Pierce, one of the Georgia delegates to the Convention, wrote character sketches of all the delegates. It is significant that he consistently singles out those who have a "compleat classical education" as being particularly well qualified for the role of American Solons and Lycurguses. Note his comments on Baldwin, Dayton, Hamilton, Ingersoll, Johnson, King, Livingston, Madison, G. Morris, Patterson, C. Pinckney, Randolph, Wilson, and Wythe.

authority of scholars, philosophers, and statesmen was all but unanimous in arguing (from the experience of history) that no republic ever could be established in a territory as extended as the United States—that even if established for a moment, class war must eventually destroy every democratic republic.[16]

These were the two lessons that Hamilton insisted, in his great speech of June 18, the Constitutional Convention must remember. These were the lessons that were stressed in John Adams's morbid anatomy of fifty historic republican constitutions. This was the theme of Madison's arguments (which the Convention accepted) for junking entirely the feeble Articles of the Confederation in favor of a government that would, it was hoped, neutralize interstate conflict and class war. It was because these lessons were accepted by so many educated men in America that the commercial crisis of 1784–1785 had become a political crisis by 1786 and a moral crisis by 1787.

Had the Revolution been a mistake from the beginning? Had the blood and treasure of Americans spent in seven years of war against England ironically produced republican systems in which rich and poor New Englanders must engage in bloody class war among themselves? Had Independence merely guaranteed a structure in which Virginians and Pennsylvanians would cut each others' throats

16. One of the chief arguments of the Antifederalists against the Constitution was that the country was too large for unified national government which in an extensive area could function efficiently only as a despotism. See the covering letter of Senators R. H. Lee and William Grayson, Sept. 28, 1789, submitting proposed amendments to the Constitution to the Virginia legislature: "We know of no instances in History that shew a people ruled in Freedom when subject to an individual Government, and inhabiting a Territory so extensive as that of the United States." "Agrippa," *Massachusetts Gazette* (Boston), Dec. 3, 1787, along with dozens of other spokesmen had made the same point over and over in 1787–1788: "It is the opinion of the ablest writers on the subject [of government] that no extensive empire can be governed upon republican principles." For a brilliant analysis of the sterile and essentially undemocratic nature of the Antifederalist attacks on the Constitution see Cecelia Kenyon, "Men of Little Faith: The Anti-Federalists on the Nature of Representative Government," *William and Mary Quarterly*, 3d Ser., XII (1955), 3–43, and the introduction to *The Antifederalists* (Indianapolis, 1966).

until one conquered the other or some foreign crown conquered both?[17]

From our perspective, 179 years later, this may appear a hysterical and distorted analysis of the situation of the United States in 1787, but we, of course, are the beneficiaries of the Fathers' practical solution to this problem that *their* reading of history forced upon them. Americans today have the historic experience of living peacefully in the Republic stabilized by their Constitution. History has reassured us concerning what only the wisest among them dared to hope in 1787: that the republican form could indeed be adapted to a continental territory. Priestley, a sympathetic friend of the American Revolution, was speaking the exact truth in 1791 when he said: "It was taken for granted that the moment America had thrown off the yoke of Great Britain, the different states would go to war among themselves."

When Hamilton presented his analysis of the vices of republicanism to his acceptant audience in Philadelphia, he also offered the traditional remedy which statesmen and philosophers from antiquity on had proposed as the ONLY cure for the evils of the three types of pure government. This remedy was to "mix" or "compound" elements of monarchy, aristocracy, and democracy into one balanced structure.[18] There was, Hamilton reasoned, little danger of class war in a state which had a king vested with more power than the political organs of government representing either the rich or the poor. The "size of the country" and the "amazing turbulence" of American de-

17. Note Franklin's speech on the final day of the Convention, Sept. 17, urging all members to sign the Constitution even if they disapproved of parts: "I think it will astonish our enemies, who are waiting with confidence to hear that our counsils are confounded like those of the builders of Babel; and that our States are on the point of separation, only to meet hereafter for the purpose of cutting one another's throats."

18. For the theory of the ideal mixed or compounded government, sometimes called balanced government, see Stanley Pargellis, "The Theory of Balanced Government," in Conyers Read, ed., *The Constitution Reconsidered* (New York, 1938), 37–49; John Adams, *Defence, passim,* in C. F. Adams, ed., *Works of Adams,* IV; Hamilton, speech of June 18.

mocracy made him despair of republicanism in the United States, without an elective monarch who once in office could not be voted out by majority rule. The people, i.e., the multitudinous poor, would directly elect the lower house of the legislature; a senate to represent the rich would be elected for life; and to guard against the poison of democracy in the separate states, they would be transformed into administrative districts with their governors appointed by the elected king.

We mistake the significance of Hamilton's proposal of an elective monarch as a solution of the crisis of 1787 if we think of his plan as either *original* or *unrepresentative* of the thought of important segments of American opinion in 1787. The strength of Hamilton's logical position lay in the fact that his proposal was the traditional, the standard, indeed, as history showed the *only* solution for the specific dangers of interclass and interstate conflict that were destroying the imperfect Union. As early as 1776 Carter Braxton had offered almost this identical plan as the ideal constitution for Virginia.[19] In May 1782 reasoning parallel to Hamilton's had emboldened Colonel Lewis Nicola to invite Washington to use the army to set himself up as a king.[20] And after Shays's Rebellion voices grew louder, particularly in the New England and the Middle States, proposing two cures for the ills of America. One cure was to divide the unwieldy Confederation into two or three small units; the other was the creation of an American throne.[21] We have Washington's word for it that the most alarming feature of this revival of monarchial sentiment was its appearance among staunch "republican characters"—men

19. *Address to the Convention . . . of Virginia . . . By a Native of the Colony* (June 1776), in Peter Force, ed., *American Archives . . .*, 4th Ser. (Washington, D.C., 1837–1853), 747–754.

20. Col. Lewis Nicola, in *Dictionary of American Biography.*

21. Madison to Pendleton, Feb. 24, 1787, in *Letters of Madison*, I, 280; Louise Burnham Dunbar, *A Study of "Monarchical" Tendencies in the United States from 1776 to 1801*, University of Illinois Studies in the Social Sciences, Vol. X, no. 1 (Urbana, Ill., 1922). The latter collects a mass of contemporary material on this topic, including the Braxton pamphlet and the Nicola letter.

who like Hamilton had favored independence in 1776 but who had become disillusioned about ever achieving order and security in a republic. Add to this group of new converts the large bloc of old tories who had never forsaken their allegiance to monarchy, and it is easy to see why Washington, Madison, and other leaders were seriously alarmed that the Union would break up and that kings would reappear in the Balkanized segments.

Furthermore, at the very time the Philadelphia Convention was rejecting Hamilton's mixed monarchy as a present solution for the vices of American democracy, leading members of the Convention most tenacious of republicanism accepted the fact that an American monarchy was inevitable at some future date. As Mr. Williamson of North Carolina remarked on July 24, "It was pretty certain . . . that we should at some time or other have a king; but he wished no precaution to be omitted that might postpone the event as long as possible."[22] There is a curious statistical study of Madison's which points to his certainty also, along with the precise prophecy that the end of republicanism in the United States would come approximately 142 years after 1787—about the decade of the 1930s.[23] John Adams's *Defence* contains the same sort of prophecy. "In future ages," Adams remarked, "if the present States become great nations, rich, powerful, and luxurious, as well as numerous," the "feelings and good sense" of Americans "will dictate to them" reform of their governments "to a nearer resemblance of the British Constitution," complete with a hereditary king and a hereditary senate.[24] Gouverneur Morris is reported to have argued during the Convention that "we must have

22. Williamson in the Convention, July 24.

23. *Letters of Madison*, IV, 21, 29–30. The statistical estimate was of probable American population growth which Madison thought, in 1829, would by 1929 be 192,000,000. This would end the nation's "precious advantage" both of wide distribution of landed property and "universal hope of acquiring property." At that time, being "nearly as crowded" as England or France, with a society increasingly polarized between "wealthy capitalists and indigent laborers," Madison feared an amended Constitution more like England's would be required.

24. John Adams, *Defence*, in C. F. Adams, ed., *Works of Adams*, IV, 358–359.

a Monarch sooner or later . . . and the sooner we take him while we are able to make a Bargain with him, the better." Nor did the actual functioning of the Constitution during its first decade of existence lighten Morris's pessimism; in 1804 he was arguing that the crisis would come sooner rather than later.[25] Even Franklin, the least doctrinaire of the Fathers—perhaps with Jefferson the most hopeful among the whole Revolutionary generation regarding the potentialities of American democracy—accepted the long-range pessimism of the Hamiltonian analysis. Sadly the aged philosopher noted, June 2, "There is a natural inclination in mankind to kingly government. . . . I am apprehensive, therefore—perhaps too apprehensive—that the government of these States may in future times end in monarchy. But this catastrophe, I think may be long delayed. . . ."[26]

The "precious advantage" that the United States had in 1787 that offered hope for a "republican remedy for the diseases most incident to republican government"—the circumstance which would delay the necessity of accepting Hamilton's favored form of mixed monarchy—lay in the predominance of small freehold farmers among the American population. Since the time of Aristotle, it had been recognized that yeoman farmers—a middle class between the greedy rich and the envious poor—provided the most stable foundation upon which to erect a popular government. This factor, commented on by Madison, Pinckney, Adams and others, helps explain why the Convention did not feel it necessary to sacrifice either majority rule or popular responsibility in their new Constitution.

25. Mason in 1792 reported this remark of Morris quoted in Dunbar, *"Monarchical" Tendencies*, 91. In 1804, writing to Aaron Ogden, Morris, like Adams and Madison, related the appearance of an American monarchy to the growth of population and poverty. Jared Sparks, ed., *The Life of Gouverneur Morris, with Selections from his Correspondence* (Boston, 1832), III, 217.

26. Franklin, June 2. It should be noted that acceptance of the deterministic theory of the unmixed democratic form swinging inevitably to the opposite extreme of despotism explains the number of prophets—Hamilton, Morris in America; Burke in England—who foretold the eventual advent of Napoleon almost as soon as the French Revolution began.

Of equal importance was the factor of expedience. Less doctrinaire than Alexander Hamilton, the leaders of the Convention realized that a theoretical best—and member after member went on record praising the British constitution as *the best* ever created by man— a theoretical best might be the enemy of a possible good. As Pierce Butler insisted, in a different context, "The people will not bear such innovations. . . . Supposing such an establishment to be useful, we must not venture on it. We must follow the example of Solon who gave the Athenians not the best government he could devise, but the best they would receive."[27]

Consequently the Constitution that emerged from the Convention's debates was, as Madison described it, a "novelty in the political world"—a "fabric" of government which had "no model on the face of the globe."[28] It was an attempt to approximate in a structure of balanced republican government the advantages of stability that such mixed governments as Great Britain's had derived from hereditary monarchy and a hereditary House of Lords.

It was an "experiment," as members of the Convention frankly admitted, but one about which most of the Fathers could be hopeful, because it adapted to the concrete circumstances of the United States of 1787 the experience of mankind through all ages as revealed by history. Driven by the collapse of the Confederation, the depression of 1785–1786, and Shays's Rebellion to take stock of their political situation six years after Yorktown had won for Americans the opportunity for self-government, the Fathers had turned to history, especially classical history, to help them analyze their current difficulties. Their reading of history, equally with their immediate experience, defined for them both the short-range and the long-range potentialities for evil inherent in a uniform human nature operating in a republican government. But their reading of history also suggested

27. Butler in debate on June 5. Cf. Bedford of Delaware's use of the same phrase from Plutarch's *Life of Solon* in debate of June 30.

28. Madison, *Federalist* 14.

a specific type of government that would remedy the evils they already knew and those worse evils they expected to come. Utilizing this knowledge, building on the solid core of agreement which historical wisdom had helped supply, they created, by mutual concession and compromise, a governmental structure as nearly like mixed government as it was possible to approach while maintaining the republican principle of majority rule. And this they offered the American people *hoping* it would be ratified, *hoping* that after ratification their "experiment" with all its compromises of theory and interest would provide a more perfect union.

If there is substance in the argument offered in the foregoing paragraphs, it should throw some light, at least, on the intellectual confusion exhibited during the last half-century by many learned commentators in discussing the nature of our Constitution. This confused and confusing debate has focused in part on the question, "Did the Fathers write a 'democratic' Constitution?"[29] The answers

29. In view of the number of able historiographical essays on the recent revisionist literature about the "critical period" and the writing of the Constitution, it seems superfluous to add merely another. Two pamphlets printed by the Service Center for Teachers of History that survey the current historical literature on the theme, through 1962, are recommended for those who wish to stand in the most modern historiographical boudoir—the contemporary historian's hall of mirrors. The first, Edmund S. Morgan's *The American Revolution: A Review of Changing Interpretations* (Washington, D.C., 1958), relates the monographic studies dealing with the period from 1783 to 1787 to the general problem of interpreting the whole American Revolution; the second, Stanley Elkins and Eric McKitrick's *The Founding Fathers: Young Men of the Revolution* (Washington, D.C., 1962), not only surveys critically historians' commentaries on the framing of the Constitution but also makes the point that the group of young men who worked most intensely to achieve a stronger national government and a more perfect union had staked their political careers on the national rather than the state scene and thus mingled their self-interest in status and power with a patriotic concern for the national welfare.

Two books and two significant essays have also been published, since 1962, that must be considered by any serious student of the "critical period." Forrest McDonald, in *E Pluribus Unum: The Formation of the American Republic, 1776–1790* (Boston, 1965), continues his analysis, begun in *We the People: The Economic Origins of the Constitution* (Chicago, 1958), of the multiple economic groups and burgeoning local economic appetites that existed in the United States, post 1783. His most

given have been almost as "mixed" as the theory to which the framers subscribed.

Part of the bother lies in the lack of precision with which the word *democracy* was used then, and the even more unprecise way that we use it now. The more a word is used, the less exact its meaning becomes, and in our day *democratic/democracy* has been extended to describe art, foreign policy, literature, etc., etc. Thus, from being a somewhat technical word of political discourse, in 1787, it has become a perfect sponge of squashy vagueness. Luckily, the context of formal theory that mixed government did imply in 1787 does allow us to recognize certain rather concrete and specific features

---

persuasive chapters show how selfish regional and state parties and economic groups—in politics these normally became Antifederalists in 1787–1788—had strained the tenuous Union to the extreme by 1787, so much so, in fact, that the success of the countervailing movement of the men who wrote and got the Constitution ratified was, in McDonald's view, a "miracle." In a 90-page introduction to an anthology of Antifederalist tracts (see footnote 16 above), Cecelia M. Kenyon provides the most thorough and wise analysis of the ideological stance of the men who opposed ratification of the Constitution in 1787–1788, and she makes it clear that the Antifederalists were not majoritarian "democrats" in any sense of the term.

Finally, two important articles in the *William and Mary Quarterly* throw light on the problem of "democracy" and our Revolution. Richard Buel, Jr., "Democracy and the American Revolution: A Frame of Reference," 3d Ser., XXI (1964), 165–190, makes the point that although Whig theory before 1776 in British-America consistently defended the right of the people to share in government, at the same time an unchecked, "simple," or "pure" democracy was uniformly condemned by all American spokesmen. Jackson Turner Main, in an essay in the same journal, "Government by the People: The American Revolution and the Democratization of the Legislatures," 3d Ser., XXIII (1966), 391–407, shows how, after 1776, "two interacting developments occurred simultaneously: ordinary citizens increasingly took part in politics, and American political theorists began to defend popular government [i.e. simple democracy]." As my essay has argued, the Constitutional Convention was dominated by men who rejected the idea that "simple" democracy was either a desirable or a safe form for the American people. To a certain extent their ideas exemplify a limited, but definite, reaction against both the institutional and theoretical "democratic" developments that Professor Main charts. This shift and change in one leader's estimate of "democracy"—a vague and noncritical view of the American people's virtue before 1776, a positive praise of this virtue in 1776, and then reservations about the wisdom and virtue of Americans, 1779ff—has been ably analyzed by John R. Howe, Jr., *The Changing Political Thought of John Adams* (Princeton, N.J., 1966).

usually associated, then, with the democratic form of government. In the first place, the very concept of "mixture" implies a relativism that modern doctrinaire democrats often forget: a political system, in 1787, was thought of as more-or-less democratic, as possessing few or many democratic features. Only in the pure form was democracy an either/or type of polity. In the second place, the simple democratic form was almost always thought of as appropriate only for a tiny territorial area—Madison in *Federalist* 10, for instance, would only equate the word with the direct democracy of the classical city-state. Third, the functional advantages and disadvantages of the pure democratic form of government were almost universally agreed upon. A government *by* the people (so it was thought) always possessed *fidelity* to the common good; it was impossible for a people not to *desire* and to *intend* to promote the general welfare. However, the vices of democracy were that the people, collectively, were not *wise* about the correct measures to serve this great end and that the people could be easily duped by demagogues, who, flattering their good hearts and muddled heads, would worm their way to unlimited power. It was this well-meaning stupidity, the capacity for thoughtless injustice, the fickle instability of the popular will, that led the classical theorists, who the Fathers were familiar with, to designate "pure democracy" as a form doomed to a short existence that tended to eventuate, with a pendulum swing, in the opposite extreme of tyranny and dictatorship.

In dark contrast to this *fidelity* of the democratic many was the vice afflicting both monarchy and aristocracy: an inveterate and incorrigible tendency to use the apparatus of government to serve the special selfish interests of the one or the few. However, the aristocratic form offered, so it was believed, the best possibility of *wisdom*, in planning public measures, while monarchy promised the necessary *energy, secrecy,* and *dispatch* for executing policy.[30]

30. Most of the modern discussion of the framing of the Constitution has concerned itself with the domestic consequences of ratification. This, I suspect, springs from the century of military security and isolation that so deeply colored American

It is in this ideological context that one can deduce some of the intentions of the authors of our Constitution. It is clear, I think, that the office and power of the president was consciously designed to provide the *energy, secrecy,* and *dispatch* traditionally associated with the monarchical form. Thus Patrick Henry, considering the proposed chief executive and recognizing that the president was not unlike an elective king, could cry with reason that the Constitution "squints toward monarchy." But it was equally possible for Richard Henry Lee, focusing on the Senate, to complain that the document had a "strong tendency to aristocracy." This was said by Lee six months before Madison, in *Federalists* 62–63, explicitly defended the Senate as providing the *wisdom* and the *stability*—"aristocratic virtues"—needed to check the fickle lack of wisdom that Madison predicted would characterize the people's branch of the new government, the lower house. Nor were there other critics lacking who, recognizing that the Constitution ultimately rested on popular consent, who, seeing that despite the ingenious apparatus designed to temper the popular will by introducing into the compound modified monarchical/aristocratic ingredients, could argue that the new Constitution was too democratic to operate effectively as a national government in a country as large and with a population as heterogeneous as the Americans'. One such was William Grayson, who doubted the need of *any* national government but who felt, if one was to be established, it ought to provide a president and a Senate elected for life terms, these to be balanced by a House of Representatives elected triennially.[31]

It is thus significant that if modern scholars are confused and disagreed about the nature of the Constitution today, so, too, in

---

thinking from 1815 to 1940. The dangers of the international jungle we live in, that now makes foreign policy our primary concern, has helped some of us recognize why a statesman like Hamilton was obsessed with the need for a strong chief executive as a prime measure of defense and security in the world of 1787, where foreign policy showed the same jungle characteristics that frighten us.

31. For convenience of reference, see Kenyon, ed., *The Antifederalists*: Henry, 257; Lee, 205; and Grayson, 282–283.

1787–1788, contemporary observers were also confused and also disagreed as to whether it was monarchical, aristocratic, or democratic in its essence.[32]

My own opinion is that the Constitution of 1787 is probably best described in a term John Adams used in 1806. Writing to Benjamin Rush, September 19, 1806, Adams, disapproving strongly of Jefferson's style as president, bemoaned the fact that Jefferson and his gang had now made the national government "to all intents and purposes, in virtue, spirit, and effect a democracy."—Alas! "I once thought," said Adams, "our Constitution was *quasi* or mixed government"—but alas![33]

"Quasi," or better still "quasi-mixed"—for, given the American people's antipathy to monarchy after 1776, and given the nonaristocratic nature (in a European sense) of the American upper class of 1787, the Constitution at best, or worst, could only be "*quasi*-mixed,"[34] since there were not "ingredients" available in the United States to compose a genuine mixture in the classic sense. So what the Fathers fashioned was a "quasi-mixed" Constitution that, given the "genius" of the American people, had a strong and inevitable tendency that "squinted" from the very beginning towards the national democracy that would finally develop in the nineteenth century.

32. Madison, in *Federalist* 38, mocked (somewhat unfairly, under the circumstances) the Antifederalists for exactly this disagreement and confusion. "This politician," Madison wrote, "discovers in the constitution a direct and irresistible tendency to monarchy [Henry]; that is equally sure it will end in aristocracy [Lee]. Another is puzzled to say which of these shapes it will ultimately assume, but sees clearly it must be one or other of them [George Mason]; whilst a fourth [Grayson] . . . affirms that . . . the weight on that side [i.e., monarchical/aristocratic] will not be sufficient to keep it upright and firm against its opposite [i.e., democratic] tendencies."

33. John Adams to Benjamin Rush, Sept. 19, 1806, in John A. Schutz and Douglass Adair, eds., *The Spur of Fame: Dialogues of John Adams and Benjamin Rush, 1805–1813* (San Marino, Calif., 1966), 66.

34. Quasi, [Latin = as if] seemingly, not real(ly), practical(ly), half-, almost. *Concise Oxford Dictionary* (1963).

҂ 6 ҂

JAMES MADISON

The Lives of Eighteen from Princeton remains an improperly neglected collection of biographical essays issued to commemorate the two hundredth anniversary of Princeton University. Adair's pithy unfootnoted study of Madison is marked by his customary fine prose and a predictable (if unusual) attention to Madison's intellectual environment.

1

EVERY COLLEGE tends to bask in the reflected glory of its famous alumni; alma mater naturally likes to hint that she is in large part responsible for the successful careers of her most illustrious sons. Yet any college which parades its distinguished graduates as proof that it is a nursery of genius lays itself open to a jibe made long ago by Adam Smith. That learned Scot complained in 1776 that educational institutions were always taking undeserved credit for the development of the talents of their students; a young man who starts his higher education "at seventeen or eighteen, and returns home at one and twenty, returns three or four years older ... and at that age it is very difficult not to improve a good deal in three or four years."

It is safe to say, though, that for eighteen-year-old James Madison, Jr., who entered Princeton six years before Smith made his cynical

SOURCE: Reprinted by permission of the Princeton University Press from Willard Thorp, ed., *The Lives of Eighteen from Princeton* (Princeton, N.J., 1946), 137–157.

remark, the undergraduate years laid the foundation he was to build on all his days. And since James Madison became one of the chief architects of our political democracy, the "father of the American Constitution," and president of our nation during its formative stage, his sojourn at Nassau Hall under the tutelage of the learned Dr. John Witherspoon was of incalculable importance to the destiny of the United States.

James Madison, Jr., born March 5 (O.S.), 1751, was the oldest child of the leading family of Orange County, Virginia. His ancestors, planters in both the paternal and maternal lines, ranked, by his own description, "among the respectable though not the most opulent Class" of Virginia society. Orange County lies in the piedmont between the fall line and the Blue Ridge. The chief families of this region, the Madisons and the Jeffersons, while a little less wealthy and aristocratic than the great tidewater families, demanded, and were accorded, the deference due to members of an established ruling class. The Madisons' wealth and political power were solidly based. James Madison, Sr., was a justice of the peace and a vestryman in the Anglican church—offices held only by men of ranking social position; he owned more than a hundred slaves, and the cultivated portion of the Montpelier plantation alone amounted to nearly two thousand acres. At birth, James Jr. entered a station of life that provided him with the values and opportunities esteemed most desirable by current Virginia standards.

Besides inherited wealth and position he had an advantage far more important—a first-rate brain. Although neither his father, nor his brothers, nor any other members of his immediate family or their descendants ever exhibited any particular intellectual distinction, James Jr., through the mysterious alchemy of the genes, was endowed with a capacity for extraordinary intellectual accomplishment. Writing his autobiography at the age of eighty, he recorded as the first important incident of his life his intellectual delight in the discovery of *The Spectator*. He was then eleven years old. The memory of the profound impact of that literary classic led him to argue, seventy years later, that from "his own experience" it was a book "peculiarly adapted to inculcate just sentiments, an appetite for knowledge, and a taste for the improvement of the mind and manners." Madison, of course, put the cart before the horse. His natural "appetite for knowledge" was the cause of his excitement over *The Spectator*, not an effect of it.

Madison's failure to become conscious until he was nearly twelve of his own "taste" for mental improvement reveals the somewhat restricted intellectual opportunities available even to a member of the Virginia aristocracy in the eighteenth century. Though born for "the intellectual pleasures of the closet," Madison grew up in an open-air society where guns and horses, dogs and stirrup cups were treated as far more important adjuncts of life than books. It was a gracious way of living, but it was also profoundly frustrating for the development of the mind and spirit. A description of colonial Virginia by George Tucker, which was read and approved by Madison himself, speaks of the gentry as generally "open handed and open hearted; fond of society, indulging in all its pleasures, and practicing all its courtesies. But these social virtues also occasionally ran into the kindred vices of love of show, haughtiness, sensuality—and many of the wealthier class were to be seen seeking relief from the vacuity of idleness not merely in the allowable pleasures of the chase and the turf, but in the debasing ones of cock-fighting, gaming, and drinking. Literature was neglected, or cultivated, by the small number . . . rather as an accomplishment and mark of distinction than for the substantial benefits it confers." When existence is as easy and pleasant as it was for the first gentlemen in the Old Dominion there can be little of the discipline necessary for sustained creative thought; the mind of upper-class Virginia, like that of most aristocracies, was marked by dilettantism and philistinism. The pleasant tyranny of social life with its endless rounds of dinners, barbecues, fish frys, and riding parties could only be resisted by a major effort of the will; and even among the best minds of Virginia there were few who succeeded in emancipating themselves. Add to these distractions the provincial nature of life on the scattered country seats, the lack of scholarly companionship to provide what Madison termed "mutual emulation and mutual inspection," and it is understandable why Virginia's colonial culture was relatively so barren of intellectual accomplishment. An individual like young James Madison could only begin to realize his own potentialities after he was exposed to ideas and scholarly habits alien to the complacency of his native state.

Madison's initiation into the larger world of ideas occurred in 1762 when he entered the school established in King and Queen County by Donald Robertson, who had emigrated to Virginia from Scotland some ten years earlier. Madison describes Robertson as "a man of extensive learning and a distinguished Teacher." Under his direction for five years the young Virginian "studied the Latin and Greek languages, was taught to read but not speak French, and besides Arithmetic & Geography, made some progress in Algebra & Geometry. Miscellaneous literature was also embraced by the plan of the School." Within this comprehensive curriculum, Robertson's standards of performance were strict; but Madison's affectionate references to his teacher in later life show that this introduction to learning was viewed as an adventure rather than a task. Here, in the Scotch classicist's library, the first of any scope to which young Madison had access, he began to discover for himself the resources hidden in books.

In 1767 the boy left Robertson's school to study under a new teacher, the Reverend Thomas Martin of New Jersey, who had become rector of the Brick Church in Orange County. Since there were now four Madison children of school age, Mr. Martin agreed to live at Montpelier and supervise their lessons. Under this arrangement the young minister tutored James for two years. Martin had been graduated from Princeton in the class of 1764. His praise of Nassau Hall influenced the Madisons to select it as the place to which James should go for his higher education. Their choice was also determined by the reputation

Princeton was rapidly acquiring under its new president, the famous
Dr. Witherspoon, as the most progressive college in America.

2

WHEN JAMES MADISON rode north to Princeton in the summer
of 1769, a vastly important chapter of his life began. He set out, an
eager intelligent boy, with no clear idea of what calling he would
follow or where his talents would lead him. He returned home some
three years later with his A.B. degree, a mature young man who
had fully developed the rigorous habits of thought that were to
mark him always and to make him the most scholarly of American
statesmen. At Princeton, the direction of his thinking was finally
set; his mind henceforward would be continually preoccupied with
the analysis and understanding of society and of principles of government. The Princeton years helped also to determine the goals of his
thought, and to crystallize the standards and values that were to
govern his political theorizing. At Nassau Hall he was immersed in
the liberalism of the Enlightenment, and converted to eighteenth-
century political radicalism. From then on James Madison's theories
would advance the rights and happiness of man, and his most active
efforts would serve devotedly the cause of civil and political liberty.

The twenty-three-year-old college at Princeton which Madison
entered in 1769 was dominated by its new president, Dr. Witherspoon. This learned cleric, who lived in a perpetual storm center
of ecclesiastical and political controversy, was a vigorous rather than
a profound thinker, markedly dogmatic in questions of politics, religion, and philosophy, but always dramatic and provocative in his
dogmatism. His reputation as a great teacher rests on the testimony
of a whole generation of undergraduates whose mental life was
aroused and guided by contact with him. In the case of eighteen-
year-old James Madison, Witherspoon fully satisfied the need that
most young men have in their formative years for a friend and
confidant in whom they feel both wisdom and authority. Stimulated

by Witherspoon's aggressive intellect, Madison's own mind bloomed. His joyous kindling to the new ideas and the scholarly discipline offered him at Princeton led the Virginian to carry double the normal load of classes, finishing the required four-year course in a little over two years. This necessitated, as Madison reports in his autobiography, "an indiscreet experiment of the minimum of sleep and the maximum of application which the constitution would bear. The former was reduced for some weeks to less than five hours in the twenty-four."

Madison was awarded his A.B. degree in the autumn of 1771. Then, as if to demonstrate that his accelerated program was the result of a voluntary and happy absorption in learning rather than a desire to finish his schooling quickly and return home, he insisted on staying on at Princeton for postgraduate work. During the winter of 1771–1772 he continued under Witherspoon's guidance, devoting his time to "miscellaneous studies" including some law, and "to acquiring a slight knowledge of the Hebrew, which was not among the regular College Studies."

It was, however, in the regular senior course labeled "Moral Philosophy" that Madison encountered the ideas which were to affect his life most significantly. The syllabus of Witherspoon's lectures in this course, which has been preserved with the list of recommended readings, explains the conversion of the young Virginian to the philosophy of the Enlightenment.

Because the French Revolution was a great drama, many people still think of the Enlightenment as a peculiarly French development connected primarily with the theories and ideas of such philosophes as Montesquieu, Voltaire, Diderot, and their circle. Actually the Enlightenment was international in scope. Every European nation produced its crop of philosophers. Moreover, while the Parisian salons were probably the chief center of advanced social thinking, the Scotch universities after 1750 were almost equally important in systematizing and disseminating the revolutionary ideas of the age. The great names in this sudden flowering of the Scotch intellect are David

Hume, Francis Hutcheson, Adam Smith, Thomas Reid, Lord Kames, and Adam Ferguson. Their books formed the core of the moral philosophy course at Princeton, and it was in these works treating of history, ethics, politics, economics, psychology, and jurisprudence, always from the modern and enlightened point of view, that Madison received his "very early and strong impressions in favor of Liberty both Civil & Religious."

A description of Madison's character as a statesman written in 1789 by Fisher Ames, when the Virginian was at the peak of his fame, shows how thoroughly he had assimilated at Princeton the ideals of the Scotch thinkers and how profoundly they conditioned his lifelong approach to politics. Ames, a political opponent, noted that Madison was "well-versed in public life, was bred to it, and has no other profession." Yet, Ames complained, politics "is rather a science than a business, with him." In this statement he paid unconscious tribute to the great Scotch philosophers Madison studied at college.

Hutcheson, Hume, Smith, and others among the eighteenth-century philosophers had conceived the bold and noble dream of reducing politics, economics, law, and sociology to a science. Their great model was Newton, who had demonstrated a century earlier that reason could discover the natural laws of the physical universe. Now in their turn the Scots aspired to use reason to discover the immutable laws of human nature. If the science of man and society was once established, it would allow reformers to reshape political, social, and economic institutions progressively so as to bring them into harmony with nature's divine plan and thus create a new social order which would guarantee liberty, equality, and happiness to all men. It was this vision that fascinated young Madison while he studied at Nassau Hall. It was to this dream that he dedicated his life. The scholarly treatises of Ferguson, Hume, and Kames, which Madison read in Witherspoon's course, did not appear to him as dusty academic exercises, but rather as thrilling manifestoes in a program of political and social regeneration. To him the arguments of the philosophers became the slogans of a fighting faith. If the social scientist could gain, by the study of history, sure knowledge of the anatomy of political society, he would be able to diagnose and cure its ills. This high concept of the function of the scholar-statesman was Princeton's greatest gift to James Madison. His complete acceptance of it throughout his life made him, with Franklin and Jefferson, one of the great American representatives of the Enlightenment.

Princeton also gave James Madison his first opportunity for intimacy with a congenial circle of friends. Nor was this a minor benefit. Like many diffident individuals the Virginian, throughout his life, showed a deep emotional need for affection. His manner tended toward stiffness and reserve, and he did not make friends easily. Even after he had become a famous statesman his self-confidence was not proof against the least suspicion of indifference or hostility in others. The comments of that famous Washington hostess Mrs. Margaret Bayard Smith are revealing in this connection. Writing of a visit made to Montpelier in 1828, she describes the brilliance of Madison's talk, "which was a stream of history . . . so rich in sentiments and facts, so enlivened by anecdotes and epigrammatic remarks, so frank and confidential as to opinions on men and measures, that it had an interest and charm, which the conversation of few men now living could have." Nevertheless, she adds: "This entertaining, interesting, and communicative personage, had a single stranger or indifferent person been present, would have been mute, cold and repulsive." Only a sympathetic environment could release Madison's deep capacity for friendship. Orange County had not provided such an environment in his youth. There is no record of any warm feeling toward his fellows at Robertson's school, or any evidence that his relations with his brothers and numerous cousins were particularly close. When he arrived at Princeton, however, he entered as an equal member a brilliant group of young men whose tastes and talents were similar to his own. In William Bradford, Philip Freneau, and

Hugh Henry Brackenridge—all of whom were to distinguish themselves in the arts and professions after leaving college—Madison
discovered a trio of friends he would cherish all his life.

It was with this group, the leaders of the recently organized American Whig Society, that Madison found what he termed "recreation
and release from business and books" while at Nassau Hall. With
them he took part in those "Diversions" and "Foibles" of student
life so charmingly described in the diary of Philip Fithian, who
entered college during Madison's last term. As Fithian speaks of the
undergraduate practices of "giving each other *names & characters;*
Meeting & Shoving in the dark entries; Knocking at Doors & going
off without entering; Strowing the entries in the night with greasy
Feathers; freezing the Bell; Ringing it at late Hours of the Night,"
one smiles at the conventionality through the centuries of student
mischief, in which young Madison presumably shared. We do know
certainly that he participated in another contemporary custom mentioned by Fithian: the "writing witty pointed anonymous Papers, in
*Songs, Confessions, Wills, Soliliques, Proclamations, Advertise-
ments* &c."[1] Preserved among the Bradford manuscripts in the Historical Society of Pennsylvania is a series of Whig satires in verse
on the members of the rival Cliosophic Society. Among them are
several of Madison's which indicate that, although he was a limping
poet, he had already developed the taste for ribald jokes which was

1. The remainder of Fithian's catalogue of undergraduate "Foibles" is worth
printing if only to round out the picture of student mores at Princeton in Madison's
day. Fithian continues: "Picking from the neighborhood now & then a plump fat
Hen or Turkey for the private entertainment of the Club. . . . Parading bad Women,
Burning Curse-John, Darting Sun-Beams upon the Town-People, Reconnoitering
Houses in the Town, & ogling Women with the Telescope—Making Squibs, &
other frightful compositions with Gun-Powder, & lighting them in the Rooms of
timorous Boys, & new *comers*—the various methods used in naturalizing Strangers,
of incivility in the Dining Room to make them bold; writing them sharp & threatening Letters to make them smart; leading them at first with long Lessons to make
them industrious—And trying them by Jeers and Repartee in order to make them
choose their Companions &c &c."

to scandalize a British ambassador when the Virginian was secretary of state.

3

WHEN MADISON left Princeton and returned home in 1772 he entered the unhappiest period of his life. After the exciting years at Nassau Hall, Montpelier seemed an "obscure corner" of the world and inexpressibly lonely. Madison's letters to William Bradford written at this time are almost pitiful in their nostalgia to breathe "again . . . your free air." To add to his spiritual desolation his health had finally cracked from the strain of overstudy; for a time he believed he had epilepsy and was oppressed with a morbid expectation of an early death. Then, as his strength slowly came back under a regimen that balanced reading with exercise, the problem of his future career filled him with doubts and hesitations. Madison was strongly inclined to a profession that would provide a "decent and independent" income as an alternative to plantation ownership for, from principle, he wished "to depend as little as possible on the labour of slaves." Yet the practice of law, toward which his intellectual interests pointed, required physical strength and ability in public speaking which he did not possess. His voice, like Jefferson's, was abnormally weak, and his self-assurance completely failed him in large public gatherings. So although Madison, during 1772–1773, started "a course of reading which mingled miscellaneous subjects with the studies intended to qualify him for the Bar . . . he never formed any . . . determination" to become a professional pleader. From the books he was buying for his library and from the comments in his letters to Bradford we rather see that his chief preoccupation at this time continued to be public law, or, as he described it to his friend, "the principles and modes of government [which] are too important to be disregarded by an inquisitive mind."

It was at this time, too, that James Madison first translated his enlightened principles into political practice. A group of Baptist preachers in Orange and Culpeper counties, whose growing congregations had attracted the unfriendly notice of the Anglicans, were prosecuted under the religious laws of Virginia and jailed for nonconformity. Although admitting that the "enthusiasm" of these dissenters "rendered them obnoxious to sober opinion," Madison could not stomach this denial of religious liberty. To quote his own words, he "squabbled and scolded, abused and ridiculed," first "to save them from imprisonment" and, when that failed, "to promote their release from it." This action on his part was to have an unexpected effect on his political fortunes, for, as he reports in his autobiography, "this interposition tho' a mere duty prescribed by his conscience obtained for him a lasting place in the favours of that particular sect." Consequently when the Anglican church was disestablished in Virginia and the dissenters were allowed to vote, Madison discovered that he could count on a solid bloc of Baptist supporters in his home district, no matter who ran against him, a decided advantage for a political philosopher who never became a colorful campaigner on the hustings.

The outbreak of the Revolution ended Madison's worries both over his future career and his poor health as "he entered with the prevailing zeal into the American Cause." Prevented from joining the army by "the discouraging feebleness of his constitution," he served during 1775 on the Revolutionary committee that ruled Orange County. Then in the spring of 1776, mainly through his family connections, he was chosen as a delegate to the convention whose task it was to establish a new government for Virginia. When he journeyed to Williamsburg in May 1776 and took his seat in this convention he found at last the profession for which talent and his training at Princeton had prepared him. Henceforth his life was devoted to the public service, and as one of the master builders of a new nation, he played a major part in framing the political institutions of the United States in accordance with the generous and humanistic creed of the Enlightenment.

Madison's role in the famous Virginia Convention of 1776 provides a striking example of the part political theory plays in revolutions. Every successful political revolution is to a large extent theoretical, since revolutionists faced with the hateful conditions that breed rebellion are forced to appeal from what is to what ought to be. They must attack current corrupt practices from the standpoint of an ideal system which they are struggling to establish. Theory, which etymologically means "vision," provides the new points of reference that replace the old norms; without theory to chart a visionary road into the uncertain future, revolt becomes no more than an incandescent blaze of unreasoning and destructive violence. The radical principles which directed the Virginia Convention's work of state building were set forth in the famous Declaration of Rights drawn up by George Mason. But it was James Madison who revised Mason's clause respecting religious freedom and in so doing made his first major contribution to American democracy.

Mason's theory of religious liberty originally written into the Declaration of Rights was revolutionary by eighteenth-century standards: "That religion . . . can be governed only by reason and conviction, not by force or violence; and, therefore, that all men should enjoy the fullest toleration in the exercise of religion, according to the dictates of conscience." Madison, viewing the problem on the basis of his reading at Princeton and his studies since leaving college, objected on principle to the inclusion of the word "toleration" in the Declaration of Rights, for it implied that freedom of conscience was a privilege that the state could grant or withhold as it saw fit. He viewed freedom of conscience as a *"natural and absolute* right" and hence completely outside the jurisdiction of government. So, while the delegate from Orange, "being young and in the midst of distinguished and experienced members," did not open his mouth during the debates in the convention, he did play an important part in its proceedings, for he prevailed on Mason to amend the clause on religious liberty in accordance with his own more advanced theory.

Thus, through James Madison's intervention, it was proclaimed for the first time in any body of law drawn up in a Christian commonwealth that freedom of conscience is a substantive right, a right which could only be secured by a complete separation of church and state. In 1776 this separation was still only an ideal; even in Virginia church and state were not divorced. Nevertheless the public and official acceptance of Madison's theory clearly defined the issue thenceforth for all Revolutionary America and designated the field of battle where the struggle for religious freedom would be fought. In 1786 Madison at last had the satisfaction of seeing his ideal subscribed to in its entirety by the Virginia legislature. In 1789 he himself was to embody the principle in the federal Bill of Rights. By the time he died in 1836 the complete separation of church and state had become the established norm throughout the United States.

Unfortunately for Madison his constituents did not appreciate his silent services in the Virginia Convention. When he sought election to the legislature in 1777 he was defeated. The austerity of the campaign principles which he conceived necessary to maintain the "purity" of republican government also contributed to this setback, for he refused to recommend himself to the voters in the traditional fashion by providing them with "spirituous liquors, and other treats." This defiance of custom was too shocking for the Orange voters; Madison's constituents, well plied with drinks by his opponents, attributed his "abstinence" to "pride or parsimony." While thus excluded for a time from elective office, the young Virginian still continued active in public life. In November 1777 he was appointed by the Assembly to the Virginia Council of State, whose eight members served as the governor's cabinet. He remained a member of this body until 1779, when, Thomas Jefferson being governor, he was appointed by the legislature one of the Virginia delegates to the Continental Congress, in which he served until November 1783.

Madison's six years of appointive office in the Virginia Council of State and in the Confederation Congress supplemented his theories of government with that subtle form of political wisdom that can come only from experience. As a councillor of state he came to know all the foremost Virginia leaders, and entered upon a deep and lasting friendship with that other enlightened philosopher, Thomas Jefferson. As a congressman he met and co-operated with distinguished men from other states, and grew steadily in awareness of the common interests shared by all thirteen.

Gradually Madison came to take a leading part in the congressional business relating to finances, national defense, trade, western lands, and international relations. Theory and experience now went hand in hand. Though his auditors still agreed that "he speaks low, his person is little and ordinary," nevertheless as they marked him in action they found that his "sense, reading, address, and integrity" made him remarkably persuasive. "His language is very pure, perspicuous, and to the point. . . . He states a principle and deduces consequences, with clearness and simplicity." Above all, his fellow statesmen were struck by his scholarly industry and marvelous grasp of fact; "he is a studious man, devoted to public business, and a thorough master of every public question that can arise, or he will spare no pains to become so, if he happens to be in want of information." It is no wonder then that on the termination of his service in Congress, James Madison returned to Virginia with a national reputation as "one of the ablest Members that ever sat in that Council."

During these years in Congress he became more than a Virginia statesman, representing as he did a national point of view that transcended class and sectional interests. Madison had entered politics with a less provincial attitude than most of his contemporaries. Now, taught by his years in congressional service, he became with Washington the most continental-minded of all the Virginia leaders. By the nature of his associations and work at Philadelphia he had been under tremendous pressure to think in national terms concerning the general welfare. When he returned home in 1783 the young statesman had gained a mature perspective which identified the cause of the American Union with the cause of liberty throughout the world.

4

MADISON'S RETURN to private life was brief. In 1784 he was elected to the Virginia House of Delegates and at once became the leader of the radical party in the place of Jefferson, who had been appointed American minister to France. During the next three years he was instrumental in finally disestablishing the Anglican church, enacting a large portion of Jefferson's revised code of laws, and strengthening the basis of state finances. Moreover, while strenuously working to make his own state a model of enlightened administration, he was increasingly aware of the larger problems confronting the nation. During these years in the Virginia legislature he steadily urged that the powers of the Confederation be strengthened. It was largely on his initiative that Virginia participated in the series of interstate conferences that led ultimately to the Philadelphia Convention of 1787.

The Convention of 1787 provided the Princeton-trained political philosopher with the opportunity of rendering his greatest service to his country. In recognition of Madison's role in the Philadelphia meeting historians have named him "the father of the Constitution." By 1787 the Confederation had declined into impotence; government credit was desperate; Congress, unable to maintain order or even to protect itself, was powerless in the face of treaty violation and foreign commercial discrimination. As the powers of Congress declined, the center of political gravity shifted to the states, which soon were engaged in a series of bitter local rivalries. Inside each of these petty sovereignties, postwar depression and deflation touched off virulent class struggles between debtors and creditors as each group strove to control the state machinery in order to protect its own economic interests. In one quarter ominous voices were heard to declare that America was geographically too large and too heterogeneous to continue under a single government; while in another it was openly stated, for the first time since 1776, that the only cure for the ills of the new nation was to liquidate the republican experiment and establish an American monarchy. It seemed to thoughtful Americans in every section that the Union, which had been the instrument of victory in winning political liberty from England, was doomed to dissolve under the tensions of postwar disagreement. Against this background of economic distress, sectional quarrels, class conflict, and ideological confusion, the Convention called to reform the Confederation met at Philadelphia in May 1787.

Long before he journeyed to Philadelphia, Madison had become convinced that the fate of republican government in America and hence throughout the world hung in the balance. As early as 1785 he had begun to warn his fellow citizens that unless the Union was strengthened there would be a competitive system of jealous sovereign states, involving "an appeal to the sword in every petty squabble, standing armies, and perpetual taxes." Internal weakness would make the disunited states "the sport of foreign politics," threaten the very existence of liberty, and "blast the glory of the Revolution." In view of the decay of the Confederation, Madison had already taken steps to approach the problem scientifically. Since Jefferson in Paris had access to the book stalls of all Europe, Madison recruited his aid in building up an extensive collection of "treatises on the ancient or modern Federal Republics." In preparation for the Philadelphia meeting he was therefore able to study in his own library the structure and principles of all the confederations described in history. The result embodied in two memoranda, entitled respectively "Notes of Ancient and Modern Confederacies" and "Vices of the Political System of the United States," is probably the most fruitful piece of scholarly research ever carried out by an American.

Madison's reading of the accounts of historic confederations, such as the Lycian League, Amphictyonic Council, the United Netherlands, was discouraging; as precedents they furnished "no other light than that of beacons, which gave warnings of the course to be shunned, without pointing out that which ought to be pursued." His studies confirmed his belief, steadily growing as he watched the American Confederation totter toward "imbecility," that it would be impossible to establish a stable federal system based on any principles tried in the past. Madison's reading underlined a further point. Never in all the history of the world had it been possible to organize a republican state in a territory as vast as America; never in the past had it been possible to frame a popular government for a population of such heterogeneous elements as those inhabiting the United States. As he discovered in his books, and as Alexander Hamilton was later to argue in the Convention, all political theorists agreed that a stable republic promoting the general welfare of a varied population could be established only in a small country. Stable empires of vast extent had been organized in the past, but they had all been held together from above by the power of a king.

It is James Madison's greatest glory as a philosopher-statesman that he accepted the challenge of the impossible. He transcended the impossible by inventing a completely new type of federal state, which while solidly resting on majority rule at the same time provided adequate safeguards for the rights of minority groups. From his reading and experience he evolved an original theory of republican federalism differing completely from the principles of any of the historic confederations. A full month before the Convention met he had elaborated his novel scheme in his memoranda and in letters to Jefferson, Randolph, and Washington. He had also commenced work on the blueprint of a governmental structure that would institutional-ize this theory. It was a brilliant intellectual achievement which won for the thirty-five-year-old Madison the right to be called the philosopher of the American Constitution. His theory, embodied in the structure of the American Union, was to prove also the greatest triumph in practical application of the Enlightenment's ideal of scientific political research.

The story of Madison's labors to get his theory elaborated into the document known as the United States Constitution is too familiar to be detailed here. The Virginian played a decisive part in every phase of constitutional creation. On the basis of his theory, which he submitted to Washington's careful inspection, he was able to persuade the general that the Convention was not doomed to impotence before it opened and that he should attend as a delegate. Washington's prestige, both at Philadelphia and during the struggle for ratification, proved of major significance in the outcome. It was Madison's theory too that provided the basis of the Virginia Plan which, after it was worked over by the assembled delegates for nearly four months, emerged as the new constitution. During the long summer days in the Convention, Madison, in the words of a fellow delegate, "took the lead in the management of every great question"; one of three debaters who were heard most frequently, he spoke from the floor 161 times. Whether in committee or in open session it was reported that "he always comes forward the best informed man on any point in debate. The affairs of the United States, he perhaps, has the most correct knowledge of, of any Man in the Union." Finally, marvelous to relate, it was James Madison, "the profound politician" blended "with the scholar," who somehow managed to find the extra energy necessary to write out daily a meticulous report of all the debates in the Convention. Although this exacting task almost killed him, as he later admitted, still he was determined that future political philosophers should have the "Debates" as scientific data requisite to carry forward the study of republican government.

Madison's labors for the Constitution did not end with the adjournment of the Convention. Almost at once the long bitter struggle to secure ratification began. During the winter of 1787–1788 the Virginian collaborated with Alexander Hamilton and John Jay in writing *The Federalist,* the classic exposition of the Constitution and the most important American contribution to the world's political literature. In the spring of 1788, elected a member of the Virginia ratifying convention, he acted as leader of the pro-Constitution party and matched himself against the great Patrick Henry, who was chief of the opposition. Until the final vote was taken the issue hung in doubt, and with it the question of whether the Constitution would be given a trial. Virginia being both the largest and the most populous of the thirteen states, her rejection would have proved fatal to the plan. In the most dramatic episode of his career, Madison faced the fiery, passionate oratory of Henry and smothered it with his quiet, lucid reasoning. When the final vote was taken, the logic of Madison and the Constitutional party had caused eight members of the opposition to disregard the express wishes of their constituents, and two more to vote contrary to specific instructions. As a result the Constitution was approved by the narrow margin of 10 out of 168 votes.

5

ALTHOUGH the new Constitution was finally ratified in 1788, it was still merely a blueprint; the task remained of transforming its paper provisions into the institutions of a functioning government. To this delicate operation the first Congress addressed itself. Madison almost missed sharing in this labor: Patrick Henry's hatred first blocked his election to the new Senate and then attempted to prevent his choice as a member of the House. Luckily for Madison his loyal Baptist supporters remembered their ancient debt and backed him solidly; and so in 1789 he began the first of his four terms as a Virginia representative in Congress. From the day he took his seat he was the leading member of the lower house. There was no act of legislative business during the first session in which he did not participate with his customary erudition. He sponsored the first ten amendments to the Constitution, which make up the federal Bill of Rights, introduced the first revenue bill, helped organize the executive department, and acted as President Washington's congressional adviser and ghost writer. It was a strenuous period full of "delays and perplexities" arising in large part from the complete "want of precedents." Many times Madison felt that "we are in a wilderness, without a single footstep to guide us." Yet the task was accomplished. By the end of the first session of the first Congress, "the more perfect union" had successfully made the transition from paper to practice.

Before the new government had been in operation a year, Madison became deeply disturbed over the trend of events in the national capital. In his view, the trouble lay in the activities and policies of Alexander Hamilton, secretary of the Treasury. To the New Yorker no federal scheme could provide a sufficiently centralized authority to subsist in so large a country; and even worse was "the disease" of democracy which afflicted America. Hamilton, therefore, seized the opportunity during the formative stage of the new government to "administer" it—the term is Madison's—so that it would more closely approach his ideal of a consolidated oligarchy. With devious brilliance, Hamilton set out, by a program of class legislation, to unite the propertied interests of the eastern seaboard into a cohesive administration party, while at the same time he attempted to make the executive dominant over the Congress by a lavish use of the spoils system. In carrying out his scheme, though he personally was above corruption, Hamilton transformed every financial transaction of the Treasury Department into an orgy of speculation and graft in which selected senators, congressmen, and certain of their richer constituents throughout the nation participated. As Madison watched Hamilton's program develop, he became disillusioned and bitter. In the Convention he had fought to create a Constitution under which "the interests and rights of every class of citizens should be duly represented and understood." Now he saw the machinery of his new government being used to exploit the mass of the people in the interest of a small minority.

Before the end of the first Congress, Madison, therefore, began to attack the Hamiltonian program as "unconstitutional" no less than antirepublican. In so doing, he probably saved the Constitution from being abrogated by the rising mass of injured citizens, and guaranteed that the American experiment in democratic government should continue on a national basis.

Hamilton's system of class government, while brilliantly successful in enlisting the loyalty of "the rich, the wise, and the well born" for the Constitution, in truth contained a major threat to American nationalism. During the struggle for ratification, a majority of the people had opposed the Constitution as containing a potential threat to their liberties. Living in an almost self-sufficient agrarian economy, they were content with the security provided by the system of independent states and saw little need for a stronger union. This majority was still deeply suspicious of the national government at its birth in 1789. Every device that Hamilton used to win the loyalty of the propertied elite tended to confirm the suspicions of the yeoman farmers and middle-class groups and to erode their faith in the new government.

Not the least of James Madison's services to American nationalism was to put himself at the head of this potentially dangerous opposition and thus guarantee that it would remain loyal to the Union. Thomas Jefferson was to prove the great organizer and symbol of the anti-Hamiltonians; but Madison had already formulated the principles of the opposition before Jefferson assumed the role of party chief. In speeches, letters, and a series of essays contributed to the newspaper edited by his fellow Princetonian, Philip Freneau, "the father of the Constitution" stressed again and yet again that it was not the federal Union that was at fault but the individuals at its head. The Constitution itself was sound; the evil lay in Hamilton's perverted "interpretation" of the document.

Thus, an aroused party which might well have developed revolutionary tendencies was marshaled by Madison under the banner of a higher loyalty and a stricter veneration of the Constitution. Once again the Virginia theorist and political philosopher had played a decisive part in fixing the pattern of future political behavior in America. Following Madison's lead, discontented groups in the

United States, even though out of power, have traditionally looked to the Constitution for the protection of their rights, and thus has been maintained that amazing balance between stability and change which has characterized our national existence. Certainly, this developed pattern of loyal opposition made the election of Thomas Jefferson and the reversal of national policies in 1800 a coup which, although "revolutionary," was still strictly constitutional.

During Jefferson's two terms as president, Madison served officially as his secretary of state and unofficially as his dearest friend and most trusted adviser. Since the president was a widower, it also came about that Madison's wife, the famous and attractive Dolly, whom he had married in his forty-fifth year, became the official hostess for the administration. As secretary of state, James Madison shared fully in the two great triumphs of Jefferson's first term: the program of domestic reform that finally identified the Union as a people's government and the Louisiana Purchase, which extended the bounds of the republican experiment clear to the Pacific. In like manner, Madison was a leader in the unsuccessful attempt during Jefferson's second administration to develop through the Embargo a system of economic sanctions to replace the use of force in our foreign relations. In 1808, through Jefferson's influence, Madison was chosen to succeed him as president.

6

As CHIEF EXECUTIVE, James Madison added few laurels to his reputation. He inherited from his predecessor the insoluble problem of preserving American neutrality in the midst of the titanic struggle between England and Napoleon. Before the beginning of his second administration the Virginian had become convinced that there was no alternative to war against England, if the United States was to maintain its maritime rights and its economic independence. Unfortunately, the talents of the philosopher-statesman were designed for peace rather than war; after the opening of hostilities Madison's inadequacies as a military chieftain soon became apparent. Throughout the conflict, he was hampered in exerting executive leadership by his theory that Congress should take the initiative in determining policy.

As it turned out, the United States was fortunate to emerge from the struggle territorially intact. Not a single American war aim was achieved; Washington was captured, and the president was forced to flee to the Virginia woods for safety; only the unexpected victories of the final months of the conflict—at Baltimore, Plattsburg, New Orleans—allowed his contemporaries to set down "Mr. Madison's War" as an American triumph. Yet the sentiment of national unity, which Madison had labored so long to inculcate by rational appeal, flowered under the irrational emotions released by the war, and the last remnants of antirepublicanism were swept away in the flood of patriotic pride. Soon after the treaty of peace, James Madison's presidential term ended and put a period to his forty years of public service.

After his retirement to Montpelier, Madison "devoted himself to his farm and his books, with much avocation, however, from both by an extensive and often laborious correspondence which seems to be entailed on Ex-Presidents." A large part of his time was spent in arranging his letters and editing for the enlightenment of posterity the carefully preserved "Notes" on the debates in the Constitutional Convention. He was closely associated with Jefferson in the founding of the University of Virginia and became its rector after Jefferson's death in 1826. When he had almost reached his eightieth birthday he reluctantly served as a member, but took no important part, in the Virginia Constitutional Convention of 1829. It was about this time that he dictated his short autobiography, nearly a fifth of which deals with his happy years at Princeton.

As Madison grew older, he withdrew as far as possible from politics. When pressed in 1830 for his opinion on a current controversial topic he wrote: "A man whose years have but reached the canonical three-score-and-ten . . . should distrust himself, whether distrusted by his friends or not, and should never forget that his arguments, whatever they may be, will be answered by allusions to the date of his birth." Yet, on the two issues of slavery and states' rights which were eventually to threaten the existence of his beloved Union, his principles forced him to break his silence. Until his death, he lent his active support to the African Colonization Society from an awareness that the "dreadful calamity" of Negro bondage was incompatible with the republican principles of liberty and equality. On one other subject also he would not hold his peace. When the South Carolinians, during the tariff controversy, tried to use his name and Jefferson's to support their doctrines of nullification and secession, he repeatedly and publicly denounced their position as constitutional heresy.

James Madison lived on peacefully to the age of eighty-six, deeply happy in his marriage, still full of "inexhaustible faith" in the future of the great democratic commonwealth he had done so much to establish. On the morning of June 28, 1836, he died quietly in his easy chair. It is reported that even his slaves wept when he was buried in the Montpelier graveyard.

7

WAS ALEXANDER HAMILTON
A CHRISTIAN STATESMAN?

One of the liveliest items in Adair's superb Hamilton bicentennial issue of the *Quarterly*, this was a collaborative effort with Marvin Harvey, a young graduate student at the University of Washington. Originating as a seminar paper on the assigned topic of Hamilton and religion, the essay was the product of Harvey's basic research and rough draft before meeting with the typically thorough editorial attention of Adair. Harvey notes that Adair rewrote sections as well as added and inserted material to the extent that the result was indeed a jointly written essay.

It was shortly after seven when the two duelists stood to their stations in the wooded clearing high above the river. At the word "Present," two reports rang out, one shortly behind the other; and the shorter of the antagonists, rising convulsively on tiptoe, staggered a little to the left and fell headlong upon his face. As the surgeon hastily examined the gaping hole in his right side, the wounded man had just strength to gasp before fainting, "This is a mortal wound, Doctor." The doctor agreed, but there might possibly be a chance to save him if he was taken back to the city at once. With the help of the boatman who had brought the party to the field, the

SOURCE: Reprinted by permission of Marvin Harvey and the *William and Mary Quarterly*, 3d Ser., XII (1955), 308–329.

unconscious figure was carried down the steep path, put aboard the barge, and rowed swiftly across the river to New York City. Once on the water, the fresh air and the doctor's liberal application of the spirits of hartshorne rubbed on his face, lips, and temples brought the dying man again to consciousness, although he complained that his vision was indistinct. By the time the New York shore was reached, he appeared tranquil and composed, although he was clearly in terrible pain as he was carried from the wharf to the nearby house of a friend on Jane Street. At his request his wife was sent for; and the doctor, although he did not now have a shadow of a hope of his recovery, asked that Dr. Post, as well as the surgeons of the French frigates in the harbor, who had had much experience in gunshot wounds, come as quickly as possible for consultation.

And fast as a spreading brush fire, the news went through New York City that Colonel Burr had shot General Hamilton in a duel—that Hamilton was dying—was already lying dead in Mr. Bayard's house at Greenwich.

But Hamilton did not die at once. In ghastly pain, despite Doctor Hosack's massive doses of laudanum, he begged, as soon as the first messenger hastened off for his wife, that another messenger be sent to bring Bishop Moore to him at once. Bishop Moore, the rector of Trinity Episcopal Church and bishop of New York, was a personal friend of Hamilton's. When the bishop arrived, Hamilton spoke from his bed: "It is my desire to receive the Communion at your hands. I hope you will not conceive there is any impropriety in my request. It has for some time past been the wish of my heart, and it was my intention to take an early opportunity of uniting myself to the church, by the reception of that holy ordinance."

Sadly, reluctantly, the bishop refused. Both his priestly office and his Christian beliefs made it incumbent on Moore to condemn dueling; moreover, while recognizing and welcoming sincere death-bed conversion, his church holds it to be its duty to take especial care that such conversions do indeed represent a new spiritual birth.

Therefore the bishop, conceiving it "right and proper to avoid every appearance of precipitancy in performing one of the most solemn offices of our religion," refused Hamilton the Communion, comforted him as best he could, and took his leave.

But the dying man would not be satisfied. Another messenger rushed off posthaste to another clerical friend of Hamilton's, the Reverend Dr. John Mason, a Presbyterian. But again, when Mason arrived, the desperate plea for the sacrament was turned down, Mason explaining that it was strictly forbidden by his sect "to administer the Lord's Supper privately to any person under any circumstances." And again the priest did what he could to comfort the wounded man with prayers and texts from the Scripture, reassuring Hamilton by reminding him that Communion is merely "an exhibition and pledge of the mercies" of Christ, and that sincere faith made this mercy accessible without the pledge. "I am aware of that," the dying man told Mason. "It is only as a sign that I wanted it." But there was nothing Mason could do, and after a time he left.

While the two priests were interviewing Hamilton and denying his request, one of his closest friends was anxiously waiting in the next room to get exact news of his condition and to offer his sympathy and aid. Deciding to delay his trip home so that he would be available if there was anything he could do to help Hamilton's family, Oliver Wolcott dashed off a note to his wife in Connecticut, explaining why he would be late returning from New York:

"I had prepared to set out to see you tomorrow morning, but an afflicting event has just occurred which renders it proper for me to postpone my journey a few days. This morning my friend Hamilton was wounded, and as is supposed mortally in a duel with Colo. Burr. . . .

"I have just returned from Mr. Wm. Bayards—where Hamilton is—I did not see him—he suffers great pain—which he endures like a Hero—Mrs. Hamilton is with him, but she is ignorant of the cause of his Illness, which she supposes to be spasms—no one dare tell her the truth—it is feared she would become frantic. . . .

"Genl. Hamilton has of late years expressed his conviction of the truths of the Christian Religion, and has desired to receive the Sacrament—but no one of the Clergy who have yet been consulted will administer it.

"Whilst there is life there is Hope, but that is all which can be said. Thus has perished one of the greatest men of this or any age. . . .

"Kiss the children and believe me Affectionately yours, Oliv. Wolcott."[1] *Meanwhile in the death room at Mr. Bayard's the minutes dragged on. Hamilton's time was running out.*

THIS LAST pitiable scene of Alexander Hamilton's life, ignored by most of his biographers, raises a number of questions that are too important to pass over. Why had not Hamilton joined some church before 1804? For years previous to his death he had been a self-proclaimed champion of Christianity, attacking the French Revolution and his American political opponents—"the American Jacobins"—as atheistic. What does "atheistic" signify in the mouth of a man who has scruples about membership in the church visible? Was Hamilton, before he died, a Christian statesman?

Here, again, the honest scholar must say there is no way at this time to answer these questions satisfactorily. Until all of Hamilton's writings have been collected and printed, until a really incisive study of the development of his mind and personality has been published, we must rest content with admissions that he is a puzzling figure and that his religious convictions are especially puzzling. The follow-

1. The detailed story of Hamilton's last hours on earth can be found in William Coleman, *A Collection of the Facts and Documents, relative to the Death of Major-General Alexander Hamilton; With Comments: Together with the various Orations, Sermons, and Eulogies, that have been Published or Written on his Life and Character* (New York, 1804) reprinted, Boston, 1904, in a limited edition of 400 copies. The accounts of Dr. Hosack (who was present at the duel), of Bishop Moore, and Dr. Mason, that have been used in reconstructing the deathbed scene are printed on 19–23, 50–57. Oliver Wolcott's letter to his wife is published in Allan McLane Hamilton, *The Intimate Life of Alexander Hamilton, Based Chiefly upon Original Family Letters and Other Documents* . . . (New York, 1910), 405–407.

ing note, then, merely defines the area where future study of Hamilton's thought and actions is insistently called for; it offers only a very tentative statement of what appear to be four distinct stages in his religious development.

The study of any man's religion in any period of history is infinitely difficult and hazardous. It is especially difficult if the subject of study lives, as Hamilton did, in an age when the very foundations of religious thought and practice are shaking and shifting under a continuing series of seismographic shocks. The general difficulty of the research problem appears in the very etymology of the word "religion" itself (variously given as *religere:* to execute painstakingly by repeated effort; or *religare:* to bind together, by the invisible bond of belief), with its reminder that religious experience is dualistic—that to talk of Hamilton's religion is to embark on a double exploration. On the one hand, religion is a man's private, personal, hidden psychic life: a subjective, continuing experience which determines that each individual will worship, thank, call on, and praise God with the unique voice of his own soul. On the other hand, religion is the overt performance of certain human activities: it is behavior in the external realm. In our civilization this behavior pattern has traditionally been, at least in part, collectivistic, a group activity. From this second perspective, according to the dogmas of certain Christian sects, Hamilton could not have been a Christian on July 11, 1804, because he was not formally affiliated with the church visible.

It is necessary to underline this dualism in religion for purposes of historical analysis, but it is necessary chiefly because it is an *unreal* dualism. For the overt, external, public "religious" behavior of any man is organically rooted in his hidden psychic experience. Thus an individual's public life is a barometer showing to some degree the intensity and the pattern of the secret inner life. The Episcopal church which Hamilton tried to join recognizes just this dualistic but unitary aspect of Christian living in its Prayer of General Thanksgiving: "And, we beseech thee, give us that due sense of all thy mercies, that our hearts may be unfeignedly thankful; and that we show forth thy praise, not only with our lips, but in our lives. . . ."

If this inner-outer relationship is the great general problem in analyzing Hamilton's career as a Christian statesman, there is another and more particular difficulty connected with the historical problem of "deism"—a problem which makes the definition of "Christian" extremely tricky in the eighteenth century. The period between the early seventeenth century and the nineteenth century is the great watershed in the modern history of religious life and belief. It is the period which saw traditional Christian thought brought into line with new scientific knowledge in the realms of astronomy, biology, and history. It is the era which saw traditional church-state relations shift with revolutionary violence, and the emergence of a new separated pattern of religious *and* political loyalty. The new cosmology, the new faith in the reasoning power of man, the rise of humanitarianism, and the growth of a spirit of secularism all combined to create a new image of deity and to produce powerful ethical and philosophical criticism of the traditional practice of Christianity, particularly as exemplified in the behavior of the existing Christian churches.

This critical attitude, called deism, never produced an organized sect; but, reaching its climax in the last half of the eighteenth century, it affected the religious thought or behavior of practically every educated man in the Atlantic civilization of which the young United States was a part. There were deists who remained orthodox enough to become bishops, and deists who reasoned themselves into radical skepticism and atheism. A deist like Voltaire could end as an enemy of Christianity; but Priestley's deism merely led him to Unitarianism. John Adams, Benjamin Franklin, Thomas Jefferson, and James Madison ended up Unitarians like Priestley, in strong revolt against the orthodox doctrines of the churches into which they were baptized. George Washington, in contrast, always remained a nominal Episcopalian. He attended church more or less regularly, served as vestryman in his parish, and recognized the value of chaplains for army discipline; but he seems to have studiously avoided mentioning the name of Jesus in any public speech or proclamation, and he conscientiously avoided kneeling in public prayer or in taking Communion.

Thus the age in which Hamilton lived, with its revolutionary debate over what was God's and what was Caesar's, its revolutionary shifts in religious thought, and its disruption of traditional sectarian behavior patterns, poses difficulties of a special nature in defining "Christian" and in exploring an individual's religious life. In every age there is some truth in the statement "the nearer to the Church the farther from God"; and Jesus' own comments on the Pharisees remind us that even anticlericalism can claim for itself Christian authority. Thus we must recognize from the beginning that Hamilton's failure to affiliate with any Christian sect during his active life is not in itself evidence of lack of piety. It is against this background that our scattered and fragmentary information on what appear to be four distinct phases of Alexander Hamilton's religious life must be viewed.

There is much persuasive evidence that the young Hamilton who landed in America seeking his fortune in 1773 was conventionally religious, but there is little evidence to show any great depth or intensity of religious feeling. Hamilton's patron and guide in the West Indies was Dr. Hugh Knox, a devout Presbyterian clergyman; the men to whom Hamilton was recommended on the mainland and who became his closest advisers on his arrival, Elias Boudinot and William Livingston, were devout Presbyterian laymen. None of these men would have backed a youth who showed signs of religious heterodoxy. Furthermore, we have specific evidence of Hamilton's practice of piety in these early years. A poem addressed to the Boudinots, with whom he boarded for a year, on the death of their young daughter, is orthodox in its treatment of immortality.[2] And his college

2. George Adams Boyd, *Elias Boudinot, Patriot and Statesman, 1740–1821* (Princeton, N.J., 1953), 23–24, prints these banal verses. Broadus Mitchell, "The

roommate, Robert Troup, describes his attentiveness to public worship and his "habit of praying upon his knees both night and morning"—a habit Troup testifies Hamilton still kept up during the first months of his military service.[3]

Troup also recalled that in college Hamilton "had read most of the polemical writers on religious subjects; and he was a zealous believer in the fundamental doctrines of Christianity; and, I confess, that the arguments with which he was accustomed to justify his belief, have tended, in no small degree, to confirm my own faith in revealed religion."[4] Nevertheless there is no evidence that Hamilton affiliated with either the Presbyterian or the Anglican church, in both of which sects he had close friends.[5] Perhaps, indeed, this pull

---

Secret of Alexander Hamilton," *Virginia Quarterly Review*, XXXIX (1953), 599, remarks that no one could have lived for a year under the roof of the pious Boudinot without kneeling regularly in prayer, or, by reaction, becoming a confirmed atheist.

3. Nathan Schachner, ed., "Alexander Hamilton Viewed by His Friends: The Narratives of Robert Troup and Hercules Mulligan," *William and Mary Quarterly*, 3d Ser., IV (1947), 213.

4. *Ibid.*

5. The young Hamilton's earliest friends and patrons on the mainland were naturally Presbyterian friends and connections of the Reverend Hugh Knox. Beside Boudinot, these included Francis Barber, instructor in the Elizabethtown Academy and graduate of the College of New Jersey; James Caldwell, pastor of the Presbyterian Church with which the academy was connected; and Richard Stockton, trustee of Princeton and Boudinot's brother-in-law. Boyd, *Boudinot*, 20. Hamilton originally planned to enter Princeton, but having been refused permission to take an accelerated course, he switched to King's College. Francis L. Broderick, "Pulpit, Physics, and Politics: The Curriculum of the College of New Jersey, 1746–1794," *WMQ*, 3d Ser., VI (1949), 53. Again he carried letters from his Presbyterian patrons to Presbyterians in New York City, among them the Reverend John Rogers and the Reverend John Mason, the father of the Reverend John Mitchell who refused Hamilton the sacrament, July 11, 1804. Once enrolled in Anglican King's College, Hamilton became a close friend of scores of Episcopalians. Troup and Mulligan, early college friends, later served as wardens and vestrymen of Trinity Church, along with other intimate personal and professional friends like John Jay, Rufus King, William Duer, James Duane, and Richard Harison. William Berrian, *An Historical Sketch of Trinity Church, New-York* (New York, 1847), 162, 360. After he became famous as a lawyer, Hamilton gratuitously handled Trinity's legal business, although not a member of the congregation. *Ibid.*, 188–189.

of competing sectarian loyalties may have made him hesitate about making any final choice of church membership at this time.

THE NEXT STAGE in Hamilton's life seems to have been a fifteen-year period of complete religious indifference. This period lasts roughly from 1777 to 1792, a time in which the unknown young immigrant shot up like a skyrocket, first winning military fame and then rising farther to dazzle the whole country with his dominance of the newly established national government. However, there is nothing in Hamilton's published letters during this era of fantastic personal success to indicate that he was emotionally or intellectually concerned with God, the Church, or any religious problems whatsoever. Indeed, this lapse into complete indifference as he reaches maturity suggests that his earlier manifestation of public piety was little more than the skin-deep and conventional religious behavior inculcated in his youth. One suspects, too, a strong element of opportunism in the early display of conventional orthodoxy. Hamilton was probably paying his devout patrons for his college education with spiritual coin of less than sterling value.

The only known mention of God or religion in the published writings of Hamilton during the Revolution is contained in two letters of 1779–1780. To Anthony Wayne he wrote: "Dr. W. Mendy is one of those characters that for its honesty, simplicity, and helplessness interests my humanity. He is exceedingly anxious to be in the service. . . . He is just what I should like for a military parson except that he does not whore or drink. He will fight and he will not insist upon your going to heaven whether you will or not. . . . Pray take care of the good old man."[6]

Six months earlier, in the same facetious vein, Hamilton had

6. Hamilton to Anthony Wayne, July 6, 1780, quoted in Nathan Schachner, *Alexander Hamilton* (New York, 1946), 93, from a MS copy in the New York Public Library. A bowdlerized version, omitting the words "whore or," is in Henry Cabot Lodge, ed., *The Works of Alexander Hamilton* (New York, 1904), IX, 200–201.

written to John Laurens listing the ideal qualifications of the wife that Laurens was to find for him in Carolina: "Take her description—she must be young, handsome (I lay most stress upon a good shape), sensible (a little learning will do), well bred (but she must have an aversion to the word *ton*), chaste, and tender (I am an enthusiast in my notions of fidelity and fondness), of some good nature, a great deal of generosity (she must neither love money nor scolding, for I dislike equally a termagant and an economist). In politics I am indifferent what side she may be of. I think I have arguments that will easily convert her to mine. As to religion a moderate stock will satisfy me. She must believe in God and hate a saint."[7] Also to these years are attributed the two wisecracks about God made at the time of the Constitutional Convention.[8]

It is during this period of religious indifference that Hamilton

---

7. Hamilton to John Laurens, Dec. 1779, Lodge, ed., *Works of Hamilton*, IX, 186–187. Hamilton ends the catalogue, "But as to fortune, the larger stock of that the better. . . . Do I want a wife? No. I have plagues enough without desiring to add to the number that greatest of all. . . ."

8. The first story alleges that when Hamilton returned from the Convention in 1787, he was pointedly asked by his old friend, Dr. John Rogers of the Wall Street Presbyterian Church, why God had not been suitably recognized in the Constitution. "Indeed, Doctor," Hamilton is supposed to have replied, "we forgot it." Isaac A. Cornelison, *The Relationship of Religion to the Civil Government, in the United States of America: A State without a Church, but Not without a Religion* (New York, 1895), 204. The second story, widely circulated in the 1820s and 1830s on the authority of Jonathan Dayton, member of the Convention from New Jersey, recounts Hamilton's purported remark on the Convention floor, when Franklin moved that each session in the future be opened with prayer. Hamilton is supposed to have replied that there was no need for calling in "foreign aid." Max Farrand, ed., *The Records of the Federal Convention of 1787* (New Haven, Conn., 1911–1937), III, 467. When directly questioned about this supposed remark of Hamilton's, Madison denied that there was any irreverence shown Franklin's suggestion, insisting that all members treated the motion with the "respect due it." *Ibid.*, 531. Madison pointedly did not commit himself to the larger point of whether the remark was characteristic of Hamilton's attitude in 1787, or whether the remark was made out of doors after the Convention adjourned for the day. The persistence of the anecdote, as well as the parallel Rogers story attributed to the same period, suggests that Hamilton did make some wisecracks about God and the Constitution in 1787.

married Betsy Schuyler, who, ironically, with her great wealth and high connections, her good figure and tender generosity, did also exhibit enough evidence of religious devoutness to be nicknamed the "Saint."[9] A staunch member of the Dutch Reformed Church, Betsy both before and after her marriage was assiduous in the practices of piety. Hamilton's marriage to her, however, did not lead him to join her church after the fashion of many indifferent husbands with devout wives.

THE THIRD STAGE of Hamilton's religious development is ushered in by the French Revolution and the revolutionaries' attacks on established religion. Although he is no longer indifferent, this period in his life hardly deserves to be praised as an era of Christian thought and practice. Rather, it is a stage of opportunistic religiosity in which Hamilton, forgetting Christ's distinctions between those things which are God's and those which are Caesar's, attempted to enlist God in the Federalist party to buttress that party's temporal power.[10]

9. See letter of Tench Tilghman to his brother William ironically referring to her as "the little Saint," in contrast to a more complaisant female friend of Hamilton's named Polly, quoted in Schachner, *Hamilton*, 108.

10. See for example the proposal to William L. Smith, Apr. 10, 1797, that, besides "vigorous preparation for war," Congress should also mobilize "the religious ideas" of Americans. "In addition to these [war measures] it may be proper by some religious solemnity to impress seriously the minds of the people. . . . A politician will consider this as an important means of influencing opinion, and will think it a valuable resource in a contest with France to set the religious ideas of his countrymen in active competition with the atheistical tenets of their enemies. This is an advantage which we shall be very unskilled if we do not use to the utmost. And the impulse can not be too early given. I am persuaded a day of humiliation and prayer, beside being very proper, would be extremely useful." William L. Smith Papers, Library of Congress. Lodge prints part of Hamilton's letter to Smith, but suppresses this paragraph. *Works of Hamilton*, X, 256. For Hamilton's own technique of utilizing religion in his warmongering against France and against his American opposition a year later at the time of the XYZ Affair, see his third essay, signed Titus Manlius, of "The Stand" (Apr. 1798), with its dreadful proofs that the French Revolution and the American admirers of France were engaged in "a conspiracy to establish atheism on the ruins of Christianity." *Ibid.*, VI, 275–277, 310–311, 317–318. For the use of religious smears against Jefferson in 1800, see Charles O. Lerche,

Unfortunately Hamilton's blasphemous attempts to use God for his all-too-human ends were extremely successful with large numbers of the clergy. Ironically, it is his insistence during these years, in tirade after tirade, that "democracy" and "Christianity" were incompatible, that Jefferson, "the atheist," was God's enemy, that has left a simple-minded American posterity with the false impression that Hamilton throughout his life was a devout Christian in both thought and practice. Actually it is during these years when religious slogans were so often on his lips that Hamilton seems farther from God and from any understanding of his Son, Jesus Christ, than at any time in his whole career. Nevertheless, the man who was attempting with all his energy to mobilize all the churches as "engines" in politics was still unwilling formally to associate himself with any church.[11] Fortified by his own ecstatic vision of self-righteous virtue,[12] Hamil-

---

"Jefferson and the Election of 1800: A Case Study in the Political Smear," *WMQ*, 3d Ser., V (1948), 467–491.

11. In 1776 Hamilton wrote down the following maxim for his commonplace book: "He (Numa) was a wise prince, and went a great way in civilizing the Romans. The chief engine he employed for this purpose was religion, which could alone have sufficient empire over the minds of a barbarous and warlike people to engage them to cultivate the arts of peace." Hamilton's summary paraphrase of Plutarch's *Life of Numa Pompilius*, written in his military paybook during the summer of 1776; see John C. Hamilton, ed., *The Works of Alexander Hamilton; Comprising His Correspondence, And His Political And Official Writings . . .* (New York, 1850–1851), I, 6.

12. Probably the most disconcerting and startling expressions of self-righteousness in all American political literature are to be found in Hamilton's "Reynolds pamphlet" of 1797. Hamilton insists that since the attacks on him by his enemies represent "a conspiracy of vice against virtue, ought I not rather to be flattered that I have been so long and so peculiarly an object of persecution? Ought I to regret, if there be anything about me so formidable to the FACTION as to have made me worthy to be distinguished by the plenitude of its rancor and venom? . . . For the honor of human nature, it is to be hoped that the examples are not numerous of men so greatly calumniated and persecuted as I have been, with so little cause." See also his proclamation of his "proud consciousness of innocence" and his pluming himself on the "delicacy of my conduct in its public relations" because he did not give his blackmailer, Reynolds, a job in the Treasury to stop his mouth. Clearly these are not the expressions of a hypocrite; Hamilton did indeed identify his

ton was still content at this time to be his own priest and prophet in what appears to be a pseudo-religion, in which his own will and his own image rather than God's will or God's image were the center of almost idolatrous worship.

It would seem that the fourth and final stage of Alexander Hamilton's religious development, reaching its climax on July 11, 1804, when he begged Bishop Moore for Communion, can be dated from approximately the spring of 1800 and certainly from March 4, 1801. Hamilton, who in the years of his early success had almost forgotten God, who in the years of his greatest power had tried to manipulate God just as he manipulated the public debt to increase that power, began sincerely seeking God in this time of failure and suffering.

For twenty-five years his genius, his driving ambition, his energy, his will had carried him from triumph to triumph. His pen and literary talent had transported him from his obscure and unhappy status in the West Indies to what seemed to be the beginning of a respectable, but dull, professional career in provincial New York. Then, providentially for the little adventurer with his obsessive ambition and his grandiose dreams of glory, his arrival coincided with the outbreak of a revolution—the type of social cataclysm that not only overstimulates ambition in some men but also provides opportunities of magnificent scope for those who dare to take advantage of them. Now his talents and luck carried him ahead by leaps and bounds. By the time he was twenty-two, Hamilton had begun that association with Washington—the most potent figure in all America—which was to serve him so marvelously for the next two decades. By the time he was twenty-five he had allied himself with

---

behavior with "virtue," "delicacy," and "proud innocence." However, in the context of a signed public confession of his sordid and adulterous liaison with Maria Reynolds, these sentiments represent an unparalleled exhibition of self-righteousness and spiritual arrogance. For the Reynolds pamphlet, see Lodge, ed., *Works of Hamilton*, VII, 372–373, 390, 400.

the Schuylers and automatically gained a top position among the elite of New York. Ten years more and he was Washington's "prime minister," the most influential man in the nation after his chief. Then after 1797, though Washington voluntarily resigned his supreme authority in the state to bumbling John Adams, the president's cabinet was still made up of Hamilton's men, who could manage Adams for him. When the first test came in the war crisis of 1798, Hamilton, in spite of Adams's violent objections, gained control of the new army recruited according to his own specifications. With his army, and with a certain French war impending, Hamilton could feel he had the game in his hands. He had enemies, it was true, but they were no longer dangerous; for now no competitor could threaten his power and his ability to drive the United States along the path he knew it ought to follow. In 1798 everything that Hamilton had willed had come to pass; everything that he still desired had almost been achieved. His virtuous pursuit of power—to be used virtuously, of course—had been successful even beyond the soaring dreams of the immigrant boy of 1772. Who can blame him for feeling omnipotent? Who can wonder that by 1799 Hamilton confused himself with God?

But within one year Hamilton's power vanished, first by slow degrees, then with sudden and cataclysmic completeness. By 1801 Hamilton, whose will had mastered every obstacle, whose power so recently had seemed firmly consolidated and impregnable, suddenly experienced the nightmare sensation of impotence. And as men do who feel completely powerless and helpless in the face of terrible adversity, Hamilton only then turned to the all-powerful Creator of the universe for support and help in his time of troubles.

We can trace the process of Hamilton's religious conversion: beginning in anger, changing to bitterness, turning to despair, and ending with what theologians would call a new birth of the spirit. This process shows in Hamilton's own letters and in the account of these later years written by his son John Church Hamilton, who was twelve when his father died.

Hamilton's fall from power, which would shortly lead him to seek God's help, began when John Adams, despite the tremendous pressure of Hamilton and his clique, declared his independence and by obstinate force of will dispatched the peace mission to France, October 1799. This event, viewed merely as a threat to his power, aroused in Hamilton chiefly anger and contempt for Adams—"a weak and perverse man." More serious was the sudden death of Washington, December 1799, evoking in Hamilton grief, of course, but more significantly "bitterness" and gloomy reflections on the "fickleness of fortune."[13] By February 1800, as it became clear that the Federalist majority in Congress—moderates who looked to Adams rather than Hamilton for leadership—were going to block any imperial military adventures, Hamilton was sadly noting that "America if she attains to greatness must *creep* to it." Ironically and bitterly he added: "Snails are a wise generation."[14] But the "snails" continued inexorably to hedge him in. In March his depression was so obvious that Henry Lee wrote urging him not to despair. Curtly denying "despondency of any sort," Hamilton contradicted himself in the very next sentence, admitting his foreboding for the immediate future by protesting: "I

13. Tobias Lear, Washington's private secretary, wrote Hamilton immediately on the general's death. Hamilton replied from New York, Jan. 2, 1800: "The very painful event which it [your letter] announced had, previous to the receipt of it, filled my heart with bitterness. Perhaps no man in this community has equal cause with myself to deplore the loss. I have been much indebted to the kindness of the General, and he was an *Aegis very essential to me*. But regrets are unavailing. . . . If virtue can secure happiness in another world, he is happy. In this the seal is now set upon his glory. It is no longer in jeopardy from the fickleness of fortune." *Ibid.*, X, 357. Cf. the frank statement to the general's widow in his letter of sympathy to her, Jan. 12, 1800: "There can be few who, equally with me, participate in the loss you deplore. In expressing this sentiment, I may, without impropriety, allude to the numerous and distinguished marks of confidence and friendship, of which you have yourself been a witness, but I cannot say, in how many ways the continuance of that confidence and friendship was necessary to me in future relations." Hamilton to Martha Washington, Jan. 12, 1800, *ibid.*, 361.

14. Hamilton to Theodore Sedgwick, Feb. 27, 1800, *ibid.*, 362–363.

feel I stand on ground which, sooner or later, will insure me a triumph over all my enemies."[15]

At the end of the following month, however, his "enemies," no longer snail-like, simultaneously struck him such a series of blows that he was driven almost insane with rage and frustration. First, Aaron Burr did the seemingly impossible by getting the Livingstons and the Clintons to combine with him in winning control of Hamilton's own stronghold, New York City, during the polling of April 29–May 1. The city's vote carried with it control of the state legislature and the guarantee of victory in the presidential election of November. Next, on May 5, President Adams dismissed McHenry and Pickering from his cabinet, with such suddenness and finality that Pickering, as he mournfully reported to Hamilton, did not even have time to rifle the State Department files for confidential information that could be used to blacken Adams's character.[16] And finally, by May 14, when Congress adjourned—the last Congress in which the Federalist party would ever have a majority—Adams had already progressed so far in dissolving the provisional army that Hamilton hopelessly resigned as commander-in-chief, June 1. It was the last public office he was ever to hold.

"Whom the gods destroy, they first make mad"; these shattering attacks on Hamilton's power and prestige produced in him a species of political insanity during 1800. Frantically casting about for any

15. Hamilton to Henry Lee, Mar. 7, 1800, *ibid.*, 363.

16. Hamilton wrote to Pickering, May 14, 1800, suggesting: "You ought to take with you copies and extracts of all such documents as will enable you to explain both *Jefferson* and *Adams*. You are aware of a very curious journal of the latter when he was in Europe—a tissue of weakness and vanity. The time is coming when all men of real integrity and energy must write against all empirics." *Ibid.*, 376. Pickering's reply of May 15 reports: "I intended to have done precisely what you suggest, respecting Mr. Adams journal, &c (very little of which I had ever read) but there was not time." Quoted in Schachner, *Hamilton*, 395. Schachner, who found this letter in manuscript in the Hamilton Papers, Library of Congress, notes that J. C. Hamilton in printing the Pickering letter deleted the quoted sentence.

means to retrieve his personal and party position in New York, he invited Governor John Jay to stage a legislative coup d'etat to preserve Federalist power. "In times like these," Hamilton wrote, "it will not do to be overscrupulous. *It is easy to sacrifice the substantial interests of society by a strict adherence to ordinary rules* [Hamilton's italics]. . . . In weighing this suggestion you will doubtless bear in mind that popular governments must certainly be overturned, and, while they endure, prove engines of mischief, if one party will call to its aid all the resources which vice can give, and if the other (however pressing the emergency) confines itself within all the ordinary forms of delicacy and decorum." Thus, "PUBLIC SAFETY" was to justify illegal retention of power as Hamilton sought by any means to prevent his greatest enemy, Jefferson, "an atheist in religion, and a fanatic in politics, from getting possession of the helm of state."[17]

Hamilton's intended coup was checked by John Jay in New York. His fear and destructive hostility were then vented on John Adams, whose solid popularity with the rank and file of the national electorate was in fact the last hope of the Federalist party for keeping Jefferson from the presidency. Hamilton's venomous pamphlet attack—not anonymous this time, but signed with his own name—designed to crush Adams and elevate Pinckney was chiefly effective in guaranteeing victory to Jefferson and Burr.[18] At the end of 1800 Alexander Hamilton, who only a year before had dominated the country like

17. Hamilton to John Jay, May 7, 1800, Lodge, ed., *Works of Hamilton*, X, 372–374. Jay endorsed the letter: "Proposing a measure for party purposes which it would not become me to adopt." This letter deserves a careful reading in its entirety if one would understand how dangerously irresponsible Hamilton had become in the spring of 1800. Lodge's characteristic comment, which misses the appalling significance of the state of Hamilton's mind at *this* particular period, reads: "The proposition in this letter was one entirely unworthy of Hamilton."

18. It is an ironic commentary on how little the religious issue really meant to Hamilton in 1800 to discover that that reliable and experienced smeller-out of "irreligion," Timothy Dwight, found that Gen. Pinckney (Hamilton's chosen candidate for the presidency) was as "atheistic" as Jefferson himself. Herbert M. Morais, *Deism in Eighteenth Century America* (New York, 1934), 142–143.

a colossus, was using the tiny shreds of influence left to him trying to block his upstart enemy Burr in order to advance his greatest and oldest enemy, Jefferson, into that highest office which Hamilton desired so much for himself.[19] And the supreme irony of this last feeble effort at manipulation lies in the fact that even here Hamilton was impotent. For his Federalist friends ignored his advice and tried their best to elect Burr, only giving way when it was clear that none of the Jefferson electors were wavering.

Perhaps never in all American political history has there been a fall from power so rapid, so complete, so final as Hamilton's in the period from October 1799 to November 1800. Twelve months earlier his party had seemed stronger than at any time since 1792. His position in the party was unchallenged and seemed unchallengeable. He had every reason to believe that soon his party would advance him to the chief magistracy. And as supreme executive he would have the opportunity to save the country by adding those "additional buttresses to the Constitution, a fabric which can hardly be stationary, and which will retrograde if it cannot be made to advance."[20]

19. It is significant that when the upstart Burr threatened to seize the helm of state in 1801, the aspect of Burr's political character that roused the greatest fear and horror in Hamilton's mind was Burr's lust for "permanent power," his potentialities for staging a coup d'etat in the style of Bonaparte, who had seized power in Paris, 18th Brumaire (Nov.), 1799. And yet Hamilton was completely ambivalent about Napoleon, using his name as a smear against both Burr and Jefferson, but also revealing a deep admiration and envy of Bonaparte's power and glory (cf. the ambivalence of Hamilton's thoughts on Caesar). Psychologists use the word "projection" to describe the process by which a man identifies in an antagonist his own secret desires. To what extent is Hamilton's analysis of Burr in 1801 a mirror of his own heart and personality? From a very superficial knowledge of Burr, I would say that he and Hamilton were much more alike both as men and as politicians than either was like Adams, or Jefferson, or Washington.

20. Hamilton to Rufus King, Jan. 5, 1800, Lodge, ed., *Works of Hamilton*, X, 359. A careful study of Hamilton's printed writings reveals a mass of evidence dating from 1787 and continuing until at least 1802, indicating his strong dissatisfaction with the Constitution and his desire to amend it, change it, reform it. But exactly what reforms he wanted the Federalists to initiate when he wrote this letter to King, it is impossible to determine. How badly we need a complete and accurate edition of all his writings! My guess would be that he favored different reforms at

But now this sudden political tempest had wrecked his hopes, stripped him of his last chance for glory, ended his power to do good for his country, and stranded him a derelict on the shoals of a petty civilian life. No wonder Hamilton felt himself a failure in 1801. No wonder he suffered the tortures of a potent man suddenly become impotent. No wonder that in his despair he finally turned to God for help and support.

Did he remember in 1801, aged forty-six and destroyed by this political tempest, the words he had written in 1772, aged seventeen, about the effect of the hurricane that had devastated St. Croix in that year?

Where now, Oh! vile worm, is all thy boasted fortitude and resolution? What is become of thy arrogance and self-sufficiency—why dost thou tremble and stand aghast? how humble—how helpless—how contemptible you now appear.... Learn to know thy best support. Despise thyself and adore thy God....[21]

We cannot know if Hamilton remembered this youthful rhetoric; we do know from his son's report that religion, beginning in 1801, suddenly achieved a new place in his life. In the words of John Church Hamilton, his father now "sought and found relief from the painful

---

different times during these 15 years, but that one reform in particular appealed to him during the whole period: the change of the tenure of the executive from a term of years to "during good behavior."

21. From Hamilton's famous letter of Sept. 6, 1772, originally published in the *Royal Danish-American Gazette*, Oct. 3, 1772, quoted in Schachner, *Hamilton*, 25. It was this letter describing the hurricane of Aug. 31, 1772, which, according to tradition, so impressed the Reverend Hugh Knox and other gentlemen of St. Croix that they decided to send Hamilton to Princeton for an education. The story is probably part myth. Certainly the style of the hurricane letter shows that Hamilton had been working on his literary prose for a long, long time. I would guess that he had done a great deal of essay writing and that everyone in that small community was aware of his "genius" long before 1772. In fact, it is a safe bet that Hamilton had probably published earlier anonymous essays in this very paper, and it is possible that a careful search of its files would reveal them. Alas for a competent editor of Hamilton's complete writings!

reflections which the growing delusion of the country forced upon him, in the duties of religion, in the circle of domestic joys, and in the embellishment of his rural retreat."[22]

As Alexander Hamilton reluctantly cultivated his garden in what had become the worst of all possible worlds, his new interest in horticulture reacted reciprocally with his new interest in the Creator.

His religious feelings grew with his growing intimacy with the marvellous works of nature, all pointing in their processes and their results to a great pervading, ever active Cause. Thus his mind rose from the visible to the invisible; and he found intensest pleasure in studies higher and deeper than all speculation. His Bible exhibits on its margin the care with which he perused it. Among his autographs is an abstract of the Apocalypse—and notes in his hand were seen in the margin of "Paley's Evidences." With these readings he now united the habit of daily prayer, in which exercise of faith and love, the Lord's Prayer was always a part. The renewing influences of early pious instruction and habit appear to have returned in all their force on his truest sensibilities. . . .[23]

Apparently the traumatic experience of 1800, the nightmare of impotence, produced in Hamilton a new birth of the spirit and a revival of religious practices previously atrophied through long disuse.

Nor was this new concern with God merely a matter of outward ritual observance. Hamilton became internally a new and different man. This psychic transformation shows forth clearly in the new focus of his family life. His children in later years always remember him in this period as the ideal father, proud of all their accomplish-

22. John C. Hamilton, *Life of Alexander Hamilton. A History of the Republic of the United States of America, As Traced In His Writings And In Those Of His Contemporaries* (Boston, 1879), VII, 499. John Church Hamilton's account of these last years is based on his own observation as well as the oft-repeated family memories of his mother, brother, and sisters. Although he was committed to the theory that his father always had been deeply religious, he was honest enough to reveal that 1801 marks a spiritual turning point in Hamilton's life.

23. *Ibid.*, 790.

ments, patient as an instructor, and joyful as a companion in play and sport. As Hamilton himself wrote his wife, "I discover more and more that I am spoiled for a military man. My health and comfort both require that I should be at home—at that home where I am always sure to find a sweet asylum from care and pain."[24] And Hamilton himself was very conscious of the change that had taken place in his character. "While all other passions decline in me, those of love and friendship gain new strength. It will be more and more my endeavour to abstract myself from all pursuits which interfere with those of affection."[25] As a consequence of this radical shift in the vital center of his personality, he publicly foreswore willingness to hold any public office whatsoever, including the presidency of the United States. Unless "called upon in the event of a foreign or civil war," Hamilton announced in the *New-York Evening Post,* February 23, 1804, he "would never again accept any office whatever, either under the General or State government."

While the sufferings and frustrations resulting from political failure started Hamilton's religious conversion, a terrible personal trag-

24. *Ibid.,* 791. His love for the military way of life, nevertheless, never disappeared. John Church remembered vividly his father reading aloud from the classics. "With what emphasis and fervor did he read of battles! When translating the commentaries of Caesar, it would seem as though Caesar were present; for as much as any man that ever lived he had the soldier's temperament. It told itself in little things: during the erection of his rural dwellings, he caused a tent to be pitched, and camp stools to be placed under the shading trees. He measured distances as though marking the frontage of a camp; and then as he walked along, his step seemed to fall naturally into the cadenced pace of practiced drill. It was his delight in his hours of relaxation to return to scenes and incidents of his early life, when fighting for his country, and praying for its protection." *Ibid.,* 792–793.

25. *Ibid.,* 791–792. From one point of view the crushing of Hamilton's political ambitions made it possible for him to be a good husband and father for the first time in his life. It was not that he did not love his wife and his children before 1800, but he was too engrossed in his pursuit of power, too busy with large affairs to be either a very considerate husband or companionable father. During these last four years of growing isolation from politics his children grew to worship him, as both John Church and James Alexander testify. And these years must have been treasured in the memory of Betsy Schuyler Hamilton, too.

edy crystallized the change. In November 1801 his oldest son, Philip,[26] was killed in a duel as a result of a political dispute. And to double this burden of grief, the Hamiltons' oldest daughter, Angelica, became permanently insane grieving over her brother's death.[27]

It is this plenitude of sorrow that accounts for a totally new note— the first echo in all his writings of "Thy will be done"—that now appears in certain Hamilton letters. "Arraign not the dispensations of Providence, they must be founded in wisdom and goodness," he wrote to an unknown friend in 1804, "and when they do not suit us, it must be because there is some fault in ourselves which deserves chastisement; or because there is a kind intent, to correct in us some vice or failing, of which, perhaps, we may not be conscious. . . . In this situation it is our duty to cultivate resignation, and even humility, bearing in mind, in the language of the poet, 'that it was pride which lost the blest abodes.'"[28] And here again we have parallel evidence that Hamilton now put into practice what he was newly preaching. In his relations with individuals the old Hamilton arrogance had disappeared, and there is an unexpected and novel attitude of tact, of consideration, even of gentleness.[29]

26. The most complete printed account of this duel, drawn from contemporary newspapers of both parties, is to be found in Henry B. Dawson, "The Duel between Price and Philip Hamilton, and George E. Eaker," *Historical Magazine*, 2d Ser., II (1867), 193–204. Price and Philip Hamilton insulted Eaker, who fought them both. After an exchange of four shots, all of which missed, between Price and Eaker, that duel ended with honor satisfied. In the second round Philip Hamilton died at the first discharge. Apparently feeling guilty because he was the aggressor, young Hamilton had shot into the air. Philip's death was a terrible blow to both his parents (his mother was pregnant with her eighth child, a boy born June 2, 1802, and named Philip after his dead brother), and Hamilton nearly collapsed at the funeral. See J. C. Hamilton, *Life*, VII, 500–501.

27. *Ibid.*, 792.

28. Hamilton to ———, Apr. 12, 1804, Lodge, ed., *Works of Hamilton*, X, 456. Cf. the change from the attitude of 1797, above, footnote 12.

29. Chancellor Kent reports a night and a day spent with Hamilton in Apr. 1804, when a storm kept Kent from returning to the city and prevented other expected guests from reaching The Grange. Kent reports: "The solicitude of General Hamilton for my comfort, and his attention and kindness, quite surprised and affected me.

His interest in politics never ceased, but his intervention in party affairs after the climactic election of 1800 was both intermittent and less than energetic.[30] It was too much to expect that he could ever view Jefferson and his cohorts with much Christian charity. Nor did he change his long-held opinion that most men are children of darkness rather than children of light. But significantly, the perspective from which he viewed the mass of Jefferson's followers—the monster mob "misshapen, huge, blind"[31]—had shifted subtly as a consequence of the change in Hamilton's own character.

This can be seen in Hamilton's startling and rather terrifying project of 1802 for a proposed "Christian Constitutional Society"— a network of interstate political clubs dedicated to the support of Christianity and the United States Constitution against the devilish Jeffersonians. Hamilton's justification for this repulsive pressure group is offered very much in his old style. "Men are rather reasoning than reasonable animals, for the most part governed by the impulse of passion." Our enemies, Hamilton continued, understanding this, have won the support of the masses by talking of equality, thus "courting the strongest and most active passion of the human heart,

---

He visited me after I had retired to my chamber, to see that I was sufficiently attended to. . . . He never appeared before so friendly and amiable. I was alone and he treated me with a minute attention that I did not suppose he knew how to bestow."In speaking of Hamilton's conversation during the next day, Kent relates: "His mind had a cast unusually melancholy. The pending election exceedingly disturbed him; and he viewed the temper, disposition, and passions of the times as portentious of evil, and favorable to the sway of evil and artful demagogues. His wise reflections, his sobered views, his anxiety, his gentleness, his goodness, his Christian temper, all contributed to render my solitary visit inexpressibly interesting." Quoted in Hamilton, *Life*, VII, 793–794.

30. In 1802, in writing to Gouverneur Morris, Hamilton was so out of touch with politics that he reported, "I often hear at the corner of the streets important federal secrets, of which I am ignorant." Lodge, ed., *Works of Hamilton*, X, 428.

31. Writing to Rufus King, June 3, 1802, Hamilton reports that the masses are still loyally supporting Jefferson, and to describe the people he used a tag from Virgil, "informe ingens cui lumen ademptum." The full quotation begins, of course, with "Monstrum horrendum" and is the poet's description of the Cyclops Polyphemus after Ulysses had blinded him.

vanity." Unless the Federalists "can contrive to take hold of . . . some strong feelings of the mind, we shall in vain calculate upon any substantial or durable result." This is Hamilton speaking in an old familiar fashion. Familiar, too, is the proposal that this society blow up the fires of religious intolerance to elect *"fit* men" to office. What is new, however, is Hamilton's additional proposal for the establishment of "charitable" institutions: immigrant aid societies and free academies to give vocational training to "the different classes of mechanics." Here for the first time in his life Hamilton talks in terms of a "Christian welfare program," which happily was never set up. But how startlingly unlike Hamilton's earlier energetic recipes for dealing with the lower orders of society! Instead of troops to overawe "whiskey boys," instead of sedition laws to discourage the likes of Callender, Hamilton was proposing Federalist "good works" to redeem the masses from their false democratic faith.[32] And when Callender turned on Jefferson and printed the charge that the Virginian kept one of his female slaves as a mistress and was the father of a mulatto son by her, Hamilton used his influence—quite ineffectually, as it proved—to try to keep Federalist newspaper editors from reprinting the scandal. In a notice in the *New-York Evening Post,* September 29, 1802, he objected to the use of this sort of filth for purposes of political attack, declaring "his sentiments to be adverse to all personalities, not immediately connected with public considerations."

It is, however, the last tragic act in his life that shows most conclusively Alexander Hamilton's sincere and strenuous efforts to act in accordance with the precepts of Christ. In contrast to the series of earlier duels which Hamilton *almost* fought, his fatal meeting with Burr was not an act of pride, but, as Broadus Mitchell has recognized, an act of resignation. In one sense Hamilton died in 1804 because of his strong new religious faith.

32. This elaborate project is described in Hamilton's letter to James A. Bayard, Apr. 1802, Lodge, ed., *Works of Hamilton,* X, 432–437.

When Hamilton reluctantly agreed to accept Burr's challenge, he was faced with an ethical and religious problem of the first magnitude. In a memorandum explaining his motives for agreeing to fight Burr, he frankly acknowledged a sense of guilt over the "extremely severe" and "very unfavorable criticisms" he had made of Burr's character. In making these criticisms, he admitted with painful honesty, "I may have been influenced by misconstruction or misinformation." Thus according to the code of honor he *owed* Burr the right to shoot at him from twelve paces. But what was his duty to Burr—his enemy, it is true, but one whom he suspected in his heart he had wronged? According to the code of honor, by accepting Burr's challenge to receive his fire Hamilton gained the *right* to kill Burr if he could. Moreover, by merely shooting at Burr, even though he missed, Hamilton's blazing pistol would help disconcert Burr's aim and would thus lessen Hamilton's chance of injury. This was the code duello. But Hamilton was now trying desperately to live by a different and higher code. Daily he repeated Jesus' words, "Forgive us our trespasses as we forgive those who trespass against us." How could he continue to say these words with good conscience, beseeching God's love and help, if his actions toward Burr, even on the field of honor, did not exemplify complete forgiveness—yes, even love—on his part? There is plentiful evidence that during the last week of June, after the duel was arranged but before the actual date for meeting had been fixed, Hamilton wrestled terribly with this problem in his soul.[33]

At last the day was set for Wednesday, July 11. On the final Sunday before the duel, July 8, 1804, Hamilton led his family at home in the Episcopal service for family worship.[34] At this service,

33. Col. Pendleton, Hamilton's second in the duel, reports a long period of vacillation on this point, with Hamilton only reaching his final decision on July 10, the day before the duel. J. C. Hamilton, *Life*, VII, 825–826.

34. J. C. Hamilton reports this service, *ibid.*, 823. On Saturday, July 7, Col. Trumbull and his wife and Col. and Mrs. William Stephens Smith (Mrs. Smith was John Adams's daughter, Abigail) had been invited to dine at The Grange. J. C.

surrounded by his children, he said aloud the noble prayer with its resolution to grow daily in goodness, dedicating his body and soul to God's service. Then in the next prayer for grace to perform this resolution Hamilton repeated, "O God, who knowest the weakness and corruption of our nature, and the manifold temptations which we daily meet with; We humbly beseech thee to have compassion on our infirmities, and to give us the constant assistance of thy Holy Spirit, that we may be effectually restrained from sin, and excited to duty." Gradually Hamilton came to see clearly what his *Christian* duty toward Burr must be.

In his memorandum on the duel, found after his death, justifying his actions he wrote: "My religious and moral principles are strongly opposed to the practice of duelling, and it would ever give me pain to be obliged to shed the blood of a fellow creature in a private combat forbidden by the laws." Consequently Hamilton concluded that when he faced Burr pistol in hand, "if . . . it pleases God to give me the opportunity, [I will] *reserve* and *throw away* my first fire, and I *have thoughts* even of reserving my second fire."[35]

Monday and Tuesday, July 9 and 10, Hamilton quietly got his affairs in order. Tuesday night he arranged for his twelve-year-old son, John Church, to sleep with him. The son never forgot how he and his father recited the Lord's Prayer in unison.[36] Before dawn on Wednesday, Hamilton rose without waking the boy, to ride the eight miles from The Grange to New York City. There he met his second, Pendleton, and together they boarded the barge in which they were rowed to the Heights of Weehawken.

Hamilton is acute in suggesting that perhaps his father intended "thus to evince to the late President his desire to part with him in peace." *Ibid.*, 822.

35. The correspondence relating to the duel can be found in Lodge, ed., *Works of Hamilton*, X, 460–470. Hamilton's memorandum on his motives in meeting Burr is printed 471–474. See also the two letters written to be delivered to his wife if he should fall, 475–476.

36. J. C. Hamilton, *Life*, VII, 827.

Did the wounded Hamilton think on these things with perhaps a touch of bitterness as first, Bishop Moore, and then, Doctor Mason refused him the sacrament? Most probably he did that terrible July morning as he lay in Mr. Bayard's bedroom with his life rapidly ebbing away.

"Almighty, everliving God, Maker of mankind, who dost correct those whom thou dost love, and chastise everyone whom thou dost receive; We beseech thee to have mercy upon this thy servant visited with thine hand, and to grant that he may take his sickness patiently, and recover his bodily health, if it be thy gracious will; and that whensoever his soul shall depart from the body, it may be without spot; through Jesus Christ our Lord. Amen." With these words Bishop Moore began the Episcopal service for the Communion of the Sick, the dying man listening all the while intently.

For the bishop had returned to Alexander Hamilton's bedside about two o'clock in the afternoon of the day he was shot, July 11, for a second interview. Then after catechizing the stricken man and being assured that he had met Colonel Burr "with a fixed resolution to do him no harm," that he bore Burr no ill will, that he received the consolations of the gospel with a "humble and contrite heart," the bishop proceeded to gratify Hamilton's wish. "The Communion was then administered, which he received with great devotion, and his heart afterwards appeared to be perfectly at rest."

Alexander Hamilton lingered on another twenty-four hours. Death finally released him from his physical agony at two o'clock on the afternoon of July 12. Undoubtedly—as eulogy after eulogy repeated during the following weeks of public grief and ceremonial lamentation—undoubtedly, "Hamilton died a Christian."

✣ 8 ✣

THE JEFFERSON SCANDALS

Written in 1960, "The Jefferson Scandals" is Douglass Adair's major hitherto unpublished essay, one on which he labored long and, to his mind, somewhat in vain. He referred to it at one time as "a horror story that I hope to rewrite and publish," and he did make numerous changes, incorporating suggestions from colleagues. "Crude as it is," Adair wrote a friend, "you will have no idea of the number of *re*writings, Part II especially. . . ." He saw "The Jefferson Scandals" as "a terrible commentary to me of how ugly human relations can become when people, whether their skins are black or white, are treated as means rather than as ends in themselves."

Regrettably he did not undertake the full documentation the subject demanded, perhaps because he considered possible publication by a mass-circulation periodical. Although he was never completely satisfied with this essay he thought it sufficiently important to justify inclusion in the book he once proposed—to be titled "The Jefferson Scandals, the Horn Papers Hoax and Other Essays."

In short, this is what Adair himself termed a "semifinished" study of what was once a delicate subject. We include it in this collection because we believe Douglass would have wanted it; and because "The Jefferson Scandals" again reflects Adair the historical detective, the fervent admirer of John Dickson Carr. We have supplied some of the documentation; these references are printed in decorative brackets. The nonbracketed notes are Adair's own comments.

1

ON SEPTEMBER 1, 1802, the following feature was published in the Richmond, Virginia, *Recorder; or Lady's and Gentleman's Miscellany*, a weekly newspaper whose masthead proudly announced "Reading Improves the Mind":

THE PRESIDENT, *AGAIN.*

It is well known that [Thomas Jefferson] the man, *whom it delighteth the people to honor*, keeps, and for many years past has kept, as his concubine, one of his own slaves. Her name is SALLY. The name of her eldest son is TOM. His features are said to bear a striking although sable resemblance to those of the president himself. The boy is ten or twelve years of age. His mother went to France in the same vessel with Mr. Jefferson and his two daughters. The delicacy of this arrangement must strike every person of common sensibilitys. . . .

By this wench Sally, our president has had several children. . . . The AFRICAN VENUS is said to officiate, as housekeeper at Monticello.

If they [the friends of Jefferson] rest in silence, or if they content themselves with resting upon a *general denial,* they cannot hope for credit. The allegation is of a nature too *black* to be suffered to remain in suspence. . . . Refutation *never can be made!*

The story was signed by the editor of the *Recorder,* one James T. Callender.[1]

Its publication set afloat a libel that has never died—a scandal that today, in 1960, after being dormant for a century, has been revived

---

1. {In the Sept. 22, 1802, issue of the *Recorder,* Callender admitted to being wrong about "one part of the statement" of Sept. 1—Sally had not sailed in the same vessel with Jefferson on the voyage to France. He continued to reaffirm the rest of the story, however.}

and is being circulated throughout the United States. And, strange though it seems, the modern renaissance of this ancient scandal—its appearance in contemporary mass-circulation publications—is motivated less by interest in Jefferson or early American history than by the story's usefulness as a weapon in current twentieth-century politics.

Ironically, just as this ugly tale in its original form is being once again broadcast through the nation, it has become possible to discover the percentage of falsity and truth in Callender's charge against Jefferson.

The motive for Callender's original publication is crystal clear. It was revenge. James Callender was a Scot who fled to the United States in 1793 to escape a jail sentence for sedition and libel in his native land. On arrival here he resumed his trade of journalist and threw his considerable literary talents into the violent party battle then raging between the Federalists, led by Adams and Hamilton, and the Republican-Democratic party of Jefferson and Madison. In this political war Callender distinguished himself by the fierceness and scurrility of his attacks on the Federalist leaders. It was a Callender exposé, for example, that forced Alexander Hamilton to admit publicly that he had had in 1792 an "irregular and indelicate amour" with the wife of a man named James Reynolds, who had thereafter systematically blackmailed Hamilton. The Callender attack on Hamilton and on President Adams played a part in the passage by the Federalist party of the Alien and Sedition Laws of 1798. These laws made it possible for the national government to prosecute and expel from the United States unnaturalized foreign libelers like Callender. The Sedition Law, however, also soon showed that, as interpreted by partisan Federalist judges, it could be used as a gag to stop even legitimate criticism of the administration. It thus was a direct denial of the freedom of speech guaranteed by the Bill of Rights of the Constitution. Between 1798 and 1800 most of the leading Jeffersonian newspaper editors, including Callender, were arrested, fined, and jailed for "sedition." Proclaimed "martyrs" to liberty by their party, they afforded the Republican-Democrats a "free speech" issue that helped defeat Adams and elect Jefferson president in the dirty, no-holds-barred election of 1800.

Jefferson had few personal relations with Callender, but he encouraged the editor's attacks on the Federalists and aided the Scot by giving him small sums of money from time to time. And, in 1801, Jefferson as president pardoned Callender, who was, however, not satisfied by this gesture. He felt his services deserved a positive reward; would not Jefferson appoint him postmaster at Richmond? Jefferson would not. So beginning in 1802 Callender began to snipe at Jeffersonian subordinates in Virginia and to hint that the Richmond post office was being run abominably. Callender's attacks were met in kind. Jeffersonian editors now cursed him as "a trimmer, a rascal, and a coward," until Callender, driven to self-righteous fury, decided to revenge himself on the president and his whole party. As Callender justified himself, Jefferson had failed to silence the pack of mongrel editors snapping at his, Callender's, heels, for the president "had it in his power, with a single word to have extinguished the volcanos ... which were showering their contents on a person, who had served him, who had been persecuted for him, and who had never injured him. With that frigid indifference which forms the pride of his character the President stood neuter."[2]

In this mood of revenge Callender published the story of Jefferson and his alleged slave-concubine, Sally.

The scandal issued into a receptive political world. It was immediately given widespread and prominent coverage in most contemporary American newspapers. Jefferson had been elected president in 1800 by a substantial majority of the popular vote, but the press of

2. {Adair undoubtedly took this quote from a Callender piece in the *Recorder* in the months following Sept. 1802, but as copies of this paper are not widely available, we have been unable to locate the passage.}

his day overwhelmingly supported the Federalists—the party of "the rich, the wise, the wellborn." In this partisan press, consequently, any attack on the Virginian was welcome whether proven or not. Indeed, having rung the changes ineffectually for six years on Jefferson's alleged atheism, his supposed cowardice during the Revolution, his financial dishonesty, and his Jacobinism—the twentieth-century equivalent would read "Communism"—Federalist editors were delighted in 1802 to work with some new material. There were congressional elections that fall in which the president's character and policies were still the main issue of debate. Even after that election was over—Jefferson's party again won easily—the Sally story was too good to drop. As long as the Virginian remained active in politics Jefferson's "Congo Harem" was an inexhaustible topic for Federalist comment.

For variety's sake, "Dusky Sally" was presented in Federalist verse as well as prose—surely she had more newspaper stanzas written about her between 1802 and 1808 than any other contemporary American female. Joseph Dennie, the editor of the genteel and popular Philadelphia literary magazine *Port Folio*, for example, composed "A Song Supposed to have been written by the Sage of Monticello." The first of its many stanzas ran:

>Of all the damsels on the green
>On mountain or in valley,
>A lass so luscious ne'er was seen
>As Monticellian Sally.

Chorus: Yankee Doodle, whose the noodle?
>What wife were half so handy?
>To breed a flock of slaves to stock,
>A blackamoors the dandy.

In Massachusetts the somewhat staid *Boston Gazette* adopted the same device of a "philosophical" song supposedly written by the president.

> Thou Sally, thou my house shall keep,
> My widow'rs tears shall dry!
> My virgin daughters—see! they weep—
> Their mother's place supply.
>
> Oh Sally hearken to my vows!
> Yield up thy sooty charms—
> My best beloved! My more than spouse,
> Oh! take me to thy arms.

Sally even stimulated poetic publication across the Atlantic by the popular Irish bard Thomas Moore ("The Harp That Once Through Tara's Halls"). Moore had toured the United States in 1803–1804, visiting chiefly in anglophile Federalist homes, and he had taken a strong dislike to American manners generally and Jefferson's in particular. He vented this dislike when he returned home in 1806 by introducing "Sally" to the London public in rhyme:

> The patriot, fresh from Freedom's councils come,
> Now pleased retires to lash his slaves at home;
> Or woo, perhaps, some black Aspasia's charms,
> And dream of Freedom in his bondsmaid's arms.

To be sure that his English audience could easily identify "The patriot," Moore added a printed footnote: "The 'black Aspasia' of the present p******** of the United States, inter Avernales haud ignotissima nymphas, has given rise to much pleasantry among the anti-democratic wits in America."[3]

---

3. ["To Thomas Hume, Esq. M.D., from the City of Washington," *The Poetical Works of Thomas Moore* (New York, n.d.), 134, a mid-nineteenth-century edition published by Leavitt and Allen. These lines are from a revised version of the poem, which appeared in mid- and late-nineteenth-century collections of Moore's works. As originally published in his *Epistles, Odes, and Other Poems* in 1806, the stanza read: "The weary statesman for repose hath fled / From halls of council to his negro's shed / Where blest he woos some black Aspasia's grace, / And dreams of freedom in his slave's embrace!" *Ibid.*, 134n. That last line apparently hung on in later

In all these contemporary repetitions of the libel few editors sought
to substantiate the charge beyond Callender's original assertion, even
though Callender was well known to be reckless with the truth. Nor
did the vehement published denials of Jefferson's friends—including
neighbors from Albemarle County—halt the pleasantries of the anti-
Jefferson wits. Since the scandal smeared and presumably hurt the
president, his detractors printed and reprinted it as though it were
established truth resting on unimpeachable evidence.

Jefferson himself never directly mentioned Callender's attack, so
far as any records show. However, in 1805, three years after the
original publication of the "Sally" story, he did *indirectly* refer to
it and indirectly deny its truth in at least two private letters. By
1805 "Sally" had appeared in a catalogue of other anti-Jefferson
smears publicly debated by the Massachusetts legislature. Since all
the libels thus became part of the official legislative record of a
sovereign state, Jefferson felt impelled to reassure the cabinet members closely associated with him in his official family and hence liable
to guilt by association. He wrote, therefore, to "particular friends,"
including the secretary of the navy, Robert Smith, and the postmaster
general, Levi Lincoln. Wishing "to stand . . . on the ground of truth,"
Jefferson told Smith, "I plead guilty to one of their charges, that
when young and single I offered love to a handsome lady"—(this
referred to Jefferson's unsuccessful attempt to seduce a Mrs. John
Walker in the 1760s—another item that Callender had dug up). "It
is the only one founded in truth among all their allegations."[4] The

---

allusions to the "scandal," as Adair shows below in quoting the forged Lincoln
charge of 1860. Some years after his American visit Moore must have regretted
the vehemence of his early anti-Jefferson verses, for he apologized to correspondents
for "the rashness I was guilty of in publishing those crude and boyish tirades against
the Americans." See Wilfred S. Dowden, ed., *The Letters of Thomas Moore* (Oxford,
1964), I, nos. 471, 554, and Howard Mumford Jones, *The Harp That Once—A
Chronicle of the Life of Thomas Moore* (New York, 1937), 78–79.}

4. {Jefferson to Robert Smith, July 1, 1805, Worthington Chauncey Ford, ed.,
Thomas Jefferson Correspondence (Boston, 1916), 115.}

note to Smith was a private letter. The public, of course, knew nothing of it at the time, nor was this letter's existence even known to Jefferson scholars before its publication in 1916.

Why to the world at large did Jefferson himself say nothing? When pressed by friends and political supporters to sue his detractors for libel or at least to issue a statement denying the worst of the charges, Jefferson steadily refused. His defense of his silence was summed up in a letter of 1816 to Dr. George Logan, a Pennsylvania friend. "As to federal slanders," Jefferson wrote then, "I never wished them to be answered, but by the tenor of my life, half a century of which has been on a theatre at which the public have been spectators, and competent judges of it's merit. Their approbation has taught a lesson, useful to the world, that the man who fears no truths has nothing to fear from lies. I should have fancied myself half guilty had I condescended to put pen to paper in refutation of their falsehoods, or drawn to them respect by any notice from myself."[5]

When Jefferson died, July 4, 1826, his lips were still sealed, apart from such private general denials. However, a codicil to his will, dated March 17, 1826, caused some talk in the neighborhood of Charlottesville when its provisions became known. In this codicil Jefferson freed five of his slaves and at the same time petitioned the Virginia legislature to allow them the privilege—forbidden by law— to continue to live in Virginia. These freedmen included Burwell, described by Jefferson as "my good, affectionate, and faithful serv- ant," who was also willed three hundred dollars to establish himself in his business of "painter and glazier"; Joe Fosset, ironworker, and John Hemings, carpenter, who were willed the "tools" of their trade and each given a log house and an acre of land. From Jefferson's comments it is clear that he counted on the University of Virginia to provide regular employment for these skilled artisans who had

5. {Jefferson to Dr. George Logan, June 20, 1816, Paul Leicester Ford, ed., *The Works of Thomas Jefferson*, "Federal edition" (New York, 1905), XI, 527n.}

now become freedmen, thus guaranteeing that his gift of liberty would not entail unemployment and economic need. Finally, in the codicil Jefferson left to John Hemings "the service of his two apprentices, Madison and Eston Hemings, until their respective ages of twenty one years, at which period respectively, I give them their freedom."[6]

It was Madison and Eston Hemings whose emancipation caused talk in the neighborhood. They were light mulattoes—indeed all the freed Negroes were mulattoes—and Eston was thought to look very much like Jefferson. Moreover, some among those members of Charlottesville society who had been entertained at Monticello were aware that the mother of these freedmen was a handsome mulatto house servant, Sally Hemings. Thus, after Jefferson's death, it was possible in the Charlottesville area itself to find some evidence that seemed to substantiate the then twenty-year-old charge by James Callender that Jefferson had taken Sally as his mistress. As a result, a strong local tradition rooted itself in the Albemarle community accepting Callender's charge as true. This tradition, handed down by word of mouth and perpetuated by generations of students at the University of Virginia, lasted all through the nineteenth century and into modern times.

In most of the nation, however, after Jefferson died the scandalous stories about his relations with Sally tended to die or at least to disappear from literature and to live on only (as in Charlottesville) as a subliterary oral tradition. There were, however, between 1830 and 1850, two schools of writing in which Jefferson's "Negro bastards" continued to be exhibited in print: first, among the travel accounts about the United States written for European audiences by unfriendly English visitors like Mrs. Trollope and, second, among Northern abolitionist tracts. Mrs. Trollope, for example, retailed the

6. {Jefferson's will is printed as an appendix to James A. Bear, Jr., ed., *Jefferson at Monticello* (Charlottesville, Va., 1967), 119–120.}

story with vividly invented details to discredit American democracy
by discrediting Jefferson the prophet of democracy, while to the
abolitionists any report that could equate slavery and sin was welcome
and used. And at least once, some thirty years after Jefferson's death,
the Sally story was revived and given national circulation for political
purposes that somewhat parallels its revival today. This was during
the bitter presidential campaign of 1860, when the issue of Negro
slavery was drawing the country into civil war. As that campaign
reached its climax a Democratic newspaper, the Chicago *Times and
Herald* (September 4, 1860) published a forged speech attributed to
Abraham Lincoln that falsely quoted Lincoln as saying: "The character of Jefferson was repulsive. Continually puling about liberty,
equality, and the degrading curse of slavery, he brought his own
children to the hammer, and made money of his debaucheries. Even
at his death he did not manumit his numerous offspring, but left
them soul and body to degradation and the cart whip. A daughter
of this vaunted champion of Democracy was sold some years ago at
public auction in New Orleans, and purchased by a society of gentlemen, who wished to testify by her liberation their admiration of the
statesman who

    'Dreamt of freedom in a slave's embrace.' "
The purpose of this forgery was to associate Lincoln in the minds
of voters with the abolitionists, who had indeed been saying such
things for thirty years. Lincoln reacted instantly, characterizing the
speech as a "bold and deliberate forgery" that he hoped would "react
upon the desperate politicians who are parties to such disreputable
tactics."[7]

From 1860 to the recent present, for nearly a century, the Jefferson
scandal lay dormant so far as widespread popular interest was concerned. Jefferson scholars knew of the story, of course, but it was

---

7. {The denunciation was printed in the *Illinois State Journal*, Sept. 6, 1860.
Lincoln to Anson G. Chester, Sept. 5, 1860, Roy P. Basler, ed., *The Collected Works
of Abraham Lincoln*, IV (New Brunswick, N.J., 1953), 111, 112n.}

scarcely a matter of public note or general concern. Then, suddenly, during the last few years it has been revived and widely circulated in national publications. In our own day the Negroes' status has once again become a major issue in American politics, as in 1860 when Abraham Lincoln was running for the presidency. And the *context* in which the Jefferson scandal is being publicized in the mid-decade of the twentieth century shows why the story of Sally Hemings is today being used by both Negroes and whites as a weapon in current politics to embitter the battle over Negro rights.

In the popular Negro picture magazine, *Ebony*, for November 1954, its five hundred thousand readers found an essay entitled: "Thomas Jefferson's Negro Grandchildren." It began: "Scattered across the nation living out their lives in total obscurity are a handful of elderly Negroes, . . . proud Negro descendants of America's third President [who] have made the long and improbable journey from the white marbled splendor of Monticello to the 'Negro ghetto' in the democracy their forebear helped to found." Jefferson, so declared *Ebony's* editors in their improvement on the original Callender charge, "fathered at least five Negro children and possibly more by several comely slave concubines who were great favorites at his Monticello house." Indeed, the editors of *Ebony* believe, *all* "the slaves that Jefferson freed in his will were his own children. At least three and possibly all five of these slaves—Burwell, Joseph Fosset, John, Madison, and Eston Hemings—were sons of the celebrated 'Black Sal,' a stunningly attractive slave girl with long pretty hair and milk-white skin." *Ebony's* article features pictures and interviews with four of the third-generation descendants of Joseph Fosset. The Fosset descendants all report that their family tradition identifies Jefferson as their grandfather's parent. All of them had heard of the connection from childhood. However, as one of the descendants told *Ebony*, "We never talked about it outside of family and close friends."

The *Ebony* revival of the Jefferson scandal, with its sensational modernized mixture of fact and fiction, is calculated to remind its

Negro readers of one of the ugliest features of Negro-white relations in American history. Its printing is designed to stir up, to quote a phrase of Jefferson's, "ten thousand recollections, by the blacks, of the injuries they have sustained." As such the publicizing today of the story of Jefferson's Negro concubines operates as a battle cry and a recruiting slogan for militant political action *now* in the battle for Negro rights.

Exactly the same note of self-righteous warfare—exactly the same use of the Monticello scandal as a weapon—but now *against* Negro demands for status, is to be seen in a current parallel publication of the story by W. E. Debnam, a white North Carolinian. Debnam, a journalist and radio commentator from Raleigh, issued in 1955 a book entitled *Then My Old Kentucky Home, Good Night!* Privately printed, it is sold today in drugstores and newsstands all over the South. It has been widely reviewed and praised in southern newspapers, and if it sells as well as the author's *Weep No More, My Lady* (1950), an attack on Eleanor Roosevelt for her stand on Jim Crow, it will gain more than a quarter of a million readers.

Mr. Debnam argues that if the South budges an inch on Jim Crow, especially if school integration should ever come to pass, then it's "good night" for civilization in Dixie. The result will be "Amalgamation and the Destruction of both the White and the Negro Race."

Debnam notices the Jefferson scandal in connection with his argument "that the Negro Race has a built-in Code of Morals several degrees below that with which the Good Lord has endowed the White Race." His logic fastens on the fact that 70 to 80 percent of the Negroes today are mulattoes: "Social contact means miscegenation. It's as certain as one and one make two. The racial arithmetic in this instance, however, is one and one make one half-breed."

How does Debnam account for this past amalgamation among the southern whites, who value racial purity so highly? His answer assumes the easy virtue of Negro women as a group—the low "built-in" moral code of all Negroes. "Out in Chicago," he reports "there's a Colored family whose proudest boast is that it can trace its ancestry back to Thomas Jefferson. Bastardy, it would seem, loses its onus when given the bonus of distinction."

Debnam's retelling of the story of Sally Hemings, while badly garbled, is more accurate than *Ebony's*. The white author's main interest, however, is to link the old scandal with modern statistics on venereal disease rates and illegitimacy among Negroes in order to demonstrate their lack of chastity. "It's a shameful situation," he feels, that there should be blacks living today with Jefferson blood in their veins—"but just because we've gotten our feet wet in a racial mud-puddle is no reason why the White Race and the Negro should jump into the Integration river and drown themselves."[8]

Debnam's local fame and popularity as a militant segregationist was widespread enough in 1956 for him to run for Congress in the Fourth Congressional District of North Carolina. His platform, chiefly consisting of the promise never to run up "the white flag of surrender to racial mixing," was almost potent enough to unseat the long-established incumbent in the office.

Given the nature of twentieth-century mass communications, given the fact that debate on the status of the Negro has now become a national issue, it was inevitable that the modern revival of the story of Sally and Jefferson, initially aimed at limited white and Negro audiences, would quickly achieve national circulation. In 1956 J. C. Furnas's popular best seller *Goodbye to Uncle Tom*, a Book-of-the-Month-Club choice, used Jefferson as a shameful example of miscegenation in slavery days and flatly stated that the great Virginian was undoubtedly the father of Sally Hemings's children. Inevitably reviews of the Furnas book, such as *Time* magazine's (June 25, 1956), picked up the Furnas judgment and the story of Sally and

8. {The Debnam quotations are from *Then My Old Kentucky Home, Good Night!*, 4, 97, 122, 123. In a footnote on 123, concerning the Chicago family, Debnam did state that the family's claim was probably "utterly false." Instead he accepted the explanation given by Thomas Jefferson Randolph, which Adair discusses below.}

Jefferson to publicize. Thus, by the mid-decades of the twentieth century, Callender's ancient attack on Jefferson was very much alive and was being regularly reprinted and circularized as "the truth" in reputable mass-media publications to millions of modern Americans.

2

"Refutation never can be made," Callender crowed in 1802. So it seemed 130 years after Jefferson's death. When scholars, such as Dumas Malone or Julian Boyd, whose intensive study of the great Virginian's career has given them an understanding of Jefferson unmatched in our generation, were asked to judge the truth or falsity of the Callender charge, their answers were bound to be ambiguous. For example, Dr. Boyd, who has long been skeptical of the Sally story, when asked in 1954 about Jefferson's reputed mulatto children was forced to reply: "I know of no single historian who would support that statement. I must also say in candor, that I know of no historian who would be able to say it is not true."

Then, unexpectedly, in four widely separated areas of the country, four different scholars independently discovered four key documents, no one of which alone solves the puzzle but which, when checked and cross-checked against each other, together throw a great blaze of light on Jefferson as a slaveholder, on the Monticello slaves, and in particular on the slaves named Hemings. Today, it is possible to *prove* that Jefferson was innocent of Callender's charges. Today, it is possible to speak with a new and firm assurance about the relations between master and slaves at Monticello, and the story of Jefferson and Sally Hemings that now emerges assumes a completely unexpected dimension. Gone is the melodramatic weapon that Callender used so effectively against the great Virginian. In its place appear tragic circumstances that knotted the lives of three generations of Negroes and whites into a tangled and twisted web. And as the outlines of this tragic drama become clear it increasingly invites compassion and pity for all the actors involved. The account of Jefferson and Sally Hemings, when one knows all the facts now available in the new documents, is not a history that either whites or Negroes can use against each other with good conscience in our contemporary political battles.

The first of the documents, in the handwriting of Jefferson himself, is his record—incredibly detailed—of all the slaves who belonged to him from 1774 until his death in 1826. This record, kept as a *Farm Book* showing the vital statistics of his plantation labor force—the births and deaths of his slaves recorded by families—was deposited in the Massachusetts Historical Society in 1898. There it remained generally unnoticed until it was reprinted in facsimile in 1953 by Professor Edwin M. Betts of the University of Virginia. The Betts edition of the *Farm Book* makes it possible to trace the genealogy of many of the Monticello slaves through four generations. Jefferson records a slave's birth and adolescence as a member of a particular family who are issued rations as a clearly designated family group. His records show the individual slave at maturity, establishing his own family and begetting his children, who in time marry and set up their families—and this record of vital statistics for the Negroes living at Monticello covers fifty years. In the words of Jean Hazelton, who, using the *Farm Book* has worked out a surprising exact family tree for the Hemingses: "The genealogical history of his slaves which Jefferson here provides is without doubt more complete than that which could be gathered for many [white] . . . families of . . . Albemarle County. Indeed, few Americans today could assemble as complete a record as this concerning their ancestry during the period 1774–1826."[9]

Thus for the first time it is now possible, thanks to the *Farm Book*, to see the relationships of the Hemingses to each other and to families like the Fossets and the Browns. It is now possible to determine

9. {Edwin Morris Betts, ed., *Thomas Jefferson's Farm Book* (Princeton, N.J., 1953); Jean Hazelton, "The Hemings Family of Monticello," 1960, typescript at the University of Virginia, Charlottesville.}

when the famous Sally was born, how many children she had, and the exact dates of their birth. But the Jefferson document does not tell all we would like to know. Significantly, the name of the father of Sally Hemings's children is not reported. Unlike many of the entries in Jefferson's *Farm Book*, which reveal the wife *and husband* in a family, Sally and her four children are shown living at Monticello with no designated slave as husband-father.

The second of these newly discovered documents is a long letter that Henry S. Randall, the earliest biographer of Jefferson, wrote to James Parton, the historian, in 1868. In his letter Randall reported on a conversation he had once had with Colonel Thomas Jefferson Randolph, Jefferson's oldest grandson, about Sally Hemings. Randall did not print Colonel Randolph's revelations in his three-volume *Life of Thomas Jefferson* (1858) because (as he told Parton) on this one topic alone Randolph had requested secrecy. And Randall himself, although completely frank with Parton, asked that he, too, keep the information about Sally Hemings off the record. Parton obeyed Randall and in his own life of Jefferson, published in 1874, made no mention of the startling secret revealed by Jefferson's grandson. But fortunately Parton did save Randall's letter with its evidence from Colonel Randolph among his private papers. These eventually were filed in the Harvard Library's manuscript collection. There the Randall letter was discovered by Professor Milton E. Flower and printed in 1952 as an appendix to Flower's monograph on James Parton.[10]

The third document, and the most amazing of all, was a short autobiography actually written or dictated by one of the Hemingses— the story of his life and his mother's life reported in the very words of one of Sally's sons—Madison Hemings. This document was not found in any manuscript archive or inaccessible library collection but had actually been printed on March 13, 1873, in a rural Ohio

10. {Milton E. Flower, *James Parton, the Father of Modern Biography* (Durham, N.C., 1951), 236–239.}

newspaper, the *Pike County Republican* of Waverly, Ohio. However, because of the small and strictly regional circulation of the *Pike County Republican,* this ex-slave's autobiography with its damning charges against Jefferson had lain unnoticed and forgotten in the newspaper files for over seventy-five years.[11]

Madison Hemings's account of his own life, and those of his mother and grandmother, reads like the plot of a lurid novel. It seemed to confirm every charge made by Callender against Jefferson and to add extra evidence of the Virginian's guilt that Callender with all his malice could never have dreamed of. For Madison, in telling the story of three generations of his family, exposed not merely one scandal at Monticello but exhibited a double scandal of sexual commerce between masters and slaves that had continued during more than sixty years and two generations.

The last of the new documents contains the reminiscences of a Monticello slave, Isaac Jefferson, dictated in the 1840s to a Virginia historian named Charles Campbell. Preserved in his papers, these memoirs eventually became the property of the Alderman Library at the University of Virginia.[12] They are among the most delightful Virginia memoirs of their period, and they provide one of the best portraits of Jefferson and life at Monticello that we possess. Born in 1775, Isaac was one of the house servants and a plantation blacksmith, as well. His father, Great George, saved the Jefferson silver from Tarleton's troops in 1781, and his mother, Ursula, the cook, was also nurse to the Jefferson children. Isaac's opportunity for knowledge of Jefferson's daily routine at home was unexcelled. His report thus

11. Madison Hemings's autobiography was rediscovered by a staff member of the Ohio State Historical and Archaeological Society at Columbus, Ohio, who called it to the attention of John Dos Passos. It is due to his generosity and to that of the director of the Ohio State Historical Society that it is quoted here.

12. {Campbell's manuscript was first published in Rayford W. Logan, ed., *Memoirs of a Monticello Slave, as Dictated to Charles Campbell in the 1840's by Isaac, One of Thomas Jefferson's Slaves* (Charlottesville, Va., 1951), which is now out of print. It has been reprinted in Bear, ed., *Jefferson at Monticello,* 3–24.}

provides us with a fine series of vignettes of the Virginian in the intimacy of his family.

It is from Isaac that we learn that while Jefferson himself always took wine at table, his visitors had the further choices of cider or rum and that although Jefferson was very fond of wine cut with water, "Isaac never heard of his being disguised in drink." In these memoirs we see Jefferson's rigid daily schedule and his insistence on absolute privacy when he was writing: "Wouldn't suffer nobody to come in his room. Had a dumb-waiter . . . turn a crank . . . water or fruit on a plate." Here too, we see Jefferson the scholar working at a difficult problem: "Old Master had abundance of books; sometimes would have twenty of 'em down on the floor at once—read fust one, then tother." Isaac often wondered "how Old Master came to have such a mighty head." It is Isaac, too, who pictures for us Jefferson's gaiety, his sunny nature, his love for music. "He kept three fiddles; played in the arternoons and sometimes arter supper . . . when he began to get so old, he didn't play. Kept a spinnet . . . his daughter played on it." "Mr. Jefferson always singing when ridin' or walkin'; hardly see him anywhar outdoors but what he was a-singin'. Had a fine clear voice."

Isaac's memoirs not only picture his "Old Master" at home but describe the members of the Monticello household, white and black. It was in this description that modern scholars got their first inkling of who the Hemings family were and why they were at Monticello. Isaac remembered going down to Williamsburg when Jefferson was elected governor of Virginia in 1779. "Bob Hemings drove the phaeton, Jim Hemings was a body servant: Martin Hemings the butler. These three were brothers: Mary Hemings and Sally, their sisters. Jim and Bob bright mulattoes; Martin, darker. . . . Sally Hemings' mother Betty was a bright mulatto woman, and Sally mighty near white. . . . Sally was very handsome, long straight hair down her back. She was about eleven years old [actually fourteen] when Mr. Jefferson took her to France to wait on Miss Polly [Maria]. She and

Sally went out to France a year after Mr. Jefferson went. . . . Harriet, one of Sally's daughters, was very handsome. Sally had a son named Madison, who learned to be a great fiddler." All of these remarks of Isaac's are extremely interesting, but it is another, ten-word sentence that provides the most significant fact about this Hemings family and offers one key to the mystery. "Folks said," Isaac remarks, almost in an aside, "Folks said that these Hemingses was old Mr. Wayles's children."[13]

Who was "old Mr. Wayles"? He was John Wayles, an Englishman, born in Lancaster in 1715, who as a young man emigrated to Virginia and became a successful planter and large slaveholder. Wayles married three times into prominent Virginia families, and his oldest daughter (by his first wife, Martha Eppes) was Martha Wayles Jefferson, Thomas Jefferson's adored wife. If the slave Isaac is to be believed, the Hemings family at Monticello were the half-brothers and half-sisters of Jefferson's wife.

On Wayles's death in 1773, Jefferson's wife, Martha Wayles Jefferson, inherited most of his slaves, including the Hemings family, who moved to Monticello. If Isaac was correct about their parentage, Jefferson and his wife, Martha, became in 1774 the owners of Betty Hemings, John Wayles's concubine, and her children by Wayles, who were Martha's half-brothers and half-sisters. Among them was the baby Sally, the youngest of "Old Mr. Wayles's" daughters, born the very year he died.

Can we accept Isaac's statement of the Hemings parentage? Probably only with great hesitation, if there was not strong corroborating evidence. But such corroboration does exist in Madison Hemings's autobiography, printed in the *Pike County Republican* of Waverly, Ohio, March 13, 1873. Madison was one of the sons of Sally freed in Jefferson's will; it was he who was remembered by Isaac as "a great fiddler." His family tradition, as known to Madison Hemings

13. {Bear, ed., *Jefferson at Monticello*, 12, 13, 4.}

("Such is the story that comes down to me"), carried his genealogy back three generations. Madison stated that Betty Hemings, his grandmother (born about 1735), was the child of an English sea captain, trading between London and Williamsburg, Virginia, and a "full blooded African" slave of John Wayles's. "Elizabeth Hemings [Betty] grew to womanhood in the family of John Wayles, whose wife dying, she (Elizabeth) was taken by the widower Wayles, as his concubine, by whom she had six children—three sons and three daughters, viz: Robert, James, Peter, Critty, Sally and Thena."[14]

Thus on this crucial matter of the Hemingses' paternity we have two different witnesses, as well as Jefferson's own records, which add exact chronological details. Robert (Isaac calls him "Bob") was born to Betty Hemings in 1762, the year after John Wayles's third wife died; James, or Jame, in 1765; Thena, 1767; Critta, or Critty, 1769; Peter, 1770; and Sally in 1773, the year of Wayles's death. John Hemings, born at Monticello to Betty in 1776 after Jefferson inherited the family, was the son of a white man, Joseph Nelson, or Neilson, according to Madison. And Jefferson's records identify him as the skilled English woodworker and cabinetmaker who was then engaged in the building of the great house.

Madison Hemings also reports that Betty, his grandmother, had seven other children by Negro fathers: six before her connection with John Wayles, and one, Lucy, born in 1777, her last child. The information helps explain Isaac's comment that Jim and Bob were "bright mulattoes; Martin, darker." And here again Jefferson's *Farm Book* allows us to identify the other five Hemings children, fathered (in Madison's words) by "colored men," who also lived most of their lives at Monticello: Mary Hemings, born to Betty in 1753; Martin, 1755; Betty, 1759; Nance, 1761; and Lucy, born in 1777. All of these were Betty's children by slave fathers, all figure prominently in Jefferson's meticulous records, as do their children. For example,

14. {Madison Hemings's reminiscences, *Pike County Republican*, Mar. 13, 1873.}

Mary, called by Isaac, Sally's "sister" (actually her half-sister), is the mother of Daniel, Molly, Joe, and Betsy. Joe is the "Joe Fosset" freed by Jefferson's will, who is no blood relation of any of John Wayles's white descendants (the Jeffersons, the Eppeses, etc.), but who *is* a cousin of Wayles's mulatto descendants through their common grandmother, Betty. Likewise, Burwell, born in 1783, Jefferson's beloved and trusted body servant, is a Hemings on his mother's side, being the son of young Bett, usually called "Bett Brown" after her marriage.

These complicated interrelations among the Hemings progeny of Monticello have been accurately worked out by Jean Hazelton, who has disentangled the lives of both the Negro and the mulatto descendants of Betty Hemings with remarkable exactitude.[15] And with the knowledge that six of Betty's children, owned by Jefferson, were fathered by John Wayles, we have one clue to the mystery of the Jefferson scandals—the secret of Jefferson's silence in the face of Callender's charges.

Even if completely innocent, Jefferson could only have defended himself against Callender's attacks by revealing who the Hemingses were and how they had come to be at Monticello. As an honorable man, he was prepared to writhe under the venomous charges of his enemies, bite his lip, and still keep silence rather than reveal that the older generation of "white slaves" at Monticello were the children of John Wayles, his father-in-law, and thus his own beloved wife's half-brothers and half-sisters.

But *was* Jefferson innocent? Madison Hemings, whose testimony helps to establish that there was "a Wayles scandal" involving those nearest and dearest to Jefferson, flatly claims that Jefferson was his father. In his autobiography, after reporting on his grandmother's life, he tells a story that must have been told him by his mother, Sally. He relates (correctly) how Jefferson and his older daughter,

15. {Hazelton, "Hemings Family of Monticello," typescript, Univ. of Va.}

Martha, in France, sent for Maria (Polly), the younger daughter, to join them.

She (Maria) was three years or so younger than Martha. My mother (Sally Hemings) accompanied her as her body servant. When Mr. Jefferson went to France, Martha was a young woman grown, my mother was about her age, and Maria was just budding into womanhood. Their stay (my mother and Maria's) was about eighteen months. But during that time my mother became Mr. Jefferson's concubine, and when he was called home, she was *enceinte* by him. He desired to bring my mother back to Virginia with him but she demurred.... In France she was free, while if she returned to Virginia, she would be re-enslaved. So she refused to return with him. To induce her to do so he promised her extraordinary privileges, and made a solemn pledge that her children should be freed at the age of twenty-one years. In consequence of his promises . . . she returned with him to Virginia. Soon after their arrival, she gave birth to a child, of whom Thomas Jefferson was the father. It lived but a short time. She gave birth to four others, and Jefferson was the father of all of them. Their names were Beverly, Harriet, Madison (myself) and Eston.... We were the only children of his by a slave woman.

Thus Madison Hemings reported in 1873 what his mother (who lived until 1835) must have told him of his parentage.[16]

16. Madison Hemings's rather vague and inaccurate report of his mother's trip abroad—a trip that occurred 15 years before he was born—can be filled out with exactitude from Jefferson's papers. Jefferson, with his daughter Martha (who was nearly 12), attended by James Hemings as a body servant, sailed from Boston for France, July 5, 1784. Maria (Polly), who was only 6 at the time, was left in Virginia with her kin, the Eppeses. In 1787 Jefferson sent for Maria to join him, and her arrival in England is reported by Abigail Adams, who wrote to Jefferson in Paris, June 26, 1787: "The old Nurse whom you expected to have attended her, was sick and unable to come. She has a Girl [Sally] about 15 or 16 [actually 14] with her, the Sister of the Servant you have with you." {Lester J. Cappon, ed., *The Adams-Jefferson Letters: The Complete Correspondence between Thomas Jefferson and Abigail and John Adams* (Chapel Hill, N.C., 1959), I, 178.} Mrs. Adams in a later letter suggests that Sally at this time was quite immature and less than adequate

Madison Hemings's report that his mother, Sally, claimed that she was Jefferson's concubine; that she had become his mistress while in France in 1788 or 1789; and that while abroad she had conceived by her master the first of the five children she was to bear him between 1795 and 1808 would seem finally to establish Jefferson's guilt past any doubt. There can be no question that Madison and his brothers and sister believed the story Sally told them of their paternity. And we too would be inclined to believe it—if we did not have evidence to prove that Sally's story contained at least one major falsification and if we did not have Colonel Randolph's report from inside the Monticello household, which points to another member of Jefferson's family as the true father of Sally's children.

Sally's falsification of fact in the story she told her children relates to the account of her stay in France, for there is extremely persuasive evidence that she was *not* pregnant when she returned to Virginia. When she arrived in Europe in June 1787, as the companion of eight-year-old Polly, Sally herself was fourteen, and when on her return she landed in Virginia, November 23, 1789, she was only sixteen. Although young, it was undoubtedly physically possible for Sally to have become pregnant while in Paris, just as it would have been physically possible for her to have borne a child "soon" after her "arrival" in Virginia. But for this detail of Sally's story to be true this first child (which she claimed Jefferson had fathered) would have been born in 1790. In fact, however, Jefferson's careful and exact records of the births of Sally's children in the *Farm Book* reveal that her first child was not born until 1795, five years after her return from Europe. Nor does it appear likely that the *Farm Book* was in error here, or that Sally bore an unrecorded child in 1790. The child

as Polly's body servant. "The Girl she has with her, wants more care than the child, and is wholy incapable of looking properly after her, without some superiour to direct her." (July 6, 1787, *ibid.*, 183.) When Jefferson and his family left Paris (Sept. 26, 1789) to return to Virginia over 2 years later, Martha was 3 months past her 17th birthday, Polly was 11, and Sally was 16 years old.

born in 1795, named Harriet, undoubtedly is the infant referred to by Madison, who identifies it as living "but a short time," for the baby Harriet lived less than two years (as Jefferson's records show), dying in 1797.[17] Thus Sally's report to her four living children that she had earlier given birth to another child and that her firstborn had died in infancy squares exactly with Jefferson's record of her family. What cannot be reconciled in the two accounts is Sally's report made later to her children that, having become Jefferson's mistress in Paris, she was carrying his child when her master brought her home from Europe.

The discovery of one major misstatement of fact in Sally's report about her relations with Jefferson certainly does not disprove the truth of other claims she made about her master. Sally's falsification even on this single point, however, does alert us to the danger of accepting entirely at face value the story as told to her son. Clearly Sally dramatized her relations with Jefferson even at the expense of truth in this instance. Clearly Sally *wanted* her children to believe that she had been Jefferson's mistress from the time she was fifteen or sixteen. Her claim that she had originally refused to return to Virginia with him and that he had begged her to, had bargained with her, and eventually had made a solemn promise that her children would be freed—all these dramatic details were given added verisimilitude by her fictitious claim that when the bargain was made she was already carrying Jefferson's child in her body. Clearly Sally's story as she tells it dignifies her role: in France her relations with Jefferson are not those of slave and master, for slave and master do not bargain as equals and slaves do not extort solemn promises from their owners. Thus Sally's account gave her children both cause for pride that Jefferson was their father and also a measure of self-

17. {As Adair points out below, Sally had two daughters named Harriet—this baby, who died a young child, and her namesake, the "handsome" girl referred to in Isaac's memoirs, above. See Fawn Brodie, "The Great Jefferson Taboo," *American Heritage*, XXIII (June 1972), 57.}

respect by making her relations with Jefferson voluntary, contractual, almost like a common-law marriage. There is pride in Madison Hemings's claim: "We were the only children of his by a slave woman."

Internal inconsistencies somewhat shake our faith in Sally's statement. However, it is Colonel Thomas Jefferson Randolph's report of Sally's relations with another member of the Monticello household that impeaches Sally's story on the crucial point of her children's paternity.

Randolph, Jefferson's oldest grandson, lived at Monticello most of his early life and, in fact, during Jefferson's later years managed the plantation. Born in 1792, he was the oldest son of Martha Jefferson and her husband, Thomas Mann Randolph, who owned Edgehill, a plantation neighboring to Monticello. As a youth, Jefferson Randolph lived about equally at Monticello and Edgehill. After Jefferson's retirement from the presidency, however, Martha Randolph kept house for him at Monticello, where the family lived until Jefferson's death in 1826. It was to Randolph that Henry S. Randall applied for basic information about Jefferson when Randall in the 1850s was writing his exhaustive biography of Jefferson.

Randolph is thus the sort of witness that the research historian prays to discover—a primary witness who was involved directly and who saw a past situation with his own eyes. Randolph then, like Jefferson, who was silent, or Isaac, who was carefully discreet on this point, or Sally, whose story we have heard, was in a good position to know the truth firsthand about when Sally's youngest children were born.

Randolph emphatically denied that Jefferson had commerce with Sally or any other of his female slaves. Since he "had spent a good share of his life closely about Mr. Jefferson—at home and on journeys—in all sorts of circumstances," he could testify that his grandfather was in sexual matters "chaste and pure"—indeed, as "immaculate a man as God ever created." Randolph remembered Sally very well, and he had many direct dealings with her, for, sharing in the management of Monticello, he gave general directions to the servants and helped distribute the food and clothing rations to them. "Sally Hening [*sic*]," Randolph told Randall, "was treated, dressed, etc., exactly like the rest." Randall also recorded that Randolph "said Mr. Jefferson never locked the door of his room by day: and that he (Col. Randolph) slept within sound of his breathing at night. He said he had never seen a motion, or a look, or a circumstance which led him to suspect for an instant that there was a particle more of familiarity between Mr. Jefferson and Sally Henings than between him and the most repulsive servant in the establishment—and that no person ever at Monticello dreamed of such a thing."

But Randolph also told Randall why visitors to Monticello on the basis of strong though circumstantial evidence would inevitably suspect Jefferson and inevitably gossip about his connection with Sally. "There was a better excuse for it," Randolph told Randall, "than you might think." Sally's children "resembled Mr. Jefferson so closely that it was plain that they had his blood in their veins." In the case of one of her sons "the resemblance was so close, that at some distance or in the dusk the slave, dressed in the same way, might have been mistaken for Mr. Jefferson." Inevitably visitors were startled by this physical similarity, for Sally and all of the children were house servants living at Monticello itself—"so that the likeness between master and slave was blazoned to all the multitudes who visited this political mecca." Randolph remembered very distinctly, he told Randall, how "a gentleman dining with Mr. Jefferson looked so startled as he raised his eyes from the latter to the servant behind him, that his discovery of the resemblance was so perfectly obvious to all."[18]

If Jefferson was not the father of the mulatto children who so closely resembled him, how had the Jefferson blood come to run in their veins? Here Colonel Randolph revealed a second scandal at

18. {Randall to Parton, June 1, 1868, in Flower, *James Parton,* 236–237.}

Monticello to match the secret of the earlier Wayles scandal that accounted for the Hemingses being there in the first place. "Mr. Jefferson," Randolph reminded Randall, "had two nephews, Peter Carr and Samuel whom he brought up in his house. They were the sons of Jefferson's sister and her husband Dabney Carr, . . . who died in 1773. . . ."[19] Sally Henings was the mistress of Peter, and her sister Betsey the mistress of Samuel—and from these connections sprang the progeny which resembled Mr. Jefferson. Both the Henings girls were light colored and decidedly good looking. . . . Their connection with the Carrs was perfectly notorious at Monticello, and scarcely disguised by the latter—never disavowed by them. Samuel's proceedings were particularly open."[20] Thus Colonel Thomas Jefferson Randolph, speaking in the 1850s to Henry S. Randall, explained the paternity of Sally Hemings's children, who had apparently been told by their mother that Jefferson was their father.

Can we trust Randolph's evidence, which is flatly contradicted by that given by Madison Hemings? Randolph in reporting his version of the truth about the Hemings children is certainly not a disinterested witness any more than is Sally herself. If, as we have seen, Sally desired to dramatize her relation with her great and famous master and was tempted to falsify the record in order to elevate her status and her children's paternity by attributing it to Jefferson, we must recognize that Randolph had perhaps as powerful a motive to invent a story that would clear Jefferson's name. Indeed, Randolph told

19. {The letter as printed *ibid.*, 236, reads "who died in 17(?)," but Adair correctly supplied the date as 1773.}

20. {*Ibid.*, 236–237.} Randolph was in error here, or Randall misquoted him. Betsy Hemings, born in 1783, was not Sally's "sister" but the daughter of Mary Hemings, born in 1753, who was Sally's half-sister. Mary, the daughter of Betty before she became Wayles's concubine, had four children (the last two by white workmen at Monticello): Daniel (1772), Molly (1777), Joe Fosset (1780), and Betsy (1783). Thus although Mary, who was 20 years older than Sally, was Sally's half-sister, Mary's daughter Betsy, who was Sally's niece and 10 years younger, was actually more nearly a contemporary. This probably explains the confusion in Col. Randolph's mind regarding the relationship.

Randall that his mother, Jefferson's daughter Martha, "took the
Dusky Sally stories much to heart," although she never spoke to
her sons but once on the topic. At that time, shortly before her death
in 1836, she abjured them with intense feeling "always to defend
the character of their grandfather" against such charges.[21] So although
we have in these documents the reports of two people—Sally Hemings and Colonel Randolph—who were in a position to tell the truth
about Jefferson and his relationship with Sally, we are still left with
the task of deciding which one in fact told the truth—a task that
recurs again and again in historical research.

In such a situation the research historian follows an ancient and
standard method. He has learned both in dealing with documents
from the past and in examining living witnesses that, while most
people are either unwilling or unable to tell the *whole* truth even
about events in which they have participated, nevertheless, even the
worst witness—the most prejudiced, the most untrustworthy—will
tell the truth on occasion, and the technique for extracting or distilling
the creditable items from a report that may be full of error is to seek
independent corroboration, detail by detail.[22]

For example, before accepting the truthfulness of Madison Hemings's prejudiced claim that his mother, Sally, was the child of
John Wayles, we turned for corroboration to the slave Isaac, who,
so far as we can judge had no temptation to lie about this matter
and hence is an unprejudiced independent witness to its truth. In
the case of Sally's testimony that she returned from Paris carrying
a child conceived by Jefferson, we sought corroboration in the neutral

21. {*Ibid.*, 237.}

22. Although the techniques and methods by which the professionally trained
historian tests for the truthfulness of witnesses were only codified and standardized
in the 18th century, in this instance the test had long been a method of criminal
law. The United States Constitution, for example, states that no man shall be
convicted of the capital crime of treason without the proof by "two separate witnesses" to the same overt treasonable act; this restates earlier English law, which
in its turn parallels the very ancient Hebrew code set down in Leviticus.

statistics of the *Farm Book* to determine that Sally was not truthful in reporting the birth date of her first child—that her first pregnancy, as verified by independent records, began in 1795. This fact, when established, increased the possibility that some other male of the Monticello household was her first child's father. Conversely, if corroboration of Sally's claim of her Paris pregnancy had been found, it would have substantially increased the *probability* that Jefferson was the child's father, since we can assume her Parisian circle of male acquaintances would have been quite restricted.

Therefore, faced with irreconcilable disagreement between two prejudiced witnesses—Sally Hemings and Jefferson Randolph—about the paternity of the Hemings children, we can accept neither with confidence unless we find independent corroboration for one or the other statement from some third and independent contemporary witness.

Such a witness does exist whose testimony corroborates Randolph's. This witness is Edmund Bacon, who was hired as overseer at Monticello in 1806 when Jefferson as president was living in Washington. Bacon remained as overseer until 1822, when he took his savings, migrated to Trigg County, Kentucky, and there established his own highly profitable plantation. In the 1860s Bacon told the story of his years at Monticello to a neighbor, the Reverend Hamilton W. Pierson, president of Cumberland College. Pierson wrote down Bacon's memoirs and also carefully transcribed Bacon's collection of letters from Jefferson on farm management. He then combined the two—the memoirs and the letters—in a delightful little book, which he published under the title *Jefferson at Monticello* in 1862, four years before Bacon's death. Here in this rare volume, which has been out of print for nearly a century, we find Bacon's observations on the Hemingses and their paternity; here is corroboration for Randolph's statement.[23]

23. {Hamilton W. Pierson, *Jefferson at Monticello: The Private Life of Thomas Jefferson* . . . (New York, 1862), 110–111. Bacon's memoir is reprinted in Bear, ed.,

Narrating for Pierson at the beginning of the Civil War, when emancipation impended, Bacon recalled Jefferson's dislike of slavery and noted that a number of his slaves were freed by his will. "I think," Bacon continued, "he would have freed all of them, if his affairs had not been so much involved that he could not do it. He freed one girl some years before he died, and there was a great deal of talk about it. She was nearly as white as anybody and very beautiful. People said he freed her because she was his own daughter." Here, thanks to Jefferson's *Farm Book*, which supports Bacon on this detail, we can recognize Sally's second daughter, Harriet, who was born in 1801 (given the same name as the infant who had died in 1797) and who left Monticello in 1822. And here, independently, Bacon supports Randolph by insisting that he knew Jefferson was not Harriet's father. "She was not his daughter; she was ———'s daughter. I know that. I have seen him come out of her mother's room many a morning when I went up to Monticello very early. When she was nearly grown, by Mr. Jefferson's direction I paid her stage fare to Philadelphia and gave her fifty dollars. I have never seen her since and don't know what became of her."[24]

Here, at last, not on the basis of Randolph's testimony alone or of Bacon's alone, but on the joint corroboration that each of these witnesses speaking independently gives the other, we have positive evidence and established ground for declaring Thomas Jefferson innocent of the charge that he fathered a mulatto family by his slave Sally Hemings. Since Pierson's ministerial discretion suppressed the name specified by Bacon as Sally's lover we still have only *presumptive* evidence, resting on the uncorroborated word of Colonel Ran-

---

Jefferson at Monticello, 27–117.} Since many of Jefferson's letters to Bacon are in the Huntington Library, it has been possible to check the accuracy of Pierson's published transcripts of the letters. They show that Pierson was careful and accurate in preparing the book.

24. {Pierson, *Jefferson at Monticello*, 110; also in Bear, ed., *Jefferson at Monticello*, 102.}

dolph, that this person was Peter Carr, Jefferson's favorite nephew. Perhaps some day, in the surviving letters of Albemarle neighbors like Professors Tucker or Dungleson of the University, who were regular visitors and knew well the whole Monticello family, such corroboration will be discovered. In the meantime, Jefferson stands exonerated, and Peter Carr stands accused, although in his case the historical verdict remains "not yet proven."

However, the skeptic may say—"Hold, not so fast, is Jefferson really proven innocent?" While the Randolph-Bacon evidence may be good enough to override the charges of a Callender, who was never at Monticello, or of casual visitors who saw that the Hemingses resembled Jefferson and drew a false inference therefrom, can even this double testimony of Randolph and Bacon actually outweigh Sally Hemings's statement to her children that she became Jefferson's mistress in France and bore him children? Randolph and Bacon perhaps indicate that Carr was the father of Sally's youngest children (Madison born in 1805, and Eston born in 1808), but does their evidence really throw light on the father of Sally's children born in 1795, 1798, and 1801? Bacon became overseer at Monticello in 1806; Randolph at that date was only fourteen years old. Thus, while we may grant their dependability as witnesses concerning the innocence of Jefferson's relations with Sally *after* 1806, their judgment of the earlier period can only be based on inference. Do we really dare decide Sally is completely untrustworthy, a falsifier regarding *all* her children's paternity, on this late and partial evidence of two unsympathetic white men?

No matter how sympathetic one is to Sally, one must conclude that she is not trustworthy about Jefferson's relations with her. We may pity her and even understand why she lied, but on this topic we cannot trust her. And this conclusion is based on three separate factors, two of which we have already noticed, but which must be reviewed and weighed with a third one. In the first place, we have seen that Sally falsified the date of her first pregnancy to buttress the story told her children that she became Jefferson's mistress in France. We have seen, in the second place, that she certainly deceived Madison and Eston when she told them that Jefferson begat them, for when they were born she was almost openly living as the mistress of some other man.[25]

The professional historian is taught to be extremely skeptical of any purported episode in a man's career that completely contradicts the whole tenor of his life and that requires belief in a total reversal of character. For example, since we *know* on the basis of an over-whelming mass of authenticated evidence that Jefferson was a very moderate drinker, that his taste invariably ran to diluted wines taken with his meals, and that he shows this pattern of behavior from early manhood until death, the discovery, say, of a hitherto unknown document that purported to prove that beginning in 1807 Jefferson became a closet drinker with such a thirst for raw brandy that he regularly ended his secret debauches in a drunken stupor—such a document, if discovered, would automatically be suspected by Jefferson experts to be either a forgery or a fiction.

Now we know a great deal about Jefferson's attitude toward women, his taste in women, and his behavior when in love, and Sally's story of Jefferson's purported affair with her simply does not ring true in this context. It is certain that Jefferson was in love twice. He fell in love first with Martha Wayles Skelton, a mature woman— a widow of twenty-three when the twenty-nine-year-old Jefferson married her in 1772. Martha was well educated by Virginia standards

25. It is my belief that Madison Hemings accepted Sally's story that Jefferson was his father in good faith, though there is the remote possibility that pride may have led him to deny Carr's paternity in favor of the more illustrious genes of his master. If Sally ceased being Peter Carr's concubine fairly soon after Eston's birth in 1808—in 1809 Jefferson returned to full-time residence at Monticello, which possibly was an inhibiting factor on Carr's nocturnal activities—the Hemings children would have still been too young to understand what was involved in Carr's visits with their mother. In 1808, Madison was only 3, Harriet only 7, and Beverly, the eldest, was only 10.

and was a talented musician. After her death, Jefferson through choice never married again, and there is much evidence to show that he cherished her memory to the end of his life. This loyalty to his dead wife did not prevent Jefferson from falling in love with Maria Cosway, whom he met in Paris in 1786—again a mature woman of twenty-eight, married, and with marked musical, literary, and artistic talent.[26] Jefferson's late marriage and the known details of his affair with Cosway remind us over and over again that even when the great Virginian's emotions were intensely engaged he was never the slave of passion—his head always to a degree governed his heart. Obviously, the women who attracted him most powerfully were those with some artistic, musical, or literary sophistication who offered intellectual as well as physical communion.

Sally, however, asks us to believe that the author of the "Dialogue between his Head and his Heart," one of the most sensitive and revealing love letters in the English language, would turn his back on the delectable Cosway, to whom it was addressed, to seduce a markedly immature,[27] semieducated, teen-age virgin, who stood in a peculiarly dependent personal relation to him, both as a slave, as half-sister to his dead wife, and as the companion and almost-sister to his young daughters. Sally would have us believe that having seduced her—a mere child—after she had conceived a daughter, he was so in thrall to his lust that when she begged to stay in France in order to remain free and in order that Jefferson's baby might be born free, the seducer beguiled her into returning to Virginia, to concubinage, and to servitude.

Such behavior is completely at variance with Jefferson's known

26. A recurring pattern in Jefferson's behavior is his taste for married women: his wife was a widow, Cosway was married, and the only known instance of youthful gallantry before his marriage was the unsuccessful attempt to make love to a married woman, Mrs. John Walker.

27. Abigail Adams, who sheltered Polly Jefferson and her attendant, Sally, when the two girls first arrived in Europe, testifies to Sally's immaturity in 1787: "The Girl [Sally] wants more care than the child"—eight-year-old Polly.

character, revealing a hypocrisy, a gross insensitivity, and a callous selfishness that he conspiciously lacked, whatever other failings are credited to him. Sally would ask us to believe that Jefferson's physical desire for her approached the obsessive—that it was the overruling passion of his later life: first consummated when the girl was fifteen or sixteen and her master forty-five or forty-six, resulting in one child born when Jefferson was fifty-two, a second when he was fifty-five, another when he was fifty-nine, a fourth when he was sixty-two, and finally, a fifth child born in his sixty-fifth year.

Consider, too, how Sally's story transforms the thin-skinned, censure-allergic Virginian into a being oblivious to and contemptuous of both the public opinion of the great world and the private judgments of his intimate family. She would try to convince us that Jefferson, traveling home from France with his teen-age daughters in the tight, enforced intimacy of shipboard, would exhibit his pregnant mulatto mistress as the fourth member of the family group; she expects us to credit the unbelievable fact that after Callender had broadcast to the world that this adulterous relationship existed, the sixty-year-old Jefferson, in the face of the transatlantic scandal, would continue to bed with her for at least six more years and beget two more children. All in all, Sally's story and the Jefferson it asks us to believe in, if credited as true, would require us not merely to change some shadings in his portrait but literally to reverse the picture of him as an honorable man, painted both by the contemporaries who know him well and by the multitude of later scholars who have studied with care every stage in his career. The personality of the man who figures in Sally's Hemings's pathetic story simply cannot be assimilated to the known character of the real Thomas Jefferson.

3

IT IS UNLIKELY that we will ever know the complete story of Thomas Jefferson and Sally Hemings in all its ramifications. Nor will we ever know the total pattern of the relations between the Hemingses and the Wayleses and Carrs. Parts of this complex web are gone past any hope of discovery. As Randall told Parton, borrowing a phrase from Walter Scott's *Ivanhoe*, "The secrets of an old Virginia Manor house were like the secrets of an Old Norman Castle."[28] Indeed it is something of a miracle—an unexpected victory over "Time's winged chariot"—that today we know much more than even Randall knew, that enough documents have survived to allow us to hear some of the dead actors in this ancient tragedy speak their lines in the very accents they used when living. As we listen intently, some themes in the plot and some roles in the drama emerge with clarity from the still-obscured background.

Jefferson's part is perhaps easiest to see now. On the basis of our new knowledge, added to what we already knew about him, we can reconstruct with a high degree of certainty the part he acted, and we can even guess at his motives. In the first place, it would appear that when John Wayles died in 1773, leaving Betty Hemings and her family as part of his inheritance to his daughter, Jefferson then knew that six of these children had been sired by Wayles and were thus blood relatives of his wife, Martha. Whether Martha realized that she had been given her own half-brothers and sisters as chattels we will probably never know, but the action that Jefferson then took suggests Martha Wayles's ignorance. It is certain, in any event, that Jefferson would have tried to keep this knowledge from his wife, and the evidence points to the probability that he did manage to keep the ugly truth both from his daughter and from his grandchildren, who seem never to have realized who was the father of Betty Hemings's children.

The Wayles inheritance of 1774 and the burden of knowledge it brought Jefferson clearly intensified his hatred of slavery. Since we now know the specific family experience to which Jefferson alluded,

28. {Randall to Parton, in Flower, *James Parton*, 239.}

we can read with deepened insight his scathing comments of 1782 on the South's peculiar institution: "The whole commerce between master and slave is a perpetual exercise of the most boisterous passions, the most unremitting despotism on the one part, and degrading submissions on the other. . . . The man must be a prodigy who can retain his manners and morals undepraved by such circumstances."[29] By this date Jefferson had concluded that slavery itself was so intrinsically evil that it could not possibly be reformed—the only cure "a total emancipation." But this general hope for the future did not solve Jefferson's immediate personal problem in 1774. What should he do about the Hemings children—Bob, James, Thena, Critta, Peter, and Sally, who ranged in age from the year-old baby Sally to twelve-year-old Bob—who were then living on the Wayles plantation? Should he leave them out of sight at one of his distant properties like Elk Hill? Isolating them would allow him to push them and the distressing relationship they represented at least partially out of mind; it would head off gossip and obviate possibly embarrassing questions. Probably Jefferson seriously considered this option, but characteristically he rejected it. His guiding principle in his relationship with all the Hemingses, revealed by his action in 1774 and thereafter in every decision affecting them until his death, was to accept full personal responsibility for their welfare and to treat them as nearly as possible as if they were members of his own family. It was his duty, as he conceived it, to give them all the fullest measure of his personal protection, to place them in an environment where they could grow up as self-respecting individuals.

In 1774 Jefferson brought every one of the Hemingses to Monticello, and from that date his home was literally their home. Twenty-eight years later, when Callender's charge that Sally was Jefferson's concubine had become a national scandal, Jefferson was under tremendous pressure to reverse this decision of 1774. His daughter and

29. {Jefferson's *Notes on the State of Virginia*, ed. William Peden (Chapel Hill, N.C., 1955), 162.}

his grandchildren, as we know, hoped and prayed he would send Sally and her young brood with the Jefferson features to Poplar Forest, the Jefferson estate in Bedford County, well out of sight. But Colonel Jefferson Randolph, who reports this unanimous family desire, also admits that no one of them, not even Martha Randolph, dared suggest it to Jefferson. At Monticello, and only at Monticello, did he feel that he could give the Hemingses the personal protection due them.

Edmund Bacon, whose twenty years as overseer at Monticello gave him the governance of most of the slaves, comments on the special status Jefferson accorded the Hemingses. He lists "Sally, Critta, and Betty Hemings" as among the house servants, who were "great favorites. . . . I was instructed to take no control of them. They had very little to do."[30] No Hemings ever felt the whip, the typical method of controlling slaves everywhere. The control, while they were little things, was exercised by Jefferson himself, helping them by instruction and example to grow up, along with his own children, as decent, God-fearing individuals, prepared at maturity to manage their own lives.

For, possibly as early as 1774, Jefferson reached a further decision: that the Hemings boys, when they were grown and after they had learned a trade and could support themselves, would be given their freedom if they wished it. And both Bob and James Hemings chose freedom in the 1790s, as is proven by two documents still preserved in the Jefferson papers. The first of these is an agreement in the form of a legal indenture drawn up in Philadelphia, September 15, 1793, by which Jefferson promises James Hemings, who has been taught "the art of cookery" at "great expence" in Paris, that if James will return to Virginia to teach a substitute how "to be a good cook . . . he shall be thereupon made free." James, who had seen Paris but did not find it too appealing, apparently had come to like Philadelphia

30. {"Private Life of Jefferson," Bear, ed., *Jefferson at Monticello,* 99.}

while serving Jefferson there, during his master's term as secretary of state. So James asked for his freedom to live in Philadelphia, and Jefferson countered with the offer in this document. James agreed to it, returned to Monticello, and presumably revealed the mysteries of French cuisine to a substitute, and on February 25, 1796, he was freed and given thirty dollars "to bear exp[ence] to Phila." A year earlier, on December 24, 1794, Bob Hemings had been given an indenture manumitting him.[31]

The significance of these indentures freeing Bob and James Hemings in 1794 and 1796 is threefold. First, they reveal Jefferson's considered policy toward the Hemings men—manumission if they wished it, when they were able to support themselves. Madison Hemings spoke not just for Sally's children when he said that it was a matter of pride for him and his brothers to know that they could go free when they were grown. All of Betty Hemings's sons had the same choice, though seemingly only two of them exercised it. In the second place, this contract of indenture drawn up for James in Philadelphia is probably the basis of the twisted story Sally told her children about the supposed contract Jefferson made with her in Paris. If so, it explains why Sally could be so sure that her children would be free when they were grown, and her fictitious account invited her sons to give her the chief credit for arranging a policy that Jefferson had already decided on. Third, the fact that James Hemings established himself in Philadelphia suggests the reason why Jefferson in 1822 took the unprecedented step of freeing a female Hemings, Harriet, Sally's twenty-one-year-old daughter. Edmund Bacon, it will be remembered, reports that Jefferson ordered him to give Harriet fifty dollars and to buy her a stagecoach ticket to Philadelphia. If James was established in that city, he would have been in a position to give Harriet a home and to offer her the

31. {Freeing of James Hemings, Freeing of Robert Hemings, in "Slaves and Slavery," Betts, ed., *Jefferson's Farm Book*, [15].}

protection that the words "home" and "family" imply, thus solving a problem that previously and tragically had baffled Jefferson.

For Jefferson's policy of freeing the Hemings men when they were grown was not applicable to the Hemings girls—especially not to Sally. There is convincing evidence that Sally was an outstandingly beautiful young girl and woman. Her advantages in early life and upbringing as a companion of Jefferson's own daughters, her years in Paris, all together seem to have given her manners, a style of behavior, and standards of taste that set her apart even from her mulatto kin and made her much too superior to associate with slaves in general. Unlike her mother, Betty, or her half-sister, Mary, Sally was never attracted to a Negro lover or to the white workmen at Monticello. By birth and upbringing, then, she was a socially displaced person in the America of 1790—even if freed there was no place for her to go, to marry, to have a normal family life. Educated above the level of the Negro community, she could never be accepted into the white community except on the terms that prevailed in such a Southern city as New Orleans. There the offspring of white fathers and Negro mothers were so numerous as to be thought of as a special social class, and it was customary for beautiful mulatto or quadroon girls like Sally either to staff the brothels that the city was famed for, or, if they were lucky, to become the mistress—the local term was *placée*—of a young creole of wealth.

Such a possibility would have been abhorrent to Jefferson. Therefore, since there was no place for Sally to go safely if she was freed, the Virginian kept her where he thought he could protect her best and best guarantee her a decent life—in the bosom of his own family.

Alas for poor Jefferson's intentions and his hopes. Sally at Monticello was indeed protected against the grosser hazards of sexual exploitation, but Jefferson's decision resulted in the liaison with Peter Carr. In doing his conscientious best to make up for the moral wrong practiced on the Hemingses by John Wayles, Jefferson found that in this instance he had actually compounded the old evil with a new one. Meaning well, his actions had resulted in ill. This guilty knowledge was the cross that Jefferson carried silently but with anguish in his soul for seven long years before Callender broadcast to the world that there was a scandal at Monticello. No wonder he writhed silently under the scourge of the newspapers, bit his lip, and stood mute. However, when Harriet, as attractive as her mother, budded into womanhood and the ancient wrong threatened to be repeated a third time, in 1822 Bacon was called in, Harriet was given her freedom and a ticket to Philadelphia, where her Uncle James had set up as a cook in 1796. Four years later, when Jefferson died, Sally herself was freed and was supported by her grown sons, Madison and Eston, until her own death in 1836.

Jefferson was spared one ironic bit of knowledge—the knowledge that Sally, the person best able to testify to his innocence, had picked up Callender's venomous charge about their relations and had passed it on to her children as the truth. Undoubtedly, if he had known this, if he had known that Sally's descendants to the third generation would believe him to have been Sally's lover, it would have added to his sorrow.

Why did Sally do it? Why did she mislead her children and conceal their true father's name from them?

An easy answer, of course, is Sally's vanity. It was flattering to her, as it would have been to most women, to have her name linked so intimately with one of the truly great men of the age. The widespread newspaper discussion of her supposed affair with Jefferson, which she undoubtedly was aware of, provided a tempting opportunity to elevate simultaneously her status in her own children's eyes and to give them as high a pride of ancestry as their situation as slaves allowed. Sally would have been less than human if the opportunity here offered had not been grasped. Hence the overdramatized report of her trip to France and the supposed adventures there. Every man's knowledge of his paternity rests on hearsay. Thus, though it is impossible to believe that Eston, Madison, Harriet, and Beverly did not hear remarks by the other servants on some occasions indicating that Jefferson was *not* their father, pride encouraged them to believe their mother's story, with its wealth of circumstantial detail.[32]

This is an easy answer, but it is not the only answer. One suspects that more is involved than Sally's vanity. Assuming that Peter Carr was Sally's lover, her denial of this fact seems especially significant in view of the lasting, almost conjugal, nature of their relations.

All of the evidence points to the notion that Sally's connection with Peter Carr was a genuine love match, exhibiting deep and lasting emotional involvements for both partners. There is no hint from any member of the Monticello household or from the record of Jefferson's *Farm Book* that Sally Hemings was to the slightest degree promiscuous. Indeed, all the evidence we have points to her strong instincts to continence. Like Jefferson himself, like the Jefferson children, Sally appears to have accepted middle-class standards of monogamy as the proper standards that ought to govern the relations of men and women, and we know that Sally inculcated these standards in her own children. Because of her special status at Monticello and Jefferson's protection, Sally, unlike most slave women, could not have been forced into a sexual relationship against her will. We can only assume then that when Peter Carr became her lover he must

32. Note that the descendants of Joe Fossett with far less ground than Sally's children came in time to accept a false family tradition that Joe was a child of Jefferson's. *Ebony*'s essay suggests the steps by which such an erroneous tradition would develop: "People say" that Jefferson freed some of his own children in his will; Joe Fossett was thus freed; Joe was a mulatto—Joe must have been one of Jefferson's sons. Q.E.D. It is a mistake, however, to consider this type of ancestral upgrading as a peculiarly Negro trait or even a peculiarly American trait, for it has been a standard and continuous feature of middle-class European civilization since the late Middle Ages. Indeed by far the largest category of forged documents surviving from the late Middle Ages are forged genealogies purporting to establish high-status ancestors for upwardly mobile descendants.

have wooed her. And apparently he won her heart once and for all, for there is no evidence of Sally Hemings's attachment ever to any other man.

The long-continued stability of the attachment is evidenced by the children born to Carr and Sally during a fifteen-year period. Their first child, the short-lived Harriet, was born when Sally was twenty-two and Carr was twenty-five, their fifth child, Eston, when the parents were thirty-five and thirty-eight respectively. Thus as a conservative estimate the intimacy between Sally and Carr lasted at least fifteen years, beginning in hot youth but enduring into middle age.

While Sally was faithful to her lover, Peter Carr, she could not as a slave ask him to be faithful to her. Two years after she bore Carr's first child and in the very year (1797) she conceived his second child, Carr married Hetty Smith, a member of a distinguished Baltimore family—one of her brothers was a senator from Maryland and another brother served in both Jefferson's and Madison's cabinets. Carr seemingly loved his wife, and he was certainly a devoted father to the four children Hetty bore him, but his marriage did not erase his affection, his desire, his deep emotional involvement with Sally Hemings. All of Sally's last three children were born after Peter Carr's marriage. Despite his wedding vows, despite his affection for his wife, he found that for at least ten years after his marriage he could not divorce himself from Sally.

It was this situation productive of fierce jealousy—of feeling of betrayal even—on Sally's part, that must be remembered in judging her repudiation of Carr's paternity of her children. In as much as Sally loved Carr, so much more must she have hated his wife, and on occasion hated him, too, for taking a wife. Her revenge was neither to refuse him her body nor to punish him by accepting other lovers but, more subtly, to deny to her children—the children who were the continuing mark of their mutual affection—that Carr was their father. Pride and revenge were equally compounded in the fictitious story she told her children about being Jefferson's mistress.

Love and rejection were strands in the twisted emotional knot that tied Sally to Peter Carr; love and guilt were strands twisted into the knot binding Peter to Sally during most of their adult lives. We have the record of an eyewitness report on Carr's confessed shame over the sorrow his attachment had caused Jefferson and the rest of the Monticello family after the newspapers began to mock the president for his supposed amours, but the guilt with love must have been present earlier. Peter Carr must have been conscious, long before Callender made Sally's name notorious, that this affair was only the most obvious and sensational way in which he had disappointed Jefferson's hopes and plans for his career.

For Jefferson, whose only son had died in infancy, looked on Peter, the child of his favorite sister and Dabney Carr, "the dearest friend I knew,"[33] almost as his own son, and on Peter's future Jefferson heavily invested his aspirations and hopes. Sometime after their father's death the Carr boys came to live at Monticello, where Jefferson personally acted as Peter's "preceptor" until he embarked on his diplomatic mission to France. At this time he asked James Madison to become Peter's guardian, recommending him as "a boy of fine dispositions and sound masculine talents," who had already mastered Latin and the rudiments of Greek, and was now ready to embark on an intensive program of advanced "philosophic" reading that would prepare him for a career of public service.[34] But Jefferson while in France was not content to leave Peter's education even to such admirable proxies as Madison and George Wythe, who acted as the boy's tutor in 1786. There was a steady flow of letters from Paris to Peter in Virginia offering guidance on his studies, his manners, and his morals. Peter was encouraged to consider his time as a precious commodity and to never waste a moment of it. He was warned that "every day you lose, will retard a day your entrance on that public

33. {Jefferson to James Madison, May 8, 1784, Julian P. Boyd, ed., *The Papers of Thomas Jefferson* (Princeton, N.J., 1950–), VII, 233.}
34. {*Ibid.*}

stage whereon you may begin to be useful to yourself," and that "the acquisition of science . . . is what (next to an honest heart) will above all things render you dear to your friends, and give you fame and promotion in your own country." To provide Peter with the "knowing head" and the necessary professional knowledge for political leadership, Jefferson carefully worked out elaborate and comprehensive reading lists (they have been preserved in his papers) of the basic books on politics and history, on natural science and mathematics that the youth should master. And from Paris came parcels of books for Peter's use.[35]

Along with the intellectual guidance came moral instruction, for as Jefferson reiterated, "a knowing head" is a secondary blessing compared to "an honest heart." "Give up money, give up fame, give up science, give the earth itself and all it contains rather than do an immoral act."[36] Morals, Jefferson told Peter, were not like astronomy, a matter of "Science," and, at best, reading books "will encourage as well as direct your feelings."[37] Above all, "lose no occasion of exercising your dispositions to be grateful, to be generous, to be charitable, to be humane, to be true, just, firm, orderly, courageous etc. Consider every act of this kind as an exercise which will strengthen your moral facilities, and increase your worth."[38]

As a practical rule which would invariably supply a sure test for honorable and right conduct, Jefferson offered Peter this advice: "Whenever you are to do a thing tho' it can never be known but to yourself, ask yourself, how you would act were all the world looking at you, and act accordingly."[39]

Peter, who worshipped his uncle, tried, as his letters show, to follow the austere regimen planned for him. Both Madison and

35. {Jefferson to Peter Carr, Aug. 19, 1785, *ibid.*, VIII, 405–408.}
36. {*Ibid.*, 406.}
37. {Jefferson to Peter Carr, Aug. 10, 1787, *ibid.*, XII, 15.}
38. {*Ibid.*}
39. {Jefferson to Carr, Aug. 19, 1785, *ibid.*, VIII, 406.}

Wythe testify to his industry and seriousness. Indeed he had progressed so well that on April 18, 1787, he was begging Jefferson to let him come to Paris to acquire European polish and to add the knowledge of men to that of books. Jefferson, however, denied the request. When he had sailed for France in 1784 he had wondered if it might not be desirable to have Peter join him in Paris, but once there he was "thoroughly cured of that Idea."[40] In fact he had come to believe that it was a great mistake for any young American boy to travel to Europe. "When men of sober age travel, they gather knowledge which they may apply usefully for their country," but young men are exposed to "inconveniences" which far outweigh any advantages to be gained. From observations "founded in experience" Jefferson feared that if Peter came to Paris he would pick up habits and manners that would "poison" the residue of his life.[41] The young American abroad "acquires a fondness for European luxury and dissipation. . . . He is led by the strongest of all the human passions into a spirit for female intrigue destructive of his own and others happiness, or a passion for whores destructive of his health, and in both cases learns to consider fidelity to the marriage bed as an ungentlemanly practice."[42] Temptation to form "a connection, as is the fashion here," would be well nigh irresistible; it is difficult for young men "to refuse it where beauty is a begging in every street." So Peter's request was denied, but Jefferson assured him: "There is no place where your pursuit of knowledge will be so little obstructed by foreign objects as in your own country, nor any wherein the virtues of the heart will be less exposed to be weakened. Be good, be learned, and be industrious, and you will not want the aid of traveling to render you precious to your country, dear to your friends, happy within yourself."[43]

40. {Jefferson to Walker Maury, Aug. 19, 1785, *ibid.*, 409.}
41. {Jefferson to Carr, Aug. 10, 1787, *ibid.*, XII, 17.}
42. {Jefferson to John Banister, Jr., Paris, Oct. 15, 1785, *ibid.*, VIII, 636–637.}
43. {Jefferson to Carr, Aug. 10, 1787, *ibid.*, XII, 17–18.}

Consequently, Peter remained in Virginia, seasoning his intensive reading with attendance at the county courts. In 1789, with Madison as chaperon, he did travel to New York to see Washington inaugurated and to meet the political leaders from all over the United States who were starting the wheels of the new federal government, but he was back in Virginia by the end of the year when Jefferson, his cousins, and Sally returned from France. In 1793, just about the time of the commencement of his attachment to Sally, he was admitted to the bar, and no young Virginian of his generation seemed to have more favorable prospects of a distinguished career. Learned, supported by both Jefferson and Madison, he came to the bar and the forum with other qualities. William Wirt, a friend who was a sound judge, found him "naturally eloquent. His voice was melody itself. He had the advantage of a large commanding figure, a countenance like his soul, open and noble." But Carr's career petered out almost at once—two undistinguished terms in the Virginia House of Delegates (1801–1804) and it was finished. Jefferson's first wish for him, that he would be "precious" to his country, was not granted.

One can be sure, too, from our knowledge of Peter Carr's inability to solve his ambiguous relations with Sally Hemings and his wife, Hetty Smith Carr, that Jefferson's third wish, made when Peter was seventeen, that he would be happy within himself, was not fulfilled. Only the second wish, that Peter would be "dear" to his friends, came true. In the obituary prepared when Carr died in 1815, aged forty-five, William Wirt wrote: "No man was dearer to his friends; and there was never a man to whom his friends were more dear." Peter Carr's great capacity to give and to inspire affection stands as his most lasting achievement, and what this involved in heartbreak for his uncle and his two families we have seen.

Here then is the story, or as much of it as we are ever likely to know, of the scandals at Monticello. Here are the circumstances that knotted the lives of the Wayles, the Hemingses, the Carrs, and the Jeffersons into the tangled web of love and hatred, of pride and guilt, of love and shame. Today it has become fashionable for some historians to defend slavery as a "good" system that had reciprocal advantages for Negroes and whites. Slavery was not really bad in itself, these scholars say, if only the master was a humane and kindly person—the evils of slavery, with its institutionalized inequality of human beings, should be attributed chiefly to the evil masters who were the rare exceptions in the antebellum South. Decent people, they argue, can transform a legalized system of unequal rights into decent personal relations. Thomas Jefferson, who was the best of masters, who had experienced the capacity of the *system* of inequalities to poison the relations of decent men and women, black and white, who were trapped in it, knew better. "The whole commerce between master and slave is a perpetual exercise of the most boisterous passions, the most unremitting despotism on the one part, and degrading submissions on the other. . . . And with what execration should the statesman be loaded, who permitting one half the citizens thus to trample on the rights of the other, transforms those into despots, and these into enemies. . . . Can the liberties of a nation be thought secure when we have removed their only firm basis, a conviction in the minds of the people that these liberties are of the gift of God? That they are not to be violated but with his wrath? Indeed I tremble for my country when I reflect that God is just: that his justice cannot sleep for ever!"[44]

44. {Jefferson, *Notes on the State of Virginia*, ed. Peden, 162–163.}

Others have commented on Douglass Adair's proclivity for engaging in widely ranging research, although an overview reveals an intriguing unity of concern. His fascination with Col. Richard Rumbold is handsomely explained in the following brief essay, the footnotes to which are as stimulating and rewarding as the text itself. Rumbold, obviously, was part and parcel of that "symbolic experience" Adair associated with the Founding Fathers.

Included here, too, as a pendant, is one more Adair reference to Rumbold, fourteen years after.

"PROSECUTIONS FOR TREASON were generally virulent," observed Benjamin Franklin to the Constitutional Convention on August 20, 1787, "and perjury too easily made use of against innocence." There was no disagreement with Franklin's comment among the other delegates who had assembled at Philadelphia during that hot summer of 1787 to write a new Constitution for the United States. These men all felt with Franklin that treason must be defined precisely in the Constitution, if political liberty were to be preserved in the new nation they had helped to create; they agreed with Franklin that

SOURCE: Reprinted from the *William and Mary Quarterly*, 3d Ser., IX (1952), 521–531.

274

individuals charged with treason must be protected with ironclad judicial procedures, if "innocence" were to be saved from the "virulence" that inevitably attends treason trials, which, by their very nature, tend to become political prosecutions. Therefore, the Convention on August 20, with a unanimity that was not always apparent in their proceedings, insisted that the Committee of Detail rewrite the treason clause in the Constitution into the form in which we know it today, carefully defining the meaning of treason against the United States and requiring that no one charged with the crime could be convicted, except on the evidence of two witnesses to the same overt treasonable act.[1]

James Madison was to explain the concern of the Convention to provide in this way a copper-riveted definition of the crime, on grounds which echoed Franklin's fears, expressed on the Convention floor, that treason trials would become political trials. "New fangled and artificial treasons," Madison wrote in *Federalist* 43, "have been the great engines by which violent factions, the natural offsprings of free government, have usually wreaked their alternate malignity on each other." Therefore, he continued, "the convention have with great judgment, opposed a barrier to this peculiar danger, by inserting a constitutional definition of the crime, fixing the proof necessary for conviction of it, and restraining the congress, even in punishing it, from extending the consequences of guilt beyond the person of its author."[2]

---

1. "Treason against the United States shall consist only in levying War against them, or in adhering to their Enemies, giving them Aid and Comfort. No Person shall be convicted of Treason unless on the Testimony of two Witnesses to the same overt Act, or on Confession in open Court.

"The Congress shall have Power to declare the Punishment of Treason, but no Attainder of Treason shall work Corruption of Blood, or Forfeiture except during the Life of the Person attainted." Article III, Sec. 3, Constitution of the United States. The most searching modern analysis of the intent of the Founding Fathers in writing this clause is to be found in Willard Hurst, "Treason in America," *Harvard Law Review*, LVIII (1944), 226–272, 395–444.

2. The Fathers did such a careful job in their strict definition of treason and in erecting safeguards against the use of perjured and malignant evidence in state trials

Why were the Founding Fathers so fearful about the invention of "new fangled and artificial treasons" as weapons in the warfare of "factions," or, as we would call them today, political parties? The answer is explained in part by their concrete and detailed knowledge of the story of treason trials in old England, for their definition of treason—as the debates in the Constitutional Convention show—was based on the famous treason statute of Edward III, revised to eliminate weaknesses in the statute revealed by the history of later English treason trials.

Among these later trials, those instituted by the Stuarts, in the seventeenth century, were of most concern to Madison, Franklin, Wilson, and the other members of the Constitutional Convention, for there were to be seen most clearly the terrible consequences, both for national unity and for individual liberty, of the use of "new fangled and artificial treasons" as a method whereby political parties wreaked vengeance on each other. Thus the Fathers' insistence on writing a precise definition of the crime into the very Constitution itself shows their determination to keep future American judges from

---

that the political trials of our day take the form, not of treason trials, but of "investigations" for "disloyalty," "un-Americanism," "security risks," and "subversive activity." All of these "crimes," vaguely labeled and impossible of exact definition, are mere circumlocutions for treason, however, and are so interpreted by the public. Therefore, to see the use of "new fangled and artificial treasons" by "violent factions" today, serving political ends much as "constructive treason" served in the Stuart courts at the time of the Popish and Rye-House Plots, one must study the procedures of the various un-American investigating committees established by Congress and the several state legislatures. The careful analysis by Lawrence H. Chamberlain, *Loyalty and Legislative Action: A Survey of Activity by the New York State Legislature, 1919–1949* (Cornell, N.Y., 1951), for example, reveals a pattern all too familiar to students of 17th-century English state trials. As one reads there of the behavior of the Lusk, McNaboe, Rapp-Coudert committees, one sees again fact-finding confused with prosecution, witnesses forced into the posture of defendants but with no procedural protection against political malignancy, innocence convicted, and public hearings transformed into public extravaganzas—all adding up to the type of judicial abattoir that the Fathers, who knew well the consequences for liberty, had tried so hard to prevent.

telling an accused prisoner, as Sir Walter Raleigh was told by Chief Justice Popham, that *his* statutory right to face his accuser in open court was no right at all—"the Statutes you speak of were found to be inconvenient," Popham remarked, "and were taken away by another law." Thus the Fathers' insistence, also set down in the very Constitution itself, that conviction of treason must rest on the evidence of two witnesses to the same *overt* act, shows their determination to prevent the sort of judicial procedures that hustled Algernon Sidney to his death in 1683, convicted, not of *acting* against the state, but of thinking "dangerous thoughts" about government and of "guilt by association."[3]

3. A brilliant account of the influence of Sidney, the Whig martyr, on the American Revolution is contained in Caroline Robbins, "Algernon Sidney's *Discourses Concerning Government:* Textbook of Revolution," *William and Mary Quarterly,* 3d Ser., IV (1947), 267–296. Sidney with five other Whig lords acted as the "Council," or strategy committee, of the Whig party after Shaftesbury's death. They were in contact with Robert Ferguson, who engineered the Rye-House Plot among a gang of broken tradesmen, ex-Cromwellian soldiers, and the like, from the Whig underworld, but Sidney, Essex, Russell, the duke of Monmouth, and the other Whig lords were given no hint of the scheme to ambush the king. Consequently, when Russell and Sidney were brought to trial, there was no real evidence against them of overt acts of treason in general, or complicity in the Rye-House Plot in particular. Nevertheless, Lord Howard of Escrick, to secure his own pardon, basely provided evidence against his companions which could be interpreted as proving their guilt. Even so, in Sidney's case, "the second witness" giving evidence of his treason could not be found. Therefore, to convict him, the crown had recourse to the manuscript of his *Discourses Concerning Government* found in his study. Excerpts read from this unpublished treatise were used to show the antimonarchical cast of Sidney's thought and his belief that it was just to resist tyrants, *vi et armis.*

Besides the "guilt by association" and the "dangerous thoughts" evidence, one other factor contributed immeasurably to bring both Sidney and Russell to the scaffold. This was the suicide of Essex in the Tower on the very day of Russell's trial, a suicide which large sections of the public inevitably misinterpreted as a confession of guilt. The tremendous effect of Essex's suicide on Sidney's fate raises one obvious question for all students with a fancy for historical parallels in treason trials. Would the abortive suicide attempt of Whittaker Chambers (just now revealed in his autobiography) have changed the verdict in the Hiss trial if Chambers had succeeded in killing himself?

Among these seventeenth-century treason trials, in which, as the Fathers knew so well, Stuart judges, acting as political partisans, turned the processes of justice into farce, one case holds a peculiar interest for Americans. It is the case of Colonel Richard Rumbold,[4] the old one-eyed Cromwellian soldier, who, in 1683, owned the Rye House, where it was proposed by an underground group of extremist Whigs that Charles II and his horrid Catholic brother James should be ambushed. The details of the Rye House Plot are obscure to this day. Certainly there was enough treasonable talk in this underground group about the possibility of the death of Charles and James to provide the crown with all the evidence needed to convict the whole gang—especially since the prosecution was less intent on discovering the truth of the plot than in using it to claim vengeance on the Whigs for Tory blood, shed during the trumped-up treason trials of the Popish Plot.[5] At any rate, Rumbold, knowing he was a dead man,

4. The story of Rumbold's life and the pattern of his personality have to be pieced together from scattered fragments. Questioning at his trial did elicit a few facts about his career, and these are most fully reported in the "Memoirs of Lord Fountainhall" printed in Charles James Fox, *A History of the Early Part of the Reign of James the Second* (London, 1808), app. IV. Born in 1622, Rumbold "owned he had been fighting against these idols of monarchy and prelacy since he was nineteen years of age." He served as a lieutenant in Cromwell's own regiment, fought at Dunbar, Worcester, and Dundee, and was one of the guard on horseback at the scaffold when Charles was beheaded. After the Restoration, he married the widow of a maltster and thus became proprietor of the Rye House. For Rumbold's part in the plot of 1683, see the testimony of the various informers and witnesses, in T. B. Howell, *A Complete Collection of State Trials and Proceedings for High Treason and Other Crimes and Misdemeanors* ... (London, 1811), IX, 294*ff*; the report of his trial in 1685 is in XI, 873–888.

A description of Rumbold's appearance in 1683, issued by the crown in the proclamation ordering his arrest, is reprinted from the *London Gazette*, June 25–28, 1683, in J. W. Ebsworth, ed., *The Roxburghe Ballads* (Hertford, 1884), V, 309. He is described there as "of middle stature, about 46 years [actually 61] of age, a smart man in discourse, having lost one of his eyes, his face somewhat thin, wearing his own hair, which is brown, and not very long; he is a round trussed man." Among the conspirators, Rumbold's one eye and his capacity for military leadership gained him the nickname of "Hannibal."

5. Since Americans in 1952, much as Englishmen of the period 1678–1688, are living in "a tyme wherein perjurie for principles passes for a Christian duty and

if caught, fled England and only returned two years later, in 1685, when Monmouth and Argyle tried to drive James from the throne by simultaneous armed landings in the west of England and in Scotland. Both rebellions were put down quickly and easily, and then the bloody work of reprisals commenced. Among the first tried and executed was Rumbold, who had been captured with Argyle's forces, after being badly wounded. Since it did not serve the crown's political purposes to have Rumbold die of his wounds, his trial was hurriedly rushed to conclusion, and he was executed, June 26, 1685.

On the scaffold, Colonel Rumbold, as was the custom, made a speech justifying his actions. One of the most striking statements in it was that "there was no man born marked of God above another; for none comes into the world with a saddle on his back, neither any booted and spurr'd to ride him." Printed on broadsides, Rumbold's speech was given wide publicity in 1685 by the Tories, to prove that he was "a republican," anti-divine-right, and hence, by definition, a traitor, who well deserved his death. Then when William and Mary, in 1688, drove James from the throne, and the Whig martyrs of the Rye House Plot were proclaimed "patriots," Rumbold's speech was printed again, to prove the Rye House Plot a sham plot and frame-up. From these contemporary printings, the speech was taken up by the English historians and political writers of the eighteenth century—and most of them who mentioned Rumbold quoted his "boots and saddle" image.

------

heroic devotion" (Sir George M'Kenzie, judge advocate of Scotland, speaking in 1681, reported in Howell, *State Trials*, XI, 86), we know from bitter experience how very little truth is needed to give popular credence to a monstrous superstructure of lies, when fears of international popish plots or Communist plots grip the mind of a nation. The actual subversive activity of a Coleman in 1678, a Rumbold in 1683, or a Hiss in 1937 merely furnishes the opportunity for unscrupulous and sinister leaders like a Shaftesbury, a Jeffries, or a McCarthy to manipulate the mishmash of truth and half-truth, provided by such pitiful and sinister figures as an Oates and a Dangerfield, a Chambers and a Budenz. To give general credit to evidence from such hysterical and shaky sources is to invite public denunciation for political and private profit to become accepted judicial procedure.

Thomas Jefferson, at some point in his careful, and, one might say, professional, study of English seventeenth-century history,[6] read about Rumbold and was struck by the dramatic strength of the old soldier's metaphor. Apparently he stored it away in his head, and when it came time for him to make his formal "dying speech," it lay ready to hand for his use.[7]

The occasion was the fiftieth anniversary of the Declaration of Independence, July 4, 1826, a date the city of Washington, D.C., planned to honor with a tremendous celebration. Mayor Roger C. Weightman wrote Jefferson, therefore, asking if he would attend the celebration, make a speech, and receive the honor due him as the Declaration's author. Unfortunately, Jefferson was far too feeble even to consider the trip. He had almost died in February 1826, and, though his strength had rallied a little, he lived through the spring

---

6. Jefferson, from 1774 on, very definitely took a *professional* interest in the meaning and history of treason in England. In the "Instructions by the Virginia Convention to their Delegates in Congress, 1774," he castigates General Gage for not knowing the Treason Statute of Edward III and for not understanding why history had proved it so necessary "to take out of the hands of tyrannical Kings, and of weak and wicked Ministers, that deadly Weapon which constructive Treason had furnished them with, and which had drawn the Blood of the best and honestest Men in the Kingdom." Julian P. Boyd, ed., *The Papers of Thomas Jefferson* (Princeton, N.J., 1950–), I, 141*ff*. In 1776, Jefferson, on the "Committee on Spies" of the Continental Congress, played the chief part in drafting the recommendation to the state governments for establishing standards of treason in the state codes; and in the "Revisal of the Laws of Virginia," it fell to him to rewrite the Virginia "Bill for Proportioning crimes and Punishment," which included treason. Boyd, ed., *Jefferson Papers*, II, 663. For an analysis of Jefferson's position on treason, see Hurst, "Treason in America," *Harvard Law Rev.*, LVIII (1944), 247*ff*.

7. The following books (and there may have been more) which quote the Rumbold metaphor were owned by Jefferson and listed in one or another of his libraries. The editions listed are those which Jefferson himself owned.

[Paul] de Rapin Thoyras, *Histoire d'Angleterre*, 2d ed. (La Haye, 1727).

[Gilbert Burnet], *Bishop Burnet's History of His Own Time* (London, 1734).

J[ames] Burgh, *Political disquisitions; or, an enquiry into public errors, defects, and abuses* (Philadelphia, [1775]).

Charles James Fox, *A History of the Early Part of the Reign of James the Second* (Charleston, 1808).

of that year at Monticello expecting death almost daily. When he wrote Weightman, on June 24, however, regretfully declining the honor, he set down in his letter his final convictions on what the Declaration of Independence and America's successful experiment in free government meant to the whole world, fifty years after 1776. "All eyes are opened or opening," Jefferson wrote, "to the rights of man. The general spread of the light of science has already laid open to every view the palpable truth that the mass of mankind has not been born with saddles on their backs, nor a favored few booted and spurred ready to ride them legitimately by the grace of God. These are grounds of hope for others. For ourselves, let the annual return of this day [July 4] forever refresh our recollections of these rights, and an undiminished devotion to them."[8] In a very real sense, this was Jefferson's dying speech—his last formal statement on democracy to his countrymen. One can be sure that old Colonel Rumbold, in whatever heaven or hell is reserved for unsuccessful revolutionaries, would have fiercely applauded both the sentiment and Thomas Jefferson's elegant rephrasing of the striking image he had used so long before on the bloody scaffold in Edinburgh.

The *Quarterly* is reprinting Rumbold's speech from a Whig pamphlet of 1689, entitled:

The
Dying Speeches
Of
Several Excellent Persons,
Who
Suffered for their Zeal against Popery,
and Arbitrary Government:
VIZ.

8. To Roger C. Weightman, Monticello, June 24, 1826, in Andrew A. Lipscomb and Albert Ellery Bergh, eds., *The Writings of Thomas Jefferson* (Washington, D.C., 1903–1904), XVI, 182.

I. Mr. Stephen Colledg, at Oxford, August 31, 1681.

II. The Lord Russel in Lincolns-Inn-Fields, July 21, 1683.

III. Col. Sidney, on Tower-Hill, December 7, 1683.

IV. Col. Rumbald, at Edinburgh, June 26, 1685.

V. The Lady Lisle, at Winchester, In September 1685.

VI. Alderman Cornish, in Cheapside, Octob. 23, 1685.

VII. Capt. Walcot, at Tyburn, in July 20, 1683.

(London, 1689).

The editors wish to express their thanks to Miss Caroline Robbins of Bryn Mawr for her generosity in lending us her personal copy of the pamphlet, from which our text is printed.

TO THE READER

Tho some of these *Speeches* were Printed some Years since, and generally received by all sorts of People with great Concern; but being in loose Sheets, they are not so well preserved, therefore I have thought fit to Collect them together that so they may be often Reviewed, and that the Present and Future may with Abhorrency behold the Iniquity of the late Violent Times, when so many Excellent Persons were destroyed by *Forms and Subtilties of Law;* and *Scribere est agere* was brought in for an Evidence (as in the Case of Col. Sydney) when no other could be found.

And whereas the Business of the *Ry-House Plot* has been received by some as an Article of Faith, and a smooth History of it has been imposed on the Nation,[9] therefore I thought good to add Colonel *Rumbald's* Speech to undeceive the World, by which it is evident

---

9. The anonymous compiler of the pamphlet here refers to: [Thomas Sprat], *A True Account and Declaration of the Horrid Conspiracy against the late King, His Present Majesty and the Government* ... ([London], 1685). Sprat, who had been made bishop of Rochester in 1684, prepared this "official" account of the "protestant plot" to express his gratitude for his preferment. Jefferson owned a copy of this work.

(if we may believe the Dying words of a good Man) that was a meer Sham-Contrivance, to bring an Odium on *Protestants*.

It has been always the Practice of the *Papists* to make *Sham-Plots*, to render *Protestants* odious, and to hide the foulness of their own Real Plots, of which this Nation has had sufficient Experience; especially in their late Damnable Plot. For when it was clearly proved on them, that they Conspired against the Life of the late King, and our Government, they presently Contrived to cast that Wickedness on *Protestants*; and too many of our easie *Church-men* were impos'd on to believe it. But through the Goodness of God, and the Auspicious Arrival of the Prince of Orange, the Eyes of the Nation are opened, and now we hope we have an Opportunity to be Delivered (if our Sins prevent not) from the Plots and Tyranny of the Church of Rome; Which God in his Infinite Mercy grant. *Amen.*

The Last Speech of Col. RICHARD RUMBOLD, at the MARKET-CROSS of EDINBURGH, with several things that passed at his Tryal, 26 JUNE, 1685.

About Eleven of the Clock he was brought from the Castle of *Edinburgh*, to the Justices Court, in a great Chair, on Mens Shoulders; where at first he was asked some Questions, most of which he answer'd with Silence; at last said, "He humbly conceived, It was not necessary for him to add to his own Accusation, since he was not ignorant they had enough already to do his Business; and therefore he did not design to fret his Conscience at that time with Answering Questions." After which, his *Libel* being read, the Court proceeded in usual manner; first asking him, *If he had anything to say for himself before the Jury closed?* His Answer was, "He owned it all, saving that part, of having Designed the King's Death; and desired all present, to believe the words of a Dying Man; he never directly nor indirectly intended such a Villany; that he abhorred the very thoughts of it; and that he blessed God he had that Reputation in the World, that he knew none that had the Impudence to ask him that Question; and he detested the thoughts of such an Action; and he hoped all good People would believe him, which was the only way he had to clear himself; and he was sure that this Truth should be one day made manifest to all Men." He was again asked, *If he had any Exception against the Jury*? He answered "No, but wished them to do as God and their Consciences directed them." Then they withdrew, and returned their Verdict in half an hour, and brought him in *Guilty*. The Sentence followed:

For him to be taken from that Place to the next Room, and from thence to be Drawn on a Hurdle, betwixt Two and Four of the Clock, to the Cross of Edinburgh, the Place of Execution, and there to be Hang'd, Drawn and Quartered.

He received his Sentence with an undaunted Courage and Chearfulness. Afterwards he was delivered into the Town Magistrates Hands; they brought to him two of their Divines, and offered him their Assistance upon the Scaffold; which he altogether refused, telling them, "That if they had any good Wishes for him, he desired they would spend them in their own Closets, and leave him now to seek God in his own Way." He had several Offers of the same kind by others, which he put off in like manner. He was most serious and fervent in Prayers the few hours he lived (as the Sentinels observed, who were present all the while.) The Hour being come, he was brought to the Place of Execution, where he saluted the People on all sides of the Scaffold, and after having refreshed himself with a Cordial out of his Pocket, he was supported by two Men, while he spoke to the People in these words:

Gentlemen and Brethren, It is for all Men that come into the World once to Die, and after Death to Judgment, and since Death is a Debt that all of us must pay, it is but a matter of small moment what way it be done; and seeing the Lord is pleased in this manner to take me to himself, I confess, something hard to Flesh and Blood, yet, blessed be his Name, who hath made me not only Willing, but Thankful for his honouring me to lay down the Life he gave, for his Name; in which, were every Hair in this Head and Beard of mine a Life, I should joyfully sacrifice them for it, as I do this: And Providence having brought me hither, I think it most necessary to clear my self of some Aspersions laid on my Name; and *first*, That I should have had so horrid an Intention of Destroying the King and his Brother.

(Here he repeated what he had said before to the Justices on this Subject.)

It was also laid to my Charge, That I was Antimonarchical.

It was ever my Thoughts, That Kingly Government was the best of all, Justly Executed: I mean, such as by our ancient Laws; that is, a King, and a Legal Free Chosen Parliament. The King having, as I conceive, Power enough to make him Great, the People also as much Property as to make them Happy; they being as it were contracted to one another. And who will deny me, that this was not the Just Constituted Government of our Nation? How absurd is it then for Men of Sense to maintain, That though the one Party of this Contract breaketh all Conditions, the other should be obliged to perform their Part? No; this Error is contrary to the Law of God, the Law of Nations, and the Law of Reason. But as Pride hath been the Bait the Devil hath catched most by, ever since the Creation, so it continues to this day with us. Pride caused our first Parents to fall from the blessed Estate wherein they were created; they aiming to be Higher and Wiser than God allowed, which brought an everlasting Curse on them and their Posterity. It was Pride caused God to Drown the Old World. And it was Nimrod's Pride in building Babel, that caused that heavy Curse of Division of Tongue to be spread among us, as it is at this day. One of the greatest Afflictions the Church of God groaneth under, That there should be so many Divisions during their Pilgrimage here; but this is their Comfort, that the Day draweth near, whereas there is but one Shepheard, there shall be but One Sheepfold. It was therefore in the Defence of this Party, in their Just Rights and Liberties, against Popery and Slavery———

(At which words they Beat the Drums;) To which he said:

They need not trouble themselves; for he should say no more of his Mind on that Subject, since they were so disingenuous, as to interrupt a Dying Man, only to assure the People, he adhered to the *True Protestant Religion,* detesting the erroneous Opinions of many that called themselves so; and I Die this day in the Defence of the ancient Laws and Liberties of these Nations: And though God, for Reasons best known to himself, hath not seen it fit to honour us, as to make us the instruments for the deliverance of his people; yet as I have lived so I die in the faith, that he will speedily arise for the deliverance of his Church and people. And I desire all of you to prepare for this with speed. I may say, This is a deluded Generation, vail'd with Ignorance, that though *Popery* and *Slavery* be riding in upon them, do not perceive it; and though I am sure there was no Man born marked of God above another; for none comes into the World with a Saddle on his Back, neither any Booted and Spurr'd to Ride him;[10] not but that I am well

---

10. Caroline Robbins (who probably knows more about the patterns of thought of the 17th- and 18th-century radical Whigs than any other living scholar), suggests that Rumbold's metaphor of the people as the horse and a tyrant as the rider may have been borrowed from the writings of the Venetian statesman and philosopher-historian Paolo Sarpi (1552–1623), famous in 17th-century England as a "Protestant champion," since he was the leading spokesman for Venice against the papacy. Zera S. Fink, *The Classical Republicans: An Essay in the Recovery of a Pattern of Thought in Seventeenth Century England* (Evanston, Ill., 1945), has shown how influential Sarpi's writings were on Milton, Harrington, Sidney, and their lesser Whig followers, especially in the 1670s and 1680s. Among these lesser Whig figures was Thomas Gordon (d. 1750), who, with his patron, Trenchard, issued a weekly paper called the *Independent Whig,* which was collected and issued as a book under that title in 1721. In *Letter II* (first published Jan. 27, 1720), Gordon, after blasting away at those among England's higher clergy whose claims had such Romish tendencies that they inevitably squinted toward kingly tyranny, concluded thus: "As *Father Paul* says of England, The Horse is bridled and saddled, and the old *Rider* is just getting upon his Back." Miss Robbins, who called my attention to this quotation, could not identify the source in Sarpi's writings, nor have I been more successful in my search.

However, a macabre use of a parallel image by Tories, venting their hatred and triumph upon the convicted Rye-House plotters, can be seen in an anonymous ballad of 1683, "Five years Sham Plots Discover'd in a True One." The final verse

satisfied, that God hath wisely ordered different Stations for Men in the World, as I have already said: Kings having as much Power as to make them Great, and the people as much Property as to make them Happy. And to conclude; I shall only add my Wishes for the Salvation of all Men, who were created for that end.

After ending these words, he prayed most fervently near three quarters of an hour, freely forgiving all Men, even his greatest Enemies, begging most earnestly for the Deliverance of *Sion* from all her Persecutors, particularly praying for *London, Edinburgh,* and *Dublin, from which the Streams run that Rule God's People in these three Nations.*

Being asked some hours before his Execution, *If he thought not his Sentence Dreadful?* He answered, *He wished he had a Limb for every Town in Christendom.*[11]

---

reads: "The Saddle is now on the right Horse, / The Whig must mount for *Tyburn* in course; / For these can be no false alarms / We have their confession: the Men and their Arms, / Make *Catch* perceive his harvest is near. / He swears if his Horse do not fail him. / He'll not take a thousand pound this year / For what his Trade may avail him." Ebsworth, ed., *Roxburghe Ballads,* V, 294. "Catch" is, of course, Jack Ketch, the executioner, and his "horse" is the scaffold, often called "the Tyburn Mare."

11. This last statement of Rumbold's must have had a familiar ring to some of the older citizens of Edinburgh, for the dying man was merely repeating the sentiments of the gallant marquis of Montrose, famous Cavalier leader in the Civil War, who was captured by the Covenanters and executed in Edinburgh, May 21, 1650.

Montrose in his "dying speech" (as quoted in Hume's *History*) said: "For my part, I am much prouder to have my head affixed to the place where it is sentenced to stand, than to have my picture hang in the King's bed-chamber. So far from being sorry, that my quarters are to be sent to the four cities of the kingdom; I wish I had limbs enow to be dispersed into all the cities of Christendom, there to remain as testimonies in favour of the cause for which I suffer."

Editor
William and Mary Quarterly
Box 220
Williamsburg, Virginia

Sir:

A note of amplification that may interest some of your readers. In the October 1952 issue of the *Quarterly* there was a short piece calling attention to the parallel between Jefferson's "last word" on the significance of the American experiment in democracy, written 24 June 1826, and the "dying speech" from the scaffold of Colonel Richard Rumbold, hanged-drawn-and-quartered at Edinburgh, 26 June 1685. The Rumbold statement: "I am sure there was no Man born marked of God above another; for none comes into the World with a Saddle on his Back, neither any booted and spurr'd to Ride him."

In Barbara W. Tuchman's *The Proud Tower* (1966), p. 22, she notes a third version offered by A. G. Gardiner, editor of the London *Daily News* in his autobiography, *Prophets, Priests and Kings*, first published in 1908. In speaking of the county oligarchy of England at the turn of the century, Gardiner wrote that they saw society made up of "a small select aristocracy born booted and spurred to ride, a large dim mass born saddled and bridled to be ridden."

There may be a moral here about progress and the persistence of metaphor.

Claremont, California Douglass Adair

source: Reprinted from the *William and Mary Quarterly*, 3d Ser., XXIII (1966), 672.

❧ 10 ❧

THE MYSTERY OF THE

HORN PAPERS

A superb exercise in historical detection, "The Mystery of the Horn Papers," which Adair coauthored with Arthur Pierce Middleton, had its origin in an investigating committee established by the Institute of Early American History and Culture under the chairmanship of Solon J. Buck (then U.S. Archivist). The Reverend Dr. Middleton was appointed secretary to the committee and charged with gathering evidence, which he did.

The Institute decided to publish a brief account of the whole affair in the *William and Mary Quarterly*—of which Douglass Adair was then the editor. Dr. Middleton recalls floundering with his wealth of material, only to be rescued by the editorial expertise of Adair. Adair's contribution took the form of restructuring and rewriting in a more impartial and judicial tone than the original report. "As a freshly-minted Harvard Ph.D.," reports Middleton, "I found him enormously helpful and only too willing to take me on as a full-fledged ally in the business of historical research and writing."

SOURCE: Reprinted by permission of Arthur Pierce Middleton and the *William and Mary Quarterly*, 3d Ser., IV (1947), 409–443. The illustrations that appeared with the essay in the *Quarterly*, the "Official Statement" of the investigating committee, and some acknowledgments made by the committee, have all been deleted from this reprinting.

I

ALMOST ANYONE who saw the substantial three volumes entitled *The Horn Papers: Early Westward Movement on the Monongahela and Upper Ohio, 1765–1795,* lying on a library table probably accepted them as an unusually impressive collection of data on local history. The respectable bulk of the books, the discreet gold lettering of the title on the black cover, give no hint of the furor excited by their publication. Everything about their external appearance is reassuringly undramatic. Yet the printing of these solid-looking volumes divided a local community into opposing camps, agitated an entire region in fierce partisan debate, and, in time, attracted the incredulous attention of the whole American historical profession.

If our same hypothetical observer, in idle curiosity, had leafed through the first two volumes of *The Horn Papers*—the volumes that provoked the bitter controversy—he still would have seen little to arouse his excitement. Here he would have found the diaries of Jacob Horn and his son Christopher whose entries, dated from 1735 to 1795, fill approximately sixty printed pages. Published with the diaries is the fifty-page court docket, dated 1772–1779, of what is described as "the first English court held west of the mountains" (I, 328). Also printed here are miscellaneous papers, court orders, and maps of the Ohio region during the last half of the eighteenth century. The last 265 pages of Volume I of *The Horn Papers* contain fifteen chapters written by W. F. Horn (a descendant of the above-mentioned diary-writing pioneers who now lives in Topeka, Kansas) on the early history of southwest Pennsylvania and the adjacent counties of northwest Virginia and Maryland. These chapters, with such titles as "Indian Wars and Massacres," "Early Forts," "Forgotten Towns," "First Courts and Court Houses," are based in large part on the data contained in the diaries and court records printed in the first 140 pages of the volume. Volume II is made up of more than 500 family histories and genealogies of the early settlers in the region and these, too, depend on the Horn diaries and records for their validity. On cursory examination, therefore, *The Horn Papers* look like just another example of the standard type of local history issued by so many county and state historical societies during the last century. As such *The Horn Papers* appeared to be an extremely valuable publication, not only for students of local history but also for professional scholars who draw much material required for building up a more comprehensive picture of the American past from works of this type.

Nevertheless the appearance in print of these innocuous-seeming historical data in 1945 drew forth a charge almost unprecedented in the annals of American scholarship. Made by Mr. Julian P. Boyd, librarian of Princeton and recognized authority on the history of western Pennsylvania, this charge appeared in the July 1946 issue of the *American Historical Review*, which as the official publication of the American Historical Association is the most influential historical journal in the United States. Mr. Boyd wrote, after a careful examination of *The Horn Papers*, "I think the conclusion is inescapable that large parts of the documentary materials in the first two volumes, including diaries, maps, court records, memorandums, and even lead plates and hieroglyphs, are sheer fabrications. I do not know of any similar publication of fabricated documents among all the thousands of documentary publications issued by American historical societies."[1]

This suspicion of forgery—the most serious charge that can be leveled at any historical writing—focused attention on the mystery of *The Horn Papers;* but it did not solve that mystery. Mr. Boyd felt sure that part of the materials was manufactured—but some of the documents had the ring of authenticity, and he confessed that

1. *American Historical Review*, LI (1945–1946), 772.

the true and the false were so intermingled that it was difficult to separate them. The situation was further complicated by the opinion of two other professional historians—also experts on frontier history—Dr. Paul Gates and Dr. Julian P. Bretz, who rejected the idea that the Horn documents were fabrications. There was no reason to doubt that in the main they were authentic eighteenth-century documents, badly edited by amateurs whose chief sin was lack of scholarly training. It was this slovenly editing, Mr. Bretz and Mr. Gates believed, that had misled Mr. Boyd and aroused his suspicions.[2]

Here was a pretty puzzle. Mr. Boyd believed there was prima facie evidence to label the *Papers* fabrications; Mr. Gates with equal emphasis called them authentic. When the experts disagree so sharply, the general historian and lay reader can only throw up their hands in despair. Both Mr. Gates and Mr. Boyd, however, were in agreement on one point: whether because of bad editing or because of tampering, the documents themselves should not be trusted in their published form. *The Horn Papers* as they stood appeared to be so unreliable, so clouded with suspicion, that no careful historian or genealogist would rely on them.

2. Mr. Gates's and Mr. Bretz's opinion of the original documents in Vol. I of *The Horn Papers* can be seen from the following quotation from their review which appeared in *Pennsylvania History*, XIII (1946), 309–310: "The authenticity of the diaries has been called into question. The diary of Jacob Horn . . . is clearly not a record of events set down at the time they occurred. The entry of April 4, 1740, six pages, is a detailed recital of events covering more than a year. It contains extensive dialogue, numerous dates, and a variety of incidents that could hardly be reported with accuracy at such a distance in point of time. While it is fair to assume that the diaries have at least been revised, there is no obvious reason for entirely discarding them. They deserve to be treated as a witness of doubtful character is treated in a court of law. The real question is whether he is telling the truth at a particular moment. . . . Some parts of the diary may be unhistorical, but for the simple doings of every-day life the pioneer does not need 'a muse of fire that would ascend the brightest heaven of invention.' To the extent that the diaries are authentic, and this cannot be exactly determined, they justify in some measure the claims of the sponsors. They add to what has been known about the dark ages of Virginia settlement, 1740–1750, on the head waters of the Potomac."

The obvious solution to this scholarly impasse was independently proposed by both Mr. Boyd of Princeton and Dr. A. P. James of the University of Pittsburgh.[3] Each suggested that a careful investigation of *The Horn Papers* by some official body was urgently required. Such an investigation would apply to the disputed materials all the various skills and techniques available to historians in dealing with questioned documents and artifacts. During the summer of 1946, with the approval and aid of Dr. Guy Stanton Ford, editor of the *American Historical Review,* a committee to investigate *The Horn Papers* was organized under the sponsorship of the Institute of Early American History and Culture at Williamsburg.

Since the challenged material dealt with the early history of western Pennsylvania, Virginia, Maryland, and West Virginia, historical societies of those states were asked to appoint representatives to the investigating committee.[4] Dr. Solon J. Buck, archivist of the United

3. Mr. James in his review of the *Papers* in the *AHR,* LI (1945–1946), 771–772, took a position halfway between Mr. Boyd and Mr. Gates. He refused to commit himself on the question of whether the documents were fabricated but insisted that they could not be accepted as genuine without further investigation.

4. The creation and membership of this committee was reported in the January issue of the *William and Mary Quarterly,* 3d Ser., IV (1947), 121*ff.* The representative for the Historical Society of Western Pennsylvania was Franklin F. Holbrook; for the Maryland Historical Society, William B. Marye; for the Historical Society of Pennsylvania, Charles F. Jenkins; for the Virginia Historical Society, Francis L. Berkeley, Jr.; for the Pennsylvania Historical Association, Lawrence H. Gipson. The other members of the committee were Julian P. Boyd; Lester J. Cappon, representing the Institute of Early American History; and Douglass Adair, editor of the *Quarterly.*

The Washington County (Pennsylvania) Historical Society was also originally represented on the committee by Mr. Earle R. Forrest. However, when Mr. A. L. Moredock, president of the Greene County Historical Society which had published *The Horn Papers,* expressed belief that Mr. Forrest had already prejudged the *Papers,* Mr. Forrest immediately resigned. Mr. Boyd also offered to resign at this time, since he, too, could be said in one sense to have "prejudged" the *Papers.* Similarly Mr. Marye could have been disqualified but Mr. Moredock replied that Mr. Boyd as well as every other member of the committee was completely acceptable to the

States, whose published works on western Pennsylvania history and long experience in dealing with dubious documents ideally fitted him for the post, agreed to act as chairman. Dr. Arthur Pierce Middleton, trained and experienced in the skills of both archeology and history, was appointed as full-time executive secretary of the committee. It was his task (under the direction of Mr. Buck) to mobilize the talents of the geographically scattered committee members, to maintain liaison with the various experts recruited to investigate the different aspects of *The Horn Papers,* and to coordinate and assay their findings.

So began the search for that elusive thing called historical truth in the matter of *The Horn Papers.* Mr. Boyd's letter had posed two major questions for an investigating committee to answer. First, were *The Horn Papers* authentic? If not, what portions had been fabricated? In the second place, if lack of authenticity was clearly proved, what was the motive for the publication of spurious documents? Every historian has heard of fake Washington signatures or of Lincoln letters sold for the pecuniary advantage of the faker; but clearly this was a case of a different sort. At no time was there ever any hint that *The Horn Papers* were printed with intent to defraud anyone or to make money for anyone. It was equally clear that the *Papers* were not intended as a hoax or a mischievous prank.

Here then is the story of the committee's attempt to unravel these puzzles. Here is the story of a search for truth—a search that entailed months of scrutinizing printed documents and unpublished manuscripts, that involved interviews with dozens of people and the unstinting labors of a corps of scholars. Before the search was ended the aid of metallurgists, of lapidaries, of experts in the analysis of ink and paper, of typographical experts, and of a specialist in eighteenth-

---

Greene County Society. He did, however, request that one additional member be appointed to the committee to represent the West Virginia Historical Society. Following Mr. Moredock's request Mr. Delf Norona, president of the West Virginia Historical Society, became a member.

century French was enlisted. The full arsenal of scientific techniques available to the historical scholar was called into use.

And now that the task is finished, has truth been captured and exhibited so that all can agree on her features? The members of the committee hesitate to make such a triumphant claim. Unfortunately for any who desire a complete and total solution neatly tied up in a tight package the committee could not follow the pattern of the fictional detective story where *all* ambiguity is miraculously dissolved in the last five pages by the phenomenal deductions of a Sherlock Holmes. The most they can say is that they have apprehended certain aspects of truth: certain facts in regard to the diaries and papers attributed to Jacob and Christopher Horn have now been established beyond question or cavil. After the events leading up to the publication of the Horn documents have been described, therefore, and after the various steps taken by the committee to test the diaries and artifacts have been set forth, it will remain for you, the reader, to judge if what has been learned during the investigation is sufficient to solve the mystery of *The Horn Papers* once and for all.

II

The Horn Papers first became a matter of public record in 1932 when the editors of the Washington, Pennsylvania, *Observer*[5] and the Waynesburg, Pennsylvania, *Democrat-Messenger*[6] each received letters from an unknown correspondent in Topeka, Kansas. Although letters to the editor are normally not saved by newspaper offices the one received by the *Observer* was so unusual that it is still carefully preserved today, fifteen years after its receipt. Since it is the earliest public announcement concerning *The Horn Papers* yet discovered,

5. Founded 1871, Republican, circulation 14,297 (daily except Sunday), in both Greene and Washington counties.

6. *Messenger* founded 1813, became *Democrat-Messenger* in 1914, Democratic, circulation, 5,267 (daily except Sunday) almost entirely in Greene County.

a transcript of the neatly written, longhand original, in which punctuation and spelling are exactly duplicated, is presented here:

Topeka, Kansas,
Aug. 15th, 1932

Editor "Washington Observer,"
Washington, Pa.
Dear Sir:

I have in my possession several pages of interesting historical notes relating to the early history of what is now Washington, County Pa., and I am writing to ask you if the "Observer" will be interested in publishing a some what lengthy article, if I prepare the article from the manuscripts which I copied in 1891, from the original diaries kept by Jacob. Horn and Christopher Gist, from 1750, to 1767, from the Diaries, and Note Books kept by John and Christopher Horn under dates from 1773, to 1798, and the same kept by John Horn, son of Christopher Horn, under dates from 1785, to 1838, with years of research work, among the records at Williamsburgh, Va, at Philadelphia, Harrisburg, and some reviews in the Carnegie Library in Pittsburgh, I have much original "data Matter" that relates to the times, and events that took place in old Augusta County, afterwards the District of West Augusta, then finally, Yohogania County, Va, before Washington County was organized in March 1781.

These original papers containing many interesting historical accounts of events were recorded in the days of which the events took place, and give a detailed account of the life and home of Jacob. Horn, at Snow Creek Virginia, of Christopher Gist, Jacob Horn, and the two French surveyors, trip from Snow Creek, to Camp Cat Fish 1, at "Spirit" Spring, on Cat Fish Run on North Tingooqua Creek, (North Ten Mile Creek) in June, 1751. *"The planting of the French Lead Plates on Dunkard Creek, at the Mouth of Casteel Run* in Morgan township, Greene, Co. The life and much history of John Canon's Career in Washington County prior to his founding Canonsburg, in 1787.

Thes records give a pretty clear account of the Jacob Horn Block House at Camp Cat Fish 1. at "Spirit" Spring and of *his Court held there in*

September, 1773, and in *June, 1774,* thence the *removal* to the *Heath's homestead,* the *division* of *the Court there,* the Court brought back to the home of John Canon, at Augusta town, in *September, 1775,* then the building of the Augusta Town Court House in the spring of 1776, by John Horn and Abiga Hough.

The *description* of *Augusta Town is Complete* with *"plat* and *Chart"* also a *description* of *Razortown in 1780.*

There are a score of other matters, and persons, mentioned that I cannot enumerate here, but which I would wish to include, if, I prepare the article as several of your City, and County people have ask me to do.

None of this has ever been published, and while much of it agrees with Boyd Crumrine's History, but goes on to clear up many things that he does not clearly settle in regard to the old Virginia Courts, &c. in the days prior to 1781.

Now if the "Observer" feels that the people of present Washington County, will be interested in obtaining a fairly clear knowledge of the "first days" in the settlement of the County *from these records.* please let me know soon, and I will prepare the article stating only varified facts, with Charts, notes, and dates of all events which the records Mentions in references.

I have been in Communication with your fellow man, Hon. J. F. Mc Farland, in relation to the relocation of the Jacob Horn homestead which to my surprise is a lost location, and while I do not know exactly where the Block House stood, My father, the late S. R. Horn, had seen it and the graves of Jacob Horn, wife, daughter, and John Hardtman, on two different occasions, in 1839, and in 1848.

Please inform me as to the wishes in this matter and I will act in accordance. also as to whether the Copy should be type written, or left in my own hand writing.

Thanking you for the favor of an early reply. I remain

Very Sincerely
W. F. Horn

2325 Topeka Ave.

It is hard for anyone unfamiliar with the local history of southwestern Pennsylvania to appreciate the impact of Mr. Horn's offer on historically minded residents of Washington and Greene counties and to understand why his articles created such a stir as soon as they began to appear in print. In effect his manuscripts, as he described them, offered solutions for a series of problems that local historians had puzzled over for years. Augusta Town and Razortown were famous "lost towns" that preceded the establishment of the present Washington; even their locality was a question of debate, and now Mr. Horn said he had a "plat and Chart" of one and a contemporary description of the other. In like manner his proffered account of the courts held at Camp Cat Fish and at Spirit Spring in 1773 and 1774 promised to be historical dynamite, for previously the earliest court in the region was thought to have been held in 1776. In 1905 the Washington County Historical Society had ceremoniously set up a granite monument marking the site of this court and describing it as the "FIRST COURT HELD BY ANY ENGLISH SPEAKING PEOPLE WEST OF THE MONONGAHELA RIVER." Mr. Horn's report of two earlier courts would therefore require the demolition of this memorial and the erection of another. In fact the Horn manuscripts, on the basis of Mr. Horn's description, would do much more than "clear up" (to use his own words) the lacunae of Boyd Crumrine's justly famous history of the region—they would require its complete revision. Imagine the excitement if a historian discovered several hitherto undreamed of diaries by companions of John Smith or William Bradford, diaries that upset long-established accounts of the founding of Jamestown or Plymouth. Transposed into local terms this is what the Horn papers promised for the early history of Washington and Greene counties.

In many parts of the United States a threat to revise drastically long-cherished local traditions or to rewrite local history would hardly cause a ripple of interest except among a tiny group. This was not the case in Greene and Washington counties. The visitor to this region cannot but be impressed by the consciousness and deep-rooted pride of the local people in their own rich heritage from the past. Washington and Jefferson and Waynesburg colleges are centers of local historical interest. Each of the counties has a flourishing historical society made up of active members greatly concerned with the region's history. If Washington and Waynesburg are the organized centers of historical activity, interest is diffused throughout the whole area, since a large percentage of the present landowners are descendants of the settlers who first entered the territory at the end of the eighteenth century. Local history is not dead antiquarian lumber to these people; it is a deeply cherished part of their everyday lives.

The editor of the *Observer*, however, delayed about accepting Mr. Horn's offer. It was, therefore, the neighboring newspaper at Waynesburg, the *Democrat-Messenger*, that printed, during 1933–1934, excerpts from the diaries and manuscripts in Mr. Horn's possession. These short samples immediately proved so popular and created so much excitement in both Greene and Washington counties that the *Observer* took up the tale. From May 1935 through January 1936, lengthy installments of *The Horn Papers* appeared as a regular Saturday feature.

The newspaper publication of the Horn articles and manuscripts in the *Democrat-Messenger* acted as a local introduction—or rather as a reintroduction—for Mr. W. F. Horn himself, who now returned to his ancestral home as something of a local celebrity.[7] Waynesburg became his headquarters, and he regularly visited that town through

7. Mr. William Franklin Horn, born in Greene County in 1870 is the son of Solomon, the great-great-grandson of Christopher and the great-great-great-grandson of Jacob, the progenitor of the Horn family in the area. In 1882 Solomon Horn moved with his wife and children to Doniphan County, Kansas, and his son, W. F. Horn, has lived in Kansas ever since. The family's ties with Greene County, however, were never completely severed. Horn relatives always have lived there, and the Kansas branch not only kept in contact through letters, but always subscribed to the local newspaper.

the remainder of the 1930s and early 1940s, sometimes staying several months at a time. He reknit old friendships, among them one with A. L. Moredock, president of the Greene County Historical Society, and gained many new friends through his infectious enthusiasm for the region's history and his knowledge of its past. Inevitably he was asked to lecture on Waynesburg's history, and here his success was marked.[8] He was always willing to help any local person trace a genealogy; nor did he charge fees for such services even though he would spend much time and fill many sheets of paper with his fine copperplate writing in working out a complete family line.[9] Mr. Horn's "historical walks," or exploring trips, through the hills and along the old paths of the area also became locally famous. Even individuals who are not personally friendly with the man speak of his ability to make the past come alive, to recreate the drama of pioneer days as he walked along pointing out the ancient landmarks of the region. Although Mr. Horn was not a young man his energy never seemed to flag on these expeditions, nor did his ability to hold an audience enthralled ever fail. By 1935, just three short years after his initial letter to the newspapers, Mr. Horn was widely accepted as the historical oracle of the Greene County Historical Society, and though he still maintained his chief residence in Topeka, Kansas, he had also become a leading citizen of Waynesburg.

Nor did his fame remain merely local. In 1939 Mr. Horn was

8. "MANY ATTEND HISTORICAL MEET IN WAYNESBURG," headlines, Washington *Observer*, Jan. 8, 1944. "Waynesburg, Jan. 7–The public meeting held Thursday night in the First Christian Church of Waynesburg by the Greene County Historical Society was a decided success and was well attended. A number of persons from outside the county were in attendance.

"Addresses were delivered by W. F. Horn, of Topeka, Kansas, and Dr. Paul R. Stewart, president of Waynesburg College."

9. Mr. Horn during an interview at Fairmont, West Virginia, July 22, 1945, announced: "I will be glad to assist anyone who is anxious to trace their genealogy while I am here and there will be no charge. The people of Marion County have been so friendly and have taken such an interest in my work that I am anxious to evidence my favor." *Fairmont Times*, July 23, 1945.

called to Uniontown to act as historical adviser in excavating what he identified as French fortifications constructed in 1747–1748 just before the outbreak of the French and Indian War.[10] In 1942 he was invited to Hagerstown, Maryland, where he lectured on the colonial history of western Maryland and received an ovation.[11] In 1945 he made the first of several speeches before the Marion County Historical Society of Fairmont, West Virginia, on the early explorations of that region. Here, too, his audiences were spellbound. In the words of the vice-president of that society, "Mr. Horn was a wonder."[12]

Few historians and few historical documents ever generate such intense and widespread enthusiasm as this. The Horn documents, however, had certain unusual features that were sure to win them acclaim wherever Mr. Horn exhibited them. One quality that struck everyone who heard him lecture from his ancestors' journals was the amazing wealth of detail provided on the "common man"—to use a modern term—of frontier history, the obscure individual in the rank and file of the westward movement whose only historical record, before *The Horn Papers* were discovered, was a name on a deed, on a petition, in a tax list, or in a family Bible. It is not surprising

10. "OLD FRENCH LINE UNCOVERED IN FAYETTE," headlines, Waynesburg *Republican*, Sept. 21, 1939. "Uniontown—Excavations in the mountains, south of the Summit Hotel, has revealed the original Maginot line, constructed by French forces during 1747 and 1748.

"W. F. Horn, historian for the Greene County Historical Society, says that forts were constructed on Mt. Calm and called Fort Contrechouer in honor of the French governor general in Canada.

"The excavation will prove, according to Mr. Horn that part of the fort was above the ground with the supply rooms and men's quarters underground, quite similar to the Maginot line in France. Work is continuing."

11. The Hagerstown *Daily Mail* reported: "Although W. F. Horn resides in Topeka, Kansas and Waynesburg, Pa. he probably knows as much if not more about the history of Hagerstown and Washington County [Maryland] than any other living person," quoted by the Washington *Observer*, Feb. 24, 1942.

12. E. E. Meredith to Guy Stanton Ford, Sept. 7, 1946. See also article by Mr. Meredith in the *Fairmont Times*, Dec. 1945, in which reference is made to Mr. Horn as the " 'wonder man from Kansas' as he is coming to be styled."

therefore that, as one listener reports, the Marion County Historical Society was overwhelmed by the body of explicit information on early settlers presented by Mr. Horn and thought him "a wonder" when he "could give dates, day, month and year, on which pioneers from whom our members descended had come into this section."[13]

Another feature that helped guarantee *The Horn Papers* instantaneous popularity was the unique documentation they provided for famous events and figures in frontier history. Jonathan Hager, Christopher Gist, John Canon, and Thomas Cresap were far from being obscure pioneers. They were the generals and chiefs of staff of the westward movement. Nevertheless historians have been baffled in trying to trace the careers of these prominent men. For certain periods in their lives there are more than adequate records, they act their historic roles on a stage brightly illuminated by contemporary documents. But for each there are periods of absolute darkness, gaps in our knowledge of where they were, or of what they were doing, or why, blank spots that historians deemed it impossible to fill. In instance after instance, however, *The Horn Papers* plugged these holes. It is understandable, therefore, why as a result of these disclosures the Hagerstown and Fairmont newspapers broke out in a rash of laudatory headlines and featured the fact that local history could now be rewritten without the unsatisfactory hiatuses and obscurities that had disfigured earlier accounts.[14]

A scarcely less popular feature of *The Horn Papers* was the supplementary collection of artifacts and relics of pioneer life that had been preserved with the manuscripts. In 1942 when Mr. Horn spoke before three hundred people at a Hagerstown luncheon he read excerpts

---

13. *Ibid.*

14. "*The Horn Papers* furnish a clue which may establish the actual founding of the town [Hagerstown] as 1740, or thereabouts, instead of the year 1762 which has been celebrated for years." Baltimore *Sun*, Mar. 2, 1942. "The revelations of Mr. Horn are likely to change the entire history of Northern West Virginia." *Fairmont Times*, Jan. 1946; cf. also issues for Aug. 13, 25, 1945.

from the Jacob Horn diary, which described his ancestor's visit to "the fur trade house" of one "Jean Le Beau" on March 19, 1739, and Le Beau's gift to Jacob of a marble cross which the latter had admired. Mr. Horn, from the details in his great-great-great-grandfather's diary, then identified Le Beau's house as the old ferryhouse situated across the Potomac from Williamsport, Maryland, a landmark known throughout the neighborhood.[15] Finally, as a dramatic climax to his talk to Mr. Horn presented Le Beau's cross, which he said had been preserved for two hundred years in his family, to the president of the local historical society.[16] At the same time Mr. Horn gave to the Hagerstown Museum another valued relic mentioned in Jacob's diary: one of the "4 new Virginia Colonial Coins" that Jacob speaks of having received from Jonathan Hager on March 4, 1740.[17] This coin like the cross, Mr. Horn reported, had been preserved by his family all these years.

The mementos presented at Hagerstown were probably the most striking example of Mr. Horn's generosity with historical artifacts. This munificence was matched on a lesser scale everywhere he went lecturing on his ancestors' documents. In West Virginia he gave arrowheads from the battlefield of Flint Top (mentioned in both the

15. "We received meat and rest at the French Post. Jean Le Beau, was friendly to us, and ask us to take meat and rest with him. He ask us where we hailed from? and where we are trailing to? Whereon John Hardtman, say: Have it known, we are Jonathan Hager's men, and we are trailing to his camp, where he is to build Fort Hager. Jean say: Have two drams each, on Jeans friendship. . . . We rested on the earthern floor surrounded by lighted tapers, and many holy crosses, and it was a strange camp to us.

"Jean say: By the grace of the Holy Father. I bestow this Holy Cross on thee, Jacob, as my desire to possess thy friendship. Where on, John Hardtman say: it is well with thee Luther.

"I still have this cross, and shall retain it all my days as a token of Him who died on a similar one for all men." *Horn Papers*, I, 6.

16. Mrs. Frank W. Mish, Jr., whose husband now owns the old ferry-house.

17. "Upon, this, he [Hager] gave each of us, 4 new Virginia Colonial Coins, in remembrance of our being at Fort Hager, and of our departure there from." *Horn Papers*, I, 11.

Jacob and Christopher Horn diaries); and the Waynesburg Museum was the recipient of a large collection of frontier relics.[18] Everywhere—in Maryland, Pennsylvania, and West Virginia—these historic objects, tangibly linking the persons and events mentioned in *The Horn Papers* with the present, aroused almost as much interest as the diaries themselves. As symbolic tokens from the long-vanished past they helped to personalize the early history of the region and challenged the imagination of all beholders to visualize the frontier life that Jacob and Christopher Horn had recorded.

Still another element in the popularity and enthusiastic acceptance of *The Horn Papers* was the appeal it made to the local pride and patriotism in those areas where Jacob and Christopher Horn's activities had centered. If one wished to write a regional folk drama or pageant based on the Horn manuscripts, there are at least four clearly discernible dramatic themes woven into the texture of the diaries. The first of these is the clash of pioneer and Indian; the second, the contest between French and English for control of the strategic Ohio area; the third, the theme of American patriot versus England; and finally there is the conflict between the virile western frontiersman and the tidewater settler east of the mountains. Each of these themes has its quota of heroes and villains; each has at least one scene which in a pageant would make a magnificent set piece—the battle of Flint Top; the planting of the French lead plates; John Canon's defiance of the English Parliament in 1774; and Jacob Horn's declaration of western independence from the trammels of tidewater politics. It would be hard to devise a record better calculated than *The Horn Papers* to promote the historical pride of the inhabitants dwelling beside the headwaters of the Ohio River.

Add all these elements together—the abundance of genealogical detail, the new information on well-known frontier figures, the arti-

18. These include 30 or 40 objects of wood, glass, metal, hide, flax, shell, and stone, besides rifles, carpenter and cooper's tools, surveyor's instruments, cannon balls, and a large collection of arrowheads and other Indian relics.

facts and maps which the diaries indicated had been made or used by the pioneers themselves, the colorful dramatization of the section's role in American history—and it can readily be seen why the Horn documents and Mr. Horn himself were assured of an eager and enthusiastic audience. Finally, when it is remembered that the preservation of the documents and their recovery by Mr. Horn was a highly romantic story in its own right, the appeal of *The Horn Papers* is manifest.[19]

If the story of *The Horn Papers* was in the main a ten-year record of dazzling success, nevertheless, a minor current of criticism and disbelief existed from the first report of the documents in 1933. Indeed the original hesitation of the Washington *Observer*, in 1932, about printing the manuscripts is evidence of an initial skepticism which increased with time. In the beginning this criticism centered in the Washington County [Pennsylvania] Historical Society, whose members, as semiofficial custodians of the county's historic tradition, found the Horn documents and Mr. Horn's newspaper articles disturbing, if only because these were so greatly at variance with long-established local history.[20] Mr. Horn himself and his sibylline books might very well be accepted as the new oracle in Waynesburg, but Crumrine's *History* had been the bible of Washington County for

19. The Horn family papers and many of the relics were stated to have been stowed away by Christopher in a chest in 1795 and the chest handed down in 1809 to his son "Young John," and by him in 1856 to his grandson Solomon, the father of W. F. Horn. The chest was carried to Kansas in 1882 and in 1891 was opened to reveal the original documents, some "written on birch bark and old linen." In order to preserve the records W. F. Horn in 1891 made with great difficulty transcripts of all the documents—because some of the papers "were so badly moth-eaten that contents could not be copied." It was fortunate that this transcript had been made for most of the original manuscripts were soon destroyed. For the account in the Christopher Horn diary of the gathering together of relics for the chest, see *Horn Papers*, I, 42; for Mr. Horn's description of the condition of the papers when the chest was opened in 1891, see Baltimore *Sun*, Mar. 2, 8, 1942.

20. The fact that Mr. Earle Forrest, a leading member of the Washington County Historical Society is also on the staff of the *Observer* helps to explain the action of the *Observer*.

more than half a century. It was too highly regarded to be upset by any series of newspaper articles. Thus a countercurrent of opinion concerning *The Horn Papers* developed in opposition to the rising tide of approval and praise. The critics were in a minority, but just as the believers in *The Horn Papers* grew in number and territorial distribution between 1932 and 1945 so, too, did the detractors.

The Horn critics, necessarily basing their strictures on the newspaper excerpts of the manuscripts and on Mr. Horn's articles and lectures,[21] focused on two major points: the doubtfulness of certain facts related in the diaries themselves and the impossibility of tracing any of the supplementary authorities that Mr. Horn adduced to buttress his ancestors' journals. As an example of the first, they pointed to the Horn story of the mob's rescue of Dr. Connolly from the Hannastown jail in 1774 during the course of the jurisdictional struggle between the Virginia and Pennsylvania authorities. The previously accepted version of this affair based on contemporary documents of unquestioned authenticity recounted the rescue of Connolly by two hundred armed Virginia sympathizers,[22] who gained their end by threatening the Pennsylvania-appointed officials. In the Horn account, however, the mob was described as having "demolished" the Hannastown courthouse and jail. And according to Jacob Horn, John Canon, their leader, announced that if the courthouse was rebuilt "he [Canon] would hang them and all who labored on it." Contrasting this story with the *St. Clair Papers* report of the affair, the critics dismissed the lurid revelations of the newly discovered *Horn Papers* as impossible.[23] Since examples of this sort could be multiplied to include discrepancies in genealogical data, dates,

---

21. The complete diaries were, of course, not available until their publication in book form in 1945.

22. *St. Clair Papers*, I, 291–294.

23. The Horn account of the Hannastown affair was first printed in the *Observer*, June 1, 1935.

and biographical details, the anti-Horn group branded the whole collection of new documents as untrustworthy.

The anti-Horn group were further disquieted by what they deemed the cavalier way in which their objections were brushed aside when they asked that the startling new history presented by the Horn journals be substantiated by other records. It is reported that Mr. Horn's usual reply was that since the data were in his ancestors' manuscripts no other authentication was necessary. Moreover, since part of the Horn materials *did* square with the established record, the pro-Horn group argued that those pages which gave a unique account of persons and events and which therefore could not be tested against unimpeachable contemporary records should also be accepted.

When urged to explain why the massacre of twelve thousand Indians at the Battle of Flint Top in 1748 (reported only in *The Horn Papers*), and the planting of three French lead plates in Greene and Washington counties (reported only in *The Horn Papers*) were not mentioned by a single contemporary document and why no nine-teenth-century historian hinted at their occurrence, Mr. Horn did provide supplementary authority.[24] He referred the skeptics to "Andrea's, Early History of Northwest Virginia, 1760–1780," a copy of which had been in his own library until 1882. A lengthy quotation from it was printed in the *Observer* (July 13, 1935) for his critics to read.[25] Further to document the diary's record of the French plates,

24. That the French did, on the other hand, plant lead plates in the Ohio Valley in 1749 to establish their claim to the area is well known and can be documented by scores of contemporary accounts. That plate-laying expedition was commanded by M. Céloron, and one of the plates that he buried has been on exhibit in the Virginia Historical Society for over a hundred years. It will henceforth be referred to as: the Céloron plate.

25. Washington *Observer*, July 13, 1935. After a lengthy quotation from Andrea, Mr. Horn gave the additional verification in the same article: "The French Consul at St. Louis in 1890 informed the writer that the French government would pay the sum of $5,000 in gold for the return of each one of these plates but I have no

Mr. Horn cited what he described as the "eminent authority" on
eighteenth-century Anglo-French relations, "Mrs. M. E. Gail" of
Paris, whose work in the Quebec and Paris archives, he said, fully
corroborated the diarist's account of the planting of the plates.[26] For
critics who questioned genealogical data in *The Horn Papers* he
produced long typewritten reports he had received from "The International Genealogical Society" of London and Philadelphia and "The
American Genealogical Society." Mr. Horn suggested that anyone
interested could write to these organizations and obtain verification
of the accuracy of the Horn journals.[27]

There is no record as to whether any of Mr. Horn's critics ever
tried to do this, but they did make every possible effort to obtain a
copy of "Andrea's History of Northwest Virginia." The effort was
unavailing—neither its author nor its title nor date and place of
publication could be traced in any bibliography, list of copyrights,
library catalogue, or rare-book dealer's inventory. However the failure to discover this nineteenth-century account of the lead plates
seemed of minor importance when two lead plates dated 1795 were
excavated on August 11, 1936, just where the maps in *The Horn
Papers* indicated they would be found.

The discovery of the two lead plates, though it did not completely
silence Mr. Horn's opponents, in effect reduced their criticisms to
offstage mutterings. Although the plates were *not* the French plates

---

knowledge of any price set on them at this date for their return." He also stated:
"The Pittsburgh Gazette of 1880 said: 'This plate three was sought for in 1854 by
the Pittsburg Committee, then endeavoring to locate this hidden plate after having
been buried for a century in Pennsylvania soil but the effort was in vain, no sign
of it being found at the time. Since then no effort has been made to locate this
plate.' "

26. "Mrs. M. E. Gail" is quoted at length (six full pages of unbroken quotation)
in *Horn Papers*, I, 190–196.

27. The headquarters of the "International Society," as revealed by the letter-
heads in Mr. Horn's possession, was 54 Canongate, London, S.W.1.

described in the Horn diaries as having been planted in 1751,[28] and although there were ambiguous circumstances about their excavation,[29] Mr. Horn's supporters could henceforth quote the newspaper account of the discovery to all who doubted. The plates which had been found, said the *Observer* report on August 12, "seemed to prove almost conclusively that the French plates had existed." Nearly ten years later when, according to Mr. Horn, the original 1751 plate with the French inscription on it was found among the effects of a deceased sister, this second discovery served further to confirm the earlier more dramatic find.

The exhumation of the lead plates in 1936 did more than fortify

28. The search for the French plates of 1751 was undertaken under the auspices of the WPA's Waynesburg history project using a Horn map. Two small plates measuring approximately 3¹/₂" x 4¹/₂" were turned up. One, dated MDCCXCV had the name "NATE O'BRINE" die-stamped on one side, and SITE OF FRENCH PLATE on the other. The second plate had stamped on it with a die: / FLINT TOP / MDCCXLVIII / C. GIST / J. HORN / X. GRENDLIER / TINGOOQUA / P. CHARTIERS / IRON POINT / MDCCLI (photographed in *Horn Papers*, I, 248*ff*). The list of names was, of course, that of the plate-laying party of 1751, X[enephon] Grendelier being one of the supposed French surveyors. But as the headlines in the *Observer* for Aug. 14, 1936, read: "FIND PUZZLES SEARCHERS." The news story goes on to suggest that O'Brine dug up the original 1751 plate in 1795, but there was no satisfactory explanation of why he buried two American plates in its place and why one was inscribed with the name and date of the battle of Flint Top.

29. The newspaper accounts of the excavation of the plates as well as the account in the *Horn Papers*, I, 249, would indicate that the WPA diggers under the directions of Mr. F. B. Jones, archeologist and curator of the Greene County Historical Society, found them. Actually they were unearthed by Mr. Horn himself during a two-hour period while the director was away. Dr. Mary Butler Lewis to Julian Boyd, Media, Pa., Nov. 22, 1946. At the time Dr. Butler was assistant state archeologist of Pennsylvania. In the excitement of the moment Mr. Horn rushed to clean up his find in a nearby creek and the exact position of the plates was forgotten. This was brought out when Mr. Jones later tried to take photographs. Members of the Greene County Historical Society were distressed that Mr. Horn had washed the plates and destroyed the archeological evidence, but as they later reported, he was so happy and excited by his discovery "skipping and dancing about like a kid" that they didn't have the heart to chide him. Statement of Mr. Jones, to Messrs. Middleton and Adair, Jan. 1947.

the faith of the Greene County Historical Society in Mr. Horn's manuscripts. The members of the society were now so thoroughly convinced of the value and importance of *The Horn Papers* that they determined to issue them in book form. This idea, it should be noted, was not originally suggested by Mr. Horn himself; all evidence points to the fact that when he first unveiled the manuscripts in 1932 he expected only newspaper publication in the *Observer* or the *Democrat-Messenger*. Now, however, under the enthusiastic urging of his Waynesburg friends he acceded to their plan of issuing *The Horn Papers* in a permanent form.

The account of the struggle to get *The Horn Papers* published is a minor epic of historiography—an amazing story of resoluteness in the face of seemingly insurmountable obstacles. Almost the entire burden of preparing the Horn manuscripts for the press and of raising the money to publish them fell on the shoulders of Mr. A. L. Moredock and of the late Mr. J. L. Fulton, president and leading member respectively of the Greene County Historical Society.[30] The record of their efforts is a tale of determination and self-sacrifice, in which any historical society could legitimately take pride.

In the beginning it was hoped that the Greene County Committee could interest either a university press or a commercial publisher in printing the *Papers*. The University of Pittsburgh, however, declined on the ground that the cost of verifying the questionable statements would be prohibitive. This discouraging reply was partly offset when a New York publisher agreed to print the book, if the Greene County Historical Society would underwrite the venture.[31] Mr. Moredock

30. Technically *The Horn Papers* were issued by a "Committee for the Greene County Historical Society," the copyright being held in the names of W. F. Horn, J. L. Fulton, and A. L. Moredock. However the *Papers* were generally spoken of as a society publication, just as Mr. Horn himself was described in newspaper accounts as "Historian of the Greene County Historical Society."

31. The stand of the University of Pittsburgh in this matter was reported by university authorities to Mr. Middleton and Mr. Adair in Jan. 1947. Putnam and

and Mr. Fulton finally resolved to finance the enterprise to the extent of their own resources and to seek the additional funds necessary by securing prepublication subscriptions from libraries, historical societies, and interested individuals. In 1938 a series of brochures was circulated for this purpose. With heartbreaking slowness the money was gradually secured.

Paralleling the difficulties of the Greene County Historical Society in raising funds were the problems of editing the manuscript which Mr. Horn turned over to them. Originally the society supposed there would be enough material for only one volume. Additional material, however, produced along with the transcript of the diaries, twenty-two maps and numerous artifacts to be photographed, and the mass of letters, reports of speeches, and genealogical data, necessitated a two-volume work.[32] The first volume was to contain the Horn diaries, the Camp Cat Fish Court docket, and Mr. Horn's commentary on them; the second, five hundred family histories based on the diaries and additional manuscripts. Although the financial burden was thereby doubled, it was hoped that the genealogical data would increase the number of subscribers to the work. Also the Greene County Committee felt that the additional materials were too valuable to omit.

After enlarging the scope of the work, the Greene County Committee found themselves saddled with an incredibly difficult editorial task. Neither Mr. Moredock nor Mr. Fulton had any editorial experience in preparing historical documents for the press. Moreover the manuscripts to be edited were in such condition that they would have baffled a veteran editor. The copies of the diaries that Mr. Horn

---

Sons, according to a letter in the society's file, offered in 1942 to print a thousand copies if $9,000 could be raised.

32. Even after the publication of two volumes had been scheduled it was impossible to find a place for all the "transcript of 1891." The 28-page manuscript about the Tygart Valley, West Virginia, exploration of 1750 was omitted, for example.

told them he had made in 1891 were in great confusion. Written on discolored, worn paper of every conceivable size and shape, they lacked any continuity of arrangement, and the editors had to put them together like a jigsaw puzzle. Mr. Moredock stated that on several occasions Mr. Horn carried off, to show to interested friends, documents or pages of the transcript that were being worked on and forgot to return them. Under these discouraging circumstances the Greene County Committee tackled the editing of the documents and began to work out rule-of-thumb editorial procedures. As an additional editorial burden Mr. Moredock and Mr. Fulton assumed the task of acquiring specialized knowledge in eighteenth-century American history outside the western Pennsylvania field.

Even before publication was undertaken the members of the Greene County Committee were sensitive about the charges that *The Horn Papers* were full of errors. They became even more sensitive as the work progressed. Laboring over the manuscripts they discovered contradictions in dates, biographical anomalies, and other errors. At the same time they found themselves exposed to a new challenge, this time from university scholars and professional historians who heard about *The Horn Papers* as a result of the publication program. Without exception, the professionals to whom the papers were submitted for opinion cautioned against publication unless the dubious parts could be verified. In spite of professional discouragement Mr. Moredock and Mr. Fulton felt committed to publication: the *Papers* had already been advertised and subscriptions accepted. Moreover, the experts while pointing to errors in the *Papers* had not denied that much of the data when tested by the scholars' own standards might be authenticated. Because scholars had produced no documents that explicitly discredited them, an impressive additional body of facts was presumed to be correct.

Under the circumstances what the editorial committee did is perfectly understandable. Where the manuscripts showed internal inconsistencies and contradictions they attempted to establish the correct reading on the basis of supplementary research. They also decided to publish with *The Horn Papers* additional historical material of unquestioned value, although these extra documents added appreciably to the cost of printing and although they were not an integral part of the Horn manuscripts. Preparations were therefore made to print in Volume II the 1790 census of heads of families of Washington County; in like manner plans were matured to issue a third volume containing maps of Washington and Greene counties prepared by the Pennsylvania Land Office.[33]

Mr. Moredock has testified to the perplexed state of mind in which the Greene County publication committee found itself as the editorial work progressed. They tried in as many ways as they could think of to test the accuracy of the *Papers* as they became fully conscious of the many scattered "errors." In Mr. Moredock's words, the committee was "well aware there are some controversial matters" that inevitably would appear in print. The editors believed, however, that the deciding factor was the need "to preserve the material for the future." Drawing an analogy from the career of the famous collector, Lyman C. Draper, who accumulated thousands of manuscripts on western history but, paralyzed by his ideal of completeness and the hope of finding one more relevant paper, never published a page of his projected history of the pioneers, Mr. Moredock observed: "Had Mr. Draper proceeded in this way [i.e. as did

33. The maps in the third volume of *The Horn Papers* are the warrant, survey, and patent maps for Fayette, Washington, and Greene counties, and show the original grantees of land in the district. They were originally prepared for abstractors of titles and business firms, such as coal companies seeking a complete chain of title from the earliest patent to the present. The Greene County Committee learned while doing their supplementary research on the Horn documents that the state of Pennsylvania had these maps for sale. Mr. Moredock reports: "We discovered that the land patents were of great assistance in scores of instances where individuals were located [in the Horn manuscripts] on certain streams, mills and valleys, these surveys verified the source." Address made by A. J. Moredock at a meeting of the West Virginia Historical Society at Morgantown, West Virginia, June 8, 1946," mimeographed.

the Greene County Historical Society] and made available to the general public the sources as he gathered them, a great benefit to history would have resulted. Perhaps some controversial matters would have been found. Even so, could we say such would have destroyed their value?"[34]

And so, what can only be described as the prodigious efforts of the Greene County Committee went on in the face of mounting financial demands, inadequate clerical assistance, wartime paper shortages, refractory printers, and their own doubts about portions of the manuscript they were editing. Throughout they were sustained by the certainty that they were rendering an important service to their own neighborhood and to the historical profession generally. At last, after nine years of editorial work and after the expenditure of approximately twenty thousand dollars (a sizable proportion of which they had advanced themselves), Mr. Moredock and Mr. Fulton saw with pride the three impressive volumes of *The Horn Papers* issue from the press in December 1945.

Six months later Mr. Boyd focused national attention on the *Papers* by branding them fabrications and calling for an investigation by an impartial committee.[35]

III

THE COMMITTEE appointed to investigate *The Horn Papers* began their analysis of the published volumes with an impartial mind. It

34. *Ibid.*

35. The Greene County Committee did not even have six months in which to relax. Almost as soon as the *Papers* were issued Mr. C. Hale Sipe, an expert on the Indian wars of Pennsylvania, commenced attacking the Horn diaries in letters to newspapers throughout the western part of the state. Focusing his attack on the account of the Battle of Flint Top, he demanded that the Pennsylvania Historical Commission remove the books from libraries where the "rising generation" of high school students would learn false history from them. See, for example, letter in the Pittsburgh *Post-Gazette*, Apr. 22, 1946.

was soon discovered that the materials published in Volumes I and II furnished internal evidence that bore out Mr. Boyd's judgment.[36]

1

THE PRIMA FACIE REASONS why portions of the documentary material in *The Horn Papers* appeared to be spurious are: (1) evidences of ineptitude in copying the original manuscripts; (2) anachronistic and doubtful words and phrases; (3) biographical anomalies; (4) historically incorrect or doubtful statements; (5) internal discrepancies; and (6) internal similarities of documents purporting to be of different authorship.

A glance at *The Horn Papers* reveals that the documentary material was carelessly presented. Although the original manuscripts are said by Mr. Horn to have been in very poor condition and partially illegible when he copied them in 1891,[37] there are few or no indications of omissions, of conjectural reconstructions of damaged pages, or of illegible or doubtful words. These deficiencies, although more heinous in connection with the documentary material, are by no means confined to it. The secondary material containing many quotations from supposed primary sources is usually without citation, and never with an adequate citation. This leads one to surmise either that the copyist was completely unfamiliar with accepted editorial techniques or that he had reason to conceal the source of his information.

Although editorial ineptitude puts the careful scholar on his guard

36. The committee unfortunately was unable to communicate directly with Mr. Horn. His daughter, Miss Mae B. Horn, in a letter to Arthur Pierce Middleton, Topeka, Kansas, Feb. 24, 1947, informed the committee that her father was too ill to reply. Miss Horn enclosed a certificate from Mr. Horn's physician, George W. B. Beverley, dated Feb. 22, 1947. Mr. Horn, however, has continued his correspondence with other interested persons. As recently as Aug. 1947, a correspondent in Fairmont is reported to have received a letter "in which Mr. Horn was quoted as saying that ... he no longer was interested in what was done about the Horn Papers." E. E. Meredith to Arthur Pierce Middleton, Fairmont, West Virginia, Aug. 11, 1947.

37. *Horn Papers*, I, xiv; brochure on *The Horn Papers*, n.d. (c. 1945); and see quotation attributed to W. F. Horn in Baltimore *Sun*, Mar. 8, 1942.

when considering specific details, it is not necessarily evidence against the authenticity of a document as a whole. Much more important evidence is the frequent appearance of anachronistic and doubtful words and phrases, for it is well known that "anachronisms are the rock on which counterfeit works always run most risk of shipwreck."[38] The documentary material in *The Horn Papers* abounds in such words and phrases, some of them quite impossible for the eighteenth century[39] and many others highly dubious.[40] Scarcely a page is devoid of them. Similarly, many passages in the diaries have the ring of nineteenth rather than of eighteenth-century phraseology.[41] Others reveal virulent opposition on the part of Jacob Horn and his fellow pioneers to the king, Parliament, and the royal government of Virginia unknown when the frontiersmen were dependent on British power to defend them against the French and Indians.[42] It is well

38. James Anson Farrer, *Literary Forgeries* (London, 1907), 2.

39. Examples: "trail," used frequently in the Horn diaries as early as 1735, to mean a path or road, belongs to a later period—the earliest reference to it in the *Oxford English Dictionary* and the *Dictionary of American English* is dated 1807; the word "stow[a]way," used in the Jacob Horn diary in an entry for 1738, first appears in the *Oxford English Dictionary* in a reference dated 1854. Other undoubtedly anachronistic words and phrases in the Horn documents are "tepee" (1740), "Virginia Blue-bloods" (1748), "braves" (1748) for Indian warriors, and "Ranch" (1748) in the expression "Gist's Mule Ranch."

40. Examples of doubtful words and expressions: "hometown" (1736), "fur trade house" (1739), "frontire spirit" (1739), "the wilds of Baltimore's Colony" (1739), "race hatred" (1772). The committee has on file a full list of such anachronisms of which the above is but a small sampling.

41. Examples: "black pirates with a just claim only to the Devil's own region" (applied to Christopher Gist's Baltimore creditors, 1770), Gen. Washington referred to in 1777 by the Napoleonic title of "the First Consul of the Colonies," the Pennsylvanians referred to as "a body of long hair, big hatted set of loud talkers for freedom and peace" (1782) and as "long whiskered peace loving brethren from the Susquehanna" (1782).

42. Examples: "the small Snow Creek Settlement are outside of Virginia Colonial directions. All men are their own masters, and say their own laws. . . . I Jacob Horn, fear God, and his Holy Laws, but fear no man. . . . Snow Creek . . . is beyond the Colonial Claims of Virginia . . . it is solely the land of the settlers, and no king, or colony hath a say over it" (1742); "I Jacob Horn am a loyal Virginia subject, so long as the King and Parliament set down no Ords" (1745); "I Jacob Horn, declare

known that this opposition developed after 1765, not in the 1740s and 1750s.

An authentic diary would be true throughout, not just in a majority of its entries. It would be true in all instances where the writer was in a position to know the truth. A genuine diary might, indeed, contain a false statement because the writer was misinformed, because he recorded hearsay that was in error, or because his judgment was faulty. But an authentic diary would under no circumstances record the appearance and activities in the writer's company of a person when that person is known to have been elsewhere or after he is known to have died. A single instance of this kind would cast doubt on the authenticity of a diary even though every other entry were correct, for it would unquestionably demonstrate that the document had been tampered with. *The Horn Papers* contain not one but many such biographical irregularities, and they form, perhaps, the most important single body of prima facie evidence against the manuscripts.[43] Closely associated with biographical errors are the many historically incorrect or doubtful statements in the Horn documents which, though too numerous to consider individually, have the cumulative effect of discrediting them. A few instances might, after all, be the result of an occasional interpolation, an inexact rendering of an illegible text, or a typographical error in transcription or typesetting. But hundreds of statements of doubtful character scattered

---

the King and Colony hath no jurisdiction over any part of this frontire settlement" (1748); Canon "declared Parliament Acts to be more of speech than of force" in Virginia (1750); "John Canon . . . heeds not the threats of the King nor the Acts of Parliament" (1750); "I, Jacob Horn, first, Virginia next, and Parliament when it is good to my will" (1754).

43. Christopher Gist appears frequently in the Horn diaries during the years 1759–1769, and his death from eating a surfeit of wild grapes and red plums is recorded at "Laurel Hill, or Little Haystack Knob" in 1769. But from unimpeachable contemporary documents we know that Gist died of smallpox en route from Williamsburg to Winchester, in 1759. Other biographical impossibilities in *The Horn Papers* involve Thomas Cresap, John Canon, Dr. Samuel Eckerlin, and Jonathan Hager.

widely through the documents render it improbable that any such extenuating circumstances might account for these errors.[44]

Also damaging to *The Horn Papers* are the internal contradictions in the documentary material. Christopher Horn variously recorded Gist's death as having occurred from November 1768 to October 1770. The references to the date of the battle of Flint Top reveal that the author of both the Jacob and Christopher Horn diaries was completely unfamiliar with the Julian Calendar (in universal use in the British colonies until 1752) and that, as a result, the references are considerably at variance. Moreover, the ignorance of the calendar change resulted in situations such as the appearance in Williamsburg of Buck Eckerlin and his brother in October 1748, after having witnessed a battle on the frontier that was not supposed to have taken place until the following month.[45]

From a purely stylistic point of view, there is evidence that the diary of Jacob Horn, the notes of Christopher Horn, the diary and daybook of John Horn, the elder, and the Camp Cat Fish docket were probably written by the same person. In the writings of both Jacob and Christopher Horn the eccentricities are identical: the same misspellings,[46] the same use of anachronistic words,[47] the same use of doubtful words and phrases,[48] and the same historically incorrect or dubious statements.[49] Another similarity between the Jacob Horn

---

44. A full list of impossible statements of this type is on file with the Institute of Early American History at Williamsburg.

45. The battle is stated in the diary to have occurred in "the 17 and 18 days of the 9th month, and year of 1748." *Horn Papers*, I, 29. The ninth month according to the Julian Calendar was, of course, November, not September. But the Eckerlins, who witnessed the battle, "trailed to Williamsburg early in October 1748." *Ibid.*, 131. Christopher Horn also interpreted the date to be "September 17 and 18, 1748." *Ibid.*, 132.

46. "Malitia"; "controll"; "corte"; and "storey."

47. "Blue Bloods"; "trail" (meaning path); "tepee"; and "brave" (Indian warrior).

48. "Wilds of," "Great Spirit," "black leaf tobacco."

49. Gist's death in 1769; the incredible slaughter of Indians at Flint Top in 1748; John Canon described as a nephew of Lord Dunmore.

diary and the Christopher Horn notes is the fondness of both for recording prophetic words of Gist and Canon.[50] On the other hand, each of these documents is written in the same peculiar literary style—an ill-matched combination of extraordinary linguistic crudities or pseudoarchaisms and outbursts of romantic sentiment couched in graceful nineteenth-century language.[51]

On the other hand there was a weight of evidence favorable to *The Horn Papers,* otherwise there would have been no disagreement about them. The mere bulk and complexity of the collection of papers, the impressive number of collateral artifacts, the absence of any pecuniary or other compelling motive for forgery, the unquestioned sincerity of the sponsoring society, the many statements in the manuscripts that agree with generally accepted facts, all strengthened the opinion that some of the Horn documents were genuine.

2

IN VIEW of this conflicting testimony the investigation entered a second phase. *The Horn Papers* certainly could not be accepted as genuine in their entirety. The search now concentrated on the problem of discovering if any were unimpeachable. It was hoped by expert examination of the physical objects—the eighteenth-century manuscripts, the lead plates, the maps, the other artifacts—to rescue some bona fide material.

The original papers upon which *The Horn Papers* are based were, according to Mr. W. F. Horn, boxed up by Christopher Horn in 1795 and the chest handed down in 1809 to his son, John, and by him in 1856 to his grandson, Solomon. In 1882, Solomon Horn moved west and took it with him to Doniphan County, Kansas. Mr. Horn reported that when the chest was opened in 1891 at Troy, Kansas, by his father and himself, it was found to contain the family records and

---

50. Examples: *Horn Papers,* I, 37, 39, 46, 47, 48, 52.
51. Examples: *Ibid.,* 17, 18, 25, 41, 45, 47, 49, 54, 56.

maps as well as a number of artifacts—small wooden boxes, tools, objects of shell and stone, and glassware. Mr. Horn also asserted that the papers, being in a poor state of preservation—or, to use his words, "very much moth-eaten"—were partially illegible. But the introduction of *The Horn Papers* states that "many, including the court docket, were preserved," and the impression that a substantial portion of the original manuscripts had survived was sustained by statements in the promotional literature.[52] The committee, however, learned from the president of the Greene County Historical Society that only the court docket and three of the maps purported to be original; everything else in the society's possession was a copy made by W. F. Horn in 1891 of original papers no longer extant. In addition the society had had two supposedly original items: (1) a torn portion of Lord Dunmore's receipt to Jacob Horn for the return of his commission as justice at Camp Cat Fish;[53] and (2) a perspective map on birch bark of the site of Turkey Foot Rock made by Jacob Horn in 1751. Shortly after the Horn papers were deposited with the society, the surviving fragment of the receipt vanished. Thereafter, the society took steps to reproduce photographically the remaining papers, a timely precaution, for almost immediately thereafter the birch-bark map also disappeared in an inexplicable manner.[54] That left only the court docket, the three maps, and the artifacts. The manuscripts, purporting to be original, upon which *The Horn Papers* are based, amount to 56 of the 141 pages of primary material contained in the work.

The court docket together with several maps and a number of

52. *Ibid.,* xiv; W. F. Horn ". . . by preserving the original manuscripts and copying the more fragmentary. . . ;" Subscription form of 1938; "Only a part of the records was legible. Some were preserved and some were copied," brochure on *The Horn Papers,* n.d. [c. 1946].

53. Mr. Horn is quoted in the Washington, Pa., *Observer,* June 15, 1935, as saying that the receipt was dated Oct. 4, 1774.

54. Reported by Mr. Moredock to Messrs. Middleton and Adair, Jan. 1947. *The Horn Papers,* I, 142, carry a copy of the birch-bark map.

sheets of Mr. Horn's transcript of 1891 were accordingly sent by the Greene County Historical Society at the committee's request to Mr. Arthur E. Kimberly, of Washington, D.C.,[55] for scientific analysis. Mr. Kimberly's report follows:

This is a report of the examination of the alleged docket of "Camp Cat Fish Corte," three manuscript maps purporting to be of the period 1770–1790, and seven sheets of manuscript in the handwriting of W. F. Horn which are said to have been copied from diaries kept by various members of the Horn family about 1770. The docket and maps are discussed in detail below.

The alleged docket is an octavo volume two inches in thickness in an oversize leather covered board jacket which is obviously not the original cover, if such a cover ever existed. The pages are blue, laid 100 per cent rag paper watermarked "Henry & Co." or "Lacourade." Neither of these watermarks is known to have been in existence during the period under consideration. The end papers and the edges of all the pages have been discolored, apparently with the same ink used in the text. The cord used in sewing the signatures together is clean and strong and the style of sewing is modern.

The text of the docket was written with a metal pen (first marketed in England in 1803) using non-ferrous blue-black ink of a type originating in Germany about 1836. This ink turns brown and tends to smudge when brought in contact with an alkali. If a sponge dampened in ammonia had been used to give the appearance of age, the observed smudging of the writing and bleaching of the paper could be explained. In some cases the first line or two on a page were not treated and so survive "unaged." Minor corrections made after "aging" also exhibit a blue color.

The largest map (10½" x 13¾") bearing the legend "MDCCLXV—Louis Map of MDCC LI by Doughty" is drawn in pencil and ink on comparatively modern paper (1860 or later). Both blue and brown ink notations are shown

55. Mr. Kimberly, who is on the staff of the National Archives, acted in a private capacity.

and the entire map has been given an ink (brown) wash followed by a coat of wax. The blue ink notations were made after the map was waxed.

The second map (5½" x 8⅞") number "39" is of the same general character as the above, but has no wax coating. The ink is of the type used in the docket, the body of the map being brown while river banks and a trail are drawn in blue.

The smallest map (3½" x 6") bearing the legend "Gist Map of MDCCL C. Horn" is on rag, laid paper and is drawn in pencil and brownish red ink. Faint ink lines have been overdrawn with modern lead pencil and the words "Cat Fish" have been added in the same pigment. Pin holes in the upper left and lower right corners suggest that this item might be a tracing.

Excerpts of the Horn diaries in the admitted hand of W. F. Horn are written in ink of the same type used in the docket and maps. The color of the ink varies from blue to brown indicating that these specimens were used in experiments on artificial aging. The handwriting resembles that of the docket in many respects.

In view of the results set forth above, it is my opinion that:

(1) The docket and maps were not produced during the period 1760–1800 as stated but were manufactured at a considerably later date.

(2) One person . . . produced all of the items examined.

(3) Although the precise determination of the age of ink inscriptions of this type is difficult, it is most probable that these writings were produced no earlier than 1930.

Washington, D.C.

April 25, 1947.   [signed] Arthur E. Kimberly

3

EXTRAORDINARY from many points of view, *The Horn Papers* are unique in the annals of American historiography in the sheer quantity of collateral artifacts advanced to substantiate them. In addition to the voluminous papers, there are three lead plates bearing inscriptions and dates and thirty or forty objects of wood, glass, metal, hide, flax, shell, and stone, besides rifles, carpenter and cooper's tools, drawing instruments, cannon balls, and a large collection of arrowheads and other Indian relics. Some of these were identified with artifacts mentioned in *The Horn Papers:* the copper coin of 1734, for example, is one of the Virginia colonial coins given by Jonathan Hager to Jacob Horn in 1740;[56] the marble cross is the one given by Jean Le Beau to Jacob Horn in 1739.[57] Many other objects, such as the unbleached flax wall pocket made by Duschea Horn in 1750, the wooden razor box made by Jacob Horn in 1737, and the wooden inkwell purchased by John Canon in England in 1762 and used by Jacob Horn at Camp Cat Fish Court were identified with the objects mentioned collectively in the Christopher Horn notes, under date of December 4, 1772, "This day we have gathered together all the belongings of our Mother and Sister who have passed on to God . . . and have preserved several of these for our children's children to behold what their kindred possessed in their day."[58] These things were said to have been placed in the Christopher Horn chest in 1795 along with the family papers, the glassware made at McCulloughtown in 1786, and other bric-a-brac, carried to Kansas when the family moved west in 1882, and opened up by Solomon and W. F. Horn at Troy, Kansas, in 1891.

To silence the skeptical, apparently, several of the artifacts were provided with labels (in handwriting similar to that appearing in the court docket and on the maps formerly thought to be original[59]) attesting the date and maker. Other objects, without benefit of label, were ascribed to particular persons, years, and places: a wall bracket was made by Jacob Horn in 1745; a wooden potato masher in 1750; a spool and flax thread in 1760; a rifle made at Augusta Town in 1776 used by Christopher Horn during the Revolution; a bell-metal brace made at Razortown in 1783; and a surveyor's plumb bob made at Augusta Town in 1777 and used in extending the Mason-Dixon Line in 1784 and in laying out Greene County in 1796.

Because of the bulk of the collateral artifact material, it was not feasible for the committee to include every known piece in its intensive investigation. In addition to the lead plates, about a third of the collection was examined and submitted to experts for opinion. This group included the objects mentioned in the Jacob Horn diary, the glassware supposed to have come from the Christopher Horn chest, and several objects that bore inscriptions purporting to be of the eighteenth century.[60] (1) The copper coin (diameter 13/16″) dated 1734 was the only object that was clearly of eighteenth-century origin, but instead of being a Virginia colonial coin, as alleged by Mr. Horn, it is a Dutch duit (eighth of a stuiver). The obverse bears a crowned shield with the lion rampant of the province of Holland and the reverse a large V with the letters O and C superimposed upon the arms of the V, and the date 1734. The VOC monogram, common on Dutch coins of the seventeenth and eighteenth centuries, was probably misconstrued to mean "Colony of Virginia." The Virginia statute authorizing the first issue of coins was passed in 1773. (2) The stone cross (length 4″, cross piece 2¼″) is of a white marble of wide distribution. It is crudely made, the sides shaped with a metal file. As the expert lapidary asserted that this kind of stone darkens upon exposure to air and to contact with other materials, the complete absence of stain on the surface clearly indicates that the cross is of recent manufacture. (3) The two pieces of glassware said to have been in the Christopher Horn chest, and therefore to antedate 1795, are quite obviously spurious. One is a pressed-glass sherbet glass (4″ high, 3½″ in diameter); the other is a small glass (2½″ high, 2″ in

60. These objects were examined by Mr. James L. Cogar, curator of Colonial Williamsburg, Inc., and by Mr. Minor Wine Thomas, archeologist of Colonial Williamsburg, Inc. The stone cross was examined by Mr. George C. Barclay, of Barclay & Sons, certified gemnologists, Newport News, Va.

diameter)—probably a toothpick holder—with a ruby-glass rim. The latter is mounted upon a white marble base of two steps ($2^{3}/_{4}$" x $2^{1}/_{4}$"). Even a novice at glass collecting would know that such items are of the late nineteenth century, if not of the early twentieth century. (4) The wooden razor box ($9^{1}/_{2}$" x $3^{1}/_{4}$" x $2^{1}/_{4}$") with brass hinges and a wooden latch. The cover of the inside compartment bears a label reading: "Penn Inn—Penns Point MDCCXXXVII I Jacob Horn made this Razor Box at Conwells Shop This Same Month By His Consent" (all block capitals except the letters "s" which are script and long, even when they appear as final letters of words). Mr. Kimberly in a report dated May 8, 1947, asserts that the ink on the label is the same type used in the court docket and "1891" transcript, that it was written with a steel pen, and that the top handle of the razor box is attached with machine-made brads and that the screws used in fastening the hinges appear to be of modern manufacture. It is Mr. Kimberly's opinion that the razor box is spurious.

4

THE MOST SIGNIFICANT OBJECTS in the Horn collection were three lead plates. Two of these—the American plates of 1795—had been unearthed by the archeological expedition of 1936.[61] These plates had been advanced as the strongest proof that there had been French plates buried in Greene County as the Horn diaries reported.[62] In 1945 the third plate, this one with a French inscription and the date 1751, turned up in Kansas among the effects of Mr. Horn's deceased sister, Miss Dora Horn.

At the same time that the manuscript court docket and maps were sent to Washington for expert appraisal, the Greene County Historical Society sent two lead plates to the research laboratories of the National Lead Company for spectrographic analysis. One plate

61. *Horn Papers*, I, 249.
62. W. F. Horn to editor, Washington, Pa., *Observer*, Topeka, Kansas, Aug. 15, 1932.

sent was the recently recovered French plate of 1751, the other was one of the American plates of 1795. At the same time the Virginia Historical Society generously loaned for comparative analysis the Céloron plate which had unquestionably been buried in the Ohio Valley by a French expedition in 1749.

The spectrochemical analysis of the three plates was revealing. The Céloron plate differed markedly both from the plate dated 1751 and that dated 1795. Both of the latter contained some nickel and a high content of silver and copper. Mr. Dunn, expert spectroscopist of the National Lead Company, for this reason attributed the lead to southeastern Missouri, the only source of lead known to him that contains nickel.[63] Although the French had mined lead in what is now Missouri prior to 1750, the mines were not then operating nor had they been for some time previous.[64] Moreover, the decided difference in composition of the lead plate dated 1751 from the genuine French plate is peculiar, especially in view of the chemical similarity of the two plates dated 1751 and 1795. The spectrographic analysis also disposed of the American plate of 1795, because the inhabitants of western Pennsylvania at that date could hardly have had access to Missouri lead.

If Mr. Dunn's report on the lead plate of 1751 left its status undetermined, the analysis of the French inscription on its face left no doubt of its spuriousness. The letter "Q" appearing in the text, for example, is a modern type form not used in French inscriptions until nearly three-quarters of a century after 1751.[65] Moreover,

63. National Lead Company Research Laboratories, memorandum No. 1612, July 15, 1947, by E. J. Dunn, Jr.

64. See Lawrence Henry Gipson, *The British Empire before the American Revolution*, IV (New York, 1939), 115, for an official French statement on this point.

65. This form of "Q" appears no earlier than 1818 in "Comparative Table of Types used by the French National Printing House from its foundation to 1825," in Daniel B. Updike, *Printing Types* (Cambridge, Mass., 1927), II, pl. 327, opp. p. 187. Sol Hess, art director, Lanston Monotype Machine Company, to Arthur Pierce Middleton, Philadelphia, Aug. 6, 1947, is also of this opinion.

the text of the inscription is not in eighteenth-century French; indeed, it was most certainly not written by a Frenchman in any century.[66]

5

TIME AND TIME AGAIN as the committee members considered the bulk and complexity of the papers and resurveyed the mountain of artifacts, they marveled that in this enormous mass nothing genuine could be found. Moreover, no reason offered to account for the manufacture of this elaborate and massive corpus of material satisfied the committee. On the face of it, the whole affair seemed impossible. Research in the history of famous forgeries, however, indicated that what appeared to be impossible had happened repeatedly.

Historic forgeries include a number of collections of documents as elaborate as *The Horn Papers*, and the existence of collateral artifacts is scarcely more proof of authenticity than the manuscripts themselves. The celebrated Vrain-Denis Lucas turned out no fewer than 27,320 spurious letters between 1853 and 1870, averaging more than four a day for seventeen years.[67] Charles Julius Bertram, an English-born resident of Copenhagen, with no ascertainable motive—unless it be vanity—fabricated an incredibly complex account of Roman Britain, published in 1747 as *De Situ Britanniae*,[68] complete with counterfeit Roman maps. Annius of Viterbo, who in 1498 published a ponderous volume of spurious documents called *De Comentariis Antiquitatum*, also carved a fake stone, the "Tabula Cibellaria," long exhibited in the local museum, to substantiate his documents.[69] Lucas fabricated his collection of letters for money, but there was no financial motive for the productions of Bertram and Annius, a

66. Marcel Reboussin to Arthur Pierce Middleton, Williamsburg, Va., Aug. 4, 1947.

67. Farrer, *Literary Forgeries*, 202–214.

68. *Ibid.*, 26–38.

69. *Ibid.*, 67–81.

fact which led many contemporaries to accept their productions as genuine but which did not prevent the ultimate exposure of both works as forgeries. Similarly, the claim that it would have required a professional historian's knowledge to bring forth the Horn documents cannot be accepted as a valid argument in favor of their genuineness. The two most celebrated literary forgeries in the English language were perpetrated by boys eighteen years of age: Chatterton's fabrication of the poems attributed to the nonexistent fifteenth-century monk Thomas Rowley[70] and Ireland's forgery of a complete play in the Shakespearean manner, *Vortigern and Rowena,* which was produced at the Drury Lane Theatre in 1796 by Sheridan.[71] The case of young Ireland is particularly curious, for when writing under the name of Shakespeare he exhibited far greater literary ability than when he cast aside the alias. For this interesting psychological phenomenon Farrer suggests the explanation, "It would seem that the mere effort of writing after an assumed model acts as a kind of hypnotic self-suggestion, and renders the intellect capable of otherwise impossible performance."[72]

6

BUT WHAT OF the numerous statements in *The Horn Papers* that are demonstrably correct, or at least plausible, and what of the occasional authentic ring that led Mr. Boyd of Princeton and other specialists in western history to suppose that they contained genuine as well as counterfeit parts? The answer was not easy to find, but once found seems clear. The perpetrator of a forgery would quite naturally be led to incorporate a number of true facts and authentic phrases in

70. Thomas Chatterton, 1752–1770, in *Dictionary of National Biography*, X, 143.

71. William Henry Ireland, *ibid.* See *Catalogue Number Sixty* (Martin Breslauer, 78 Stamford Court, Goldhawk Road, London, 1946), 61–62.

72. Farrer, *Literary Forgeries*, 246.

his fabricated documents. And it can be shown that the forger of the Horn manuscripts drew heavily on such works as Boyd Crumrine's *Old Virginia Court House at Augusta Town, Near Washington, Pennsylvania, 1776–1777* (1905). Crumrine proved to be an excellent quarry for material: he was candid enough to admit the extent of every hiatus in his knowledge of the history of the period and region about which he wrote, thereby virtually inviting a creative artist to fill gaps with imaginary data. Moreover Crumrine provided suggestions that were elaborated upon by the author of the Horn saga. For example Crumrine spoke of a map showing the extent of French claims in western Pennsylvania published in M. Robert's *Atlas Universel* (Paris, 1757), purporting to have been based on surveys made by Christopher Gist in 1751.[73] The fabricator of the Horn diaries fastened on this single fact and elaborated it into the romantic fictitious story which forms one of the spectacular tableaux of *The Horn Papers*, about the appearance of the French surveyors in 1751, the bribery of Christopher Gist with French gold to be their guide, their alliance with the Indians, and the plate-laying expedition in the Monongahela Valley to claim the region for France. The product when threshed was one single grain of Boyd Crumrine wheat and a ton of Jacob Horn chaff.

Throughout the early stages of *The Horn Papers* controversy, the protagonists derived great comfort from the geographic accuracy of the diaries and the physiographic exactitude of the Horn maps. Their owner on being taken through Tygart's Valley for the first time was able to identify and impute historic associations to tributaries, hills, Indian sites and paths to the amazement of his guides,[74] who had hunted and fished along the river all their lives. This exact geographic information was attributed solely to the Jacob Horn diary, which

73. Crumrine, *Old Virginia Courthouse* . . . (Washington, Pa., 1905), 37–38.
74. Articles by E. E. Meredith in *Point Marion* [Pa.] *News*, Apr. 17, 1947, and in the *Fairmont Times*, May 9, 1947.

was found by the local people to be so full of explicit and accurate details that Mr. Charles Snyder of Fairmont was able to trace the day-to-day progress of Jacob's alleged exploring trip of 1750 on the modern, large-scale map in the Monongahela Power Company's office.[75] Similarly, the president of the Greene County Historical Society asserted in a public address that the Horn maps must have been drawn by someone familiar with the territory because one of them revealed "the nearness of head springs of Muddy Creek to the main stream of South Ten Mile, *something not recognized by cartographers until the United States Geological survey was made.*"[76] But in view of what is now known about *The Horn Papers*, it is apparent that the creator of the diaries and the maps carefully worked over the modern geological survey maps and may even have traced portions of them.[77] Moreover there is evidence that details were added to the maps after 1930. In consequence, the fabrications assumed accuracy and minuteness of detail that astounded and delighted the believers in the Horn documents, who in their enthusiasm lost sight of the fact that genuine maps and diaries of the period seldom contain such details. Consequently, they quite understandably construed this feature of the *Papers* to be one of the strongest proofs of the authenticity of the manuscripts, whereas, in reality, the very profusion of accurate topographical detail was one of the most convincing proofs that they were counterfeit.

Here then is the account of the mystery of *The Horn Papers* as it developed in its fantastic form for more than ten years; and here, too, is the account of the scholarly investigation of that mystery

---

75. *Fairmont Times*, Mar. 28, 1947.

76. Address by A. L. Moredock, president of the Greene County Historical Society, at Morgantown, W.Va., June 8, 1946. The italics are ours.

77. The fabricator of the Horn maps exhibited extraordinary skill in deducing from the physiographic features of a region the probable routes of forgotten Indian paths and the probable sites of forgotten Indian villages.

which extended over another year. But the story of *The Horn Papers* is still not ended, for the noxious influences of the *Papers* are already fermenting and will continue to work for an indeterminant time. Many genealogists have already incorporated Horn data in their reports of various family lines, and as a result the national headquarters of the Daughters of the American Revolution has had to take precautions to cope with them. The praiseworthy campaign to raise funds to restore the Jonathan Hager House in Hagerstown, Maryland, is meeting opposition from individuals who were *always* against expending money on such projects, and who now cite *The Horn Papers* affair as reason for noncooperation. Thus the poison works on. And, undoubtedly, for years to come some unwary individuals will continue to be misled by the documents' fascinating historical fictions, and other persons will continue to use the story of the false diaries as a weapon against legitimate and valuable historical enterprise.

The Horn Papers will also live on in another fashion, as will the reputation of the mysterious creator of the Horn saga.[78] The fantastic counterfeiter, whoever he was, and whatever his genuine abilities as a student of regional history were, is henceforth disqualified among scholars. His creative feat, however, may well be regarded by posterity as ranking him in that fascinating and devious company which includes Lucas, Bertram, Chatterton and Ireland. Indeed he is the *only* American deserving to be mentioned with that celebrated group of European artists. Beyond a doubt, also, the impressive first and second volumes of *The Horn Papers*, which, by reason of this investigation, now seem worthless to their purchasers, will in time become collectors' items in the field of literary curiosities. As such, their

78. Mr. Moredock in Jan. 1947 advanced the hypothesis that "Old John" Horn, the grandfather of Mr. W. F. Horn, possibly fabricated some of the Horn documents as a joke on his own family. Since Mr. W. F. Horn was too ill to communicate with the committee, it has been impossible to learn his opinion of this theory.

pecuniary value will very likely exceed the original purchase price, for they will be sought and treasured with comparable fabrications on the grand scale—fabrications which possess the peculiar worth such efforts have in illuminating the strange uses to which some men put their talents.[79]

79. See Breslauer's *Catalogue Number Sixty,* section entitled " 'The Tenth Muse,' Being the Catalogue of a Collection illustrative of Forgery and Alleged Forgery in History, Science and Literature in Manuscript and Print including Major and Minor Rarities of English and Continental Literature," 38–68.

II

REVIEW ESSAYS, NOTES, AND DOCUMENTS

THE NEW THOMAS JEFFERSON

In his younger years Adair was a prolific and provocative reviewer. He
wrote frequently for the *New York Times* and the old New York *Herald
Tribune* as well as for professional journals. It is rare that a review gains
any lasting currency, but Adair's essay on "The New Thomas Jefferson"
proves it can happen. His overview of Jefferson's historiography remains
useful as does his dry humor. At least one scholar feels this review suggests
the significant book on Jefferson and the intellectual tenor of his times that
Adair wanted to write and never did.

Jefferson Himself: The Personal Narrative of a Many-Sided Ameri-
    can. Edited by Bernard Mayo. (Boston: Houghton Mifflin Com-
    pany, 1942. Pp. xv, 384.)
The Complete Jefferson: Containing His Major Writings, Published
    and Unpublished, Except His Letters. Assembled and arranged by
    Saul K. Padover. (New York: Duell, Sloan and Pearce, Inc., 1943.
    Pp. xxix, 1,322.)
The Life and Selected Writings of Thomas Jefferson. Edited, with an
    Introduction by Adrienne Koch and William Peden. (New York:
    The Modern Library, 1944, Pp. xliv, 730.)

THE PUBLICATION of these three books is an event of importance
for historians; for they collectively stand as a sure sign that we are

SOURCE: Reprinted from the *William and Mary Quarterly*, 3d Ser., III (1946),
123–133.

just now entering on a new era of Jefferson historiography. From now on professional scholars who discuss the great Virginian, as well as the informal historians who parade the "Sage of Monticello" in editorials, advertisements, sermons, and radio broadcasts will write on a "new" Thomas Jefferson subtly changed both in *stature* and *quality* from the Jefferson known to their fathers. It is worthwhile, therefore, to consider at some length these three anthologies and their background. For although they contribute no details to the specialist's knowledge of Jefferson, being primarily composed of selections from his best-known writings, still they do present his portrait in a fresh perspective that promises to be official for many years to come.

In the first place, it is clear that the new Jefferson who appears in these books looms larger as a hero and as a symbol of Americanism than the Jefferson whom earlier generations of scholars discussed. It was only during the last decade that Thomas Jefferson's fame came to full flower. Today for the first time since his death he has achieved symbolic status as a national hero of the highest order, ranking next to the myth-encrusted figures of Washington and Lincoln. Since this apotheosis is of so recent a date, and since it will inevitably condition all future consideration of Jefferson's career, it is pertinent to review the history of his reputation in some detail. Only thus will it be possible to appraise the artistic selectivity which created the portrait offered us by Messrs. Mayo and Padover, and Miss Koch and Mr. Peden.

Jefferson was accorded secular sainthood of a sort even while he lived, nor has he ever entirely lacked, since his death in 1826, a devout congregation of worshippers. On the other hand, no American leader was ever more bitterly hated during his lifetime than Jefferson; and until very recently the praise of his believers was always offset by the complaints of heretics, who denied all his claims to glory. Thus, during the nineteenth and early years of the twentieth century Jefferson was sometimes revered as a party leader, or as a class leader, or as the spokesman of a particular section, but never as a figure above the strife of partisan politics. Inevitably this restricted the appeal of his name, so that during no period before the 1930s did all Americans, rural and urban, rich and poor, North and South and West accept him as a major representative of the great tradition of Americanism.

In the beginning Jefferson was hated by the self-chosen elite of "the rich, the wise, and well-born," who voted the Federalist ticket; New England ministers, publicists, and political leaders, especially, viewed with horror his "atheistic" and "leveling" ideas. As these old-line Federalists died off, Jefferson's fame rose perceptibly in the North, but at the same time its luster dimmed in his own section. Southerners, after 1830, subscribing to the constitutional gospel according to Calhoun, found the Virginian's majority-rule principles and his heterodoxy on slavery increasingly distasteful. The abolitionists and the "free-soilers" moreover, had been quick to claim him for their own. Thus by the 1850s Jefferson was becoming a prophet without honor in his own neighborhood, while the most ardent Jeffersonians, such as Abraham Lincoln, had made him the patron saint of a new sectional party organized in the North and deliberately christened "Republican" to trade on the prestige of the Virginian's name.[1]

Thomas Jefferson did not long remain the Republican party hero. That title was soon given to the martyred Lincoln. After 1865, Jefferson's memory went into deep eclipse. In Virginia and the rest of the South, Lee's had become the great name. In the North during the Gilded Age, when progress was popularly conceived of as industrial expansion and businessmen were worshipped as demigods, it was inevitable that the Virginian's ideal of an agrarian republic would

1. The only general account of the vicissitudes of Jefferson's fame is to be found in Dixon Wecter's delightful and thoughtful study, *The Hero in America: A Chronicle of Hero-Worship* (New York, 1941). A suggestive discussion of the use of Jefferson's name by Lincoln and the creators of the Republican party is in Wilfred E. Binkley's *American Political Parties: Their Natural History* (New York, 1943).

seem quaint or wrongheaded. He had been far too forthright in his denunciation of bankers and manufacturers to suit the mores of the day; the fact that he had been a slaveholder and a believer in states' rights also counted strongly against him with official and unofficial molders of public opinion. And so, while Alexander Hamilton's fame rapidly revived, Jefferson's reputation, like his home, Monticello, fell into rank decay.

It was only toward the end of the century that Jefferson's name again became a dynamic political slogan. Farmers who had found that the West was not golden, and city dwellers who had discovered that progress could mean poverty, rejuvenated Jefferson's fame as a critic of industrial capitalism and as the farmer's friend. Then as the Populist revolt was transformed into the ferment of Progressivism, the significance of Thomas Jefferson's career was reevaluated by the historians. The most notable of these revisions were written by Frederick Jackson Turner and Charles Beard; together these two historians succeeded in making "Jeffersonianism" intellectually respectable for the first time since the Civil War.

Turner presented Jefferson, somewhat incongruously costumed in a coonskin cap, as the first great spokesman for the pioneer West— and hence for unadulterated Americanism— against the conservative and semi-European East. Thus Jefferson became a key symbolic figure in the frontier version of American history, which, aside from its scholarly importance, exerted a powerful emotional appeal by emphasizing the unique origin and destiny of American democracy. Charles Beard, likewise, in a series of brilliant studies helped increase Jefferson's historic stature by revealing the continuing vitality of the Jeffersonian economic tradition in American politics.

The writings of these two men and of lesser historians around the turn of the century, together with the publication of a sizable part of Jefferson's own writings, guaranteed that his name would no longer lie ignored. His renewed popularity, however, did not go unchallenged even in orthodox Progressive circles. Theodore Roosevelt thought him a mollycoddle; Woodrow Wilson considered Alexander Hamilton a far abler statesman; and Albert L. Beveridge, a very paladin of Progressivism, wrote in his classic *Life of Marshall* the most sustained and thorough attack ever made on Jefferson and all his works. Nevertheless, the tide had turned; the Virginian's prestige was steadily and slowly rising.

As the 1920s opened and the United States returned to Republican "normalcy," although Jefferson's fame was continuously growing, he still remained for most Americans a distinctly minor prophet of the national faith. On this point we have the convincing evidence gathered by the present senior senator from Michigan, Arthur H. Vandenberg, at that time a Grand Rapids newspaper editor. In 1921 Vandenberg polled a hundred leading citizens in politics, education, the church, and the professions to discover who was "The Greatest American."[2] Forty-nine voters unhesitatingly named Lincoln.[3] George Washington was the outright choice of thirty-two pollees, and four others named Washington and Lincoln as equally great. Thomas Jefferson was obviously not considered worthy of comparison with these gods in the national pantheon. There was but one lone vote cast for him as the greatest American by James M. Cox, the Democratic candidate for president, who had lost to Harding.[4] It is true that three prominent southern Democrats had listed Jefferson as greatest after Washington, and he was mentioned with approval

2. The report of this poll is contained in Vandenberg's biography of Hamilton, *The Greatest American: Alexander Hamilton. An Historical Analysis of his Life and Works Together with a Symposium of Opinions by Distinguished Americans* (New York, 1921).

3. One of these Lincoln voters, ex-Governor Ferris of Michigan, justified his choice thus: "The Declaration of Independence is the greatest exposition of America's ideal. Abraham Lincoln was the incarnation of that ideal."

4. Other great Americans who, with Jefferson, got one vote were: Roger Williams, Alexander Hamilton, Daniel Webster, and Samuel J. Tilden. Theodore Roosevelt was listed several times with Washington and Lincoln, and Ben Franklin got two votes, one of them from a southern university president who begged to remain anonymous for fear his neighbors would "misunderstand" his choice of a Yankee.

by two professional historians and two liberal newspaper editors. Nevertheless it is clear that Thomas Jefferson in 1921 was still considered a hero of relatively small stature even by Virginians.[5]

Few Americans in 1921 could have foreseen that Jefferson's fame would soon grow so prodigiously that he would far overshadow all other Americans except Washington and Lincoln. Yet within ten years this had come about, and within twenty years Jefferson had become easily our most widely quoted and most enthusiastically praised historic leader. In part this new Jefferson popularity of the late 1920s was due to the general preoccupation with the American past generated by the superheated nationalism which followed World War I.[6] It was at this time that general histories and biographies of dead Americans began with increasing regularity to make the best-seller lists. It was then that students and the reading public became aware of the fact that it was impossible to write accurately about the American Revolution and the early Republic without writing about Thomas Jefferson. He had either participated in or penned copious comments on every major political and social development in American history from 1769 to 1826. He had known and written about all his famous contemporaries. As scholarly interest, egged on by national pride, then went on to explore the origins of American architecture, American science, American economic thought, American agriculture, American inventions, American music, and American education, student after student found his research trail leading to Jefferson himself or Jefferson's writings.

5. Jefferson did not get a single vote from Virginia for win, or place, or show, even though one of the several Virginians answering the poll was Pres. A. E. Alderman of Jefferson's own university. He explained his choice of Washington as "greatest" and R. E. Lee as next, by affirming that "character is greater than genius."

6. Vandenberg's book was clearly one of the products of this historical nationalism. Consider his argument, which is typical of many in the volume: "If the familiar cry—'Back to the Constitution'—is an apostrophe to sanity and wisdom, the story of the Constitution is the starting point for the crusades. In a word, no one thing would go farther or do more toward Americanizing America than to make American History fashionable."

In very short order a number of scholars and amateur historians rediscovered the true greatness of Mr. Jefferson. Claude Bowers, famous for his keynote speeches at Democratic Conventions, proclaimed in 1925 that Jefferson was the greatest Democrat of them all; A. J. Nock a year later showed him to be "the father of American democracy"; Vernon Louis Parrington exhibited him in 1928 as our greatest "liberal"; while Gilbert Chinard in 1929 proved that Jefferson was "the Apostle of Americanism." All of these books were widely circulated. There was, besides, a heavy increase in articles in newspapers and magazines quoting and discussing Jefferson; and it was during this period that Monticello was made a national shrine.[7] And so when Gutzon Borglum in 1927 began sculpturing the colossal heads of America's four greatest leaders on Mt. Rushmore there was no loud complaint when Jefferson emerged beside Washington, Lincoln, and Theodore Roosevelt.

The final canonization of Thomas Jefferson was not consummated, however, until after Franklin D. Roosevelt entered the White House. In the years between 1933 and 1937 both of our major political parties at last accepted the master of Monticello as a statesman of supreme vision. For while Jefferson, as the decade drew to a close, was officially proclaimed as the patron of the New Deal, he was simultaneously hailed as holy by those who most hated FDR. In fact, for a time the anti-Roosevelt voters were much warmer than the Democrats in their glorification of Jefferson.

It was not Jefferson but Andrew Jackson who was first recruited by the Democratic publicity staff to symbolize the early New Deal; the reviewing stand erected before the White House for Roosevelt's second inaugural parade was a replica of the Hermitage, not of Monticello. It is true that during the campaign of 1932 Roosevelt praised

7. The *Reader's Guide to Periodical Literature* entries under Jefferson's name show the development of interest in him exhibited in periodicals from 1921 to 1932:

| 1919–1921——2 entries | 1925–1928——35 entries |
| 1922–1924——9 entries | 1929–1932——18 entries |

Jefferson highly in two major speeches. Nevertheless, after the election the Virginian was quickly thrust into the background by the Democrats. The cause for this coolness becomes apparent when it is remembered that the years from 1933 to 1936 saw the greatest peacetime centralization of federal authority in American history. The power of the executive was drastically extended at the expense of the legislative. Government costs leaped to astronomical heights. Increasingly the state intruded itself into the "private business" of its citizens. In all these matters the New Deal ran contrary to the gospel of good government expounded by Thomas Jefferson.

The anti–New Dealers did not remain silent on this point; dissident members of Roosevelt's own party, calling themselves "Jeffersonian Democrats" denounced his heresy. The Liberty League, spending nine hundred thousand dollars to educate the voters, paid a good proportion of this sum reprinting Jefferson's remarks on government economy, on states' rights, on bureaucracy, and on the beauties of laissez-faire. For the first time since Lincoln's day Jefferson was accepted as a seer by the Republican party.

Inevitably Franklin Roosevelt, whose sense of history was most acute, was bound to consider Mr. Jefferson a somewhat ambiguous patron for his first administration. Consequently it was Old Hickory, who had mastered the bankers a century earlier, that was paraded in 1936 as the first New Dealer; and it was at a Jackson Dinner that FDR opened his campaign for reelection. It required the Supreme Court fight—in which Jefferson furnished the president with his most potent weapons against the judges—to make the Democratic high command openly acknowledge what rank-and-file New Dealers had known all along. The Roosevelt administration was using Hamiltonian means to achieve Jeffersonian ends.

It was only then in 1937, as if to make belated amends for the earlier coolness, that the New Dealers set out to give tangible proof of their homage to Jeffersonian ideals. The great marble temple, set beside the Tidal Basin to rival the Lincoln and Washington Memorials, was rushed to completion. The buffalo and Indian head vanished from the nickel to be replaced by Jefferson and Monticello. By a clever change in postal designs it was arranged that the Jefferson three-cent stamp would be the most popular issue.[8] Finally the government sponsored what promises to be the most enduring of all monuments to Jefferson, a complete edition of his writings. The mere proposal that the government should memorialize Jefferson in any one of these ways would have loosed a storm of outraged objections twenty years earlier.

It was Adolph Hitler and the terrifying growth of Nazi power that added the last few cubits to Jefferson's new stature. As Americans after 1938 came rapidly to understand the threat of fascism, Jefferson's figure was raised entirely above all partisan struggles of domestic politics. The whole pattern of democratic rights, the whole scheme of democratic values with which his name was associated took on fresh and dramatic meaning as European democracy recoiled before the advance of the dictators. And so when America engaged in the war in 1941 there could be no question of the Virginian's place in our hierarchy of saints. As we once again risked "our lives, our fortunes, and our sacred honor" in battle, Thomas Jefferson's memory was a living force to give us faith, to set our goal, and to strengthen our courage.

THE THOMAS JEFFERSON who appears in the anthologies of Messrs. Mayo and Padover, and Miss Koch and Mr. Peden is the rediscovered militant democrat whose life was dedicated to the advancement of freedom and the happiness of man. In the pages of these books Jefferson speaks again to us and to all our contemporaries who have

8. The postage stamp in most use had traditionally been the Washington head. Under the new system, planned in 1937, all the presidents were arranged in chronological order with the first president on the one-cent stamp, the second on the two-cent, etc. The Jefferson three-cent issue thus became the most used stamp under existing postal rates.

looked on the face of tyranny with power and moving intensity. Each of these volumes contains his great documents on government by consent, on equality before the law, on freedom of speech and worship, which are landmarks in the development of democracy. All of the anthologists also add to the cumulative effect of Jefferson's greatness as a political philosopher by leaving out the questionable part of Jeffersonian doctrine that is dated and irrelevant to our day. With deft selectivity they have skillfully refrained from overburdening their pages with Jefferson's praise of laissez-faire, with his innumerable expositions of free trade and the tariff, and with his warnings against a positive national state. The portrait they present of the great Virginian was clearly painted after Pearl Harbor and after the triumph of the New Deal social-service state.

Since no book containing three hundred pages of Mr. Jefferson's writings could lack merit, the prospective purchaser is here faced with a choice of virtues. Each of these three volumes has its own particular qualities to recommend it; each will appeal to a different type of reader.

Mr. Mayo's *Jefferson Himself* is the most unusual anthology and the most artistically satisfactory book of the three. The editor, not content with merely printing separate selections of the best of Jefferson, has synthesized the passages into a continuous running narrative of the Virginian's life in Jefferson's own words. He has quarried the diaries, the public papers, and approximately six hundred of the private letters, and the brilliance with which Mr. Mayo has joined the various bits of material into a unified and proportioned whole cannot be too highly praised. He had indeed ably succeeded in the task he set himself, to present "an intimate and rounded portrait of a great and many-sided American." If one were asked to name the best single book with which to introduce Jefferson to the average American, the answer would be Mayo's *Jefferson Himself*.

In *The Life and Selected Writings of Thomas Jefferson* Miss Koch and Mr. Peden have done a more conventional anthology. After a competent introductory sketch of Jefferson's career, they offer in slightly abridged form his "Autobiography," written in 1821 and recounting his life through his French ambassadorship; a small part of the "Anas"; short selections from the "Travel Journals"; the "Essay on Anglo-Saxon"; his biographical sketches of Washington, Franklin, and Wythe; and, likewise slightly abridged, that typically eighteenth-century classic, the "Notes on Virginia." The next section, labeled "Public Papers," running to fifty-five pages, is made up of: "Summary View of the Rights of British America," the Act for Religious Freedom, the Report on the Government of the Western Territories, the most famous reports as secretary of state, and the most notable presidential addresses. These selections in the first half of the Koch-Peden book fill over three hundred pages; the last half, covering approximately the same number of pages, is made up of over two hundred of Jefferson's private letters. Few of the letters are printed in entirety, but the choice is excellent. It is this part of the volume that recommends it over Mayo's and Padover's for the person who knows Jefferson and who wishes to own a fine sample from his marvelous "epistolatory" file. It is a pity, however, that Miss Koch and Mr. Peden did not insist that the publisher let them index their selections. No anthology, especially one so largely composed of letters, should ever be printed without this indispensable aid for the reader. Even so the book would still be a great bargain at triple the price.

Mr. Padover's *The Complete Jefferson* is obviously the book of the three that will appeal most to students of American history or any scholar who uses the Virginian's writings in a professional way. For, besides its pretensions to completeness, Mr. Padover's volume possesses the virtue that professionals must demand: all of the Jefferson documents included, except the small store of letters, are printed in full and ably indexed. *The Complete Jefferson* is a big, solidly packed book that contains practically all of Jefferson's formal writings. Here in the 280-page section on "Politics and Government" are all of the Virginian's resolutions, declarations, bills, constitutional opinions, and reports on agriculture, commerce, and the currency. Two hundred pages encompass all of Jefferson's speeches and addresses. The "Notes on Virginia," the "Autobiography," the "Travel Journals," and the private diaries are published in their entirety. A hundred pages are given to Jefferson as an educational theorist and the founder of a university; equal space is allotted to his thoughts on religion and philosophy and his scientific projects. Here are the two Jefferson essays on Anglo-Saxon; here are fifteen biographic sketches of his contemporaries; and included here is the discussion of the American language and the notes on English prosody.[9] *The Complete Jefferson* runs to 600,000 words, and though the inclusion of only 80 out of the 18,000 letters that Jefferson wrote makes the title grossly misleading,[10] Mr. Padover has indeed offered us a one-volume Jefferson library.

These three volumes together insistently raise one question about the "new" Jefferson that cannot yet be answered—a question that bears on the *quality* of Jefferson's eminence rather than on his stature as a great man. No informed person will object when our four editors applaud the Virginian as one of the world's chief democrats. One must, however, cry "not proven" when Jefferson is nominated as a universal genius in other areas of human endeavor outside of politics. Yet all of the anthologists suggest that the Virginian was a unique superman, mastering and adding to all fields of knowledge. Miss Koch and Mr. Peden call him "the American Leonardo"; Mr. Mayo underlines his cosmic versatility; and Mr. Padover goes completely overboard in claiming that there has never been anything to equal the "incredible" brilliance of Jefferson's mind "since the Italian Ren-

9. Also included in this section is Garrick's poem, "Lovely Peggy," which Padover mistakenly attributes to Jefferson.

10. Approximately 70 percent of Jefferson's letters *have never been published*, so until the promised Boyd edition is issued it is impossible for any anthologist to get even a "complete" sample of them.

aissance." Such sweeping statements are suspect on two counts: they ignore the age in which Jefferson lived and, more important, they falsely assume that we possess an exact knowledge about Jefferson's ideas, which in fact is still lacking.

Jefferson was only one of the great amateurs in a period that swarmed with them. He was a contemporary of such titans as Franklin and Goethe. Every philosopher of the Age of Reason took all learning to be his province and despised the specialist—who dominates our era—as a vulgar groundling unfit to move in polite and leisured circles. The briefest check on the careers and interests of such friends of Jefferson as Priestly, Dupont, Paine, and Rush would reveal that they, too, exhibit the same breathtaking many-sidedness that marks the Virginian. All of these men, like Jefferson, were amateur scientists or inventors, all of them were educational reformers, all published creditable tracts on economics or political theory, all speculated on philosophy and religion, all were writers of merit, and each man was up to his ears in politics. Clearly Jefferson's versatility was not as uncommon in his day as it would be in a modern statesman. It is necessary, therefore, for anyone who would parade Jefferson as *the* universal genius of the eighteenth century to show with detail and exactness the Virginian's contributions to the accumulated knowledge of his own age.

Unfortunately we lack adequate studies of just this aspect of Jefferson's life; we know relatively little about his ideas in the context of the total civilization of which he was a part. American historians for fifty years have bayed down the false scent laid by Turner and have viewed Jefferson as a peculiarly American product of his "frontier" environment. Consequently few students have analyzed the agreements and divergences between Jefferson's theories and statements and those of his European contemporaries.[11] Therefore, as of today

11. Carl Becker, Gilbert Chinard, and Adrienne Koch are among the few who have done outstanding studies of this type.

it is still impossible to go through Jefferson's writings on any topic and to say with assurance, here Jefferson is breaking new ground, here he is making his own original contribution, and here he is merely repeating the borrowed idea of someone else.

The evidence we do have should make us extremely wary of characterizing Jefferson as an important innovator in any field except politics and, perhaps, architecture. It is quite possible that scholars twenty years from now will dismiss many of Jefferson's remarks on religion, philosophy, education, and science included in these anthologies as the superlative product of an intellectual middleman, whose literary skill made him an ideal popularizer of other people's thoughts. Take, for example, Jefferson's statement, included in the Mayo and Koch-Peden volumes, that "the mass of mankind has not been born with saddles on their backs, nor a favored few booted and spurred, ready to ride them legitimately by the grace of God," and lay it beside the speech of Rumbold, one of the Rye House plotters executed in James II's reign.[12] Is it legitimate to quote this as "Jefferson himself"? How should we label Jefferson's discussion of the doctrines of Jesus and Epicurus, which Mr. Padover and Miss Koch reprint, now that Professor Chinard has shown it to be a paraphrase taken from Enfield's encyclopedia of comparative religion? Would a study of the Virginian's "Thoughts on English Prosody," which can be found in Mr. Padover's book, reveal the same sort of borrowings from Dr. Johnson or Lord Kames? Even the Virginian's political theories—the area of thought which elicited his deepest interest and most sustained efforts—must be studied with discrimination. For did not Jefferson himself state that in writing his most famous document,

12. *Bishop Burnet's History of His Own Time* (London, 1734) reports that Rumbold said "he did not believe that God had made the greater part of mankind with saddles on their backs, and bridles in their mouths, and some few booted and spurred to ride the rest." Cf. also the slightly different version of this speech (which Jefferson had read too) in the first chapter of James Burgh's *Political disquisitions* . . . (Philadelphia, [1775]).

the Declaration of Independence, his purpose was "not to find out new principles or new arguments . . . but to place before mankind the commonsense of the matter . . . "? These are not picayune questions, for they relate directly to the quality of Jefferson's greatness. Was not his incontestable genius as leader of a popular revolution due in part to the fact that Jefferson was not a disturbingly original thinker?

Here then is one aspect of the "new" Jefferson that clearly needs further study. Until all of Jefferson's ideas and projects are carefully examined against the background of contemporary European developments, and until his theories are appraised as part of the great tradition of Western social thought, we will be unable to take the true measure of the man. It will be a big task requiring the labors of many students. In the meantime Mr. Mayo, Mr. Padover, Miss Koch, and Mr. Peden have done their share by making available at small cost a solid body of Jefferson's writings. Jefferson himself has been lavish with clues showing where the search should begin. Now if specialists in all phases of eighteenth-century life and thought will study the Virginian as a typical philosopher-statesman of the Enlightenment we will finally be able to finish the portrait of the "new" Jefferson.

❧ 12 ❧

THE CATALOGUE OF THE
LIBRARY OF THOMAS JEFFERSON

The long-awaited publication of the first three (of five) volumes of Millicent Sowerby's superb Jefferson library catalogue furnished Douglass Adair with a marvelous occasion to remind his readers of the relevance of Jefferson's books to any understanding of their owner.

The Catalogue of the Library of Thomas Jefferson. Volumes I, II, and III. Edited by E. MILLICENT SOWERBY. (Washington, D.C.: Government Printing Office, 1952–1953. Pp. xv, 562, 433, 481.)

"I CANNOT LIVE WITHOUT BOOKS," Jefferson confessed to John Adams in 1815. From his earliest youth, Jefferson labored "grievously," as he put it, "under the malady of Bibliomania"; until the day of his death, books were "a necessity of life" to him. Jefferson's books, therefore, offer scholars one unsurpassed approach to the innermost citadel of his personality—an approach that reveals significant traits of his character both as private citizen and public man. Jefferson's libraries are the hyphen in the phrase now commonly used to describe him as the young Republic's most spectacular "scholar-statesman."

SOURCE: Reprinted from the *William and Mary Quarterly*, 3d Ser., XI (1954), 637–641.

An admirer of Sir Francis Bacon—he was often to group Bacon, Locke, and Newton as the three most acute thinkers of modern times[1]—Jefferson subscribed to the Baconian dictum *Abeunt studia in mores* and early began a systematic collection of books designed to further his studies. Catalogued by Jefferson in accordance with Bacon's analysis of the chief "faculties" of the mind, under the heads of History (Memory), Philosophy (Reason), and Fine Arts (Imagination), this vast collection of books made Monticello to some degree a curious equivalent, set on a mountaintop in the backwoods of America, of "Solomon's House" as described by Bacon in his utopian *New Atlantis*—a shrine and research center dedicated to the proposition that "knowledge is power," that the great heroes of civilization most worthy of praise by posterity are those scientists, inventors, and philosophers who have contributed to the expansion of the human mind and thus by their discoveries advanced the happiness and liberties of mankind.[2]

1. In this Jefferson followed Voltaire, whose *Lettres sur les Anglais* (1734) first established this trinity of philosophers as the great secular saints of the Enlightenment.

2. "Solomon's House" as described by Bacon was a strange combination of temple, museum, and research institute. In one wing of the buildings were exhibited "patterns and samples of all manner of the more rare and excellent inventions"; in the other wing were displayed effigies and statues of "all principal inventors." Members of the order of scholar-priests who governed Atlantis daily celebrated in Solomon's House with "hymns and services" and "forms of prayer," imploring God's "aid and blessing" for the "illumination" of the members' research projects "and the turning of them into good and holy uses."

Visitors to Monticello during Jefferson's lifetime (as well as in modern times) noted and were sometimes puzzled by the museum-like aspect of the mansion, an aspect which is especially striking as one enters the main entrance hall. Here on display were pictures and busts of "great men" (including Bacon, Newton, and Locke); also conspicuously in evidence were all manner of excellent inventions and gadgets; and here, during Jefferson's life, was exhibited what must have been a rather cluttered collection of Indian artifacts, fossil mammoth bones, etc., etc. And the library at Monticello, as will be seen, was designed and indexed, as in Solomon's House, to make immediately available for use all "discoveries" from the earliest times in all sciences and all arts.

It is for these reasons that the publication by the Library of Congress of Miss Sowerby's brilliantly edited *Catalogue* of Jefferson's greatest library (among several he assembled during his long life) is a major event in the field of Jefferson studies. For it does not take the gift of prophecy to predict that Miss Sowerby's reconstruction of the library at Monticello will be the starting point in the immediate future of a larger number of fruitful studies of Jefferson and his age than any other single block of known Jefferson papers.

Thanks to Miss Sowerby and her patron, the Library of Congress, we find here a marvelous guide to the intellectual world of Jefferson—a world which a few earlier scholars have glimpsed but have hardly yet begun to map—a key to the whole circle of late eighteenth-century politics, science, and arts. And since Jefferson's power as a thinker did not depend on originality, it is a key which will serve wonderfully well, if used intelligently, to open up for inspection the common pattern of libertarian ideas, in all fields of knowledge, prevailing on both sides of the Atlantic during Jefferson's lifetime.

Under Miss Sowerby's creative editing the *Catalogue* is a "bio-bibliography" of the books sold by Jefferson to Congress in 1815 to replace the Congressional Library burned by the British in 1814. The collection at that time represented Jefferson's purchases, systematically made in Europe and America over a period of forty-five years, and additions from other sources, the whole totaling approximately five thousand titles and between six and seven thousand volumes. It has been the purpose of Miss Sowerby's annotations, as Mr. Luther H. Evans points out in a graceful foreword to the *Catalogue*, to reveal "not only what volumes Mr. Jefferson had acquired but, when possible, where and why he had acquired them and, most important, how he had made use of them. Thus the form which the catalogue was to take became something more than a bibliography and something less than a biography. Essentially, however, it is a study of the mind of a scholar, a philosopher, and a statesman as reflected in the books he assembled about him."

The great fire of 1851 which destroyed two-thirds of the original Jefferson collection, the Library's failure to place any of the Jefferson volumes in a separate collection until the closing years of the nineteenth century—the surviving volumes are now shelved in the Rare Book Room—demanded of Miss Sowerby a major feat of detection in reconstructing the library as it was when delivered to Congress in 1815. However, by using both the manuscript catalogue that Jefferson himself began to keep in 1783 and the printed short-title catalogue of the Library of Congress issued in 1815, the editor has succeeded admirably in her task. Here is described with precision for the first time what books made up Jefferson's greatest and most comprehensive library.

The reconstruction of the original collection, the mere publication of the titles of the books, the identification of the editions Jefferson owned, and the description of those volumes that survive, would alone be sufficient to mark these handsomely printed volumes as a great scholarly accomplishment. However, for students of the eighteenth century, for Jefferson scholars, indeed for any modern bibliophile, the feature of Miss Sowerby's work which evokes the deepest gratitude is the inclusion of Jefferson's revealing comments, recommendations, glosses, and criticisms on specific volumes and specific authors. These comments allow us as never before to determine which of his books Jefferson "tasted," which he "swallowed," and which he "chewed and digested"; these critical glosses on the literature of many fields, thus systematically assembled, show us how Jefferson transmuted the "experience" of the printed page and the "reality" of life and thought there made accessible to him, both into "delight" in "privateness and retiring," and into "ability" in the "judgment and disposition" of public business.

These are sweeping claims for the importance of Miss Sowerby's work, but they are claims that can be substantiated in detail.

For example, consider some of the implications of Miss Sowerby's detective work in identifying the component units of the many volumes that arrived at the Library in 1815, labeled merely "Religious Tracts" or "Political Pamphlets." Three of these volumes of religious writings known heretofore only by this catchall heading now become fifty-seven specific titles—replies to Paine's *Age of Reason*, analysis of Swedenborg, and so forth. Many of these tracts were sent by admirers; some were gifts with a string attached (the hope of a literary plug or a political job); but the sheer *number* of these pamphlets which Jefferson read and commented on is startling, even to the so-called Jefferson expert. The Sowerby edition of his library affords persuasive evidence of the never-ending religious interests of Jefferson, the man whom his enemies tagged "atheist." Apparently he was always willing to "taste" anything in print on that topic.

If Miss Sowerby enables us to see how avidly Jefferson tasted these sectarian and controversial religious pamphlets, she renders another major service in recalling obscure and forgotten writers whose works Jefferson appears to have "swallowed whole." How many American historians today could identify a single work by Conyers Middleton? Yet Jefferson could affirm in 1813 that on certain of Priestley's theological works and *"on Middleton's writings"* rested "the basis of my own faith." Some day, when an adequate study of Jefferson's deism is written, Miss Sowerby's volumes, with their ready-made catalogue of Jefferson's reading and his comments thereon, will be foundation stones of that study.

Clearly, however, both the number of the books in the library and the quality of the comments indicate history and politics as the area where Jefferson was determined to "chew and digest," in order to transform the recorded experience of other ages and other peoples into "judgment." And here the evidence exhibited by Miss Sowerby reveals how powerfully Jefferson was committed to research in the modern sense. When faced with any problem, Jefferson consistently launched an exhaustive investigation in the best printed authorities with the aim of discovering truth based on critically established fact.

A wonderful vignette of Jefferson, the research man, at work in his library, appears in the recently published *Memoirs* of the Monticello slave, Isaac. "Old master had a abundance of books," Isaac recalled; "sometime would have twenty of 'em down on the floor at once: read fust one, then tother. . . . When they go to him to ax him anything, he go right straight to the book and tell you all about it." Miss Sowerby's anatomy of the library confirms Isaac's picture time after time, and it also reveals, as Isaac could not, that Jefferson was sophisticated in his research techniques, that he generally followed procedures that remain the tools of professional scholars today.

For example, Jefferson was always intent upon confronting one authority with another in order to establish a critically acceptable truth. Thus for every important treatise on the history of classical republics—the only significant precedents the eighteenth century had on the dangers and potentialities of the republican form of government—Jefferson acquired the best available texts plus numerous commentaries and translations. Of Thucydides, the great source on the glory and suicide of ancient democracy, his library contained, besides the best current Greek and Latin texts, two "modern" translations, Hobbes (1629) and Smith (1753). Of Sallust's bitter account of the corruption of Rome's aristocracy, he bought four Latin editions. Of Tacitus ("the first writer in the world," Jefferson proclaimed in 1800), besides the best original text of this morbid anatomy of tyranny, he owned the Gordon and Murphy translations. In contrasting these latter two in a letter of 1813, Jefferson showed his acute perception of the problem faced by every translator: the literalness which may kill the spirit, and the freedom which may falsify the original.

This critical and comparative approach to truth is evident very early (see the annotations Miss Sowerby lists from Lord Kames's *Essays on the Principles of Morality*, one of the rare survivors from Jefferson's youthful library at Shadwell), but it is perhaps best illustrated by the method used in preparing the so-called Jefferson Bible. Here the doctrines of Jesus were compared both with those of classical religion and philosophy as well as Mohammedanism (Jefferson owned the Sale translation of the Koran [1734]); the texts of the Gospel were correlated; and an attempt was made to produce a compendium of the words and parables that could be attributed to the historic Jesus.[3]

It is this dependence on the research approach that explains the overall plan of Jefferson's library, its attempt to provide the most recent standard authorities in every field of art and science with pretension to completeness in the fields of republican politics and modern history. It was highly appropriate, then, for Jefferson's great collection to go to Washington to serve Congress; for by conscious design it was shaped (after the model of "Solomon's House") to be a *public* library.[4]

3. Jefferson was the author of only one book, the *Notes on Virginia*, but the reader is soon made aware by the Sowerby *Catalogue* of the number of volumes he played midwife to, by providing the author with documents, arranging for translation, reading proof, and on occasion preparing prefaces.

4. As this number of the *Quarterly* goes to press, the editors have learned that the Thomas Jefferson Memorial Foundation, which administers Monticello as an historic site, has begun to assemble a collection of books, based on the Sowerby list, in an effort to restock Jefferson's home with a substantial selection of its original owner's favorite volumes. Since books played so large a role in Jefferson's life and thought, this is a highly welcome and appropriate step.

❧ 13 ❧
THE FEDERALIST PAPERS

Handed four new editions of *The Federalist*, Adair was happily provoked into an excellent summary of their relative virtues—including their measure of agreement with him on the question of disputed authorship. As an introduction to *Federalist* scholarship his review essay has obvious value; as an opportunity to discover Adair's own updated judgments on recent scholarship it is no less rewarding.

NINETEEN SIXTY-ONE was a banner year for our ambiguous classic, *The Federalist*. Four editions of Publius were printed in the United States,[1] all four of significant scholarly value, and each making its contribution in a different way. Clearly we are in mid-course of a new era of *Federalist* scholarship. Certainly by 1987, the two-hundredth anniversary of Publius' work, Norman Cousins's prayer of 1958 will

SOURCE: Reprinted from the *William and Mary Quarterly*, 3d Ser., XXII (1965), 131–139.

1. Five editions, in fact, if one counts the reissue of the Everyman edition, printed in London and New York, 1961, with new introduction, replacing that of the first issue of 1911. The old introduction was by W. J. Ashley; the new is by W. R. Brock, of Selwyn College, Cambridge University. The four editions discussed here are: *The Federalist Papers*. Selected and edited by Roy P. Fairfield. (New York: Anchor Books, 1961. Pp. xxviii, 328.) *The Federalist*. Edited with an introduction by Benjamin F. Wright. (Cambridge: The Belknap Press of Harvard University Press, 1961. Pp. 572.) *The Federalist*. Edited, with introduction and notes, by Jacob E. Cooke. (Middletown, Conn.: Wesleyan University Press, 1961. Pp. xxx, 672.) *The Federalist Papers*. With an introduction, table of contents, and index of ideas by Clinton Rossiter. (New York: Mentor, 1961. Pp. xxxi, 559).

be answered: "Over the years," wrote Cousins, "I have searched in vain for a fully annotated and carefully indexed edition of *The Federalist* papers, suitable for detailed reference work."

This new era of *Federalist* studies has accumulated a substantial body of fresh knowledge about the writing of the book, a much surer understanding of the aims of its authors, and a juster estimate of its nature as a world classic. The new era dates from sometime after 1937—a year which saw the United States at the climax of a "constitutional crisis"that had dominated politics since 1935, and a year which was celebrated by the American Historical Association in Philadelphia as the sesquicentennial of the Constitution. There was much lively debate at Philadelphia in 1937 and much learned disagreement about the Constitution, about FDR, and about judicial review. Inevitably Publius was quoted there scores of times (as so often during the preceding months in the newspapers and on the air), but one feels today that the interest then in *The Federalist* was topical rather than scholarly.

There was, it is true, a "Sesquicentennial Edition," but it did not register a consumer demand and it was not undertaken by a commercial publisher in hope of a profit. The edition was subsidized by the Carnegie Foundation, and the graceful, ritualistic introduction, as to a little-read sacred document, by Edward Mead Earle is most revealing in showing that Publius in 1937 could be taken pretty much for granted. The essays were one of "the givens" (to use Daniel Boorstin's telling phrase) of American constitutional discourse and as such seemed to present few problems of interpretation or comprehension. Their chief value was as commentary on the political practices that had developed under the Constitution. No questions need be asked about the motives of Publius, about his philosophy, about his technique of authorship, or about the place of the book in American or world history. Indeed the sesquicentennial edition was explicitly offered to the American common reader—the average educated citizen, who Earle was sure, would find it "one of the most rewarding documents of American History"—as completely available and entirely accessible to his understanding if only Mr. Everyman would read it "with care and thoughtfulness."[2]

One can speculate about the various reasons for a changed perspective on *The Federalist* between 1937 and 1961 and for the renewed concern of scholars with questions about the work, but of the new perspective there can be no doubt. In the Bibliographical Appendix of the Fairfield edition there are three closely printed pages of references that cover, in the editor's words, "the major body of *Federalist* scholarship." All but a handful of these journal articles, dissertations, and books have been written in the last twenty years. Very striking in this scholarly writing is a shifted focus from the view of Publius as a somewhat parochial commentator on the peculiarities of our Constitution and the peculiarities of federal systems, to Publius as a major political theorist, who while advocating a particular constitution also addressed his searching analysis to the enduring and universal problems of every democratic state.[3]

2. This edition, which is still in print, was originally issued under the imprint of the National Home Library, one of the early and abortive ventures of the 1930s in the field of inexpensive paperbacks. In 1941 this edition was taken over by Random House and added to its Modern Library list. That Earle's view of Publius as merely a holy national document, almost entirely concerned with American political practice, was the accepted scholarly view at that time is substantiated by the curious fact (noted by Professor Wright) that George H. Sabine's deservedly famous textbook of 1937, *A History of Political Theory*, whose literary felicity and comprehensiveness made it the bible of a generation of doctoral candidates, contains no single reference to *The Federalist*, to Hamilton, or to Madison, although many of their lesser contemporaries in the field of theory—Malby, Coleridge, Holbach, Godwin, d'Alembert, Hartley—are singled out for notice.

3. A comparison of Professor Brock's introduction, in the 1961 Everyman edition, with the earlier Everyman is revealing in this connection. Professor Ashley in 1911 explained that "there has hitherto been no English edition of *The Federalist*, because the general English public has hitherto been but little interested in questions of federal government," but that now after the creation of the Canadian and Australian federations, and with the possibility of an Irish federal system, Publius, "a dignified and worthy commentary, upon the creation of the greatest federal constitution the world has yet seen," is of increasing interest to Britons, and deserves a place on the shelf with Freeman's *History of Federal Government*, Mills's *Representative*

This Bibliographical Appendix of the Fairfield *Federalist*, besides its handy summary of modern *Federalist* scholarship, also includes a list of all editions of the work published here and abroad through the year 1960.[4] Of value, too, are the twenty-six pages of substantive annotations on the text itself, which set, for example, Publius' eighteenth-century discussion of the difficulties of treaty making in a federal system against modern European judgments of the problems. Professor Fairfield's text includes only fifty-one of the eighty-five essays; but his edition provides the best available guide to writings about *The Federalist*, as well as the most extensive and useful annota-

----

Government, Dicey's *Law of the Constitution,* and Sedgwick's *Elements of Politics.* Ashley, however, warns that a basic weakness will always limit the work's value to the political scientist or statesman, and this is the "complete absence in it [*The Federalist*] of the idea . . . of development or evolution. There is no suspicion that the needs of the future will ever render any substantial change necessary."

In contrast Brock in 1961 views this universal and timeless quality of Publius' writing as its most striking feature. He comments on the "air of maturity" that marks the work in which "political theory and political action meet . . . in a way which was almost unique." The great triumph of Madison's and Hamilton's collaboration (as Brock sees it) lies in their insight and honesty in facing and offering a "theoretical and practical solution to the fundamental problem of all free government": the acceptance of popular sovereignty as "the only source of authority which is both expedient and just," coupled with the recognition that the sovereign people "could be brutal, arbitrary, and unwise." Brock himself finds *Federalist* 10, 14, 39, 48, and 51 especially rewarding and argues that these alone are sufficient to "establish Madison as one of the leading theorists of the dangers and opportunities which are latent in the modern democratic state."

4. The last careful bibliography of early editions was Paul Leicester Ford's of 1898 showing 30 to that date. Fairfield lists 68 editions through 1961, some reissued as many as 7 times. One of the interesting modern developments shown by the Fairfield bibliography is the increasing number of foreign editions in translation of the whole or a part of *The Federalist*. Since 1951 the work has been printed (in the native tongue) in Italy, Austria, France, Britain, in Mexico, Argentina, Brazil, and in Beirut (Arabic), India (two editions, one Bengali, one Assamese), Korea, Vietnam, and Japan. Previously, between 1788 and 1911, there had been two French (1792, 1902), two Brazilian (1840, 1896), one German (1864, abridged), one Argentinian (1868), and one British (1911) imprints. This contrasting score adds up to: a mere 7 foreign editions in the 119 years between 1792 and 1911, as against 14 editions in the single decade 1950 to 1960.

tions available on the text printed in any existing edition. And the price is right.

Professor Wright's edition, which contains no annotations on the text, is notable for its commentary on *The Federalist*, offered in an eighty-six-page introduction. There he—one of the wisest interpreters of the classic for our generation—sets down his matured thoughts on the work. In a series of nine "chapters" he discusses with insight and learning such topics as Publius' view of human nature, Publius on direct and representative democracy, on separation of powers, on fundamental law and judicial review. Wright makes the point that *The Federalist* is unlike most other treatises in the great canon of Western political philosophy, for it ignores dozens of traditional problems and begins where most treatises end, by analyzing with philosophic and theoretical profundity *how* certain objectives of politics are to be achieved. Because the Revolution had committed Americans to republicanism it was quite unnecessary—nay, even inappropriate—for Publius to discuss certain issues associated with monarchial and aristocratic governments; nor do the authors spend pages debating the origins and necessity of government, the nature of law and sovereignty, the grounds for political obligation. An American political consensus, an accepted tradition (Wright aptly calls this consensus "The Spirit of '76") on so many political issues, allowed Publius to take these for granted, and to discuss at length the problems of order, stability, and strength—contemporary theory held that these were not characteristics of republics—in a republican system and to argue, at less length, that when the proposed constitution had provided for *them*, justice, welfare, and liberty would also be gained and preserved.

Professor Wright does not offer a commentary on every *Federalist* essay or on many of the themes of Publius that were traditionally associated with monarchies and aristocracies. His introduction does, however, provide analysis and interpretation of many major ideas of the work. Many of his views and suggestions will be familiar to readers of earlier Wright lectures and journal articles, but it is good to have this integrated general commentary. Anyone interested in American political theory, or in the ideas of Hamilton and Madison, will find Professor Wright's introduction both enlightening and stimulating to the highest degree; the more pity that the price charged for this handsome volume puts it in the luxury class for many readers.

The Cooke *Federalist* is a product of the Columbia University editorial office now publishing the welcome complete Hamilton *Papers*. In preparation for printing Hamilton's Publius essays among the collected writings,[5] Professor Cooke studied the text of the complete *Federalist*, and, happily for scholars, he determined to print this separate edition embodying his discoveries. He ends at last our previous ignorance in two important areas: first, in recording the printing history of the individual essays in the four New York papers where they originally appeared; second, in reporting all the changes that Publius (Hamilton and Madison) made (or sanctioned) in the primary newspaper text when it was reissued in book form in 1788, 1802, and 1817. Cooke's edition, thus, is the first definitive, variorum edition of the text of this much reprinted classic.[6]

The textual changes are greatest in number, Cooke shows, between the newspaper printings and the book publication by McLean: Volume I, March 22, 1788; Volume II, May 28, 1788. Most of the changes here relate to capitalization; the shift of singulars to plurals; a's to an's, and other such grammatical polishing. In the 1802 edition (published by Hopkins), a friend of Hamilton's "corrected" the text

5. Harold C. Syrett and Jacob E. Cooke, eds., *The Papers of Alexander Hamilton* (New York, 1961–), IV, reprints all the Hamilton essays, some of Madison's ("disputed"), and parts of the introductory matter from Cooke's complete *The Federalist*.

6. Wright, who follows the 1788 McLean text (with corrections of its typographical and grammatical errors), notes that Lodge's edition (1888) of McLean carelessly repeated many of the original typos and added quite a few transcription errors of its own, and that it was the Lodge version of McLean that was uncritically copied in most subsequent reprints of *The Federalist*, which carefully reproduced the Lodge-McLean errors.

by the substitution, chiefly, of more elegant for (supposedly) less elegant language in the McLean text. Hamilton approved these emendations, and so Cooke also shows these variations. Finally in 1817, the edition published by Jacob Gideon included a relatively small number of Madisonian revisions, and these, too, are indicated by Cooke.

Before Professor Cooke undertook this demanding and tedious job of collation—the text runs to 180,000 words—scholars were uneasily aware that they were dealing with an ambiguous text, but, daunted by the inaccessibility of the newspaper version and the size of the task, even the conscientious were willing to settle for less than complete checking; they were also partially reassured by the pronouncement of Henry Dawson, who had collated the texts in the 1850s and reported that the changes he discovered were unimportant. Cooke's labors confirm Dawson's judgment in the vast majority of cases. The texts that students have used are marked with multitudes of minor changes and typographical errors rather than infected with major corruptions from Version I through IV.

There are, however, some instances where textual changes may indicate substantive changes of meaning. In one instance, at least, the difference between newspaper essay and McLean's text does add definite evidence to the sum of our knowledge of Madison's collaboration with Hamilton. It has always been clear from the date of publication of McLean's edition that Hamilton assumed the responsibility for seeing the volumes through the press and for whatever proofreading was done on the galleys. However, recently the argument has been advanced by Professor Richard Morris (Cooke, oddly, appears to subscribe to it) that Hamilton *edited* and *corrected* Madison's text between newspaper printing and book publication. Cooke's chronology of the appearance of the newspaper essays shows that Madison's last contribution to the series was in print two days before he left New York City; and Cooke's collation of changes in the text between newsprint and McLean in *Federalist* 51 offers strong evidence that Madison was his own editor, possibly correcting in the margins of the newspaper the essays that were reprinted in McLean's second volume after he had returned to Virginia.

Clinton Rossiter's *The Federalist Papers,* in the Mentor paperback series, on first glance would seem to be an edition chiefly designed for the student meeting Publius for the first time. There is no annotation of the text (it is McLean's purged of typos and solecisms), no bibliography, and the introductory commentary is merely historical-descriptive, identifying the three authors and describing briefly the circumstances under which the book was written. Rossiter, also with the wisdom of the experienced college teacher, recognizes that most purchasers of his edition will lack "the energy and fixed purpose" to read all of the eighty-five essays, so he lists the twenty-one he considers to be "the cream" of Publius—ten by Hamilton, ten by Madison, and one by Jay. However, at the end of his edition Professor Rossiter has printed the Constitution itself, collated with Publius' discussion of each article and section—a useful feature—and, finally, an especially good index "compiled with particular attention to the interests of students of political theory and constitutional law." In my judgment this index is better than that in any previous *Federalist* edition, including Wright's and Cooke's, which are each indexed more extensively than earlier editions.[7] For example, Professor Wright's index, appropriately, shows fifteen references to "human nature" in Publius' text, but Rossiter lists twenty-eight references (as does Cooke), and Rossiter then indexes seventeen *more* specific references under subheads, such as "altruism; ambition; avarice; bellicosity; bright side of; irrationality; pride; selfishness; weak side of," etc. Thus, though it has been Wright's role to alert scholars to the

7. Fairfield, whose index is very brief, suggests that readers of his volume desiring a more complete descriptive analysis, as well as one that compares concepts in *The Federalist* with those in other classics of political thought, should turn to the Synopticon volumes indexing the 1952 Great Books edition of Publius.

great significance of Publius' assumptions about human nature, it is Rossiter's index that allows us to find most easily Publius' words on the subject. Again, each of the three editions is helpful in indexing Publius' comments on "history" and his historical examples, but both Cooke and Wright reveal an occasional carelessness that does not show in Rossiter's more extended and precise indexing. In Cooke's, for example, under "History of Ancient Confederacies," the only entry: "Essays 18–20," shows errors both of omission and commission: Numbers 19 and 20 do not mention any *ancient* confederacy but rather the contemporary Holy Roman Empire, Switzerland, Poland, and the Netherlands; while Hamilton's Number 9, ignored in this entry, does comment on the ancient Lycian league. In like manner the searcher of Wright's index under "History, Greek and Roman [*sic*] confederacies" will find "Venice" listed, as well as "Junius," which perhaps sounds Roman but is in fact the pseudonym under which Sir Philip Francis excoriated George III and his ministry, 1769–1771. One final example that reveals the superior comprehensiveness and carefulness of the Rossiter index is seen in the handlings of the theme of "responsibility." According to the *Oxford English Dictionary on Historical Principles* the word itself is an American invention, and its first appearance in the language is credited by the *OED* to the long discussion of senatorial "responsibility" in Madison's *Federalist* Number 63. There the word appears four times in two paragraphs (the first English occurrence is credited by the *OED* to Burke in 1792). There is an equally long discussion of executive "responsibility" in Hamilton's Number 70 (the word appears three times) and in Number 77 (two times). Of the three indexes under consideration Rossiter's is the only one to deal satisfactorily with the word and the important idea it represents. Wright does not index the term; and Cooke notices only the comments in *Federalist* Number 70. Rossiter, in happy contrast, indexes senatorial responsibility in Number 63, presidential responsibility in Numbers 70 and 77, and judicial responsibility in Number 79.[8] Therefore, no matter how many hard-cover copies of *The Federalist* a scholar owns, this inexpensive Mentor edition with its outstanding index should be added to his shelf if he has any expectation of studying the book seriously or using it as a reference work.

In conclusion, the appearance of these editions of *The Federalist* signalize the end of the controversy over the authorship of the disputed essays. All of the editors, while indicating that Hamilton claimed entire authorship of Numbers 49–58, 62–63, and coauthorship of Numbers 18–20, accept Madison's counterclaim to these essays as (in Cooke's word) "superior." Thus this dispute was pretty well settled by traditional historical analysis even before Professors Mosteller and Wallace reported the results of their four-year statistical study of the prose styles of Hamilton, Madison, and Jay. I am not competent to explain their application of Bayes's theorem to Publius' writings, but their conclusions are overwhelmingly persuasive even to the statistically illiterate. The odds for *all* the disputed essays, to quote their paper delivered at the joint Presidential Session of the American Statistical Association and the Biometric Society (September 9, 1962), are "strongly in favor of Madison," running

---

8. The word "responsibility" is apparently a coinage of James Madison; its first obscure appearance (that I have found) is in Madison's committee report to the Continental Congress on the Quartermaster Department [July 22, 1780], in William T. Hutchinson and William M. E. Rachal, eds., *The Papers of James Madison*, II (Chicago, 1962), 44–45. There is some evidence that it was used with some frequency by Madison and some of his colleagues in the Federal Convention. At any rate James Wilson on Dec. 4, 1787, in the Pennsylvania ratifying convention is talking about presidential responsibility without any self-consciousness (Jonathan Elliot, ed., *The Debates of the Several State Conventions on the Adoption of the Federal Constitution* ..., II [Philadelphia, 1863], 480); and by the close of that convention (Dec. 11, 1787) both Federalists and Antifederalists seem to be making use of the term. *Ibid.*, 530, 532. It appears unobtrusively in Madison's *Federalist* 48 and 57 (Feb. 1, 19, 1788) and in Hamilton's Number 23 (Dec. 18, 1787) prior to the eye-catching and extended use in Numbers 63 and 70 (Mar. 1, 15, 1788). Jay also uses it in Number 64 (Mar. 5, 1788). And so Publius in Mar. 1788 definitely fixes this word in the language once and for all.

as high as 3,000,000 to 1 in Number 51, and to only slightly less astronomical figures in Numbers 63, 57, 62. The lowest odds—the only "low odds" by statistical criteria—in favor of Madison showed in Number 20 (where borrowing from Sir William Temple sophisticated the Virginian's style to a noticeable degree) and in Number 55, where the odds favoring Madison over Hamilton dropped to a mere 240 to 1. Statisticians, historians may conclude, are astonishingly conservative, for most of us would think 50 to 1 or 100 to 1 quite a good bet.

The Mosteller-Wallace study, just published in its entirety,[9] will stand as a landmark and model for future detective work in statistical literary analysis. Their system was used this past year to identify the anonymous authors of a series of polemical pamphlets attacking Tory policies, incident to the British parliamentary election of 1964. More important, in the future, if any historian really wants to identify all of Franklin's anonymous newspaper essays, or to sort out what sections of the *Annual Register* Burke wrote, the techniques tested by Mosteller and Wallace stand ready to hand, offering a precision of identification never before achieved in statistical comparison of prose styles. In the meantime, as a by-product of the statistical study Mosteller and Wallace are preparing a *Federalist* concordance—the ultimate in indexing for our ancient classic that should satisfy even Norman Cousins.

9. Frederick Mosteller and David L. Wallace, *Inference and Disputed Authorship: The Federalist* (Reading, Mass., 1964).

HAMILTONIAN SIDELIGHTS

I. Hamilton on the Louisiana Purchase:
A Newly Identified Editorial from the
New-York Evening Post

II. A Note on Certain of Hamilton's Pseudonyms

III. What Was Hamilton's "Favorite Song"?

Adair made substantial contributions beyond the call of editorial duty in compiling his well-known Hamilton bicentennial issue in 1955. The essay on "Hamilton as a Christian Statesman," written with Marvin Harvey, was in this issue, along with the three notes reprinted here, which Adair curiously left unsigned. If he had revealed his authorship publicly in the issue, it would, perhaps, have made it uncomfortably clear that the editor had himself written close to half of the material in it. Julian Boyd termed the issue, Adair's last, "a splendid swan song" and found particular favor with the essay on Hamilton's favorite song ("a beautiful piece of detective work").

SOURCE: Reprinted from the *William and Mary Quarterly*, 3d Ser., XII (1955), 268–281, 282–297, 298–307.

I

Hamilton on the Louisiana Purchase: A Newly Identified Editorial from the *New-York Evening Post*

ALEXANDER HAMILTON was notoriously independent and individualistic as a party leader. His friends insisted that this trait was proof of a transcendent patriotism that never for a moment sacrificed his country's good for party advantage; while his enemies charged the same trait to his monstrous egotism, his inability, because of his rule-or-ruin complex, to work within the pattern of compromise and mutual concession required for the development of responsible party government.[1]

For whatever reasons, the news that Napoleon had sold Louisiana

1. For a favorable interpretation of Hamilton's individualism and lack of party regularity, see John C. Hamilton, *Life of Alexander Hamilton. A History of the Republic of the United States of America, As Traced in His Writings and in Those of His Contemporaries* (Boston, 1879), VII, 654. "Hamilton never for a moment forgot his country for party." In contrast, see the judgment in 1800 of Noah Webster, a staunch Federalist, on Hamilton's bad habit of breeding intraparty strife, specifically, in his attacks on President Adams, the head of the party: "Think not, Sir, that all the monstrous schemes of daring ambitious men to overawe and control the constitutional powers of our government are either hidden or approved by Federal men. . . . I reprobate your policy. I know that most of the hardy sons of freedom in the northern states want no standing army to overawe domestic factions nor to resist foreign foes, unless under circumstances that do not now exist. . . . And it is surprizing that your boasted wisdom and foresight should have, in this instance, yielded to the impulses of your military zeal. Indeed, it would be incredible, had not other instances occurred in which your passions had blinded your reason. But what can be expected from a man whose prominent talents have given him a confidence in his influence that disdains public opinion and overleaps all the ordinary maxims of prudence. . . . Your ambition, pride, and overbearing temper have destined you to be the evil genius of this country." Noah Webster, *A Letter to General Hamilton Occasioned by his Letter to President Adams* (Sept. 1800), reprinted in Harry R. Warfel, ed., *Letters of Noah Webster* (New York, 1953), 223–226.

to the United States stimulated Hamilton to act this role of political maverick—to take a stand upon the Purchase definitely at odds with the vast majority of other Federalist spokesmen. An editorial in the *New-York Evening Post* of July 5, 1803, which can now be definitely identified as expressing Hamilton's convictions on the subject, shows him departing from the Federalist party line on Louisiana, but not abating one whit his partisanship. His estimate of the ultimate value of Louisiana to the United States is also of significance in revealing how clouded could be his prophet's crystal ball upon occasion.

Hamilton, like all of the leading statesmen of the day, early recognized the strategic and commercial importance of New Orleans for the United States and by 1798 had decided what ought to be done about it. It was a characteristic Hamilton policy, exemplifying his favorite quality of "energy" in both foreign and domestic affairs. Correctly predicting that France would probably regain Louisiana from Spain, arguing that our very "independence and liberty" were already threatened by this "most flagitious, despotic, and vindictive government" in its march "with hasty and colossal strides to universal empire," he suggested that the United States seize the initiative, create a navy, and, more important, "raise with the utmost diligence a considerable army." This army, Hamilton insisted, was the key measure; yet he prophesied that it was the measure "which will meet with the greatest obstacles." Nor did he conceal his reasons for believing that loyal troops available to the government were perhaps more necessary even than a navy: not only would trained soldiers be required to repel French invasion of the United States if England collapsed (a "possibility" which seemed not to be "chimerical"); they would also be ready to forestall the French "acquisition of Louisiana, [by which] the foundation will be laid for stripping her [Spain] of South America and her mines; and perhaps for dismembering the United States." Finally a standing army was absolutely necessary to control the "treason which lurks at the core" of Jefferson's faction. "The people of this country must be infatuated indeed, if . . . they are at a loss for the true source of the evils they suffered, or may hereafter suffer from the despots of France. 'Tis the unnatural league of a portion of our citizens with the oppressors of their country."[2]

John Adams, by his independence and by his determination to avoid war with France, effectually blocked Hamiltonian schemes for a defensive-offensive conquest of New Orleans in 1798–1799. And, when the Louisiana issue once again erupted into the very center of politics in 1801, Hamilton and Adams and their divided party were out of power.

The events that precipitated the Louisiana crisis of 1801 are well known. By 1800 Napoleon's pressure on Spain had become so great that, in the Treaty of San Ildefonso, Louisiana was ceded back to France.[3] Hamilton, now a private citizen, successfully practicing law and less successfully practicing politics in New York City, received early news of this "portentious" development from a friend in Paris. He at once passed on his information to his ex-friend James Madison, the new secretary of state;[4] and then watched, not without pleasure,

2. "The Stand," written by Hamilton in Mar. and Apr. 1798 (contemporaneous with the beginning of the XYZ Affair), signed Titus Manlius, and printed in seven parts in the New York *Commercial Advertiser;* reprinted in Henry Cabot Lodge, ed., *The Works of Alexander Hamilton* (New York, 1904), VI, 259*ff.* Part IV (p. 284) discusses the danger of Louisiana in the hands of France; Part VI (pp. 307–309) pleads the absolute necessity for an army; while Part VII (pp. 311–318) identifies the domestic traitors who must be suppressed. See also Hamilton's private letters to Pickering, Mar. 27, 1798, and to Harrison Gray Otis, Jan. 26, 1799, advocating conquest: "I have been long in the habit of considering the acquisition of those countries [Florida and Louisiana] as essential to the permanency of the Union." *Ibid.,* X, 338.

3. Hamilton denies in "The Stand" that the Jay Treaty (which Professor Bemis suggests should be more correctly called "Hamilton's Treaty") had any effect on French policy toward the United States (and Louisiana). *Ibid.,* VI, 249*ff.* Modern scholars, however, are unanimous in feeling that the Federalist pro-British orientation even before 1794, climaxed by the treaty, precipitated the French Foreign Office's determination to regain Louisiana from Spain as a secure continental base to support France's vulnerable Caribbean possessions.

4. A friend, Constable, wrote Hamilton a two-sentence note from Paris dated Mar. 23, 1801, informing him that he had sure information that Louisiana was once again France's. Hamilton must have received the letter in May, for, with an

while Jefferson and Madison struggled to solve the dilemma created by the new developments.⁵ By the end of 1802, Hamilton and the Federalists in Congress had decided what their party line would be, and early in 1803 Hamilton spelled out for Jefferson and Madison the correct policy which he thought they ought to follow. This advice appeared in an essay signed Pericles in the *New-York Evening Post*, the paper which he had set up as his personal organ.

As Pericles pointed out, Napoleon's control of Louisiana "threatens the early dismemberment of a large portion of the country; more immediately, the safety of all the Southern States; and remotely, the independence of the whole Union." Hamilton was sure that:

---

endorsement of May 20, he sent it on to Madison, secretary of state. Madison returned it with formal thanks and word that the department had already had the news. This exchange appears to be the only correspondence between Madison and Hamilton after their break in 1793. The letters are printed in John C. Hamilton, ed., *The Works of Alexander Hamilton; Comprising His Correspondence, And His Political And Official Writings* . . . (Boston, 1850–1851), VI, 524–525.

5. Hamilton to Charles Cotesworth Pinckney, Dec. 29, 1802: "Amidst the triumphant reign of democracy, do you retain sufficient interest in public affairs to feel any curiosity about what is going on? In my opinion, the follies and vices of the administration have as yet made no material impression to their disadvantage. On the contrary, I think the malady is rather progressive than upon the decline in our Northern quarter. The last *lullaby* message, instead of inspiring contempt, attracts praise. Mankind are forever destined to be the dupes of bold and cunning imposture. But a difficult knot has been twisted by the incidents of the cession of Louisiana, and the interruption of the deposit of New Orleans. You have seen the soft turn given to this in the message. Yet we are told that the President, in conversation, is very stout. The great embarrassment must be how to carry on the war without taxes. The pretty scheme of substituting economy to taxation will not do here. And a war would be a terrible comment upon the abandonment of the internal revenue. Yet how is popularity to be preserved with the Western partisans if their interests are tamely sacrificed? Will the artifice be for the chief to hold a bold language, and the subalterns to act a feeble part? Time must explain. You know my general theory as to our Western affairs. I have always held that the *unity of our empire* and the best interests of our nation require that we shall annex to the United States all the territory east of the Mississippi, New Orleans included. Of course I infer that, in an emergency like the present, energy is wisdom." Lodge, ed., *Works of Hamilton*, X, 445–446.

"Two courses only present: First, to negotiate, and endeavor to purchase; and if this fails, to go to war. Secondly, to seize at once on the Floridas and New Orleans, and then negotiate." Hamilton being Hamilton, it is not surprising that he felt the only sensible plan was to go to war at once.[6] "The army should be increased to ten thousand men, for the purpose of insuring the preservation of the conquest." The navy should be increased; forty thousand militia should be prepared for emergencies. "Negotiations should be pushed with Great Britain, to induce her to hold herself in readiness to co-operate fully with us, at a moment's warning."[7]

In conclusion Hamilton explained why he had some faint hopes—though very faint—that the administration might follow this policy: "These ideas have been long entertained by the writer, but he has never given himself the trouble to commit them to the public, because he despaired of their being adopted. They are now thrown out with very little hope . . . yet with the encouragement that there is a strong current of public feeling in favor of decisive measures. If the President would adopt this course, he might yet retrieve his character, induce the best part of the community to look favorably upon his political career, exalt himself in the eyes of Europe, save the country, and

6. Pericles, reprinted, *ibid.*, VI, 333–336.

7. In a characteristic example of the lazy and incompetent editing he gave to Hamilton's writings, Henry Cabot Lodge printed the following annotation with this Pericles essay: "It is a very interesting paper, as it shows how completely Hamilton parted with his party on the Louisiana question and how unswervingly national he was in every thing." Lodge's footnote, *ibid.*, 333.

If Lodge had even looked into the *Annals of Congress*, Jan.–Apr. 1803, he would have seen that Pericles was actually voicing party policy at this date; that the Federalists in Congress were bending every effort to force Jefferson into war with Napoleon over New Orleans or, failing that, to detach southern and western voters from his party by pillorying the administration as unwilling or unable to defend American rights on the Mississippi. Hamilton broke with his party only *after* Jefferson disappointed Federalist expectations by getting New Orleans and all Louisiana without war. It was only then, when the party leaders began to talk of secession, that Hamilton refused to stay in line.

secure a permanent fame. But, for this, alas! Jefferson is not destined."[8] Jefferson did not disappoint Hamilton. While confessing
privately that Napoleon's occupation of New Orleans would indeed
force us to "marry" the British fleet, he nevertheless continued to
put his trust in negotiations.

But to Hamilton and other readers of the *New-York Evening Post*,
the Louisiana crisis seemed more and more hopeless as winter turned
to spring and spring to summer. On June 11 the *Post* published a
"Letter from a gentleman at the Natchez to his friend in Washington,
dated April 13, 1803," complaining of the lack of "manly measures"
on Jefferson's part. The Administration, this gentleman felt, was all
too much "like Sterne's ass, which when we are kicked, cuffed, and
spat upon, turns up his piteous, imploring eyes and says 'pray don't
beat us.' " Americans would have no choice but to reconcile themselves to the despotism of Bonaparte or quit the territory.[9]

Then came news from abroad on June 16 that set Louisiana in a
new light—news so important that it interrupted for nearly three
weeks the *Evening Post*'s serial reprinting of scandalous stories on
Jefferson's private life—news that France and England were on the
verge of war, or already had gone to war.[10] Nor was there much time
for editorial speculation as to what this promised for the United

8. Pericles, *ibid.*, 336.

9. *New-York Evening Post*, Apr. 13, 1803. The *Post*, at this time a four-page
daily, printed nothing but advertisements on pp. 1 and 4; thus all news items
hereafter quoted appear in columns on pp. 2–3.

10. *Ibid.*, June 16, 1803, under the headline "WAR, WAR!" reporting that the
London newspapers, just arrived on the ship *American* (30 days from Londonderry),
carried news of Addington's having told the House of Commons that the British
ambassador in Paris had been given his passports. The same issue carried the first
of a series of articles on the charge by Gabriel Jones of Virginia that Jefferson had
cheated him by welching on a private debt. With all the exciting foreign news
during the following weeks, the editor could not find space to take up the Jefferson
scandal again until July 7, when it was resumed, "to enable the public . . . to judge
more correctly of the principles of that man's heart, whom a deluded portion of
our citizens seem still disposed to support, *through thick and thin.* . . ."

States. On Thursday, June 30, William Coleman, editor of the *Post*, featured the same breathtaking announcement in three separate letters:

The following letter is just handed us by a friend, who received it on this morning's Eastern mail.

IMPORTANT

Paris, April 29, 1803.

We have now the moral certainty of being paid in the United States what France owes to Americans. . . . Government cedes Louisiana for a certain sum. . . .

Paris, May 9, 1803.

. . . The American Creditors are to be paid by the American Government in exchange for Louisiana. The thing is fixed. . . .

Another letter to a New York citizen.

Paris, April 28.

The American creditors will be paid soon, and it is believed by the United States, in part compensation for Louisiana, which is to be ceded to our government.[11]

This unofficial information that the nation had purchased Louisiana was so momentous that Hamilton apparently began composing an editorial almost at once:[12]

---

11. *Ibid.*, June 30, 1803.

12. Hamilton and Coleman must have started work on the editorial at once, for in Saturday's paper, July 2, 1803, the following notice appeared: "The necessity of reinserting this evening the great number of advertisements left out yesterday . . . induces us to defer the leading editorial article, which had been prepared on the subject of Louisiana." From this it would seem the editorial was finished by Saturday morning.

NEW-YORK EVENING POST.

Tuesday, July 5. [1803]

Purchase of Louisiana.—At length the business of New-Orleans has terminated favourably to this country. Instead of being obliged to rely any longer on the force of treaties, for a place of deposit, the jurisdiction of the territory is now transferred to our hands and in future the navigation of the Mississippi will be ours unmolested. This, it will be allowed is an important acquisition; not, indeed, as territory, but as being essential to the peace and prosperity of our Western country, and as opening a free and valuable market to our commercial states. This purchase has been made during the period of Mr. Jefferson's presidency, and will, doubtless, give eclat to his administration. Every man, however, possessed of the least candour and reflection will readily acknowledge that the acquisition has been solely owing to a fortuitous concurrence of unforseen and unexpected circumstances, and not to any wise or vigorous measures on the part of the American government.

As soon as we experienced from Spain a direct infraction of an important article of our treaty, in withholding the deposit of New-Orleans, it afforded us justifiable cause of war, and authorised immediate hostilities. Sound policy unquestionably demanded of us to begin with a prompt, bold and vigorous resistance against the injustice; to seize the object at once; and having this *vantage ground,* should we have thought it advisable to terminate hostilities by a purchase, we might then have done it on almost our own terms. This course, however, was not adopted, and we were about to experience the fruits of our folly, when another nation has found it her interest to place the French Government in a situation substantially as favourable to our views and interest as those recommended by the federal party here, excepting indeed that we should probably have obtained the same object on better terms.

On the part of France the short interval of peace had been wasted in repeated and fruitless efforts to subjugate St. Domingo; and those means which were originally destined to the colonization of Louisiana, had been gradually exhausted by the unexpected difficulties of this ill-starred enterprize.

To the deadly climate of St. Domingo, and to the courage and obstinate resistance made by its black inhabitants are we indebted for the obstacles which delayed the colonization of Louisiana, till the auspicious moment, when a rupture between England and France gave a new turn to the projects of the latter, and destroyed at once all her schemes as to this favourite object of her ambition.

It was made known to Bonaparte, that among the first objects of England would be the seizure of New-Orleans, and that preparations were even then in a state of forwardness for that purpose. The First Consul could not doubt, that if an English fleet was sent thither, the place must fall without resistance; it was obvious, therefore, that it would be in every shape preferable that it should be placed in the possession of a neutral power; and when, besides, some millions of money, of which he was extremely in want, were offered him, to part with what he could no longer hold it affords a moral certainty, that it was to an accidental state of circumstances, and not to wise plans, that this cession, at this time, has been owing. We shall venture to add, that neither of the ministers through whose instrumentality it was effected, will ever deny this, or even pretend that previous to the time when a rupture was believed to be inevitable, there was the smallest chance of inducing the First Consul, with his ambitious and aggrandizing views, to commute the territory for any sum of money in their power to offer. The real truth is, Bonaparte found himself absolutely compelled by situation, to relinquish his darling plan of colonizing the banks of the Mississippi: and thus have the Government of the United States, by the unforseen operation of events, gained what the feebleness and pusillanimity of its miserable system of measures could never have acquired.—Let us then, with all due humility, acknowledge this as another of those signal instances of the kind interpositions of an over-ruling Providence, which we more especially experienced during our revolutionary war, & by which we have more than once, been saved from the consequences of our errors and perverseness.

We are certainly not disposed to lessen the importance of this acquisition to the country, but it is proper that the public should be correctly informed of its real value and extent as well as of the terms on which it has been acquired. We perceive by the newspapers that various & very vague opinions are entertained; and we shall therefore, venture to state our ideas with some precision as to the territory; but until the instrument of cession itself is published, we do not think it prudent to say much as to the conditions on which it has been obtained.

Prior to the treaty of Paris 1763, France claimed the country on both sides of the river under the name of Louisiana, and it was her encroachments on the rear of the British Colonies which gave rise to the war of 1755.— By the conclusion of the treaty of 1763, the limits of the colonies of Great Britain and France were clearly and permanently fixed; and it is from that and subsequent treaties that we are to ascertain what territory is really comprehended under the name of Louisiana. France ceded to Great-Britain all the country east and south-east of a line drawn along the middle of the Mississippi from its source to the Iberville, and from thence along that river and the Lakes Maurepas and Pontchartrain to the sea; France retaining the country lying west of the river, besides the town and Island of New-Orleans on the east side.—This she soon after ceded to Spain who acquiring also the Floridas by the treaty 1783, France was entirely shut out from the continent of North America. Spain, at the instance of Bonaparte, ceded to him Louisiana, including the Town and Island (as it is commonly called) of New-Orleans. Bonaparte has now ceded the same tract of country, and this only, to the United States. The whole of East and West-Florida, lying south of Georgia and of the Mississippi Territory, and extending to the Gulf of Mexico, still remains to Spain, who will continue, therefore, to occupy, as formerly, the country along the southern frontier of the United States, and the east bank of the river, from the Iberville to the American line.

Those disposed to magnify its value will say, that this western region is important as keeping off a troublesome neighbour, and leaving us in the quiet possession of the Mississippi. Undoubtedly this has some force, but on the other hand it may be said, that the acquisition of New-Orleans is perfectly adequate to every purpose; for whoever is in possession of that, has the uncontrouled command of the river. Again, it may be said, and this probably is the most favourable point of view in which it can be placed, that although not valuable to the United States for settlement, it is so to Spain, and will become more so, and therefore at some distant period will form an object which we may barter with her for the Floridas, obviously of far greater value to us than all the immense, undefined region west of the river.

It has been usual for the American writers on this subject to include the Floridas in their ideas of Louisiana, as the French formerly did, and the acquisition has derived no inconsiderable portion of its value and importance with the public from this view of it. It may, however, be relied on, that no part of the Floridas, not a foot of land on the east of the Mississippi, excepting New-Orleans, falls within the present cession. As to the unbounded region west of the Mississippi, it is, with the exception of a very few settlements of Spaniards and Frenchmen bordering on the banks of the river, a wilderness through which wander numerous tribes of Indians. And when we consider the present extent of the United States, and that not one sixteenth part of its territory is yet under occupation, the advantage of the acquisition, as it relates to actual settlement, appears too distant and remote to strike the mind of a sober politician with much force. This, therefore, can only rest in speculation for many years, if not centuries to come, and consequently will not perhaps be allowed very great weight in the account by the majority of readers. But it may be added, that should our own citizens, more enterprizing than wise, become desirous of settling this country, and emigrate thither, it must not only be attended with all the injuries of a too widely dispersed population, but by adding to the great weight of the western part of our territory, must hasten the dismemberment of a large portion of our country, or a dissolution of the Government. On the whole, we think it may with candor be said, that whether the possession at this time of any territory west of the river Mississippi will be advantageous, is at best extremely problematical. For ourselves, we are very much inclined to the opinion, that after all, it is the Island of N. Orleans by which the command of a free navigation of the Mississippi is secured, that gives to this interesting cession, its greatest value, and will render it in every view of immense benefit to our country. By this cession we hereafter shall hold within our own grasp, what we have heretofore enjoyed only by the uncertain tenure of a treaty, which might be broken at the pleasure of another, and (governed as we now are) with perfect impunity. Provided therefore we have not purchased it too dear, there is all the reason for exultation which the friends of the administration display, and which all Americans may be allowed to feel.

As to the pecuniary value of the bargain; we know not enough of the particulars to pronounce upon it. It is understood generally, that we are to assume *debts* of France to our own citizens not exceeding four millions of dollars; and that for the remainder, being a very large sum, 6 per cent. stock to be created, and payment made in that. But should it contain no conditions or stipulations on our part, no "tangling alliances" of all things to be dreaded, we shall be very much inclined to regard it in a favorable point of view though it should turn out to be what may be called a costly purchase. By the way a question here presents itself of some little moment: Mr. Jefferson in that part of his famous electioneering message, where he took so much pains to present a flattering state of the Treasury in so few words that every man could carry it in his noddle and repeat it at the poll, tells us, that "experience too so far authorises us to believe, *if no extraordinary event supervenes, and the expences which will be actually incurred shall not be greater than was contemplated* by Congress at their last session, that we shall not be disappointed in the expectations formed" that the debt would soon be paid, &c.&c. But the first and only measure of the administration that has really been of any material service to the country (for they have hitherto gone on the strength of the provisions made by their predecessors) is really *"an extraordinary event,"* and calls for more money than they have got. According to Mr. Gallatin's report, they had about 40.000 to spare for contingencies, and now the first *"extraordinary event"* that *"supervenes"* calls upon them for several millions. What a poor starvling system of administering a government! *But how is the money to be had? Not by taxing luxury and wealth and whiskey, but by increasing the taxes on the necessaries of life.* Let this be remembered.

But we are exceeding our allowable limits. It may be satisfactory to our readers, that we should finish with a concise account of New-Orleans itself.

The Island of New-Orleans is in length about 150 miles; its breadth varies from 10 to 30 miles. Most of it is a marshy swamp, periodically inundated by the river. The town of New-Orleans, situated about 105 miles from the mouth of the river, contains near 1300 houses, and about 8000 inhabitants, chiefly Spanish and French. It is defended from the over-flowings of the river, by an embankment, or *leveé*, which extends near 50 miles.

The rights of the present proprietors of real estate in New-Orleans and Louisiana, whether acquired by descent or by purchase, will, of course, remain undisturbed. How they are to be governed is another question; whether as a colony, or to be formed into an integral part of the United States, is a subject which will claim consideration hereafter. The probable consequences of this cession, and the ultimate effect it is likely to produce on the political state of our country, will furnish abundant matter of speculation to the American statesman.

If reliance can be placed on the history given of the negociation of *Louisiana* in private letters, from persons of respectability residing at Paris, and who speak with confidence, the merit of it, after making due allowance for the great events which have borne it along with them, is due to our ambassador, Chancellor Livingston, and not to the Envoy Extraordinary. "The cession was voted in the Council of State on the 8th of April, and Mr. Munro did not even arrive till the 12th." Judging from Mr. Munro's former communications to the French Government on this subject, we really cannot but regard it as fortunate, that the thing was concluded before he reached St. Cloud.[13]

13. The striking thing about this editorial is the paradoxical mixture of acuteness and obtuseness, of genuine patriotism and blind partisanship. Modern scholars would applaud Hamilton's sharp analysis of France's difficulties in Haiti and the shifting balance of power in Europe as important ingredients in the American diplomatic triumph. They would also add as important, Spanish dilatoriness and the cold winter of 1802 that froze up Gen. Victor's Louisiana expedition until late spring 1803. But few modern scholars would deny any credit at all to the administration and its representatives in France.

This editorial is unsigned, and it has never been printed in any of the editions of Hamilton's writings as his. Nevertheless, thanks to the efforts of his son, James A. Hamilton, twenty years after his father's death, it is possible to identify the essay as Alexander Hamilton's.

In the family campaign to keep their great sire's fame from going into complete eclipse during the era of Jeffersonian ascendancy,[14] James A. Hamilton collected material on two topics in particular: proof that Hamilton had written Washington's Farewell Address, and evidence to prove that Hamilton had never shared in the disunion plots of the sort that had damned the Federalist party past any hope of salvation after the Hartford Convention of 1815.[15] In order to

---

It is also significant that Hamilton in the last year of his life was pertinaciously holding to the dogma that no free republic could be established and maintained in a large geographical area. It was this dogmatic conviction (shared with the "anti-Federalists of 1788") that led him to insist in 1787 that the Constitution, as originally written, was so weak as to be unworkable.

14. Someday someone will write the fascinating story of the Hamilton family's heroic battle against oblivion waged on behalf of the dead statesman in the period 1815–1860. With his party smeared with the stigma of treason after 1815, with the rising popularity first of Jeffersonian, later, of Jacksonian democracy, Hamilton by 1850 was the most undervalued of the Founding Fathers in the popular mind. Against this tide of opinion the family struggled, almost singlehandedly at first, to get Hamilton recognized both as a great man and as a great American. For a sketchy but suggestive outline of the ebb and flow of Hamilton's fame in the 19th century correlated with the rise and fall of Jefferson's and Madison's reputation in the same period, see Douglass Adair, "The Authorship of the Disputed Federalist Papers," *William and Mary Quarterly*, 3d Ser., I (1944); "The New Thomas Jefferson," *ibid.*, III (1946); and "The Tenth Federalist Revisited," *ibid.*, VIII (1951) [essays 2, 3, and 11 above].

15. The story of James A. Hamilton's research on his father can be found scattered in the early pages of his *Reminiscences of James A. Hamilton; or, Men and Events, at Home and Abroad, During Three Quarters of a Century* (New York, 1869). Especially interesting is his account of the difficulty the family had in getting Hamilton's letters to Washington and drafts of the Farewell Address from an inner circle of Federalist leaders, who had decided that this material should stay secretly locked up in the possession of Rufus King. The purpose was to prevent publication, which would show Hamilton's role as Washington's ghost-writer, and thus lessen the authority of the Farewell Address by revealing it as a Federalist manifesto

further this latter research he solicited information from friends and contemporaries of his father regarding Hamilton's position on the Louisiana Purchase, which had stimulated so many Federalists to talk of disunion in 1804.[16] The most interesting material came from William Coleman, editor of the *New-York Evening Post* in 1804, who wrote to James Hamilton on February 23, 1829, with copious detail about "your Father's opinion" of the purchase of Louisiana:

> . . . it so happens that that opinion was, after repeated conversations with me, committed to writing in my own phraseology, indeed, for the purpose of publication in the *Evening Post;* and so desirous was he of having his ideas on this important measure of government expressed with the greatest precision, neither restricted nor extended in any degree, that being informed at what time the proof sheets would be ready for inspection, he came to the office and examined it after it had been corrected and was all ready to go to press, and having with great deliberation carefully perused the whole, declared it contained the identical idea he had wished to express on the subject.
>
> That article I have not seen for some years, but a little research will discover it when I again go down to my office.[17]

On Coleman's testimony, then, the *Post* editorial of July 5, 1803,

---

disguised as nonpartisan advice. The Hamilton family finally had to go to law to secure the documents. *Ibid.*, 24–34. It is suggestive that these Federalist leaders who loved Hamilton and who knew of his intimate association with Washington nevertheless wished to keep exact knowledge of the association from the public; the family, on the other hand, was naturally anxious to emphasize the intimacy in order to refresh Hamilton's withering laurels in the period from 1820 on.

16. Among the people questioned on this topic was John Quincy Adams. He, King, and Hamilton were the only prominent Federalists not in outright opposition to the Purchase in 1803. For Adams's report of a conversation with James A. Hamilton on the subject, see Charles Francis Adams, ed., *The Memoirs of John Quincy Adams, Comprising Portions of His Diary from 1795 to 1848* (Philadelphia, 1874–1877), VIII, 110, under date Mar. 11, 1829.

17. William Coleman to James A. Hamilton, Feb. 23, 1829, in J. A. Hamilton, *Reminiscences*, 94. Whether Coleman ever looked for the editorial and sent it to the family is uncertain.

contains Hamilton's "identical idea" on Louisiana, "expressed with the greatest precision, neither restricted nor extended in any degree."

But should not the essay be identified as a collaborative work of "Coleman and Hamilton"? Coleman, after all, speaks of its being written "after repeated conversations" in "my own phraseology." Fortunately we have much more exact evidence on the writing partnership of the editor and the sponsor of the *Post* than is contained in this letter to James A. Hamilton.

Jeremiah Mason, the famous lawyer and Federalist senator from New Hampshire, who knew Coleman intimately as a young man, reports in his "Autobiography" how "surprized" he and other friends of Coleman were "by the ability of some of his editorial articles" when Coleman first began managing the *Post*:

Having a convenient opportunity, I asked him [Coleman] who wrote, or aided in writing those articles. He frankly answered that he made no secret of it; that his paper was set up under the auspices of General Hamilton, and that he assisted him. I then asked, "Does he write in your paper?" "Never a word."—"How, then, does he assist?" His answer was "Whenever anything occurs on which I feel the want of information, I state the matter to him, sometimes in a note. He appoints a time when I may see him, usually a late hour of the evening. He always keeps himself minutely informed on all political matters. As soon as I see him, he begins in a deliberate manner to dictate, and I to note down in short-hand" (he was a good stenographer); "when he stops my article is completed."[18]

This statement made by Coleman to Mason elucidates the puzzling elements in Coleman's letter to Hamilton *fils*.

18. G. S. Hillard, ed., *Memoirs of Jeremiah Mason; Reproduction of Privately Printed Edition of 1873* . . . (Boston, 1917), 31–32. Mason's "Autobiography," which makes up the opening of the *Memoirs*, was written in 1844 when he was 76 years old and contains material on Coleman's early life available nowhere else. Coleman fully deserves a biography of his own, and Mason's revelation of his editiorial relationship with Hamilton literally begs for a study of *Post* files between 1800–1804 and the identification of other Hamilton editorials.

Adding this statement of Coleman's to what we know from other sources of Hamilton's method of composing political manifestos, we can reconstruct the actual composition of the editorial on Louisiana with a fair degree of certainty. Hamilton *did* have "repeated conversations" about Louisiana with Coleman during the years 1801–1803, but he did *not* have "repeated conversations" on that topic between June 30, 1803—the date that news of the Purchase reached New York—and Saturday morning, July 2—the date that Coleman announced the editorial as finished. For Hamilton did not compose in small accretions in a fashion analogous to the building of a coral reef. All observers who had knowledge of the writing of his great state papers, his political pamphlets, and polemics describe his method as single bursts of tremendously concentrated and extremely rapid production, resulting in essays or editorials that were so well organized, so finished on the first draft that they seldom needed either revision or polish.[19]

Thus we are safe in assuming that probably late either Thursday night, June 30, or Friday night, July 1, 1803, William Coleman sat, notebook in hand, transcribing Hamilton's ideas and very *words* on the significance of the purchase of New Orleans, on the insignificance of all the trans-Mississippi West, and on the detestable pusillanimity of Thomas Jefferson.

II
A Note on Certain of Hamilton's Pseudonyms

THE DEMOCRATIZATION of modern politics has made the pseudonym in political pamphleteering practically obsolete. During the late eighteenth century, however, writing under a pseudonym was

---

19. Compare Madison's description of the speed with which Hamilton wrote his share of the *Federalist* essays, Elizabeth Fleet, ed., "Madison's 'Detached Memoranda,' " *WMQ*, 3d Ser., III (1946), 564–565.

standard procedure, even in countries like England and the United States where the press was relatively free.[1] Almost all books, pamphlets, squibs, letters to the editor on controversial issues—which naturally meant most political issues—were either unsigned or signed with a pen name. During the American Revolution and the early years of the Republic, the pseudonym is thus the norm. Some publicists like Samuel Adams adopted a score of names and a score of personalities and created the impression of a host of Massachusetts opinions, all "patriotic," of course, and all squinting with suspicion toward England in the years before the Tea Party; in contrast, the impact of the single pamphlet of the author who signed himself *Common Sense* was so powerful that Paine used this nom de plume, almost like a modern trademark, for the rest of his life.

Thus the essay with some such signature as Junius, or Publius, or the plain, unpretentious American Farmer is one of the conspicuous marks of the difference between the "style" of eighteenth-century and modern politics. And since the nom de plume is an overt sign of difference between then and now, it hints that perhaps the function of public opinion in politics at that time differed both in degree and kind from its function today; and it invites studies of the pseudonym as a point of departure leading to a deepened understanding of various aspects of eighteenth-century politics and the politicians who used them.[2]

1. It was, of course, fatal not to write under a pseudonym where the press was not free. And although in both England and America the liberty of the press was broadening down from precedent to precedent during the 18th century, the right to criticize government was not definitely won in either country before 1800. Undoubtedly the class structure of 18th-century society and the aristocratic ethos of politics are also related to the continued use of pseudonyms even after freedom of the press was won. A gentleman lost caste if he wrote professionally in competition with mere scribblers; and conversely, a lower-class professional writer concealed behind a nom de plume could gain authority by writing as if he were a gentleman. Probably, too, the prevalence of the code duello fortified continuance of the practice, even though in most cases the identity of the man behind the pseudonym was an open secret.

2. For example, Dr. Richard Hooker has demonstrated that a study of the toasts at celebrations where conviviality and politics mingled in alcoholic amity provides

It would seem, for example, that some study of the pseudonyms used by Alexander Hamilton would provide valuable insights both into his intent as manipulator of public opinion and into his estimate of the public whose opinion it was necessary to control if his favored policies were to be followed.[3] The most prolific pamphleteer among the leading statesmen of the young Republic, he almost always wrote under nom de plumes. And almost always the nom de plume seems to have been carefully picked to match the thrust of the argument in the pamphlet.

In many instances the pseudonym shows merely the standard and rather crass device of appropriating for Hamilton's side of the controversy a positive and popular name that put any opponent on the defensive and associated him with an unpopular and false alternative. For example, no leader in 1793 wanted to be thought of as anti-Pacificus, for peace and real neutrality was the passion of every responsible American statesman;[4] in like manner, no opponent

---

a significant barometer of political tensions in pre-Revolutionary America. Would not a study of the increasing use of such nom de plumes as Brutus, Hampden, Cromwell, Sidney before 1776 perhaps provide equally suggestive material on the rise of antimonarchical sentiments?

3. The pseudonyms discussed below are signed to pamphlets that are all printed in Henry Cabot Lodge, ed., *The Works of Alexander Hamilton* (New York, 1904). Lodge in his lazy way did not try to identify any pamphlet that had not been already identified and printed in John C. Hamilton's edition, *The Works of Alexander Hamilton; Comprising His Correspondence, And His Political And Official Writings* ... (New York, 1850–1851), merely adding to J. C. Hamilton's published corpus the famous Reynolds pamphlet (which was signed) and *The Federalist*, which was readily available in many reprint editions. How many other Hamilton essays disguised with pseudonyms remain to be identified in the periodicals of the period, it is impossible to say.

4. Madison in answering Pacificus naturally did not sign himself Bellicose, but shifting the issue to Hamilton's claim for executive prerogative in foreign affairs, warned against executive tyranny in signing his essays Helvidius. As every reader of Tacitus recognized immediately, this was a reference to Helvidius Priscus, the Roman Stoic and patriot whose opposition to imperial aggrandizement first gained him banishment under Nero and, eventually, death under Vespasian.

Publius, the pseudonym shared jointly by Madison, Jay, and Hamilton, was picked from Plutarch for obvious reasons. Publius Valerius was the great hero who, after

of Hamilton's warmongering against France in 1796 and 1797 liked the implication that disagreement with the policy advocated by the New Yorker was simply un-Americanus.

Most interesting of Hamilton's pseudonyms are a group borrowed from historic personages of antiquity who were described by Plutarch: Phocion (1784); Tully (1794); Camillus (1795); Pericles (1803).[5] A study of the pamphlets to which Hamilton signed these borrowed names readily reveals in each instance the appropriateness of the particular pseudonym for the policy advocated.

Every educated man (for in 1794 by definition "education" meant "classical education") who read Hamilton's attacks on the Whiskey Rebels, signed Tully, must have been quite conscious of the author's desire to stimulate memory of Cicero's invective against the horrid

Lucius Brutus overthrew Tarquin, the last king of Rome, consummated the revolution by establishing a stable and just republican government. As Plutarch reports: "He resolved to render the government, as well as himself, instead of terrible, familiar and pleasant to the people, and parted the axes from the rods . . . to show in the strongest way the republican foundation of the government. . . . But the humility of the man was but a means, not, as they thought, of lessening himself, but merely to abate their envy by his moderation; for whatever he detracted from his authority he added to his real power, the people still submitting with satisfaction, which they expressed by calling him Poplicola, or people-lover. . . ."

5. In 1798 Hamilton used another classical pseudonym, Titus Manlius, for the series of six inflammatory papers, contemporary to the XYZ Affair, collectively entitled "The Stand." Titus Manlius Torquatus (fl. 215 B.C.) was not included in Plutarch's gallery of heroes, but is described by Livy as one of the great leaders who came forward, when Rome was most menaced by Carthage, to advocate a policy of total war on land and sea. He was against even treating with Hannibal for the release of the Roman soldiers captured at Cannae. It seems probable that Hamilton used this alias as appropriate to the argument in the text of these essays, that the conflict between France and the rest of the world, led by England, had become of the same deadly and irreversible sort as the duel between Rome and Carthage. The United States for its own safety must take an active and energetic stand, with arms in its hands, beside Britain—there could be no neutrals any more. It was also a most appropriate pseudonym in view of the specific area in which Hamilton most wished the United States to attack France. For Titus Manlius' most famous military triumph was an expedition against Carthage's allies on Rome's own doorstep, the Sardinians—just the sort of triumph that Hamilton hoped to achieve by invasion of New Orleans, held by France's ally, Spain, on our doorstep.

conspiracy of Catiline, when "Rome itself was in the most dangerous inclination to change on account of the unequal distribution of wealth. . . . So that there wanted but a slight impetus to set all in motion, it being in the power of every daring man to overturn a sickly commonwealth."[6] And many readers of Hamilton's tract must have been aware that the author's demand for a crushing and severe lesson to the rebels was fortified by Cicero's parallel insistence on the extreme penalty for conspirators.

Likewise the name Phocion signed to a pamphlet of 1784 in its very syllables carried a plea for magnanimity, generosity, and justice even to ex-enemies. For as Plutarch describes Phocion, the Athenian general and statesman "never allowed himself from any feeling of personal hostility to do hurt to any fellow-citizen. . . ." Indeed, "he would befriend his very opponents in their distress, and espouse the cause of those who differed most from him, when they needed his patronage." Phocion, among all the Athenian leaders of his day, exerted himself most to have pardoned and recalled those who had been banished; he sought to protect prisoners of war when demagogues were likely to "persuade the people in their anger into committing some act of cruelty." No better name than Phocion thus could have been found by Hamilton for a tract pleading with the citizens of New York to end the post-Revolutionary proscription of tories and to restore their full civil rights.

The situation described in the very opening sentences of Plutarch's sketch of Camillus parallels to a degree the situation in the United States in 1795 when Hamilton as "Camillus" wrote his defense of

6. "Cicero," in Plutarch, *The Lives of the Noble Grecians and Romans,* translated by John Dryden, Modern Library Edition (New York, no date). All the following quotations from Plutarch will be from this translation, the most popular English version of the classic in the 18th century, and one undoubtedly known to Hamilton. How early he read Plutarch cannot be determined, but there exists in his military paybook for 1776 a series of maxims culled from Plutarch's lives of Demosthenes and Numa, and his son reports that Plutarch and Alexander Pope were his favorite authors before he came to the United States.

the Jay Treaty. For "the state and temper of the commonwealth," during the time of Camillus, saw "the people, being at dissension with the senate. . . ." Camillus, like Hamilton, was concerned with the threat of the "Gauls" to the republic; and it was the old Roman who drove off the Gallic warriors when they were attacking the very capitol itself. Nevertheless, though Camillus was "styled a second founder of Rome," yet demagogues "railed against [him] . . . as a hater of the people, and one that grudged all advantage to the poor. Afterwards, when the tribunes of the people . . . brought their motion . . . to the vote, Camillus appeared openly against it, shrinking from no unpopularity, and inveighing boldly against the promoters of it, and so urging and constraining the multitude that contrary to their inclinations they rejected the proposal but yet hated Camillus." So, too, Hamilton stood forth without shrinking against the mob, which stoned him almost into insensibility for defending the British Treaty. But in the end, like the old Roman's, his cause triumphed also.

In 1803 Hamilton, signing himself Pericles, was arguing like that famous Grecian that his country, to be worthy of its destiny, must make itself an imperial power. Specifically, it must conquer the Island of New Orleans. And his argument, as his readers who knew their Plutarch would have recognized, paralleled almost exactly the argument with which Pericles justified the great war against Sparta: *our enemy, Napoleon, is "already all but in actual hostilities"* against us.

Clearly all four of these Plutarchian pseudonyms used by Hamilton carried immediate implications for his classically educated audience that our generation misses. Each of the four names used as a disguise was chosen with symbolic intent to further the argument made in the text of the tract. Each is fitting and appropriate in four different ways for four different policies being advocated by Hamilton at four different times.

However, even more interesting than the symbolic differences of these four pseudonymic figures are certain characteristics that all four of these ancients share in common. As Plutarch describes the characters of Pericles and Phocion, of Camillus and Cicero, the reader becomes aware of a connection that joins them all into one pattern. And here one discovers that there are two levels of symbolism in these names used by Hamilton. The first and more superficial level, described above, relates these dead heroes' policies of war or peace, of severity or magnanimity, to comparable policies advocated by Hamilton. The second and more profound level of symbolism throws light on the character of Hamilton himself and the role his nature forced him to play in American politics.

All four of these men of heroic virtue from four different eras of Greek and Roman history share in common a profound contempt for the people whom they rule and serve so devotedly. Camillus we have already seen winning the hatred of the plebs by driving them through sheer force of will to follow a correct policy which, in their shortsighted greed and ignorance, they wished to reject. Cicero, who made his countrymen reluctantly "prefer that which is honest before that which is popular . . . ," took as his maxim the recipe given him by the Delphic oracle: that he must make "his own genius and not the opinion of the people the guide of his life. . . ." Pericles, though he came to power as leader of the "party of the people" against the "party of the few," then ceased to be "tame and gentle and familiar as formerly with the populace. . . . Quitting that loose, remiss, and, in some cases, licentious court of the popular will, he turned those soft and flowery modulations to the austerity of aristocratical and regal rule; and employing this uprightly and undeviatingly for the country's best interests, he was able generally to lead the people along . . . and sometimes, too, urging and pressing them forward extremely against their will, he made them, whether they would or no, yield submission to what was for their advantage."[7] Phocion,

7. Hamilton, too, was no doubt aware of Plutarch's analysis of Pericles' method of controlling the "distempered feelings" among the populace "in an especial manner, making . . . use of hopes and fears, as his two chief rudders . . . ," and addressing

too, prided himself on his "free-spoken expostulation" which the ignorant people "construed into contempt." He was "so far from humouring them or courting their favor, that he always thwarted and opposed them. . . . And when once he gave his opinion to the people, and was met with the general approbation and applause of the assembly, turning to some of his friends, he asked them, 'Have I inadvertently said something foolish?'"

Not only do all four of Hamilton's selected prototypes show their profound disdain of the people, but all four in their biographies are seen to be misjudged, betrayed, persecuted by the miserable populace whose safety and well-being depend on the superman's abilities and services to the state. Camillus and Cicero were banished because of their superior talents. When the plague broke out in Athens, "the people, distempered and afflicted in their souls, as well as in their bodies, were utterly enraged like madmen against Pericles, and, like patients grown delirious, sought to lay violent hands on their physician, or, as it were, their father." He was driven from office and crushingly fined. And Phocion, blackguarded by the tongues of "demagogues" and "disfranchised citizens," was condemned to death by

---

"the affections and passions, which are as it were the strings and keys to the soul. . . ." It is also probable that Hamilton strongly identified his own incorruptibility with Pericles' "manifest freedom" from personal corruption (though Pericles did use the common treasury of the Delian League to buy his way to power in Athens) and his "superiority to all considerations of money. Notwithstanding he had made the city of Athens . . . great and rich . . . he, for his part, did not make the patrimony his father left him greater than it was by one drachma." There is also the pitiable point of identity that Hamilton, in 1803, could make with Pericles in the terrible sorrow suffered in the death of a favorite son.

As *Pericles* in advocating war, Hamilton may also have remembered the use which Plutarch reports that Camillus made of war for purposes of domestic politics: "And although he [Camillus] perceived it would be no small work to take it [the city of Falerii], and no little time would be required for it, yet he was willing to exercise the citizens and keep them abroad, that they might have no leisure, idling at home, to follow the tribunes in factions and seditions; a very common remedy, indeed, with the Romans, who thus carried off, like good physicians, the ill humours of their commonwealth."

the assembly of the citizens he had served so wisely for twenty years. "The populace . . . [cried] out they were oligarchs, and enemies to the liberty of the people, and deserved to be stoned; after which no man durst offer anything further in Phocion's behalf."[8]

But if the people crucified their political saviors, the people inevitably were punished horribly and collectively for their repudiation of their supermen in the subsequent disasters that befell the state. "A very little time and their own sad experience soon informed" the Athenians, who had given Phocion the hemlock, "what an excellent governor, and how great an example and guardian of justice and of temperance they had bereft themselves of." Camillus, smarting from the "mock and scorn of his enemies" and driven into exile, "went silently to the gate of the city, and there stopping and turning round, stretched out his hands to the Capitol, and prayed to the gods, that if, without any fault of his own, but merely through the malice and violence of the people, he was driven out into banishment, the Romans might quickly repent of it; and that all mankind might witness their need for the assistance, and desire for the return of Camillus." Naturally the gods testified their displeasure with the Roman people, and "such a punishment visited the city of Rome, an era of such loss and danger and disgrace so quickly succeeded . . ." that only the return of Camillus to dictatorial power saved the state.[9] Nor was the

8. Plutarch notes in the biography of Phocion: "It is commonly said that public bodies are most insulting and contumelious to a good man, when they are puffed up with prosperity and success. But the contrary often happens. . . . So fares it in the body politic, in times of distress and humiliation; a certain sensitiveness and soreness of humour prevails, with a weak incapacity of enduring any free and open advice, even when the necessity of affairs most requires such plain-dealing. At such times the conduct of public affairs is on all hands most hazardous. Those who humour the people are swallowed up in the common ruin; those who endeavour to lead them aright perish the first in the attempt."

9. See the toast to Hamilton printed in the *New-York Evening Post*, July 15, 1802, quoted in Nathan Schachner, *Alexander Hamilton* (New York, 1946), 412: "*Alexander Hamilton*—As like in virtue as in suffer'd wrongs, so may he prove the *Camillus* of America, to drive from power by fraud obtain'd, the modern Gauls and Vandals."

account of Pericles, which Hamilton read with relish in Plutarch, different in its moral: "The course of public affairs after his death produced a quick and speedy sense of the loss of Pericles. Those who, while he lived, resented his great authority, as that which eclipsed themselves, presently after his quitting the stage . . . readily acknowledged that there never had been in nature such a disposition as his was. . . . And that invidious arbitrary power, to which formerly they gave the name of monarchy and tyranny, did then appear to have been the chief bulwark of public safety; so great a corruption and such a flood of mischief and vice followed. . . ."

Ancient wisdom has it that as a man "thinketh in his heart, so is he." All the psychological evidence, clinical and sociological, accumulated in recent years confirms this point, anciently recognized by historians, too, that the characters, real or fictional, with whom any man identifies and whom he emulates are of crucial importance in crystallizing his own personality. Each of us, in choosing his heroes and in defining his villains, reveals his own evaluation of himself, displays his own estimate of his potentialities, and exhibits his secret desires and hopes concerning the role that he himself wishes to act on the stage of life.

It is for this reason that the heroic characters from Plutarch deliberately picked by Hamilton to reveal his public sentiments seem of unusual significance too in revealing his own estimate of his destiny. In his private letters and public writings Hamilton is little given to self-analysis. When he does give autobiographical details, they cannot be trusted. It was Hamilton himself who misled historians for two centuries into misdating the year of his birth by a deliberately written ambiguity; and his false statements about his share in writing *The Federalist* are so flagrant in their errors as almost to pass belief. So, willy-nilly, we must seek the man within by indirection; we can see him only in the moments when the public mask slips briefly, revealing the personality behind it. And are not these choices of the role of

Phocion-Camillus-Tully-Pericles just such revelatory flashes which define the texture and flavor of Hamilton's ambition?[10]

Certainly Hamilton's mask slipped completely off just for an instant in the spring of 1791, revealing with frightening clarity the identity of Hamilton's greatest hero. And this figure, too, bulks large in Plutarch's pages. Jefferson tells of the event, a cabinet meeting held in his lodgings at Philadelphia, probably in April 1791, while Washington was on his southern tour: "The room being hung around with a collection of portraits of remarkable men, among them Bacon, Newton, and Locke, Hamilton asked me who they were. I told him they were my trinity of the three greatest men the world had ever produced, naming them. He paused for some time: 'the greatest man,' said he, 'that ever lived, was Julius Caesar!'"[11]

The Caesar of Plutarch that Hamilton knew and admired is not the Caesar modern Americans know chiefly through Shakespeare.

---

10. Thirty years ago Carl Becker in reviewing Bernard Faÿ's *L'Esprit Révolutionnaire en France et aux États-Unis à la Fin du XVIIIᵉ Siècle* (Paris, 1925), begged for research in exactly this field. "Will not someone write a book showing how the revolutionary state of mind of the eighteenth century was also nourished on an ideal conception of classical republicanism and Roman virtue? Just why did Madame Roland often weep to think that she was not born a Spartan? Just why did John Adams ask himself if Demosthenes, had he been a deputy to the first Continental Congress, would have been satisfied with non-importation and non-exportation agreements? To know the answers to these questions would help much to understand both the French and the American revolutions." *American Historical Review*, XXX (1924–1925), 810. Taking up Becker's challenge, Harold Talbot Parker, in *The Cult of Antiquity and the French Revolutionaries: A Study in the Development of the Revolutionary Spirit* (Chicago, 1937), brilliantly demonstrated how much light a study of the uses of classical history, particularly Plutarch, could throw on the ambitions and careers of such figures as Robespierre, Desmoulins, Brissot, Saint-Just, *et al.* Parker's research, however, does not exhaust the topic for the French Revolution, and, alas, there is not even a beginning on the classics in Revolutionary America.

11. Thomas Jefferson to Benjamin Rush, Jan. 16, 1811, Andrew A. Lipscomb and Albert Ellery Bergh, eds., *The Writings of Thomas Jefferson* (Washington, D.C., 1903), XIII, 2.

Plutarch's Caesar is the hero of the world's most sinister success story—a man of transcendent genius who could find self-fulfillment only in the exercise of unchecked power over his fellows. "Caesar is said to have been admirably fitted by nature," Plutarch reports, "to make a great statesman and orator [in the traditional and constitutional manner], and to have taken such pains to improve his genius this way that without dispute he might challenge the second place. More he did not aim at, as choosing to be first rather amongst men of arms and power, and, therefore, never rose to that height of eloquence to which nature would have carried him, his attention being diverted to those expeditions and designs which at length gained him the empire." Caesar's disdain for money and the groveling arts of money-makers early became notorious, though no leader was ever more calculating in using men's love of wealth to make them his tools: "By incurring [profuse] expense . . . to be popular . . . he was purchasing what was of the greatest value at an inconsiderable rate." His "love of honour and passion for distinction" led him to court dangers in battle from which his rank would have normally exempted him. Conscious of his genius and certain of what he most desired, he recognized in the social instability and political disorders of Rome the typical revolutionary circumstances which could be exploited in his own pursuit of power, a power which would be used to restore social order and gain him immortal fame. "There being two factions in the city, one . . . which was very powerful, the other . . . which was then broken and in a low condition, he undertook to revive this [latter] and make it his own." Little by little the power of Caesar's clique grew as his influence over the clique became more and more pervasive. Eventually he was able to use a foreign war to make himself both independent of the Senate's control and strong enough to challenge its authority. At last he had risen so high that only two or three men could challenge his position, "which now openly tended to the altering of the whole constitution," but the very possibility of challenge spurred him to consolidate his power by mastering these last few rivals and seizing the supreme authority in the state. "In his journey, as he was crossing the Alps, and passing by a small village of the barbarians, with but few inhabitants and those wretchedly poor, his companions asked the question among themselves by way of mockery, if there were any canvassing for officers there. . . . To which Caesar made answer seriously, 'For my part, I had rather be the first man among these fellows, than the second man in Rome.' "

This was the personality and career that even on the surface suggest a series of parallels with Hamilton's own character and career through the year 1800. Like Caesar he considered himself "born to do great things, and had a passion after honour." Like the Roman, when faced with the alternative paths to distinction offered either by law and oratory or "arms and power," he never hesitated in his choice. In his military vocation, again like Caesar, his soaring, eagle-like spirit penned in a weak and sickly body drove him to overexert himself in action to the verge of physical collapse; and like the ancient hero he was a staff officer who insisted on leading infantry charges in person against the enemy. Caesar's contempt for the low and sordid ambition of moneymaking that obsessed so many men was matched by that of Hamilton, who described himself in 1797 as "a character marked by indifference to the acquisition of property rather than by avidity for it." But, again like Caesar, he could be prodigal in "his unsparing distribution of money," showing his followers "that he did not heap up wealth . . . for his own luxury, or the gratifying his private pleasures. . . ." Through this means, following the technique that had worked in ancient Rome, Hamilton revived a party in the Republic that was low and broken in 1783 and made it his own. Finally, the American, like his classical hero, ended by determining "to make himself the greatest man in Rome"; each man fixed his eye on the highest office in the state—the office that combined in its prerogative control over the military, the financial, and the diplomatic resources of the Republic—and ruthlessly struck down every rival who stood between him and that office.

It would seem that perhaps the most significant feature of Hamilton's confession of 1791 that he admired Caesar above all men who had ever lived lies in its suggestion that by that date Hamilton's private and personal ambition had become focused on the office of president of the United States. In his secret heart he did not think of himself at that time (if, indeed, he ever had) as a follower of Washington so much as his successor in this supreme constitutional office. The love of fame—"the ruling passion of the noblest minds," Hamilton called it—which had obsessed Caesar, too, had committed him even while secretary of the Treasury to envision himself "seated on the highest summit of his country's honors."

There is every reason to believe that even if Hamilton had *lacked* obsessive personal ambitions for the presidency, he nevertheless would still have pressed for his domestic financial system and his favored foreign policy. But if it is recognized that every part of his program between 1789 and 1800 carried the additional cargo of his private ambition, some of the enigmas of his political behavior in this decade are explained. In particular, we can understand Hamilton's violent and aggressive enmity toward any first-rate man close to Washington, as well as his intrigues against John Adams. He was committed by both his vision of how the Constitution should be strengthened and his vision of his own personal destiny to consider first Jefferson and later John Adams as deadly rivals and public enemies who must be destroyed.

John Quincy Adams is only one among Hamilton's contemporaries who recognized the significance of the New Yorker's craving for the presidency; but Adams, fortunately for the historian, was acute enough to suggest some of the unhappy consequences for Hamilton himself. And we can see today how these consequences for a man enamored of the Phocion-Camillus-Caesar style of statesmanship carried a terrible threat to the shaky new Constitution of 1787 and to the infant Republic whose union depended upon it. Hamilton's "talents were of the highest order," Adams noted, "his ambition transcendent, and his disposition to intrigue irrepressible . . . he was of that class of characters which cannot bear a rival—haughty, over-bearing, jealous, bitter and violent in his personal enmities, and little scrupulous of the means which he used against those who stood in the way of his ambition."[12] Talents, ambition, propensity to intrigue, all three of these characteristics must be viewed in dynamic interaction if we would evaluate the final personal tragedy of Hamilton's statesmanship in the 1790s.

There has never been any disagreement about the first of the trinity of characteristics attributed by Adams to Hamilton; friends and foes who knew him personally all agree on his "genius." There is no doubt that Hamilton had executive talents commensurate to the presidency of the United States. Indeed, Talleyrand, that shrewd judge of statesmen, rated him as a political personality greater even than Charles Fox or Napoleon.

Nor can there be any debate on the question of Hamilton's "transcendent ambition." It was only on the nature of Hamilton's ambition that his contemporaries divided, some finding it praiseworthy, others fearing it as potentially dangerous to the liberty of the Republic itself. George Washington, in a letter to John Adams, September 25, 1798, reveals this disagreement with exactness: "By some he is considered as an ambitious man, and therefore a dangerous one," Washington wrote President Adams. "That he is ambitious I will readily grant, but it is of the laudable kind, which prompts a man to excel in whatever he takes in hand." And here again we must agree with Washington, at least in part. It was in no way inappropriate or censurable for Hamilton to wish to be president. No one can blame

12. Quoted in Adrienne Koch and William Peden, eds., *The Selected Writings of John and John Quincy Adams* (New York, 1946), 329–330.

him for dreaming of himself as Washington's heir apparent. From 1787 to the present, it has been the pride of Americans that their republican system invites every talented man in the United States to dream of occupying this supreme office with its noble opportunities for patriotic service and glory.

The crux of the Hamilton problem lies not in his original ambition—his dream of the presidency—but in the methods he chose to translate his dream into actuality. And since means tend to control ends, we can see, as George Washington could not, that Hamilton's once laudable ambition had *become* dangerous by 1798. Poor Hamilton was America's first major statesman whose imagination was fevered by presidential aspirations. It was his misfortune to seek that high office at a time when the road by which a candidate advanced to it was not marked out in any way; there was no "custom of the Constitution" governing the presidential succession in 1792, 1796, or 1800. Consequently in attempting to realize his dream, he was tempted to intrigue for the post; and when his intrigues raised up an overwhelming host of enemies, he was finally tempted to the ultimate in political libertinism. Hamilton's personality was not fixed and static from birth, as his enemies claimed; indeed, during the deadly power struggle of the 1790s Hamilton's character appears to exhibit greater dynamic changes than that of any of his major contemporaries and rivals. The Alexander Hamilton who confessed to Jefferson that Caesar was his hero in 1791 was not in his heart meditating Caesar's road to power at that time; but the Alexander Hamilton of 1799–1800 had been transformed by the attrition of political warfare into a leader dangerously close to the image of Caesar painted by Plutarch.

In 1791, with his financial system taking shape, Hamilton might well assume that his office as secretary of the Treasury would be the stepping-stone to the presidency. There was at that time no precedent for the vice-president to step into the office, as happened in 1796 and again in 1800; there was no precedent that the secretary of state was the heir-apparent, as between 1808 and 1824. The nearest thing to a precedent, or rather, what Hamilton hoped to convert into a precedent, was the function of the Treasury office as it had been developed by Sir Robert Walpole in the British cabinet. Just as Hamilton, to prop the "frail" new Constitution in America, copied the Walpole financial program—funding, bank, excise—which had been used to support the shaky Hanover dynasty in England, so, too, he converted his office as secretary of the Treasury into that of "prime minister" under Washington. Perhaps if he had only been a bit more patient, tactful, and sensitive to the necessities of American coalition politics, he would have been successful in his double-barreled program of personal and party power. As it turned out, he was only half successful: his legislative program was passed because of his influence over Washington, but in the process the program itself, plus his rash and overbearing leadership and his intrigues, had created a powerful opposition party whose leaders hated and feared Hamilton. Under the gentlemanly mores of the day, office had to seek the man; intrigue as he might to get it, Hamilton could not *appear* to want the presidency or even to be working for it; and now the growing personal opposition, which pictured him as the symbol of all evil, was making it impossible that Hamilton should ever be carried into the highest office by popular acclaim. If Hamilton was the first of our statesmen to be bitten by the presidential bug, he was also the first to discover himself "unavailable" as a candidate for popular election. By 1795 Hamilton realized with bitterness that his great services to the nation as secretary of the Treasury were not going to win him the reward he wished. He therefore resigned his office and watched a man he considered to be weak and silly succeed Washington.

With that penetrating insight of which he was at times capable, Hamilton had described in 1788 a situation in which he was to find himself in 1798. In analyzing the desirability of allowing the president to succeed himself, in *Federalist* 72, he had noted that an ambitious man who has held great power, if suddenly deprived of his power or frustrated from achieving power, is tempted to usurpation. "An ambitious man," he had then written, "when he . . . reflected that no exertion of merit on his part could save him from the unwelcome reverse; such a man in such a situation would be much more violently tempted to embrace a favorable conjuncture for attempting the prolongation of his power, at every hazard. . . ." The XYZ Affair presented Hamilton with both this favorable conjuncture and his final temptation. Blocked from attaining "the summit of his country's honors," which he felt to be rightfully his due, he sought in the "crisis" of a foreign war and in control of a standing army an alternative road to the presidency.

Give an army to any man who lusts for supreme power and who sees no legitimate road to power under existing institutions, and existing institutions are at once in danger. "Emergencies" and "crises" in this situation provide tremendous temptations to use force in "solving" simultaneously both the political crisis and the private dilemma of frustrated ambition. And here self-righteousness, consciousness of talent, even religion and patriotism become distorted inducements to attempt the short and easy way of usurpation of power outside the constitution. Is there any evidence that Alexander Hamilton, who never pretended in private that he thought the Constitution of 1787 was adequate, would have been able to withstand the temptation of "reforming" it by force if he had had the "emergency" of a consummated war crisis in 1799?

Especially in the last years of his life he does not appear to be a statesman cut to the traditional modern pattern: he was a son of revolution, who appears to have been haunted by one specific type of glory and power that revolution makes available to greatly talented, daring, and supremely ambitious men. Was not Alexander Hamilton the one major leader among our Founding Fathers who had the desire, the will, and the capacity to attempt a policy of Caesarism in which he was the destined Caesar? Is he not the one leading personality among the Revolutionary generation who had the potentialities, and who almost created for himself the opportunity, to try the role successfully played by his contemporary Napoleon?[13]

Granted that no crisis in the United States in 1799–1800 would have been so severe as to allow a successful military coup d'etat, nevertheless the very attempt to use the army to seize emergency power would have shattered the Union, overthrown the Constitution, and aborted the birth of the party system as the only legitimate way to gain power.[14] The party system we know, the Constitution which we accept as setting the rules of the political game, the American political way of life, probably could only become established, stable, and secure *after* the personal ambitions and the ultimate private goals of Hamilton were defeated in 1799–1800.

These are questions that cannot be answered with exactness until more is known about Hamilton as a person. Certainly of prime significance in this research will be an analysis of Hamilton's use of Plutarch, and how the former's vision of classical antiquity and the

13. Hamilton's opinion of Napoleon Bonaparte (who, with him, felt Caesar to be the greatest man who ever lived) would be worth analysis. In 1798 he speaks of him as "that unequalled conqueror, from whom it is painful to detract" (Lodge, ed., *Works of Hamilton*, VI, 276); and on Apr. 10, 1801, in addressing a New York meeting of Federalists, he praised Napoleon for the coup d'etat of Brumaire which subdued the "monster" of Jacobinism. John C. Hamilton, *Life of Alexander Hamilton. A History of the Republic of the United States of America, As Traced in His Writings and in Those of His Contemporaries* (Boston, 1879), VII, 498. Yet Hamilton used the term Bonaparte as a smear word against Jefferson, Burr, and Gallatin, just as he charged Jefferson and Burr with potential Caesarism.

14. Hamilton's desire to use military force against the Virginians in 1799 is clearly revealed in his letter to Sedgwick of Feb. 2, 1799. He felt that the Virginia and Kentucky Resolutions provided ample justification, but warned Sedgwick that since the militia could not be trusted, this emphasized the need of professional troops—during the Whiskey Rebellion, he reminded Sedgwick, he had "trembled every moment lest a great part of the Militia should take it into their heads to return home rather than go forward." With a professional army he would have no hesitation in marching in "to subdue a *refractory and powerful State.*" His suggestion was that a special committee of the Senate should sanction the counteraction. "In this case let a force be drawn towards Virginia for which there is an obvious pretext—& then let measures be taken to act upon the laws and put Virginia to the test of resistance." Quoted in Schachner, *Alexander Hamilton*, 387.

great man's role in history affected his view of his own destiny and the policies appropriate to achieve it. Until such studies of Hamilton are undertaken and the puzzles of his personality solved, we must be satisfied with tentative estimates of the enigmatic figure who looms so large in the politics of the infant Republic, dazzling many of his contemporaries with his genius and frightening others.

But no matter how tentatively we say it, until more evidence comes to light, Hamilton would appear to be a statesman who could thus be described in neoclassical rhetoric: "Curse on his virtues; they have *almost* undone his country." And to some scholars at least, it will appear, until contrary evidence is presented, that the "almost" which blocked Hamilton's final move toward Caesarism was also Plutarchian in flavor and moral impulse.

Between 1789 and 1796, Hamilton was checked and limited in his personal aims because he had to work with and through Washington, a man who in his youth gave allegiance to the ideals of Cato the Younger,[15] who in his maturity behaved like Fabius,[16] and who even

15. For the youthful Washington's admiration of Cato the Younger, see Samuel Eliot Morison, *The Young Man Washington* (Cambridge, Mass., 1932), 19–21, 41. This is the Cato who killed himself when Caesar triumphed over his country's liberty. Washington's introduction to the Roman was not directly through Plutarch (though he probably read the *Parallel Lives*), but through Addison's enormously popular play *Cato*, perhaps the most famous tragedy written during the 18th century. It was from Addison's *Cato* that Patrick Henry paraphrased his familiar "Give me liberty or give me death," and Nathan Hale drew, "I regret that I have but one life to give for my country!" Washington caused *Cato* to be performed at Valley Forge to boost morale in the army.

16. It was entirely natural for his contemporaries to compare Gen. Washington, whose army-in-being hovered on the edges of the stronger British forces without risking formal battle, with Fabius, who worked the same strategy against Hannibal. The young Fabius is thus described by Plutarch: "His slowness in speaking, his long labour and pains in learning, his deliberation in entering into the sports of other children . . . made those who judge superficially of him, the greater number, esteem him insensible and stupid; and few only saw that this tardiness proceeded from stability, and discerned the greatness of his mind, and the lionlikeness of his temper. But as soon as he came into employments, his virtues exerted and showed themselves; his reputed want of energy then was recognised by people in general as a freedom of passion; his slowness in words and action, the effect of a true prudence; his want of rapidity and his sluggishness, as constancy and firmness."

in his declining years emulated with every spark and fiber of his being the role of Cincinnatus.[17] From 1798 to 1801, John Adams, who thought of himself as a combination of Lycurgus and Solon,[18] refused to act as Hamilton's tool or further his cherished "crisis," and thus effectually ended Hamilton's political career. And, luckily for the future history of the United States, the beneficiary of the power struggle between Adams and Hamilton, Thomas Jefferson, while not unmoved by Plutarch's glorification of the savage, archaic, military virtue of his heroes, nevertheless had chosen as his secular saints the modern, civilian, rational philosopher-scientists: Bacon, Newton, and Locke.

III
What Was Hamilton's "Favorite Song"?

ON JUNE 27, 1804, Colonel John Trumbull, artist and one-time aide to Washington, landed in New York City after a European sojourn of ten years.[1] His reception in the city by his friends, he reported

17. Cincinnatus is not a Plutarchian hero but a figure who appears in Livy's *History* of the early days of Rome.

18. Lycurgus was the inspired legislator who drew up the Spartan constitution and code of laws; Solon, the Athenian statesman who worked out the proper balance between the democracy and the oligarchy by which justice could be secured for both the rich and the poor and the commonwealth secured against faction. Adams believed with both Solon and Lycurgus that the legislator's first duty is to ensure moral education. The best accounts of the struggle between Adams and Hamilton over the question of war or peace with France, 1798–1799, are to be found in Charles Francis Adams, ed., *The Works of John Adams, Second President of the United States* ... (Boston, 1850–1856), I, 508ff, and Manning J. Dauer, *The Adams Federalists* (Baltimore, 1953), *passim*. On hearing of Hamilton's death, John Adams commented, "Mr. Hamilton's imagination was always haunted by that hideous monster or phantom, so often called a *crisis*, and which so often produces imprudent measures." *Ibid.*, IX, 289.

1. Trumbull had left the United States in 1794 to act as secretary to John Jay during the negotiation of the British Treaty. After the treaty was signed, it was Trumbull who, having memorized its provisions, was sent to Paris to report them to Monroe if Monroe would promise on his honor not to communicate the terms to the French government—a promise Monroe refused to give. Trumbull then spent the next ten years traveling on the Continent and living in England, supporting

in his *Autobiography*, "was cordial and pleasant." On the Fourth of July, he noted, "I dined with the society of Cincinnati, my old military comrades, and then met, among others, Gen. Hamilton and Col. Burr. The singularity of their manner was observed by all, but few had any suspicion of the cause. Burr, contrary to his wont, was silent, gloomy, sour; while Hamilton entered with glee into all the gaiety of a convivial party, and even sung an old military song."[2]

In 1804 the Fourth of July fell on a Wednesday; by the following Wednesday, Trumbull, the Cincinnati, and all other citizens of New York knew what had transpired between Hamilton and Burr. For Hamilton was dying with Burr's bullet in his body.

What was the song that Hamilton sang and Burr heard on this last social occasion together before they met, pistol in hand? The occasion was a gathering of veterans who had proved their courage in battle so publicly that it seems fantastic that Hamilton or any one of the group felt the need of re-proving it in a private vendetta.[3] So far as is known, Trumbull's report of the song is the only one written down by any of the group of Cincinnati who heard it. Unfortunately, Trumbull gives no title and says no more than that it was "an old military song." John Church Hamilton, the son who made a lifelong career of amassing details about his father, did, however, in 1850, supply a title in his description of this dramatic gathering of the Cincinnati and Hamilton's singing:

On the fourth of July, Hamilton and Burr met at the anniversary dinner of the Cincinnati, Hamilton officiating as President-General of the Society;

---

himself by a mixture of art, business speculations, and odds and ends of diplomatic jobs done for the State Department.

2. Theodore Sizer, ed., *The Autobiography of Colonel John Trumbull, Patriot-Artist, 1756–1843* (New Haven, Conn., 1953), 237–238.

3. Trumbull makes this point about the duel. "It always appeared to me, that the obvious and honorable reply of Gen. Hamilton [to Burr] might have been: 'Sir, a duel proves nothing, but that the parties do not shrink from the smell of gunpowder, or the whistling of a ball; on this subject you and I have given too many proofs, to leave any necessity for another, and therefore, as well as for higher reasons, I decline your proposal.' " *Ibid.*, 238.

and, except that his manner was more than usually affectionate, with his accustomed cheerfulness. He was urged to sing, and he replied,—"Well— you shall have it." He sang once his favorite song, "The Drum." Burr conversed little, did not mingle with the company, and, except when he spoke and put on his gracious smile, his countenance was that of a "disappointed, mortified man." The single thing that roused him was the song of Hamilton. Sitting on his left, he raised his head, and placed himself in a posture of attention. Hamilton sang with his usual glee.[4]

Unfortunately, John C. Hamilton's account, while it suggests a title for Hamilton's song, does not supply either the words or the tune.

A set of verses entitled "The Drum" was printed in 1910, however, by Allan McLane Hamilton in his life of his grandfather:

THE DRUM

'Twas in the merry month of May
When bees from flower to flower did hum,
Soldiers through the town marched gay,
The Village flew to the sound of the drum.

The clergyman sat in his study within
Devising new ways to battle with sin:
A knock was heard at the parsonage door,
And the Sergeant's sword clanged on the floor.

---

4. John C. Hamilton, *Life of Alexander Hamilton* . . . (Boston, 1879), VII, 821– 822. This biography was first issued 1857–1864 under the title *History of the Republic of the United States of America, As Traced in the Writings of Alexander Hamilton and of His Cotemporaries* [sic]. James Parton's *The Life and Times of Aaron Burr, Lieutenant-Colonel in the Army of the Revolution, United States Senator, Vice-President of the United States* (New York, 1859), 348, reports substantially the same scene but adds the information, probably drawn from contemporaries of Burr and Hamilton, that the song was not only a favorite of Hamilton's but the "only" song friends ever knew him to sing.

"We're going to war, and when we die
We'll want a man of God near by,
So bring your Bible and follow the drum.[5]

This version vouched for by a grandson has been the one generally accepted by scholars since that time, apparently relying on the authority of the *Intimate Life*.[6]

The bother about accepting this as Hamilton's song lies in the fact that while the first four lines, beginning " 'Twas in the merry month of May," are indeed the refrain of a comic recruiting song named "Follow the Drum," there is a very strong probability that this particular song was not written before Hamilton's death in 1804. Sabine Baring-Gould's *English Minstrelsie* offers five stanzas of this song, the first, second, and fifth of which are printed below:

FOLLOW THE DRUM

'Twas in the merry month of May,
When bees from flow'r to flow'r did hum,
Soldiers through the town march'd gay,
The village flew to the sound of the drum.
From windows lasses look'd a score;
Neighbours met at ev'ry door,
Sergeant furl'd his sash and story,
And talk'd of wounds, of honour and glory.
Refrain: 'Twas in the merry month of May,
When bees from flow'r to flow'r did hum,
Soldiers through the town march'd gay,
The village flew to the sound of the drum.

5. Allan McLane Hamilton, *The Intimate Life of Alexander Hamilton, Based Chiefly upon Original Family Letters and Other Documents, Many of Which Have Never Been Published* (New York, 1910), 47. The biographer does not cite the source of this version.

6. See for example, Claude G. Bowers, *Jefferson in Power: The Death Struggle of the Federalists* (Boston, 1936), 250.

Then Roger swore he'd leave his plough,
His team and tillage all, by gum,
Of a country life he'd had enow,
He'd leave it all and follow the drum.
He'd leave his thrashing in the barn,
To thrash his foes right soon he'd larn;
With sword in hand he would not parley,
But thrash his foes instead of the barley.

Refrain

Three old women—the first was lame,
The second was blind, the third nigh dumb—
To stay behind were a burning shame,—
They'd follow the men, and they'd follow the drum.
Our wills are good, but lack aday!
Where there's a will, there is a way,
To catch the soldiers we will try for it!
And march a mile tho' we die for it!

Refrain[7]

Unfortunately, Baring-Gould offers no exact date for this song. He identifies it as: "A song by Hudson, written to an old English Country Dance. Blewitt, Hudson, and other comic singers of their day, were accustomed to make use of old airs which they altered to suit their fancy, much as Tom Moore doctored up Irish melodies; and unhappily in many cases completely vulgarized them. This is not the case with the dance tune to which Hudson set the capital words of Follow the

7. S[abine] Baring-Gould, *English Minstrelsie: A National Monument of English Song* . . . (Edinburgh, 1895–1899), II, 9–11. The other two verses report the cobbler throwing by his awl to "attend glory's call" and the tailor dropping his needle in order to wheedle the foe with a sword. There is no verse printed by Baring-Gould that shows the parson following the drum as in Allan McLane Hamilton's version.

Drum." The date of the unidentified tune to which Hudson is said to have set these words is given by Baring-Gould as in the period "1750–1800." But the words themselves, if Hudson was indeed the author, can hardly have been written by 1804. For Thomas Hudson (1791–1844) was at that date only a lad of thirteen, and had not yet entered on the career that was to make him one of the most famous figures of the early Victorian music hall.[8] Thus until someone can produce evidence that these verses were written before 1804, scholars will have to assume that they are *not* Hamilton's song but a later song that achieved a spurious authenticity by being printed in Allan Hamilton's *Intimate Life*.

If the scholars who cited " 'Twas in the merry month of May" in their own texts had carefully read all of the footnotes in Allan Hamilton's *Intimate Life*, they might have hesitated before accepting the Hudson version of "The Drum" as correct. For Allan Hamilton, though an amateur historian and not too sure in testing historical evidence, was an honest and conscientious biographer. On page 389 of his *Intimate Life* he set down in a footnote that James Edward Graybill suggested a different version of Hamilton's swan song from that printed in his text on page 47.

James Edward Graybill, invited to address the Alexander Hamilton Post of the Grand Army of the Republic, utilized the opportunity to prepare a study of Hamilton's military career which was printed as a pamphlet under the title *Alexander Hamilton, Nevis-Weehaw-*

---

8. For Hudson see Charles Douglas Stuart and A. J. Park, *The Variety Stage: A History of the Music Halls from the Earliest Period to the Present Time* (London, 1895), *passim*. Hudson was the author and singer of the song "Jack Robinson" from which our colloquial phrase comes.

The editors of the *Quarterly* would like to express their deep appreciation to Mr. William Lichtenwanger, Associate Reference Librarian, Music Division, Library of Congress, for his generous help and expert suggestions in guiding them in this tricky field of 18th-century musicology. It was he who identified Hudson's "Drum" for us and suggested various other possibilities. They are also extremely grateful to the Reference Department of the New York Public Library for their helpful suggestions.

ken. *A Lecture on the Military Career of Alexander Hamilton.*[9] Among the topics touched on by Graybill was Hamilton's song. In the course of his research he wrote to Schuyler Hamilton, another grandson, and received a long letter in reply, of which the following paragraphs contain the pertinent material:

I have always been of the opinion, from what I have heard from my father and uncles, that the song sung by my grandfather at the dinner of the Cincinnati, where Colonel Burr was present, was General Wolff's famous camp song, which begins with the words, "How stands the glass around?" I enclose you a copy of it. Colonel Burr was seated on the left of General Hamilton at this dinner. My informants told me, and they had it from their fathers, who were present, it was the song, "How stands the glass around?"—as well it might, which aroused Burr's attention.

Mr. Edmund Lincoln Bayliss, a grandson of General Lincoln, of revolutionary fame, told me the song sung on that occasion was Wolff's song, and scouted the idea of General Hamilton singing, before the Cincinnati, "The Drum," which, he said, was a common tavern ballad.

"The Drum," to which I suppose you refer, was a favorite camp song in both the British and Continental armies. It appears as part of "The Jolly Beggars," in Robert Burns' works, and begins, "I am a son of Mars;" tune, "Soldiers' Joy." It is like many of the camp songs of that day—un-nice, and, with a duel before him in a few days, it is altogether out of keeping with my grandfather's character for him to have sung it, Colonel Burr being by his side.[10]

This Schuyler Hamilton letter, dated January 4, 1897, obviously raises some problems, but it at least specifically identifies two genuine

9. The New York Public Library owns the copy examined for this essay. Graybill points out, incidentally, that the verses about a drum in George Alfred Townsend's ("Gath's") romantic novel *Mrs. Reynolds and Hamilton* (New York, 1890), 166–168, are an invention of the novelist himself.

10. *Alexander Hamilton, Nevis-Weehawken. A Lecture on the Military Career of Alexander Hamilton, with Elaborate Notes on the Important Events of His Life, and Full Particulars of the Hamilton-Burr Duel,* 2d ed. (New York, 1898), 72.

"old military songs" which Hamilton could have sung on July 4, 1804.

Schuyler Hamilton's reasons for rejecting the Robert Burns "Drum" are not in themselves very persuasive. Clearly any song that was deemed "un-nice" by him and such of his friends as Mr. Bayliss—"a common tavern ballad"—was not an appropriate swan song for his illustrious ancestor. Thus Schuyler Hamilton rejects the Burns ballad as "altogether out of keeping with my grandfather's character." There is, however, stronger evidence against Burns's "Drum" than he seems to have been aware of. "The Jolly Beggars" was indeed written as early as 1793, but like so many of Burns's poems it circulated only in manuscript among his friends for a long time before it was published posthumously in Glasgow in 1799. Schuyler Hamilton was evidently mistaken, then, in thinking that the Burns verses were "a favorite camp song in both the British and Continental armies" during the American Revolution. It was not impossible, of course, for Hamilton or some other member of the Cincinnati in 1804 to have learned and performed the Burns ditty, but if it was sung at the July 4, 1804, meeting, it would have had to be offered as a brand new hit, rather than as an old familiar song dating back to the days in which the group were comrades-in-arms. And this sort of solo, it must be confessed, does seem out of character both for Hamilton in particular and in general for convivial singers at a veterans' gathering, either of the Cincinnati, the GAR, or the American Legion.

The most likely candidate, then, as the song sung by Hamilton is the so-called "General Wolfe's Song"—the song which Wolfe was *supposed* to have written the night before his glorious death on the Plains of Abraham:

GENERAL WOLFE'S SONG

How stands the glass around?
For shame, ye take no care, my boys!
How stands the glass around?

Let mirth and wine abound.

The trumpets sound,

The colours they are flying, boys,

To fight, kill, or wound:

May we still be found

Content with our hard fare, my boys,

On the cold, cold ground.

Why, soldiers, why

Should we be melancholy, boys?

Why, soldiers, why?

Whose business 'tis to die!

What! sighing? fie!

Damn fear, drink on, be jolly boys!

'Tis he, you, or I;

Cold, hot, wet, or dry,

We're always bound to follow, boys,

And scorn to fly.

'Tis but in vain,

(I mean not to upbraid you, boys),

'Tis but in vain

For soldiers to complain:

Should next campaign

Send us to Him who made us, boys,

We're free from pain;

But should we remain,

A bottle and kind landlady

Cures all again.[11]

11. W[illiam] Chappell, *Popular Music of the Olden Time* . . . (London; my copy of this encyclopedia of old songs has no date, but the first edition appeared in the 1850s), II, 669, supplies both the words and music. Chappell points out that the last two verses of the song, under the title, "Why, soldiers, why?" were sung in the play *The Patron, or The Statesman's Opera* in 1729, two years after Wolfe was born, but thinks it possible that Wolfe sang it the night before his death. Robert Wright, in the first scholarly study of Wolfe, *The Life of Major-General James Wolfe* . . . (London, 1864), 572–573, denies even this possibility. "Neither does there

Rather slowly and firmly.

How stands the glass a - round? For shame, ye take no care, my boys! How stands the glass a - round? Let mirth and wine a - bound. The trum - pets . . sound, The co-lours they are flying, boys, To fight, kill, or wound : May we still be found Con - tent with our hard fare, my boys, On the cold, cold ground.

"HOW STANDS THE GLASS AROUND?"
Tune: "A Soldier's Song"

(Reprinted from W. Chappell,
Popular Music of the Olden Time
[London, n.d.], II, 669.)

exist a particle of evidence . . . to prove that Wolfe so much as sang the song at a farewell carouse with his officers; on the contrary, it appears he was otherwise occupied on the eve of his last day upon earth." Wright also cites the study of Sir Henry Bishop (*Illustrated London News*, Jan. 24, 1852), who found a version of "Why, soldiers, why?" printed as early as 1710. Bishop believed that some enterprising music seller in 1759 slightly altered the meter of the 50-year-old song, added the first verse, and cashed in on the enormous fame and popularity of the dead Wolfe by inventing the pathetic story of Wolfe composing the song before he died.

Air.

I am a son of Mars, who have been in ma-ny wars, And show my cuts

and scars wher-ev-er I come; This here was for a wench, and that

oth-er in a trench, When wel-com-ing the French at the sound of the drum.

My pren-tice-ship I past where my lead-er breathed his last, When the blood-y die

was cast on the heights of A-bram: I serv'd out my trade when the gal-lant game

was play'd, And the Mo-ro low was laid at the sound of the drum : I

served out my trade when the gal-lant game was play'd, I served out my trade when the

gal-lant game was play'd, And the Mo-ro low was laid at the sound of the drum.

AIR FROM BURNS'S "THE JOLLY BEGGARS"

Tune: "Soldier's Joy"
(Reprinted from George Gebbie, ed., *The Complete
Works of Robert Burns* [New York, 1909], I, 161.

There will always be an ad man! The hoax was completely successful. The song
gained instant popularity, was repeatedly reprinted and used in such plays as Shield's
The Siege of Gibraltar. While Wolfe's close friends and family knew the truth, the
public did not; it was only in the mid-19th century, long after Hamilton's death,
that this successful advertising fraud was exposed. Even so, Schuyler Hamilton and
Graybill in the 1890s still believed that Wolfe wrote the song.

If indeed this was the song sung by Hamilton, it is no wonder that Burr, fully aware of the dramatic irony of the verses, would have listened mute and glum; for an examination of the second stanza reveals how pointed it must have seemed to the melancholy Burr. And we can recognize, too, in the third verse, a terrible and dramatic prophecy that was to be fulfilled for both duelists—Hamilton dead and freed from pain; Burr cursed to live on and on, his engaging character and tremendous talents steadily eroded away with an endless succession of bottles and complaisant landladies.

In contrast, the air from Burns's "Jolly Beggars," even though it has a drum, seems (if one reads the verses carefully) intrinsically a most inappropriate song for the Cincinnati meeting, a most unlikely song for Hamilton to sing, and one unlikely to elicit any direct response from Burr:

From THE JOLLY BEGGARS (Tune: "Soldier's Joy")

I am a son of Mars who have been in many wars,
    And show my cuts and scars wherever I come;
This here was for a wench, and that other in a trench,
    When welcoming the French at the sound of the drum.
                      [Lal de daudle, &c.]

My prenticeship I past where my leader breathed his last,
    When the bloody die was cast on the heights of Abram:
And I serv'd out my trade when the gallant game was play'd,
    And the Moro low was laid at the sound of the drum.
                      [Lal de daudle, &c.]

I lastly was with Curtis among the floating batt'ries,
    And there I left for witness an arm and a limb;
Yet let my country need me, with Elliot to lead me,
I'd clatter on my stumps at the sound of a drum.
                      [Lal de daudle, &c.]

And now tho' I must beg, with a wooden arm and leg,
  And many a tatter'd rag hanging over my bum,
I'm as happy with my wallet, my bottle and my *callet* [i.e., trull],
  As when I used in scarlet to follow a drum.
                        [Lal de daudle, &c.]

What tho' with hoary locks, I must stand the winter shocks,
  Beneath the woods and rocks, oftentimes for a home,
When the tother bag I sell, and the tother bottle tell,
  I could meet a troop of hell, at the sound of a drum.
                        [Lal de daudle, &c.][12]

But verse two of the "Jolly Beggars" air does suggest a possible answer to the question of how John Church Hamilton came to report that his father's "favorite song" was "The Drum." The peg-legged hero of the Burns ballad is a soldier of Wolfe's, who learned his trade on the Plains of Abraham, and who followed the drum in the Seven Years' War. Would it have not been possible during the early decades of the nineteenth century, when Burns's songs were extremely popular all through the English-speaking world, for this particular drinking song *about* Wolfe's soldier to be confused with *the* "Wolfe" drinking song?

In this hypothesis the key word is "Wolfe," and if we recall the unique glory and romantic appeal attached to that hero's name from the date of his triumphant death in 1759 until the end of the century, it would seem to increase the probability past any doubt that it *was* "Wolfe's Song" that was Hamilton's life-long favorite.

For General James Wolfe, conqueror of an empire for Britain and dead at thirty-two, was the only successful English general available for romantic hero worship between 1715 and 1800. Between Marlborough and Wellington, England had brave privates by the thousands, efficient staff officers by the score, but its list of commanding generals

---

12. George Gebbie, ed., *The Complete Works of Robert Burns* (New York, 1909), I, 161–162.

was a uniformly dull and sorry lot until Wolfe flashed like a shooting star across the sky.[13] Hence the glamour and apotheosis of the general who was the most spectacular military success in the Empire for two generations. Hence the popularity of a run-of-the-mill drinking song falsely attributed to his authorship; hence the fact that during these years he was the idol par excellence of every small Britisher who lusted for military fame and martial glory.

We know that Alexander Hamilton was just such a boy, growing up in Nevis and writing at the age of fourteen in the earliest letter of his that has survived, "I contemn the grovelling condition of a clerk or the like . . . I wish there was a war."[14] We know also that his dream of military glory never died—when he reached maturity it was Caesar whom he described as "the greatest man that ever lived."[15] It is entirely in character, it is exactly fitting that this ballad associated with Wolfe, carrying a cargo of wish fulfillment and lust for military glory, should very early become Hamilton's favorite song—possibly his "only" song—and remain so until the death he faced with such manic elation. Why should he be melancholy?

> Why, soldiers, why?
> Whose business 'tis to die!

13. Wright in his *Wolfe* points out, in explaining Wolfe's almost fabulous fame, that in 1755 the military reputation of England was at its nadir; that although England at this period had a large number of veterans who drew the pay of generals, none of them seemed capable of winning victories. Part of the appeal of the Wolfe legend that made him available as a hero to ambitious young commoners like Hamilton was the proof he gave that genius could triumph against birth and connections even in the army. For Wolfe, spotted by the great Pitt, was jumped to command of the Quebec expedition at the age of 32 for sheer merit, although he lacked "parliamentary interest, family influence, and aristocratic views."

14. To Edward Stevens, Nov. 11, 1769, Henry Cabot Lodge, ed., *The Works of Alexander Hamilton* (New York, 1904), IX, 37–38.

15. Jefferson reports that at a cabinet meeting held in his lodgings at Philadelphia in the spring of 1791, Hamilton told him: " 'The greatest man . . . that ever lived, was Julius Caesar!' " Thomas Jefferson to Benjamin Rush, Jan. 16, 1811, Andrew A. Lipscomb and Albert Ellery Bergh, eds., *The Writings of Thomas Jefferson* (Washington, D.C., 1903–1904), XIII, 2.

✶ 15 ✶

CLIO BEMUSED

Despite his deteriorating health during the mid-1960s, Adair found the time and energy to give increasing attention to the problems of teaching history. One result was his acceptance of Henry Cord Meyer's invitation to address an Advanced Placement Conference in History held at Pomona College on a drizzly day in June 1965. The result was a serious effort by Adair to examine some of the classroom implications of his own research and writing; at least one listener thought Adair learned as much from Adair as did his audience. He always had an infinite capacity for surprise, especially at himself.

WHEN I WAS A BOY, American history had a fairly neat shape and structure. It was the story of the transplantation of European "seeds" in the American wilderness. The institutional seeds planted in seventeenth- and eighteenth-century America recapitulated English social institutions. They were aristocratic, hierarchical. In the American colonies one had refugees from Europe, but these only selectively rejected a small part of the European heritage. So in the northern colonies the refugees established landlord and merchant aristocracies, and in the southern, planter aristocracies. They maintained political power by property qualifications for voting, economic power by privileged manipulation of politics, and the maintenance of such feudal

SOURCE: This essay was prepared from a tape recording of Adair's address and has never been previously published.

devices as primogeniture and entail. These colonial aristocracies were threatened somewhat by poor farmers to the west and by city artisans, but the colonial aristocrats, supported by British imperial authority, managed to maintain their positions until the Revolution came along. Then after 1760, needing allies to challenge England's tax policy and reorganization of the empire, they encouraged artisans to riot in Boston and New York, encouraged westerners to support them in the name of British rights, and found themselves in 1776 with a genuine revolution on their hands, which had transformed itself, in Carl Becker's words, from an argument for "home rule" into one over who should rule at home.

I was taught that then this farmer-labor party of democratic western farmers allied with eastern artisans used the revolutionary situation to put through a series of social reforms, as Jameson suggested, more far-reaching than that put through by the French revolutionaries. But in 1787 the old colonial aristocracy, the survivors from the old regime, kidnapped, as it were, this lower-class revolutionary movement, and utilizing the postwar depression of 1786, presided over a Thermidorean reaction, the writing of an undemocratic Constitution that tipped its hat in the direction of democracy but attempted to reestablish an aristocratic polity. The aristocratic-oligarchical tendencies of the Constitution were clearly revealed by Alexander Hamilton's financial and political administration of the Treasury during Washington's presidency.

Now the lovely thing about this version of early American history was that it also suggested a marvelous dialectic account of American history in the nineteenth and twentieth centuries. Arthur Schlesinger, Sr., who had written a generation ago about colonial merchants being kidnapped by the artisans they had triggered into political action, had a son who could write after World War II about the Jacksonian period as a time when once again a farmer-labor movement revolted against the oligarchical big-business dominance of the Bank. The story of the late nineteenth-century Populists and

Progressives was told as the story of farmers—debtor-farmers—and eastern laborers combining to reform the Robber Barons. Today Arthur Schlesinger, Jr., moving from the Jackson period to the period of Franklin Roosevelt, continues to treat Roosevelt II as the lineal successor of the revolt against Hamilton's oligarchy, as the lineal successor of Jackson, who attacked the economic-royalists, as the godchild of the Populists and Progressives.

The bother, of course, with this neat dialectic, which made it easy to teach American history from the beginning as the "growth of democracy," or "the rise of democracy," or "the progress of democracy" is that various disturbing characters—termite-like—have chewed the foundations from under the structure in the seventeenth and eighteenth century. Fred Tolles, for one, has produced evidence that the Revolution of 1776 had few elements of a social-reform movement. Robert E. Brown indicates that it is quite ridiculous to talk about aristocracy in seventeenth- or eighteenth-century European terms in describing the eighteenth-century American gentry. What we are left with is a structure with a beam pulled down here, a cornice loosened there. The old building seems to stand, mainly because historians repeat themselves. There is naturally an enormous inertia in our textbooks, but nonetheless the dialectic, the neat argument for linear progress, seems today far less than an adequate account of American history. In the eighteenth century, as Brown's researches seem to show, the availability of cheap land made it possible for practically every white man over twenty-one who wanted to, to vote.

Most of the time a large part of the legally qualified did not bother to vote, but this is another problem and raises other questions. The point is that the traditional account that turns the rebellion of 1776 into a movement of the disenfranchised struggling to gain political rights just doesn't happen to be true. Our textbook treatment that makes our Revolution the first of an established aristocracy by a farmer-labor class just doesn't hold up after one looks at the evidence carefully. The "spirit of '76" was not the midwife to the baby "democracy."

Yet it is fairly obvious that the political practices of eighteenth-century America do have a different style from twentieth-century politics. If the right to vote was more widely spread through the total population than in any contemporary polity as a consequence of the wide diffusion of property ownership, nevertheless to stop with calling eighteenth-century America "democratic" is to invite misunderstanding. It was "democratic" in an eighteenth-century political and intellectual context, and to acknowledge this contextual difference is to recognize that there are differences in the eighteenth-century meaning of "democracy" as important as the likeness with our twentieth-century democracy.

Students of language have warned us repeatedly that abstract nouns such as "democracy" are like sponges: the more they are used, the more times they are squeezed through our mouths, the more connotations they absorb, the less precise and exact becomes the meaning, the more they become burdened with extra implications. Now the word "democracy" has in the last seventy-five years become one of the most widely used honorific terms in politics. It has in the United States become a sacred cow that has escaped from its original pasturage in the field of politics, and grazes in the fields of literature, art, diplomacy. An eighteenth-century man like Jefferson would be amazed, I suspect, to hear such terms as "industrial democracy," "democratic art," or a war designed "to make the world safe for democracy."

Faced with this bloated and swollen modern aspect of the term "democracy," it would seem that the teacher of American history, whose commitment is to examine American politics, past as well as present, might well find it wise to try to recover the eighteenth-century usage of the term. If one is to understand the changes as well as the continuities in American democratic polity such an inquiry would seem essential.

We are furthermore urged to such an endeavor by the results obtained analogically by two of America's greatest scholars: Francis Parkman and Samuel E. Morison. Parkman, to escape from the anachronizing knowledge he had of the feeble civilized and Christianized Indians of the East, traveled west on the Oregon Trail in the 1840s to see for himself wild Indians. Only thus did he feel he could write with understanding of the wild Indians of the seventeenth-century New England. Morison, likewise anxious to tell truthfully the exploits of Columbus, followed his voyages of exploration by boat. In both the case of Parkman and Morison the results of placing themselves in the landscape, in the geographical contexts of their subject was wonderfully justified. I suggest, too, that their method offers a model for the recovery of the primitive meaning of our word "democracy."

In politics the physical geography, the landscape in which voting takes place, is less significant than the geography of the mind. Can we recapture the mental landscape of eighteenth-century statesmen? Of greatest significance in this regard is the fact that a clear majority of the signers of the Declaration of Independence and a substantial majority of the fifty-five men who took part in forming our Constitution were college-trained men. The leaders of the Revolution had been formally instructed—brainwashed if you will—as to an accepted estimate of democracy as a feature of their intellectual coming of age.

It does not seem impossible then, or useless, to try to recapture the context of the eighteenth-century discussion of democracy as the Founding Fathers had been introduced to it formally, systematically, in their educational training. One of the extremely interesting things that comes out of this inquiry is the standardization in Virginia, in the Middle Colonies, in New England—at Pennsylvania, at Princeton, at Yale, at Columbia. All students were fed the same intellectual pablum. We talk about conformity today as a problem in American education; in most ways the eighteenth century, as befits a pre-Darwin age, was tradition-directed and was far more conformist in its educational ideas than we are today.

I understand that currently there is only one economics text that is used universally in introductory courses at colleges, but as we are well aware, this is not true in history or the other social sciences today. In the last half of the eighteenth century, however, the standard text that summarized all the social sciences, used at Columbia, Harvard, William and Mary, and Yale, was Francis Hutcheson's *Short Introduction to Moral Philosophy*. Oddly enough it was not the assigned text at Princeton, for President Witherspoon was a public critic of Hutcheson's religious ideas. But I was amused and horrified to discover he had plagiarized the moral philosophy text for his course syllabus but did not admit that it was Hutcheson's book that he had used. It was only after Witherspoon's death that people dug up his carefully copied notes and published them—Witherspoon naturally had not allowed his lectures to be printed while he was alive. So it is possible today to see that they reveal this very curious form of academic theft. And Princeton students, too, learned exactly the same lesson about government that their eighteenth-century contemporaries learned.

One of the things that seems very clear is that for the eighteenth-century student of politics, the word "democracy" is never used or very seldom used before the French Revolution except as a technical concept. Moreover, it is a concept that normally compares "democracy" with both monarchy and aristocracy. Madison at Princeton, Hamilton at Columbia, Jefferson at William and Mary, Adams at Harvard, all learned that there were three pure or simple forms of government; monarchy, aristocracy, and democracy. And all of them learned, too, that not one of these pure forms, not one of these simple forms was good or adequate or safe in itself.

Let me present to you the argument that Witherspoon gave the Princeton seniors in his moral philosophy course—the course which treated systematically of any government: "There are four things that seem to be requisite in a system of government and every form is good in proportion as it possesses or attains them. 1) Wisdom to plan proper measures for the public good; 2) Fidelity to have nothing but the public interest in view; 3) Secrecy, expedition and dispatch, in carrying measures into execution; and 4) Unity and concord, so that one branch of the government may not impede, or be a hinderance to another."

Notice this is a functional analysis of government that was in the eighteenth century allocated, translated, into the functional strengths and weaknesses of the three pure forms. The first one, monarchy, "has plainly the advantage in unity, secrecy, and expedition. Many cannot so easily nor so speedily agree upon proper measures, nor can they expect to keep their designs secret; therefore, say some, if a man could be found wise enough, and just enough for the charge, monarchy would be the best form of government." Its weakness, on the other hand, is the probable lack of virtue—lack of fidelity to the public good in the monarch—the possibility of the monarch treating his own interest as predominant to the public interest. Also, wisdom is not hereditary.

The second pure type is aristocracy. "Aristocracy has the advantage of all the others for wisdom in deliberations; that is to say, a number of persons of the first rank must be supposed by their consultations to be able to discover the public interest. But it has very little or no prospect of fidelity or union. The most ambitious projects, and the most violent and implacable factions, often prevail in such states.

The last type of government, democracy, "has the advantage of both the others for fidelity; the multitude collectively always are true in intention to the interest of the public, because it is their own. They are the public. But at the same time it has very little advantage for wisdom or union, and none at all for secrecy and expedition. Besides, the multitude are exceedingly apt to be deceived by demagogues and ambitious persons. They are very apt to trust a man who serves them well with such power as that he is able to make them serve him."

A pure democracy, so the Founding Fathers had been taught, is like a child; it means well but has not the capacity, is too flitter-brained, is too unstable to be a safe form for liberty, security, and union. A key word applied to the people is that the public, the people, do not think and reason in politics but instead act out their feelings—moreover they overreact. In quiet times public opinion will not plan ahead; in a crisis the tendency is to explode into frenzied energy in a terrific short-run burst, which, based on fear and feeling, is as likely to do harm as to do good; and then when the crisis lessens they quickly relapse into thoughtless torpor.

It is interesting that modern commentators on the strength and weakness of foreign policy in democratic governments like Britain and the United States echo these estimates made in the eighteenth century about the hazards of popular decision and diplomacy. For example, Gabriel Almond's study, *The American People and Foreign Policy* (New York, 1960), does not use the ancient literary metaphor comparing the popular will with the fluctuating instability of the ocean, but he describes the same instability in the terms of "mood-swing." He points out that before the Pearl Harbor attack it was difficult to mobilize a large segment of public opinion, first, to face seriously that our security might be threatened by Germany and Japan, and second, to face that the choice of war or peace was not a unilateral decision that Americans alone would decide. The mood of perhaps a majority of the population before 1941 was a compound of fatalism plus apathy, a mood that in policy terms didn't want to do anything decisive in hopes that the war would go away from our door. Then came Pearl Harbor, and the mood of hysteria swung public opinion from semipacifism to the extreme of ruthless and total war. The Japanese and Germans became devils—the embodiment of evil; our war aims called for total defeat and unconditional surrender. And all enemies of our enemies were baptized as "democrats," "peace-loving," "liberty-loving," folk. Stalin, just a plain old-fashioned fellow, became "Uncle Joe"; the Chinese were our favorite Asians.

The swing twenty-five years later of public opinion is almost as extreme. Our favorite people today are the devils of 1942: the Japanese and the Germans—our only dependable friends and democratic allies. For the majority of Americans the devils today are our Russian and Chinese ex-buddies. And it is this sort of instability—this aspect of popular will—that caused the Fathers to doubt whether a completely democratic polity was the best for all aspects of governance.

You will notice that in those terms democracy is not thought of as a monolithic entity, a unitary system either democratic or nondemocratic, which recalls the old joke about the parson's egg, which was a little stale. Eggs unlike social systems are either/or, either fresh or rotten. The eighteenth century had a view that looked on political institutions as capable of being mixed, with democratic elements diluted or supplemented by monarchical or aristocratic elements. The view held that if all the functions of fidelity (the democratic function), wisdom (the aristocratic function), and energy, secrecy, and dispatch (the monarchical functions), could be held in balance, this would provide the best of all possible commonwealths.

In these terms it is not inexact to note that what the members of the Constitutional Convention of 1787 did was not Thermidorean, was not anti-democratic except in the qualifying eighteenth-century sense. Although rejecting monarchy and aristocracy, they were dubious about the weaknesses of pure democracy. The Constitution that they wrote is essentially a democratic, a popular instrument with, however, the Senate constructed as a quasi-aristocratic body and the president as a quasi-monarchical elective king. I say "quasi," for the indirectly elected Senate showed the effort, in Madison's word, "to refine" the will of the majority and to produce in a more permanent, more stable governing body, the wisdom, the ability to make long-range plans, that was not expected of the directly elected pure democracy of the House of Representatives.

Also anticipating the continuance of a jungle world of international relations, where the expectation was that war would be more normal than peace, the founders constructed the presidency to be the closest thing possible to an elective king—that seeming contradiction in terms—a democratical monarch, not chosen by the people's vote directly but responsible to majority will. In these terms of constitutional creation one finds, I suspect, the most searching criticism of what has been the American ideology, the main thrust of the traditional teaching of American history: that human nature in America is different; that we are the direct descendants of Adam before Eve and original sin appeared; that we are more innocent and virtuous than any other people. We defined ourselves by insisting America had escaped the corruptions of the Old World. Alas for this complacent theory! The argument of *The Federalist* papers is the argument of the possibility of the corruption of human nature in America. It is an argument that human nature everywhere, in America as in the rest of the world, though it has rare capacities for nobleness, by and large has more obvious and normal capacities for self-interest, delusion, irrationality. And that doesn't mean "those other people yonder," it means you, and me, and all of us Americans. The justification for our Constitution carried an explicit rejection of laissez-faire. Ours is a government that was planned to regulate the citizen's conduct because human nature cannot be left to itself to produce an inevitable harmony without governance.

Those of you who are interested in examining the Founding Fathers' estimate of our common human nature might check through *The Federalist* on this issue. For this purpose let me recommend to you the most inexpensive edition of *The Federalist*, available in paperback and edited by Clinton Rossiter. This edition is the one that is far and away most useful to scholars because of Rossiter's superb and careful index. If you examine this index under the head of "human nature," you will find fourteen entries under the black side of human nature, and why, "since Americans are not angels," they require government.

One must also notice that although *The Federalist* depicts the black side of our nature, the final judgment on it is "gray." The government established under our Constitution, while dubious about our virtue, is nevertheless in some ways the least pessimistic about the potentialities of human nature and politics of any government that existed in the eighteenth century. This more favorable judgment, looking to the white side, though muted, is most clearly stated by James Madison. Speaking to the Virginia ratifying convention, Madison replied to Patrick Henry's argument that to set up a republican government in a large state like the United States would take congressmen too far away from their constituents and that congressmen would be crooked unless their constituents could keep one eye cocked right on them. Responding to Henry with muted confidence, Madison declared, "I go on this great republican principle, that the people will have virtue and intelligence enough to select men of virtue and wisdom. Is there no virtue among us? If there be not, we are indeed in a wretched situation. No theoretical checks, no form of government can render us secure. To suppose that any form of government will secure liberty or happiness without any virtue in the people is a chimerical idea."

I would suggest that this statement of Madison's also throws light on the somewhat less muted democracy of Thomas Jefferson. Jefferson came to stand in the nineteenth century as a symbol of the idea that "the voice of the people is the voice of God," but in practice the Jeffersonian system was an attempt to use the democracy of the people's choice to translate the numerical quantitative majority into a qualitative intellectual elite—a "natural aristocracy." In a wonderful exchange with John Adams, in 1813, Jefferson speaks of his belief that there is "a natural aristocracy" and that that form of government is best which selects out the natural *aristoi* from the artificial aristocracy of wealth and birth. It is worth noticing that he describes the function of the people as that of separating "the wheat from the chaff"—note well the words "wheat from the chaff." The Jeffersonian program of reforms in Virginia culminated in a complete three-level educational system and was designed to train the people to exercise their choice by electing the wise and good as rulers and representatives. The people are to guarantee the function of fidelity in separating the wheat from the chaff. And here we get in Jeffersonian democracy the echo of his early college training in standard eighteenth-century mixed government, mixed democratic theory as presented in the standard moral philosophy texts. The people have a key role but a very limited and circumscribed function that does not require of them the knowledge and foresight and technical information that they lack. In Madison's words, the people as a whole have enough "virtue and intelligence" to select out of their mass a limited number of men with the virtue and the wisdom that the mass lacks to be leaders and rulers.

In Jefferson's three-leveled educational system, only the elementary level would be open to everybody; a small number would be chosen on the basis of stringent competitive examinations for the grammar school—to be taught Latin, which was the narrow language gate through which one entered the professions; and finally, a tiny segment would then be chosen for university training. If, as I have suggested, it was the function of the people to choose their rulers, it is very clear that Jefferson expected and hoped these rulers would be chosen from the university-trained people. And this is the way that Jeffersonian democracy functioned in practice.

Last year Sidney Aronson published his monograph entitled *Status and Kinship in the Higher Civil Service: Standards of Selection in the Administrations of John Adams, Thomas Jefferson, and Andrew Jackson* (Cambridge, Mass., 1964). As Aronson shows, Jefferson's criteria for appointment—and he is supposed to have been the enemy of "the rich, the well-born, the well-educated"—continued to be an advanced education, which implied both wealth and a family tradition of officeholding. Jefferson's percentage of appointment into the highest civil service, of people whose family tradition had given them office earlier and, above all, of people who had had the training of

higher education is roughly the same as John Adams, the Federalist. Moreover, Aronson's study of appointments by Andrew Jackson, in the era which proclaimed that "the voice of the people is the voice of God" casts doubt on whether the so-called Jacksonian revolution did change greatly the elitest aspect of the higher civil service.

This crude summary that I have offered you of what's involved in looking at American democracy in its eighteenth-century context brings me back to my opening remarks. However we view the American Revolution, the writing of the Constitution, and the structuring of the two-party system under Jefferson, it obviously cannot be fitted into the traditional syllabus of the dialectic between good American democrats and bad anti-democratic oligarchs. Our old syllabus has very much "gang a glae."

I am myself uncertain about what new patterns for teaching the story of America may emerge in our classrooms. I do feel that it's a good thing in many ways that the complacent history of America as pure and unadulterated progress—the triumph of triumphant democracy—will probably become less common. I believe with Madison and Hamilton and Washington and Adams that one of the desirable lessons of our history lies in the lesson that though the American people have been favored by Providence above all others in many ways, this luck does not mean we were chosen by God to be immune from unoriginal sin, foolishness, and irrationality—*and* perhaps disaster.

The Founding Fathers' reservations about popular government such as we have today were rooted in their fears that a pure democracy was the least functionally safe in a world where foreign policy and the threat of war dominated politics. This is why the president and the Senate under the Constitution had prime jurisdiction in this sphere.

Oddly enough, though our government had the oldest great power constitution in the world, it has been tested least in just this dangerous political area of exterior relations. The nineteenth century demonstrated that our system was viable in domestic politics—in internal affairs the story of American democracy *was* a success story. It still remains for the last half of the twentieth century and the twenty-first century to show whether the story of America as a world power is a success story.

Until that time, to teach our students that the story of America is a story of inevitable progress with a built-in and guaranteed happy ending is to validate Voltaire's remark about history being a pack of tricks played on the dead to confuse the present about their future. Other more vulgar terms would make our teaching of history like a bustle: "a fictitious tale attached to stern reality."

DOUGLASS ADAIR

A Select List of Writings

The Power to Govern: The Constitution—Then and Now. With Walton H. Hamilton. New York, 1937. (A paperback edition with an introduction by Adair was issued by W. W. Norton in 1967.)

"The Intellectual Origins of Jeffersonian Democracy: Republicanism, the Class Struggle, and the Virtuous Farmer." Ph.D. dissertation, Yale University, 1943.

"The Authorship of the Disputed Federalist Papers." *William and Mary Quarterly,* 3d Ser., I (1944), 97–122, 235–264.

"James Madison's Autobiography." Edited with an introduction. *William and Mary Quarterly,* 3d Ser., II (1945), 191–209.

"James Madison." In *The Lives of Eighteen from Princeton,* edited by Willard Thorp. Princeton, N.J., 1946.

"The New Thomas Jefferson." Review essay. *William and Mary Quarterly,* 3d Ser., III (1946), 123–133.

"The Mystery of the Horn Papers." With Arthur Pierce Middleton. *William and Mary Quarterly,* 3d Ser., IV (1947), 409–445.

The Candidates; Or The Humours of a Virginia Election. By Colonel Robert Munford of Mecklenburg, in Virginia. A Comedy; in Three Acts. Edited, with an introduction, with Jay B. Hubbell. Williamsburg, Va., 1948. (Originally published in the *William and Mary Quarterly,* 3d Ser., V [1948], 217–257.)

"Good Newes from Virginia, 1623." A broadside, edited with an introduction. *William and Mary Quarterly,* 3d Ser., V (1948), 351–358.

"The Tenth Federalist Revisited." *William and Mary Quarterly*, 3d Ser., VIII (1951), 48–67.

"The Autobiography of the Reverend Devereux Jarratt, 1732–1763." Edited with an introduction. *William and Mary Quarterly*, 3d Ser., IX (1952), 346–393.

"Rumbold's Dying Speech, 1685, and Jefferson's Last Words on Democracy, 1826." *William and Mary Quarterly*, 3d Ser., IX (1952), 521–531.

"The Stamp Act in Contemporary English Cartoons." *William and Mary Quarterly*, 3d Ser., X (1953), 538–542.

"The Catalogue of the Library of Thomas Jefferson." Review. *William and Mary Quarterly*, 3d Ser., XI (1954), 637–641.

"Hamilton on the Louisiana Purchase: A Newly Identified Editorial from the *New-York Evening Post*." *William and Mary Quarterly*, 3d Ser., XII (1955), 268–281.

"A Note on Certain of Hamilton's Pseudonyms." *William and Mary Quarterly*, 3d Ser., XII (1955), 282–297.

"What Was Hamilton's 'Favorite Song'?" *William and Mary Quarterly*, 3d Ser., XII (1955), 298–307.

"Was Alexander Hamilton a Christian Statesman?" With Marvin Harvey. *William and Mary Quarterly*, 3d Ser., XII (1955), 308–329.

"Chancellor Kent's 'Brief Review of the Public Life and Writings of General Hamilton': A Newly Identified Document." Edited with an introduction. *The Historian*, XIX (1956–1957), 182–202.

" 'That Politics May Be Reduced to a Science': David Hume, James Madison, and the Tenth *Federalist*." *Huntington Library Quarterly*, XX (1956–1957), 343–360.

"They Come for Gold and Die in the Sheets: A Diary of the California Gold Rush." Edited with an introduction. *Claremont Quarterly* (Winter–Spring 1957).

"The Evans Bibliography of Early American Imprints in the Honnold Library." *Claremont Quarterly* (1960).

"The Jefferson Scandals." Written in 1960.

Peter Oliver's Origin and Progress of the American Rebellion: A Tory View. Edited with John A. Schutz. San Marino, Calif., 1961.

"The Federalist Papers." Review essay. *William and Mary Quarterly*, XXII (1965), 131–139.

"Clio Bemused." Paper presented at the Advanced Placement Conference in History, Pomona College, Pomona, Calif., June 1965.

" 'Experience Must Be Our Only Guide': History, Democratic Theory, and the United States Constitution." In *The Reinterpretation of Early American History: Essays in Honor of John Edwin Pomfret*, edited by Ray Allen Billington. San Marino, Calif., 1966.

The Spur of Fame: Dialogues of John Adams and Benjamin Rush, 1805–1813. Edited with John A. Schutz. San Marino, Calif., 1966.

"Fame and the Founding Fathers." In *Fame and the Founding Fathers*, edited by Edmund P. Willis. Bethlehem, Pa., 1967.

INDEX

Abolitionists, 236, 337

Adams, John, 5, 10, 214, 350, 429, 430; on youthful ambitions, 8; to R. H. Lee on fame, 28–29; passion of, for fame, 28–29, 33; death of, 52; and scientific study of republics, in *Defence*, 137, 153, 158–63, 168; on use of history, like *boudoir*, 153; self-image of, as Lawgiver, 159, 405; on dangers of pure democracy, 159–60; on need for strong executive, 160; praises British constitution, 160, 168; political determinism of, 161–62; to B. Rush, on "quasi-mixed" Constitution, 175; as Unitarian, 205; actions of, weaken Hamilton, 213, 215, 371, 405; and Alien and Sedition Laws, 229–30

Adams, John Quincy, 52, 111–12, 398

Adams, Samuel, 386

Addison, Joseph, 12, 17, 404n

African Colonization Society, 199

Albemarle County, Va., 233, 235

Alien and Sedition Laws, 51, 229–30

Almond, Gabriel, 426

American Revolution: as catalyst for Founding Fathers' greatness, 6, 8–10, 27, 33, 212; nonphilosophical nature of, 133; importance of Jefferson in period of, 340; use of pseudonyms during, 386

American Whig Society, 184

Ames, Fisher, 182

"Andrea's History of Northwest Virginia," 307–8

Anglican church in Virginia, 186, 190, 207, 207n

Annius of Viterbo, 327

Antifederalists, 165n

Anti-intellectualism, 178–79

Aristocracy, 361; and political determinism, 161–62; as part of balanced government, 166; compared with democracy, 173–74, 424; nature of, 425, 428. *See also* Democracy; Monarchy

Aristotle, 17n, 92n

Army, standing, 370

Aronson, Sidney, 430

Ashley, Robert, 12

Ashley, W. J., 58, 68n, 105n, 359n

Atheism, 133, 211

Augusta Town, 298

Bacon, Edmund, 255–57, 263, 264, 266

Bacon, Sir Francis: in Jefferson's trinity of great men, 18, 19, 351, 351n, 405; in *Essays*, on fame and honor, 19–20; in *Advancement of Learning*, on fame and honor, 22–23, 25; in Voltaire's trinity of greatness, 25–26; as prophet of philosophy,

This book is set in Aldus, with Castellar display. Aldus was designed by the eminent German type designer Hermann Zapf expressly for text setting and was first made available in 1954. Castellar, a set of monumental capitals issued in 1957, was designed by John Peters.

Book design by Sandra Strother Hudson, Athens, Georgia
Typography by Monotype Composition Company, Inc.,
Baltimore, Maryland

9 780865 971936